The Road Bends

An Autobiography

The Road Bends

SAMI YAFFA

An Autobiography *with Tommi Liimatta*

Translated by *Hanna Hurme and Sami Yaffa*

RARE BIRD

Los Angeles, Calif.

THIS IS A GENUINE RARE BIRD BOOK

Rare Bird Books
6044 North Figueroa Street
Los Angeles, CA 90042
rarebirdbooks.com

FIRST NORTH AMERICAN HARDCOVER EDITION

Originally published in Finland as *Tie taipuu* by Like Kustannus in 2016.

Cover Photographs by Meeri Koutaniemi
Design by Hailie Johnson

The Road Bends is also available in English as an e-book,
and as an abridged vinyl audiobook narrated by Sami Yaffa,
featuring music by Sami Yaffa and Janne Haavisto, from Rare Bird Books.

An unabridged audiobook narrated by Sami Yaffa in English
is also available from Tantor Media.

For more information, address:
Rare Bird Books Subsidiary Rights Department
6044 North Figueroa Street
Los Angeles, CA 90042

Set in Dante
Printed in the United States

10 9 8 7 6 5 4 3 2 1

Library of Congress Control Number: 2021951456

Publisher's Cataloging-in-Publication data available upon request.

1963–1979

From Tapiola to Lepakko

"Playing music puts you in this state of being that's a really good place to be in.
In a way, you're not yourself,
you're not necessarily totally conscious
of what your fingers are doing."

1963–1969

Grandpa's Harmonica & Honky Tonk Women

A bus.

That's my earliest memory. Also, the very first words I even uttered were "a bus." I was sitting in my stroller on a sunny afternoon when everyone around me was buzzing like mad because I'd said something intelligible. Little did I know then that I would end up spending the rest of my life in buses.

I was born in the Helsinki Women's Clinic on September 4, 1963, at 12:15 a.m. From there, I was whisked off to the Tapiola neighborhood of Espoo, Kelohongantie 14 F 32 to grow up and live for the next sixteen years. My parents, Ingrid and Lauri, or Lasse, sister Maarit and brother Jouni made up the family.

The garden city of Tapiola was designed as the suburb of the future, a model design city that architects and tourists from around the world would come to visit and marvel at. The street I lived on, Kelohongantie, sloped up from the Oravannahkatori ("squirrel skin square," in English) miniature strip mall. Our building had three stories and seven stairwells, from A to G. The so-called Taskumatti buildings were right next door; the whole area was built in harmony with nature, with lots of wooded areas to run around in. In the late sixties, the neighboring town of Mankkaa was totally rural, just dirt roads, forest, and fields. We'd buy our vegetables straight from the farmers.

My first memory of my dad is him in a welding helmet, crazily spraying paint from a can in each hand, giving birth to an abstract painting on a large canvas. I was sitting in my mom's lap in the basement studio, wearing an Abraham Lincoln top hat that Dad had made me out of black cardboard. I remember wishing that things could always be like this.

Dad was born poor in 1930, in the Pohjanmaa region of Finland, famous for its knife-wielding outlaw gangs at the turn of the century. His mother died when he was four. His father was crushed by the death of his wife and took to the bottle; he couldn't take care of his child. Dad was brought to a farm, where he labored as a child and was brought up by a strict religious matriarch. He was not allowed to sleep in the main house but in the barn. At sixteen, in 1946, he moved to Helsinki, which was a pretty brutal place to be right after the war, full of ruins and broken people. Dad got a job working the lathe in a machine shop, did all kinds of odd jobs, and managed to go to art school at night. Easy to say that Pops didn't take to whining too kindly.

Throughout the fifties, Dad worked as an assistant to somewhat legendary designer Timo Sarpaneva and designed ad campaigns for Iittala glass. Dad also made sculptures and painted until he started a family and had to earn a better living. He continued to paint until his death, never showing his works publicly. Later on, he worked at the Taucher advertising firm as a graphic designer and as an artistic director at the international agency Interplan. Dad's fingerprints can be found all over, like on the World Chess Federation Logo, the one Bobby Fischer and Anatoly Karpov played under.

Toward the end of his career, Dad scaled down to just one client: a Finnish paper producing giant, Finnpap. Which was enough. He did all of Finnpap's campaigns.

He got me a modeling job in a Serlachius toilet paper ad. Mom brought me to the shoot. I was really young, maybe three. The studio had bright lights and a set with a strange woman sitting on the couch, who was supposed to play my mom in the ad. I didn't wanna go near her, 'cause I thought my real mom should have been on the couch. "I'm not gonna do this, this is some other mom!!" I wasn't feeling it. Somehow they enticed me to do the job, probably with some candy. That was my first commercial gig.

There was an animation studio down the street from our apartment that I'd often go to. I'd sit quietly in the dark and watch the figures grow from black-and-white sketches to moving in full color. It was pure magic. The second-best place in the world was the bakery downstairs from the production company, where you could get soda, meat pies, and doughnuts.

My mom's mom, Ingeborg Haugene, was from Fagernes in Western Norway, not far from the glaciers of Jotunheimen, the land of the giants in Viking legends. I was told we're descendants of Harald Fairhair, but who knows? At eighteen, Ingeborg went to Finland as a maid to a wealthy Norwegian couple and fell in love with Emil Kesäluoto, ten years her senior. Grandma was gentle, strong, and understanding, whereas Grandpa was a train conductor who excelled in sports and played the violin and harmonica, with a taste for gambling.

Mom lived through the Soviet bombings in Helsinki. After things with the Russians got too heavy, Grandpa evacuated her off to Norway with her mom to flee the war, but they had to do a quick turnaround and head back to Finland when the Nazis invaded Norway.

We'd go to Grandma's apartment in Hiekkaharju on the local train. Grandpa would show up down the train hallway in a blue conductor's uniform, hat, and a cool coin belt. He would give me some used train tickets, which I'd use to play games with other kids. When I think of Grandpa, I remember a green rocking chair, his warm presence, big hands, and the soothing sound of the harmonica.

Grandpa's harmonica is probably my first musical memory, but the Rolling Stones' "Honky Tonk Women" was the first big one that hit me upside the head! I was five. It was definitely love at first sound when I heard it on my brother's turntable. Jone—eight years my senior—and his friends had built me a little guitar and beautifully carved the names Rolling Stones, Monkees, and Manfred Man on it…I strummed that guitar endlessly and dreamed of having Jimi Hendrix's hair. We had a pretty sick record collection at home of all the heavyweights: Janis Joplin, Memphis Slim, John

Coltrane, Stones, Zappa, etc. Dad listened to Django Reinhardt and Ornette Coleman, Mom to Demis Roussos and classical music, my brother and sister were heavy into late sixties R&R but already starting to lean toward jazz. My head was filled with all that good stuff from a very young age.

I remember watching the 1968 Finnish presidential elections on TV. The Cold War was in full effect. Reading the votes out loud left four-year-old me with the impression that there was no other candidate but Kekkonen, Kekkonen, Kekkonen, Kekkonen. That one name dominated the others and got stuck like a mantra in your head. The US sent Apollo 11 to the moon in the last summer of the decade, and the TV showed Neil Armstrong and the other astronauts leaping around on the moon. The waving American flag made me wonder, "Wow, there's wind on the moon, too?" And of course, being Yanks, they had to drag a car to the moon.

1970–1974

Are there any dull knives in the house?

The name Pelé was heard a lot in the summer of 1970 when Brazil won the Soccer/Football World Cup in Mexico City. I'd jump out of bed in the morning, pull on my swim trunks, and go run to the yard to practice my scissor kick endlessly. Of course my jersey had to be number ten, same as Pelé.

Every building in my neighborhood had its own little gang or clique. We jumped from trees, scrambled up the rocks, and played rock war using the old First World War trenches behind Kino Tapiola movie theater as our battlefield. Sometimes things got a little out of hand and someone got knocked in the head by a rock, but usually things were pretty harmonious. Sometimes we'd pedal to a bar in Oravannahkatori to bum some free chocolate milkshakes.

The Tapiola power plant's giant smokestack was right in my backyard, which sent black exhaust up into the sky. Big green oil trucks delivered heating oil all day long to feed the gaping maw of the plant. I'd watch the smoke curl up to the sky and think about what kind of toxic shit was in it, it sure as hell couldn't be healthy.

Haukilahti beach was a bike ride away. At that time, Haukilahti was a pretty fancy place even if Cisse Häkkinen, the bass player from the Hurriganes, lived there. Cisse was the biggest celebrity living in the Tapiola region. Jaana Ukkola, who later became a model and owner of a modeling agency, was one of our neighbors. Jaana's mom, Eila-Iiris, hired me to model a couple of times. When I was seven, I modeled some underwear for a women's magazine, *Kotiliesi*: I wore long johns, briefs, an orange boiler suit, and "manly stockings with a reinforced foot." The legendary Hexi Riihiranta lived a few hundred yards from us. He played defense for the HIFK hockey team. He and Vellu Ketola were the first Finns to play in the NHL, which was a big deal. When my sister got caught smoking weed at thirteen and needed a lawyer, it ended up being another hockey player, Juha Rantasila, one of Finland's best known defensive players.

The older guys of Kelohongantie chopped up old Jawas, Moto Guzzis, and Nortons in front of the bike shed. One guy tuned a Tunturi moped to rocket sixty miles an hour and got so hurt in a fall that his leg had to be shortened a couple of inches.

There were two old American cars in the yard too. The Kansi family had a blue Thunderbird, and Keltti the taxi driver had a Plymouth. There's a picture where I'm sitting in Keltti's Plymouth dressed as Batman. Keltti was sometimes found passed out under our stairwell even though he lived four doors down. Must have been a rough day at work. Us kids were freaked out wondering if he was dead. An old lady from the building went to shake him and figured out what was going on. "A lotta nerve you got to pass out drunk in front of all the kids in the middle of the day! Get movin'!"

Watching the TV news on one of the two TV channels was the evening ritual in every family. Foreign minister Ahti Karjalainen droned on in his slow and incomprehensible English, making everybody ashamed, but also providing comedy with his heaaavy Finnish accent. Henry Kissinger mumbled in that creepy robot voice about the necessity of war, because if the United States didn't continue to arm up and fight, the Communists would take over the world. Americans seemed to be real worked up about communism.

Vietnam was the first televised war. Every night I'd watch carpet bombings and unbelievable suffering until my mom shooed me away from the TV. Dirty and ragged American soldiers plodded through the rice fields, hand-rolled cigarettes dangling from slack jaws. The jungles exploded into giant Napalm flameballs. The Vietnamese peasants fled burned and naked on muddy roads. Dad paced angrily back and forth in front of the TV cursing. "Fucking Americans...goddamn Nixon."

In a little kid's brain, this all left the impression of a world in complete chaos. It seemed like the old was giving way to the new. There was rioting in the cities around the world, hippies and Black Panthers challenging the status quo, no justice no peace. Change in human societies doesn't happen often without chaos and destruction. There was a war on the home front as well, and this one was between Mom and Dad. Doors were slammed and furniture got smashed. Sometimes we'd end up fleeing to Grandma's in the middle of the night because of the fights. Lots of nights I went to sleep with my head under the pillow to drown out the dismal soundtrack while my brother tried to calm me down. There was fighting at home, on the TV was the Vietnam War, and it was all set to the music of Miles Davis, Rolling Stones, The Doors, and especially Jimi Hendrix's "Machine Gun." It was all so heavy. We had that iconic Che Guevara poster on our wall next to Herman's Hermits and Hendrix.

I started school the fall that Hendrix died. I remember when the news hit; it hit my brother and sister hard. Brian Jones had died a year before. Janis Joplin, Jim Morrison. It felt like they'd all died at the same time.

The neighborhood was full of families, and everyone ate at home; back then, no one ate at restaurants, because there weren't that many and they were expensive. Kitchen knives were like treasures. We had a couple of good ones. Mom always used the same one for cooking. When the knives got dull, they needed to be sharpened. A knife sharpener used to come by, door to door, to fix the knives. You could hear him in the hallway. "Are there any dull knives in the house?" This guy had an absolutely legendary look, straight out of a French gangster film: cigarette butt dangling from his mouth, a crumpled fedora pushed far back on his head, a faded brown suit, and the wide sharpening strap slung over his shoulder. He stank of sweat, stale booze, and garlic. He was terrifying, almost like bringing the horrors of the war in Vietnam to the front door. One day I needed to go out when he was doing his thing, but didn't dare to do so. After some procrastinating, I figured out that I could just run by him like a maniac, and I did. It worked.

One time when I spurted past him, the knife sharpener stopped me and grabbed me by the arm. My heart blocked my throat. This was the end: I'M GONNA DIE! But once I looked into his kind brown eyes, I realized that he was probably a pretty okay guy after all. He muttered, "Calm down, kid. I ain't gonna kill you." My fear of the knife sharpener vanished that day.

There's a guy driving around Brooklyn to this day whose family has been sharpening knives since the beginning of the twentieth century. He comes around in an old truck with three pit bulls in the back with all his sharpening gear. He also has his own jingle, so that everyone knows to bring their knives downstairs. He doesn't do it for the money, he has another means of making a living, but makes the rounds a couple times a month for the fun of it and to keep the tradition alive. The tradition will be gone after he's gone, or when he decides to quit.

In the summertime, Dad and I would spend a couple weeks camping on the island of Gåsgrund. We'd fish, eat canned food, drink water from the well. A supply boat would come by every four days or so to sell food and necessities; my dream was to one day be the captain of that boat. Days on the island went by fast: running around, inspecting the island, looking at birds, fishing, carving wood, and floating on an air mattress in the freezing cold Baltic summer sea.

In the winter, Grandma stitched me a military-like snowsuit. I wrestled myself into it and went out into the woods to practice my defense tactics with a toy machine gun, in case Russia invaded again or the craziness on TV made its way to Tapiola. Playing war as kids was a big thing.

The huge stones in the forest around our house all had names, some after mythological forest beings and animals, like Hiidenkivi and Otsonkivi, or just because the rock looked like letter A: Aakkoskivi. One time I was going to play hockey and was running downhill in the woods, skates around my neck and a hockey stick in hand. Toward the bottom, the path had a blind turn behind another one of these massive boulders. I turned the corner and ran right into a moose's muzzle. I just about pissed my pants. I bolted right back up to where I came from. The path felt like it had gone vertical, and I felt the enraged moose on my tail, foaming at the mouth. Once I got to the top of the hill, I realized the beast hadn't been following me at all. Just as scared of me, it had boogied off full speed the other way across the road.

A different sort of people lived in a shack town called Viinamäki—Booze Hill in English—down the hill from our neighborhood. The drunks' dwellings were only slightly better than our homemade huts made out of discarded planks of wood and cardboard.

Viinamäki was less than half a mile from the center of Tapiola, right next to the hockey and soccer fields. You had to tread carefully in the forest if you didn't want to run into the winos. Whoever was brave enough to sneak into the camp while the drunks were snoring away to gather bottles for the deposit money was a true hero. One morning I crept up to the outskirts of the shantytown, peeking out from behind a rock from a distance to see if anyone was awake. They were definitely awake. Viinamäki was having a full-on party. The drunks were sitting in a circle on rocks and boxes, shouting, clapping, singing, and passing bottles around. In the center of the circle, an old couple, beaten up by life, were rocking back and forth on top of each other in time with the applause. What the fuck were they doing? Then I realized those two old winos were getting it on. It was a pretty grim visual. That image would come back to me later while reading Bukowski.

The contrast was pretty jarring. Behind the well-manicured lawns and nice houses was a forest where a debauched group of forgotten people—the homeless alcoholics, many of them veterans from the Second World War—were getting wasted and living in misery.

We'd go play the slot machines and pinball in the bakery with the money we'd get from the bottle deposits. If we won money from the slot machines, we'd go to Dipoli in Otaniemi to play pool. Viinamäki was torn down when the city built a jogging track in the forest; the poor bastards had to move elsewhere. Some of them probably ended up in the flophouse in Ruoholahti that later became Lepakkoluola.

Because of Dad's advertising work, our house was full of all kinds of paper, pens, rulers, markers, brushes, and paints. I drew whenever I could, wherever I could, on my schoolbooks, fences, bus stops, my hands, and a LOT on paper. I drew caricatures of friends and family, magical beings, ghosts, nature, war, sports, dictators, politicians, etc. Sometimes I tried to copy Picasso's work. On the weekends, my parents dragged me to the Ateneum Art Museum and other galleries in central Helsinki to check out the abstract art that was happening in the late sixties and early seventies. Art shows, museums, and galleries were a dreamworld that'd stick with me for the rest of my life.

I got it in my head to look for treasure. I started examining rocks with a little pick and hammer, taking little samples to the geology lab which was a bike ride away. I wanted to know what my findings were and what kinds of rocks and stones existed in my area. The guy at the lab was patient and helpful. He'd tell me what types of rocks I'd brought and gave me a box of samples and explanations of different rocks so I could compare my findings against those. I kept on chipping away; more and more rocks fell into my bag. If the shards were even a little bit unusual, like a freshly cracked surface of rock that shone like gemstone, I'd put it in my bag and haul it in for inspection. It became a thing in the lab: here comes that little kid again with his bag of rocks. Finally, the guy said, "That's enough, PLEASE don't bring any more rocks."

Sand glitters in the sun, but in New York, it's the sidewalks that glitter, with bits of broken glass in the asphalt. "Even the streets in New York are paved with gold," they say.

×××

On TV, there was this music program called *Iltatähti* ("Evening Star" in English) that showed the very first music videos. As special effects, the bands used psychedelic swirling colored water and oil that they superimposed on the background, or on the artists themselves. It was all elastic pictures to elastic rock 'n' roll. We had a black-and-white TV, so the trippy LSD psychedelia was even more nonsensical. I thought our TV was broken.

My brother Jone went nuts over the saxophone when he saw the Norwegian sax player Jan Garbarek live at the Tapiola Disco sometime in 1971. I was eight, and my bro was sixteen. He bought a sax immediately and practiced it like a maniac. I noticed how hard he practiced and realized that blowing that horn for ten hours a day was his escape from anxiety.

I got used to doing my homework and falling asleep to the sound of that sax. It was cool to see how seriously my brother got into it. Jone would also test me at times. He'd clap out a rhythm sequence and ask me to clap after him—three, one, pause, two, pause, four, and so on. When he played his records, he asked me to tell him what I heard, my ear always zeroed in on the bass line.

At eight or nine, I built a drone bass from the coils of a table lamp. I stretched the coils on a piece of board with nails and taped a mike underneath. For the amp, I used a reel-to-reel tape recorder we had at home. I strummed the lamp coils for hours on end and was in some kind of a trance zone. It was an even, percussive, rough space hum that sounded like the drone of a sitar, only on a very low bass frequency.

I fought pretty frequently with my sis, Maarit, until we made a deal on a bike trip that the fighting had to stop. After that, we never fought again, period. My sister had started playing the guitar and taught me how to play Howlin' Wolf's "Spoonful" with one finger. Just two notes; there's a third one too, but you can leave it out, so it's really just two notes. Getting the rhythm right was the main thing.

My sister was hanging out with a gang of twenty or so hippies. Out of all of them, only my sister and one other guy are still alive. They'd hang out in Silkkiniitty Park in their hippie gear smoking weed, dropping acid, and taking whatever else they could get their hands on. Whenever our parents were away, there'd be big parties at our house, incense burning, people nodding off, and murky music playing. They'd try to get me to go to bed early, but it never worked because I was too intent on being the center of attention, perched on the knee of a pretty girl taking drags off a cigarette.

Dad worked like a dog, and when he was home his presence was palpable. He was unpredictable. You'd never know when or what would make him lose it. Usually he was okay, and there were moments of calm too. I had a chronic stomachache from the ages of seven to ten or so, due to the tension and fighting in the house. Headphones were my escape. When the storm started to gather, I'd pull them over my ears and crank 'em up. Dad had given me the Rolling Stones' *Beggars Banquet* album as a present, which is still my favorite Stones record. It's mostly an acoustic album where

Keith Richards does the bulk of the guitar playing: "Street Fighting Man," "Sympathy for the Devil," "Dear Doctor," "No Expectations." Jagger sounds like he's from Mississippi, not from Dartford, England. In the sixties and seventies, most of the English singers wanted to sound American.

I escaped from the world's bullshit through music and reading. Some books are now mentally linked to music. IRA, Belfast, The Troubles, and all that insanity on the TV felt so close in the seventies. I read a lot of books about the IRA and the Vietnam War in the seventies and eighties. My memory of the first Stiff Little Fingers record is paired with this one book I can't remember about the IRA. Iggy Pop's *Idiot* album is etched in my mind with a book called *Chickenhawk* about the Vietnam war.

Mom had been a stay-at-home mom until she went to work at the children's hospital, and after that at RAY, Finland's Slot Machine Association. That's when the good times began. I got to buy singles discarded from jukeboxes, ten cents a pop. Alice Cooper, Sweet, Slade, Suzi Quatro, David Bowie, Rory Gallagher, Sparks, Beatles, Stones, Hendrix, you name it!

I played these 45s on our Lenco record player nonstop. The Stones were always badass, but so were the Beatles in their Beatles way: "Back in the USSR," "Get Back," "Penny Lane," "Eleanor Rigby," etc. Paul McCartney would have made history just for his bass lines. But my first loves that were all mine was Alice Cooper, Sweet, and Slade. My brother and sister absolutely hated them. "Do we really have to hear 'School's Out' for the thousandth time?"

The only R&R music program that was on the radio, once a week, played the New York Dolls' first album in its entirety, and I recorded it on a cassette; the other side was Bowie's *Diamond Dogs*. There had been a tiny color picture of the Dolls in a music magazine, which mesmerized me.

Holy shit, I could just stare at it and stare at it like holy mama, what a fucking crew. All of a sudden Sweet didn't seem so tough.

Music lessons at school were a drag. We were made to listen to classical music and learn about long-dead composers. Rock 'n' roll wasn't culture, so it wasn't part of the curriculum.

My brother dressed up good: a neck scarf, tight pants, and hair down to his ass. He'd gotten his hands on a Harlem slang dictionary. I flipped through the book trying to think of what I wanted to know. Well, how about what's the slang for "Jesus" in that city of Harlem, NYC? I looked up the letter "J" and read: "Jesus Christ—Jerusalem Slim."

After the military coup in '73, some students from Chile appeared in our school. A Chilean family moved into the next building. Their parents were artists. I started hanging out with the immigrant kids more than my old buddies. The Chileans were more interesting; their families and lives had a totally different vibe from us Finns. At school, some kids would yell shit like "fucking Commies" at them. How does a ten-year-old know what the fuck communism is? All that stuff comes from home, learned from the ignorant parents.

Then one sunny day, Mom and Dad took me to the local bakery for a doughnut and soda. They told me that they were getting a divorce.

"Thanks. It's about time. I'll finally get some peace and quiet around the house," was my response.

1974–1977

I still remember what Jonna's beanie smelled like

I moved from elementary school to middle school at eleven. Hakalehto was the closest option. My last grade at the elementary school, fourth, wasn't a great success. At one point my brother was the worst student on record at Hakalehto High School; he'd gotten the most failing grades ever, though he did graduate at the end of it. My sister was a pretty close second as far as problem students go. The school board must have said no way in hell when they saw another Takamäki coming, so I had to go to a school in Lauttasaari, in the Helsinki school district. I had to get up extra early to catch the right bus. If I missed it, I'd miss the first period.

I started to hang out with Asko Erwe, Jussi "Ykä-Kossu" Yrjö-Koskinen, and Ari Lehtovaara that first fall in Lauttasaari. They had a cardboard box band—cardboard drums, ratty homemade electric guitar, homemade amp, one microphone. They called themselves the Crazy Boys. We'd get together, jump around like rabbits, and make a lot of noise. Our repertoire consisted of only one song, "Summertime Blues" by Eddie Cochran. We found the tabs in a book of rock songs and the three chords were easy enough for us to play.

That winter, the Hurriganes' *Roadrunner* was the soundtrack to every house party in Lauttasaari, probably in all of Finland too. Once the song "I Will Stay" came on, it was time to slow dance with a girl or find a dark corner to make out.

The Hurriganes were HUGE when *Crazy Days* came out in the fall of 1975. As much as I dug Albert Järvinen, who was the great guitarist on *Roadrunner*, and the greatest Finnish R&R guitar player in history, the follow-up album, *Crazy Days*, and Ile Kallio on guitar were also a big deal. I went to see the Hurriganes play in Leppävaara at Maxi Market Super Market.

I biked all the way there and back. The sound at the place was awful. I remember standing next to a rack of women's clothing and checking out the show. But honestly, the show was absolutely insane. The power that rolled off the stage was magical. Remu, the drummer and singer, was a scary mofo and very intense. Cisse, the bass player, was ultracool in his tiger-striped jacket, slicked-back hair, and sunglasses, and Ile, the guitar player in a badass Western shirt and cowboy boots, simply kicked ass!! My sister was hanging out with Jyri Rautakoura, who was close friends with Ile Kallio. One day, they took me along to meet him.

We met in front of the Bio Rex movie theater in Helsinki. Ile was wearing, again, a Western shirt, Beavers brand jeans, and cowboy boots. But first, Ile had to go to the bank to do some biz, so we went along. He dropped a fat stack of hundreds onto the counter and had them deposited into his account. I eyeballed that money on the counter and suddenly it clicked that you could actually make that kind of cash playing guitar here in Finland too.

At the end of the afternoon, Ile gave me all kinds of *Crazy Days* swag and stickers and a card signed by the whole band. Remu had added: "Sammy—Keep on Knockin'!" I treasured that card.

×××

In the fall of 1976, I was able to transfer to a school district closer to home, in the north of Tapiola. Lauttasaari had been a good time, as far as good time in school goes, but it was nice to not have to run for the bus every fucking morning. The new school was walking distance.

I turned thirteen and found some kindred spirits at my new school: Janne Haavisto, Ile Hilden, Pasi Ervi, Mika Jussila, and Pepe Seivo. Antti Sajantila, who's now a prominent coroner and criminal pathologist, also went to the same school. We had been classmates since elementary school.

Pepe Seivo and I quickly became the best of friends. He was obsessed with getting his own drum kit and was constantly banging out beats on his legs in anticipation of getting the real thing. Pepe introduced me to Arto Tamminen, who was a year older and was going to night school, which was really weird at the time. Just the mention of "I wanna go to a night school" got daggers from both Mom and Dad. Arto's big brother Epa had dated my sister, and their father had invented a very successful battery patent. It was a lot of fun to hang out at their place, listen to music, and noodle on the instruments they had lying around the house. Arto played the cello, a bit of piano and drums, but he was an absolute mf on the electric guitar. He idolized Hendrix, which you could hear in every note when he cranked it up. When it came to songwriting, he was all about the Beatles. Arto was way ahead of his age as a musician and just generally, as a person. Over the next year, I learned a ton about playing music from Arto.

We'd go drool over the Japanese Guyatone guitars and basses at the music shop in Tapiola, but I didn't have the kind of money to get one. I couldn't even get a summer job. I'd gone to ask around at the gas station, but Dad was all, "No son of mine works at the gas station!!" Guyatone made great copies of the more well-known brands and also came up with their own models. Some of them are worth a boatload of money nowadays.

One lazy afternoon, Arto and I were staring at his *The Who Live at Carnegie Hall* poster on the wall. He turned to me to say that someday, he was going to play Carnegie Hall too.

The fifties rockabilly look and culture was the in thing back then with the teenagers. If you let your hair grow past your ears, kids at school or people on the street would call you names, fucking junkie, dirty hippie, fucking faggot, etc., real inventive stuff. Personally, I didn't give a fuck of what the sheeple thought and let my hair grow out. My brother Jone was playing the sax in a fusion band called the Himalaya Band. One of the members, the bass player, Silu Seppälä, became something of an idol to me. He looked like a Ramone before the Ramones: leather jacket, T-shirt, worn-out jeans, and tennis shoes, long greasy hair.

Later he gave me some advice about why to play the Fender Jazz bass. "You can rest your liver on the top curve of its body."

Jonna Järnefelt was my first love. I still remember what her beanie smelled like. Within a year, she broke my heart.

I played ice hockey since I was a nipper with my buddies, but suddenly it got all serious when I joined a team. The coach, Karl-Gustav Kaisla, was famous for refereeing the Hockey World Cup and Olympics.

He made us play a practice game against a team of older kids. The age difference wasn't really that big, a couple of years, but the goal was to toughen us up as players. I was playing left wing and was going full speed to the corner after the puck, when out of nowhere, a defender from the other team plowed over me with his arms crossed. I went flying backward and slammed my head on the ice. I got a concussion and spent the next week bedridden and hallucinating. I saw swirling colors, a bit like the black-and-white TV's music videos, but now in color. I saw some sort of "beings" come in and out of my vision. That's when I decided to put an end to my budding hockey career. The guy who smashed me, Timo Blomqvist, ended up playing for the New Jersey Devils. Right career choices for the both of us.

I spent the midsummer holiday in 1977 sailing with Arto Tamminen on his family's boat. We'd scraped off the old varnish, paint, and barnacles back in March to get the Renata ready for summer. The Renata was a pretty big boat, so there was a lot of room for friends, and some older guys came along, like our classmate Rotta Raatikainen's big brother.

We set course for the archipelago off Porkkala. Everyone was getting drunk as soon as the trip started. It didn't take long for people to drop like flies, one by one. Arto was at the helm and had a bit of a buzz going himself. He pointed out an island in the distance. "A few hundred feet off the shore, drop the front anchor, then the back one, then furl the sails." I was thirteen and knew fuck all about sailing. It was a windy day and the waves were a couple feet high. The boat was bouncing, and we were going really fast, but I followed Arto's directions. I ran up front, threw the first anchor, ran to the back, threw the other, and started pulling down the sails. I didn't want to look, but could tell that the island was getting closer and closer. I ran to the back, crouched down, and braced myself for impact, but the anchors did catch and the boat slowed down. Finally, the Renata came to a halt. I got up and walked to the bow.

We'd stopped a couple feet from the rocks. I guess Arto knew all along what he was doing.

I grabbed a bottle of red wine—some real cheap stuff—jumped down to the island, tied the boat to a tree, opened the bottle of wine, drank it in a couple of gulps, and passed out on a big rock. I woke up hungover and sunburned. Everyone was snoring and everyone, except Arto, was unaware of our near miss, which to him wasn't a near miss.

I've loved sailing ever since that trip. Years later, in Florida, I used the couple days of downtime between shows to rent a catamaran, and I went out into the Caribbean. The waves can change real fast out there. The way out was calm and easy breezy, but the direction and power of the wind changed on the way back to shore. I spent hours weaving side to side. I was wrecked by the time I got back to the shore.

1977–1979

Aria Diamond

There was a rehearsal space in our school basement with some amps, a piano, and some other stuff. Janne Haavisto, Ile Hilden, Pepe Seivo, Antti, and I jammed for a month with the school's gear until Pepe finally got his own Premier drum kit. We got a small storage room from his building to use as a rehearsal space and moved our operations there. Then Arto Tamminen came in the picture. We thought it would be a great idea to start brewing our own beer. The space next door was an AA clinic; those poor souls were just trying to keep it together while the smell of our little brewery was wafting everywhere.

Pepe had drums and Arto had all the gear to play guitar, so now it was my turn to get my hands on a bass, which wasn't as easy as I'd thought. Dad wanted to make sure I was serious. He promised me half the money if I could figure out the other half. How in the hell was I, a thirteen-year-old, supposed to get my hands on that kind of cash? Dad pointed at my record collection.

This was seriously fucked; my record collection was the apple in my pie, but I figured that I could always replace the records later on down the road. My dad, brother, and I went into the city to a used record shop, and I sold my records. Goodbye, Sparks, Stones, Bowie…but I have to admit I wasn't too broken up about parting with Elton John's *Captain Fantastic and the Brown Dirt Cowboy.* I only held onto Alice Cooper's *Billion Dollar Babies.*

It was love at first sight with my Aria Diamond: the sunburst colors, the feel of the wood, the thick strings, the switches, the knobs, the white pickguard, but most of all, that sound. I got my bass in the beginning of September. If memory serves me correctly, it was the same day Weather Report played at the Kulttuuritalo in Helsinki. My brother and sister had bought me a ticket for my fourteenth birthday. The show blew my mind! Alex Acuña, Manolo Badrena, Wayne Shorter, Joe Zawinul, and Jaco Pastorius. Jaco's bass playing blew my brains out to Saturn and back!

I started practicing as much as my brother. The bass felt like home; the rhythm and the low end was my thing. "Lady Madonna" and "Dizzy Miss Lizzy" were the first songs I got a handle on. Poor Mom tried to enjoy watching TV while I banged out scales. She was living in hell: Jone still lived at home, and I was playing bass all the time. My brother's room was next to Mom's, while I'd taken over the kitchen. Jone practiced ten hours a day and I wasn't far behind. At first, my playing was kind of like "doo-doo…oh, wait…doo…I mean…" After a while, Mom would get fed up and explode. "SIIIIIIILENCE!!"

The tension was thick after one of her outbursts. Both my brother and I would just sit in our rooms, itching to play again. Little by little, we'd start over again, first very quiet, barely touching the strings, then the noise would start building up again louder and louder.

I didn't have an amp, but there was an old radio lying around the house. Converting a radio into an amp is a time-honored tradition. I wired the RCA plugs into a quarter-inch jack, pressed down the aux button, and voilà: Sound! The radio held up for a couple of months before it started to smoke and finally blew up! One of Grandma's friends had a big old Telefunken Concertino radio that stood up to the punishment a little longer until that one eventually exploded as well.

Seems like everyone's grandma had a Telefunken Concertino in those days. I think my friend Timo Kaltio still has one. The radio was something like five watts, but the sound was mean.

The makeshift amp wasn't cutting it, though, so I had to get my hands on a real thing. Dad had finally gotten the picture that I was serious about the bass, so he asked an electrical engineer friend of his to build me an amp.

I got into prog and jazz rock through my bro and sis, and some of my friends from school listened to it. The big influences I was trying to learn from were Weather Report's *Heavy Weather* and *Black Market*, Jeff Beck's *Wired* and *Blow by Blow*, Stanley Clarke's *Journey to Love* and *School Days*, Mahavishnu Orchestra's *Birds of Fire*, and Billy Cobham's *Spectrum*. But the most important album of all, if not prog rock exactly, was Hendrix's *Electric Ladyland*. That record is just absolutely unbelievable and magic and it never gets old. All those Stratocaster players pulled their whammy bar springs down to three from five when they saw the back of his guitar when Hendrix played with his teeth. Hendrix had learned a lot from a certain guitarist from the fifties named Jimmie Rodgers, who was playing guitar behind his neck already back then. Everyone's got a predecessor.

Jimi Hendrix was the bible for my bass: "Can You See Me," "Fire," "Manic Depression," "Purple Haze," "Hey Joe." *Band of Gypsys* was this close to soul, a heavy record with heavy riffs. The best way for me to practice was to put on some headphones and play along. I was also kind of getting used to reading notes thanks to Carol Kaye's bass book. It was a shitload of fun to learn to play; my little fingers were always in blisters or covered in blood.

Years later, I got to record in Electric Lady Studios. I already knew that the actual studio room where you would record was all round with no hard edges and there I was, ready to do some recording of my own. The mural Jimi had commissioned was still on the wall, and so was some of the original gear next to all the up-to-date, modern stuff. Other than that, I'm not sure how much of it is original and what's new. The magic place is still going strong.

×××

Sometime in late 1977 or early 1978, I saw a short news report on TV. All of the UK was freaking out about a new thing called punk rock; the Sex Pistols were at the forefront. The story even showed a clip of "Pretty Vacant."

Well, well, well. What do we have here!!? The volume and intensity knocked me on my ass! I HAD to get my hands on a copy of that record right then and there. I started looking around for other punk bands: the Clash, the Damned, the Stranglers, the Ramones, the Members, the Saints, Stiff Little Fingers, etc. For the first time, music and its message made me think! It felt real and true. All my old favorites suddenly seemed old and tired, even if I still loved Bowie, the Dolls, Alice Cooper, and the Stones.

Weird as this may sound, I was very fortunate that my brother and sister got me listening to a lot of Tomasz Stanko, Edward Vesala, Art Ensemble of Chicago, Sonny Rollins, Jan Garbarek, and Niels-Henning Ørsted Pedersen in addition to all that punk and rock 'n' roll I was listening to. You've gotta feed your brain and soul with a large palate of music, keep finding more and more of the different forms of musical expression, both old and new, as without the past, there's no future. My friend Ile Hilden's older brother lived in Copenhagen, in the freetown of Christiania. He smoked strange-smelling "cigarettes" and would play us all kinds of music we'd never heard of whenever he was visiting home back in Finland. It all sounded like it had come from outer space! Much later on I realized it was all dub reggae: Lee "Scratch" Perry, King Tubby, Prince Jammy, all the giants of early and mid-seventies dub from Jamaica.

I finally got the amp from my dad's engineer friend. It had twenty-five watts and one fifteen-inch speaker with volume and EQ controls. It wasn't quite loud enough next to Arto, armed with a Strat, a bunch of pedals, and a Vox AC30 amp, and Pepe banging away behind us. I'd have to REALLY lay it on with a heavy hand and at full blast just to be heard. That's where my right-hand pick style came from.

I came up with our band name: the Bablers. Maybe it wasn't exactly the best name ever, but it was good enough for the guys and was easy to remember.

I'd pretty much stopped playing sports by then. My hockey coach, Karl-Gustav Kaisla, called my dad to say, "Tell Sami to quit playing that banjo and get back to playing hockey."

Getting into the "banjo" ruined my burgeoning hockey career...but I still go skating every now and then. Some years ago I found a pair of used seventies Bauer Black Panther ice skates on the net and I just had to get them. Sometime at the end of the eighties, Mickey Finn, the singer from Jetboy, bragged a bit about what a great skater he was, so we went skating together once. I thought he knew how to take a tackle, so I slammed right into him against the boards—gently, I thought. He busted a rib. Still sorry about that.

Taking bass lessons with Erik Siikasaari helped a lot. When you start playing as a kid and you're not quite strong enough yet with your hands, you can learn bad things that are hard to correct later. Doing things the wrong way feels easier at first, but it ends up being a bad idea in the long run. It might feel natural to get your power from your body, but you end up having your hands, arms, and body the wrong way. Erik gave me chromatic exercises up and down the E string, then A, D, and G. It was frustrating to practice, but worth the effort to build strength and also to learn where exactly on the neck all the notes were.

My brother went to a pop and jazz school in the Oulunkylä neighborhood of Helsinki. I got it in my head that I should study there too, so I signed up for a summer camp just to check things out. The camp was outside Pori, in Western Finland, at some convention center in the middle of the woods. There were rooms for the students, a few bigger buildings for the lessons, and a bunch of garages converted into practice spaces. Klaus Järvinen, who was a big name in music pedagogy, gave the opening speech at the camp orientation. All the teachers looked kind of strict. I got assigned Pekka Sarmanto as my teacher; he was famous from playing as a studio musician, backing big artists, and playing in TV bands. For some he was kind of a bass guru.

All us kids got split up across dorms. There were maybe a hundred of us in total. Drummer Janne Haavisto, keyboardist Tomi Ervi, and his tenor sax–playing brother, Pasi Ervi, were all there from my neighborhood. Fortunately, we were all together in the same dorm.

Pekka Sarmanto was a bit stuck in his ways and seemed kind of disinterested in the whole teaching thing. Not a whole lot of it stayed with me. I couldn't really care less about Country and Western bass. Okay, this is how you progress from C to the next chord, which is D, you can put the half note in there. Whatever. Country music to me, then, was mind-numbing, and the whole thing was so unbelievably stiff and soulless. My opinion about country music changed after I heard Hank.

Some of us kids decided to have a jam session. We obviously needed beer; jam sessions need beer. We got the oldest-looking sixteen-year-old student with the monobrow onto a bike with some cash and sent him to town, about a mile away, on a beer run.

At the end of the day, we got our case of beer and snuck into the garage, shut the door, and plugged in. The beer greased our fingers and spirits. We'd been jamming on Herbie Hancock's "Chameleon" for about fifteen minutes or so when the garage door violently rolled up. In walks the jefe, Klaus Järvinen, in his pajamas, and he's pissed. What in the hell did we think we were doing!!? There we were, eight of us kids, having a grand old time, beer bottles scattered on the amps. "We're jamming, Klaus."

He had some advice for us. "This is an academic environment and there is to be no jamming, or any other kind self-serving nonsense."

I realized that studying music in an academic environment really wasn't my thing. From then on, jamming, asking advice from other musicians, and learning from records were the only school I needed.

My first gig—maybe I had played a song before at school—was at the end of the summer of 1978 at a terrace in Tapiola, with Arto Tamminen on guitar and Hirkka Hirvonen on drums. It was a nice sunny day. We banged the shit out of Hendrix's "Who Knows," Earl King's "Come On (Let the Good Times Roll)," and Lead Belly's "Goodnight, Irene." The crowd was into it. I was hooked and wanted to play more gigs right away. Playing with a band puts you in this specific mental state; it feels absolutely brilliant in every way.

Mikko Lankinen played guitar at some of the Bablers shows. He and Janne Haavisto both later played with the amazing Laika and the Cosmonauts, and the Finnish musician J. Karjalainen and his band. At some point, we got into a big fight with Arto, who kicked me and Pepe out of the band. Arto, Mikko Lankinen, Janne Haavisto, and Juha Mieskoski put out an album or two as the Bablers a few years later.

Arto was a pretty amazing songwriter. He was born again at some point and stopped making music altogether for a while. Our lives took off into such different directions that I had no idea that Arto had had a big radio hit in Finland sometime in the mid-nineties and wrote a bunch of songs for other artists.

Arto called me a few years back to catch up. He told me his son was learning how to play guitar. Arto was more pissed off than anything that his son wanted to learn how to play Hanoi Rocks' "Tragedy." "Why couldn't he at least pick a good song?" but he handed the phone over to his son anyway. Of course I cheered him on, told him to keep practicing, and that he should listen to his dad because his pops was an amazing guitarist. It's pretty funny though that out of all the songs the kid could have picked, he picked "Tragedy."

The bass consumed my life and took up all of my time. No more sports or other kid stuff. School was even less interesting than it had been. I got held back a grade in 1979 for a bad average, so in the fall, I had to repeat ninth grade.

There were music associations popping up all around the country, organizing all kinds of gigs and club nights. Punk, DIY ethic was in full force. At Elmu, the local branch in Tapiola, I heard of a spot called Lepakkoluola (Finnish for "bat cave") in the Ruoholahti neighborhood of Helsinki. Ruoholahti wasn't at all residential back then, just lumber yards and industrial buildings until it all got torn down. Lepakkoluola had been a flophouse for hundreds of alcoholics and down-and-out people for years. The city had wanted to kick the bums out, tear it down, and build office buildings. At the same time, the younger generation didn't have any cultural outlets or places to go to, to rehearse, start bands, put on shows or theatre plays, or do anything meaningful, other than get wasted and get into street fights.

At the end of the summer of '79, the kids from Elmu told the city to go F themselves and occupied Lepakko. I went to check out the place as soon as I heard about it, which was maybe a couple of weeks after the takeover. The occupation was followed by a standoff, with barricades and lookouts to keep out the cops. Everybody was ready to fight. Some of the more hardcore punks had Molotov cocktails ready to go.

Soon enough, I was hanging around Lepakko more than I was at home or school. My crowd changed completely. I started hanging out with punks like Panda Nikander, Kääriäinen, Ölli Hildén, Saku Paasiniemi, Njassa, and guys like Rane Raitsikka or Kellogs Bollocks from bands like Woude, Lama,

Widows. These were my people. The rockabilly gangs, like the Steissi gang and the Nalle gang, would come by to flex their muscles, start trouble and fights, bust up windows, and destroy what we had built the previous day. But we just kept cleaning, scrubbing, and fixing things up, no matter how long it was going to take. The downstairs cellar area at Lepakko didn't have anything but a giant space to clean up and build up. The stench at the place, after years and years of hundreds of alcoholics living there in squalor, was unreal. The big room still wasn't ready a year later when I moved to Stockholm with Hanoi Rocks. But little by little, Lepakko built up its spaces and turned the place into a proper cultural center and operation, with rooms to rehearse and perform, a café—of course, being Finns, it needed a sauna—and the first independent radio station. The city finally caved and agreed to a long and cheap rental agreement.

Right around the beginning of Lepakko, Pepe Seivo and I started a band called Suopo with Markojuhani Rautavaara aka Kobo, who also sang in a band called Kärsäräkä (Snoutsnot). Ile Hilden and Ilari Rantala played the guitars. I got my hands on a Czech-made 200-watt WEM transistor amp and a Hiwatt 4x12" amp. Now I was finally getting some volume. I traded in the Aria Diamond for a Japanese Marchis Jazz bass. I swapped out the Marchis for a Fender Precision while playing with Pelle, and then made the switch to a Gibson Thunderbird with Hanoi. I ended up trading that '64 Precision for a Gibson EB3L. I still don't know what the hell I was thinking, must've been high.

Suopo played mostly songs that Kobo had written. Some of 'em were by the whole band. I had started writing some discopunk kind of stuff. We did a version of the Stranglers' "Something Better Change" in Finnish: "Mitkä tsäänssit sulla on."

Suopo played a lot of gigs, especially around Tapiola. We got around in an old moving van that had room for three up front; everyone else had to sit in the back with the gear. We were a local band, playing at suburban youth centers and events. There was a gig in the middle of the woods where we got paid in beer. Sometimes I'd perform in a jacket that had belonged to Kobo's dad, a famous Finnish classical music composer named Einojuhani

Rautavaara. Suopo had two fangirls who followed us from show to show. You could spot them from a mile away in their white coveralls.

Our BIG show was at a venue called Dipoli where I used to go to play pool as a kid, because we got to open up for the punk gods Pelle Miljoona and 1980. I played at Dipoli again less than a year later, but this time as a member of Pelle Miljoona Oy.

×××

The good thing about repeating a grade was that I ended up in the same class as Janne Haavisto. Janne and I built a delay effect out of a tape player by adding a playback head. We used it to record our version of the theme music from *Close Encounters of the Third Kind*. I got to know Janne's brother, Olli, and sister, Susanna. The Haavisto family was pretty cool, and Janne was a sick drummer. He was playing Billy Cobham stuff at thirteen.

Ölli Hildėn was in a band called Pohjanoteeraus, which I loved and even played with for a bit when the original bassist faded away. Ölli was Michael Monroe's cousin and he later played for Backsliders. Ölli was known as the loosest guy in Lauttasaari because he moved like he didn't have any bones.

Pohjanoteeraus had a big hit with the punks, "Hulluna on hyvä olla" (it's good to be nuts), that always got the crowd pogoing. I was running on beer and playing music every weekend. And that was that for the seventies.

1980

Moottoritie on kuuma (The highway is hot)

I came home from school on your average cold, dark day in January 1980. I was in a bad mood and tired. The phone rang. "Hi, it's Tumppi Varonen from Pelle Miljoona. Would you be interested in coming by to try out for the band?"

I thought one of my friends was messing with me. I slammed the receiver down. The phone rang again. "Listen up now. This *is* Tumppi, and if you're interested, here's the address…"

Pelle Miljoona had a rehearsal space in the Herttoniemi area of Helsinki. I was supposed to go out there in a couple days. WTF just happened?

Their last album, *Viimeinen syksy*, was my favorite record at the time, and Pelle Miljoona 1980 was pretty much the only Finnish band I could stand to listen to. This was fucking wild. When I was younger, I had listened to Finnish stuff like Hector ja Hullujussi. Dave Lindholm was for my brother's generation and just wasn't working for me. Pelle was something altogether different. A real homegrown punk band with a message.

I put Pelle's records on and started checking out the bass lines. When the day came to go for the audition, I jumped onto the bus and headed to the other side of town. I was nervous and still a bit in disbelief. I was just a sixteen-year-old punk kid who played in small local bands, like Suopo and Pohjanoteeraus. Pelle Miljoona had written basically every big Finnish punk song up to then.

All these years, I thought Tumppi Varonen had talked me up to Pelle Miljoona, but Ari Taskinen, the band's guitarist and keyboard player, recently told me, "By the way, I was the one who recommended you because I knew your brother from the pop and jazz school and I'd seen you play at Lepakko with Suopo." Suopo had played Lepakko just about every weekend in the fall of 1979. I'd seen Taskinen there in the crowd a bunch of times. Apparently he'd asked my brother for our home number and told Tumppi to call me. I'd been wondering for ages why Tumppi had called me, a sixteen-year-old kid from the suburbs, to ask if I wanted to join the biggest band in Finland. Was it because of those Suopo gigs at Lepakko? All I know is that I've always played with a heavy hand, banged the shit out of the bass. Taskinen had played the bass in Pelle up until then, but he wanted to transition over to the guitar and keyboard.

×××

I got off and switched buses at the central station. I got off the bus and walked over to the old, abandoned neighborhood school where Ari Taskinen and Tumppi Varonen lived, as did some other punks, like Stefan Piesnack and members of Sehr Schnell. The classrooms had been divided up into smaller spaces with plywood walls. This breeding ground for Finnish punk was later fixed up and is now a school again.

Tumppi, Taskinen, and some other guy were sitting up on the third floor. That third guy looked a little out there: red pompadour, lipstick, a big old nose, leather pants, and a leather jacket. When this weird-looking guy opened his mouth, an even weirder Finnish accent came out of it. "So, you some kinda bass player? I'm Andy."

"Yeah…I'm Sami…"

Pelle showed up and we all went downstairs to the rehearsal room. Red lights, Persian rugs, posters, and paintings. We plugged in and those songs that I'd loved for the past couple of years blasted out like a shotgun shot: "Mulla menee lujaa," "Mä vaan pogoon," "Lähdetään kiitämään," all dem classics.

It seemed like everyone was pickin' and grinnin'. Something was happening: chemistry, magic, something, it was definitely working. Pelle, the singer, was a bit older, very powerful but with a warm and kind spirit. Drummer Tumppi was a no-nonsense tough street punk with a giant heart. Taskinen was an eccentric, talented, weird guy with a heavy stutter; it would take him days to get his point across. Andy was distant, sullen, and cool, with a habit of sucking in his cheeks and bumming smokes off me. Andy's cheeksucking, I guess in his mind, made him look cool. I finally put two and two together that he'd played with Briard, the first Finnish punk band to get a record made (*I Really Hate Ya,* 1977). I'd seen the end of a Briard set in 1977 and their whole show in 1978 or 1979. Andy's stage presence and guitar playing was already then, for a fourteen or fifteen-year-old kid, pretty fucking intense.

I got the message the next day that I was in the band and we were leaving to play some shows that weekend. We'd be rehearsing up until then. I called my best friend right away. He didn't believe me. No one did. Everyone at school knew Pelle Miljoona. Their last record *Viimeinen syksy* had been a huge deal in Finland and had a number-one single on it, "Tahdon Rakastella Sinua."

Up until then, I hadn't played any shows other than around Espoo, or at Lepakko or in and outside of Helsinki. Now all of sudden I'd be playing all over Finland, Rauma in Western Finland or Saarijärvi in Central Finland. I went straight from behind a school desk to a tour bus. I didn't know a whole lot about the rest of the country. My family was all in the Helsinki area or in Norway. My dad was an orphan, and Mom was an only child. I had no other family except for my immediate family. I'd been to a couple of cities like Pori, Tampere, and to friends' summer cottages not too far from Helsinki. That's about all I had seen of Finland.

It was about ten below outside and not a whole lot warmer in the tour bus. A broken window had been covered with cardboard and it was letting cold air in. We were all shivering under our blankets, sitting on the old busted-up seats. We were traveling with a couple of old-school roadies, Puosu and Illi, plus all the band gear and the band's blue PA system.

The road into Rauma greeted us with a sign: "Make yourself at home, ya hear." The audience was boozing it up in the freezing cold outside the venue, getting good and ready to party and fight.

A thousand people showed up and packed the venue. My biggest audience up until then had been maybe a hundred people at Lepakko. Well, turn it up and get into it! And sure enough, like always, the music took over. When a band really clicks together and starts to flow during a live show, it's spiritual. Your mind goes off to some other space and time, the same way music-induced trances have done to people for thousands of years.

I was grooving on the edge of the stage, like a real fucking star. The girls in the front row reached out to feel up my legs. Suddenly they kept going all the way up to my crotch. I freaked out and froze up! I backed up all the way to play in front of the amps. Maybe I'd just take it easy here for the rest of the show. That kind of fan thing, grabbing onto limbs and touching musicians, didn't really fly in the Helsinki punk clubs. It was a total no-no. The shock wore off pretty fast though.

We went backstage after the show, and my adrenaline was pumpin'! Tumppi had a little bottle of rum with him. I took some swigs which started bringing down the rush. I knew then and there that I had to keep doing this. Playing music was my thing and there was nothing else I wanted to do.

I kept going to school but had totally lost interest in it. I played shows from Thursday to Saturday, sometimes on Wednesdays too. The tour bus would drop me off at home sometime around four in the morning on Sundays, leaving me, bass, and a big wad of cash in hand.

Mom would wake me up Monday morning and ask me how all the gigs had gone. It was just me and Mom at home then, since my brother and sister had moved into Helsinki. Mom was understanding and supportive. I'd give her some money from time to time, just to help with rent and food, even though I don't think I needed to. It just felt like the right thing to do.

The music magazine *Suosikki* put out an article about Pelle's new project that was now known as Pelle Miljoona Oy. We took some pictures at Pelle's house for the article. When the magazine hit the newsstands a few weeks later, someone at school pasted up the story on the cafeteria bulletin board. So all at once, everyone at school found out I was playing with Pelle. And I sure did hear about it. For the most part people were pretty into it, but I did get some comments along the lines of "Who do you think you are," "Fucking rock star," "Fucking punk," "So you're now famous or something?" But I still hung out with the same friends in Tapiola, Lauttasaari, and at Lepakko. The only difference was that now I was playing shows all over Finland on the weekends, and I finally had some money for equipment, smokes, or whatever. No more thinking about if I could afford to buy this album or if I had to sell a record to get it. Now I could also buy beers for my friends.

The way to rehearsals was kind of sketchy. The war between punk and rockabilly gangs was at its peak those days. When I switched buses by the Central Station, I had to dodge past ten or so greasers just itching to beat up some punks. In order to get to my bus to rehearsals, I would have to hide behind a bus, wait until it started moving, and walk alongside of it to get behind the next bus and wait until that one started moving and walk next to it to the next stop, total cat and mouse on the crowded bus depot with the grease heads on the lookout. There'd always be some problems with 'em. Andy and I ended up running into a shopping center, guitar cases in hand, with a bunch of rockabillies on our tail. We'd run down a side street behind the Ateneum museum. From there, you could cut through one of the shops— "Psst! Over to the left! To the right!"—and out through the back door. We had to outsmart the rockabilly idiots and get onto our bus for the rehearsal, what a ritual.

My old band, Pohjanoteeraus, had qualified for the Finnish rock music competition, Rock SM, held that spring in Tampere. A crew of about thirty to forty punks piled into a bus at Lepakko to go show our support. Once there, we got some booze, went nuts cheering for Pohjanoteeraus and jeering the other bands. I met Ismo Alanko there for the first time. His band, Hassisen Kone, ended up winning the competition. Later on, everyone in Lauttasaari and at Lepakko thought he had ripped off a Pohjanoteeraus song for one of his own. "Hulluna on hyvä olla" (It's good to be nuts) became "Rappiolla on hyvä olla" (It's good to be on the bottom). Sadly Pohjanoteeraus never recorded anything.

Ismo Alanko himself hasn't changed a bit over the years; he's just as down-to-earth as he ever was, a legend.

×××

When I was a kid, we had a record of protest songs at home called *Lautanen Guatemalan verta* (*A Plate of Guatemala's Blood*). I had noticed the Love Records logo, which I saw again later on Kaj Chydenius and Hurriganes records. It seemed like all the Finnish music worth listening to came out on Love Records.

People always say that, for example, Bob Dylan's lyrics are brilliant and political, which they are, but they're not going to mean a thing to you if you don't understand English, right?

All through the late sixties, early seventies, Love Records put out protest albums and showed that Finnish language music could also be socially conscious, inspiring, and political. To me the new form of protest music came a-knocking around 1978–1979 with the explosion of Finnish punk. Finally there was something I could understand and feel like it was my music, it talked to me. "Olen työtön" (I'm unemployed), "Pelko ja viha" (fear and hate), and all those great late seventies Finnish punk songs. And there it was again, that logo, Love Records—yes, of course! Who else in Finland but Mr. Atte Blom, the leading rebel of Love Records, would release Pelle's music? He was a huge cultural mover and shaker in Finland all through the sixties to nineties.

Viimeinen syksy was released on Johanna Records, which was also Atte Blom's label that he started after Love finally went under. Now it was my turn to meet the grand old man of the Finnish rock-and-roll business.

Atte Blom was and still is a kind spirit. An art and music lover, a fixer, a good ear for music, simultaneously easygoing and a worrier. Atte didn't work for money; he worked for the love of music. Money was only important to keep the show going. Atte released jazz and prog and folk on Love, and he wasn't scared of punk the way a lot of his generation was. Punk was actually perfect for Atte; he was highly opinionated and always rooting for the underdog. It makes perfect sense. That's why it's so good to see his FB updates; up yours powers that be!! He's still a rebel.

The Johanna office was in the Helsinki neighborhood of Eira. Tiina Vuorinen and Sini Perho worked there alongside Atte. In the summer of 1980, they moved shop to right above the concert venue Tavastia. Our concert booking was done by another old-school character named

Lido Salonen. I hate to say it, but Lido was kinda slippery; he would have fit into seventies Forty-Second Street perfectly, a hustler and a wheeler-dealer. I never really trusted him, but I was just a little brat thrown into the business straight from the school bench.

We'd start honing and rehearsing the new songs for the upcoming album as soon as we wrote them. I don't remember a lot of planning about the song order or which song would be on the new record or not. That stuff was all up to Taskinen, Tumppi, and Pelle.

We recorded a single: "Olen kaunis" (I'm beautiful) / "Älä äiti itke" (Don't cry, Mom). It was done in a day. Pelle has a spoken intro at the beginning of "Olen kaunis," and we all followed his lead on when to start playing, there was no count in.

I'd been to a recording studio once before; it was a friend's uncle's barn with some archaic reel-to-reel recording equipment. Next thing I knew, here I was, recording at the top studio in Finland, Finnvox, with the legendary Risto Hemmi as our engineer. I was pretty nervous, but I had my poker face on, like I'd been recording my whole life. I learned fast how Pelle, Taskinen, and all of those guys wanted to do it. This was punk, why get stuck with polishing everything? All the songs were played live in a few takes. Fuck-ups didn't matter as long as the take had a good vibe going on. If the vibe was off, we'd play it again. At first it was weird when Risto played the tracks back individually, just one instrument at a time, it sounded like crap. All together, though, it sounded great. It's that chemistry thing of playing together as a group which easily gets ruined nowadays because of the tendency to try and fix up all the imperfections in post-production, thinking it's going to make the song sound better. R&R needs the push and pull, swing.

I don't have a lot of memories from the recording sessions because it all flew by so fast. The songs weren't really too hard to play, but there are times you can hear my hands were not necessarily strong enough yet. The ideas are all there, though, and some of them stick out loud and clear. Most of the bass lines were improvised on the spot, especially the ones that we didn't have time to go through at the rehearsals prior to entering the studio. I'd switched from my Marchis bass to a Fender Precision 64. The verse melody and main hook for "Moottoritie on kuuma" was written on

Taskinen's keyboard. He asked if I could just double that on bass. The bass line for the chorus of the song was all mine and came out without much thought. A sixteen-year-old doesn't necessarily think a lot about what they're playing. The way to go is by instinct. I'd studied music theory and knew my major seventh and ninth chords and all them scales, when not to play a particular note. You fuck up a note with the bass, everybody notices.

The guitar solo in "Moottoritie on kuuma" was Andy's Middle Eastern vibe. It started already then, even before Andy started listening to flamenco. Andy was already a badass at fourteen while playing in Briard. The manic solo in "Moottoritie" was Andy's own take on an Arabic scale. He made his own version of everything.

Recording was sporadic, two or three days here and there. Maybe we'd have some recording sessions at Finnvox on Tuesday and Wednesday, then Thursday we'd go play some shows. Same thing the next week. The single for "Olen kaunis" was coming out, and during the spring I decided to leave school. I'd already found my own path. My teacher wouldn't let me go that easy, though. "What are your plans if the band breaks up?" Well, then I'd start a new one.

I got along best with Andy since we were about the same age. I was sixteen and Andy seventeen. Pelle was my brother's age, so he was like another older brother. Tumppi and Taskinen also felt a lot older and were already in their twenties. We were all close, but Andy and I spent more time hanging together.

Andy and I found our groove, so to speak, one day in some hotel room in Middle of Nowhere Finland. We had a day off between shows. We got ourselves some booze and sat around telling stories and laughing our asses off. We got a great idea and started throwing empty bottles against the wall. Shards of glass were flying everywhere. I eventually got tired, undressed, and passed out. I woke up the next morning hungover and covered in blood. There were little shards of glass all around me. In my stupor I hadn't noticed we had been busting the empties on the wall above MY bed. Andy laughed his ass off while I tried to pick the shards off myself in the shower.

After we finished playing shows for the weekend, I'd sometimes go over to Andy's in the Vuosaari neighborhood of Helsinki. His unbelievably huge

Rottweiler, Ali, would freak me out every time, getting up on his hind legs with his paws on my shoulders to lick my face. Andy had a real nice family—brother Ikke, sister Kaisa, and their parents. His dad was a bit of a nutter, though. I stayed over there a lot because we always had a lot to talk about.

Toward the end of the winter, Andy brought along a very strange character to Pelle rehearsals. Despite the way-below-zero-Celsius freezing weather, he was wearing just a thin leather jacket, torn-up jeans, a ratty T-shirt, and sneakers. His big blond hair was teased up, and he had a face like Brigitte Bardot covered in makeup, earrings, and jangly bracelets. I remember thinking that I was gonna punch him if he came any closer.

This freak was jumping maniacally from instrument to instrument, drums to bass to guitar to Taskinen's keyboards. He could play them all. At the end he pulled a harmonica out of his jacket pocket and played a Little Walter song. This guy was unbelievable! This Makke Fagerholm/Michael Monroe. A week later, we got on the same bus and made acquaintance properly.

I heard later on that Andy had tried to get Makke into Pelle as the bassist. It wouldn't have worked out anyway. Kind of like having Mick Jagger on the bass. Michael was destined to be a front man.

The original lineup of Hanoi Rocks also practiced in the same space in Herttoniemi. Back then it was Makke, Nasty Suicide, Stefan Piesnack, who used to play guitar for Pelle, Nedo Soininen, and Peki Sirola. Andy hung out with all of them and there was a lot of whispering and scheming going on. I had no idea that Andy wrote songs, but it became apparent because this band was playing them, along with some MC5 and Cheap Trick covers.

Andy wasn't part of the first Hanoi Rocks lineup that played a handful of shows that summer, but I got the feeling it was only a matter of time before he joined. Andy was working with them clandestinely; he and Michael had a vision for the future.

Michael had suggested Chinese Rocks for the band name, as a nod to the Johnny Thunders and the Heartbreakers. Andy turned it into Hanoi Rocks.

Johanna released a summer compilation called *Helleaalto* (heatwave) that included Pelle Miljoona Oy playing a Finnish version of the Specials' "A Message to You Rudy," "Viesti (teille kovikset)," which had been recorded in the spring. My brother played sax on the track. Jone and I haven't played together on anything other than that song and Pelle Almgren's EP from 1986. Jone also played on Maukka Perusjätkä's song "Vaatteet on mun aatteet" (clothes are my concepts). Fun fact: in the song's video, Michael Monroe "plays" the saxophone solo. It was Michael's first time performing on TV.

The *Moottoritie on kuuma* LP was coming out later that summer. We were playing the songs live long before they were released, and the crowds were really getting into them. We could tell the record would be a hit. Kari Riipinen took the picture for the cover of *Moottoritie* in the basement bathroom at Lepakko. Kari said he'd picked up some clown outfits. I said absolutely not but was down to dress up like an Orthodox Jew or Amish instead. Andy got it in his head that he wanted to dress up as a ballerina with a tutu and nothing underneath. The shoot came out great.

We took a break from touring at the beginning of June. Andy and I took a weekend trip to Stockholm. We stayed by Slussen with Andy's girlfriend, Anna Jederby, in her grandfather's apartment. He'd played the double bass for Charlie Parker during a Scandinavian tour. Later on, Anna ended up becoming the mother of my son, so the boy's got some bass in his blood.

We bounced around Stockholm and bought punk records you couldn't get in Finland. I bought the Clash's *Black Market Clash* EP, a single from the Swedish band Chatterbox, the Dickies' LP *Dawn of the Dickies*. I also bought a pair of checkerboard pants from a punk shop; those ended up in a lot of pictures.

Andy knew a drummer in Stockholm, Gyp Casino, real name Jesper Sporre or Jeppe. We jammed with Jeppe in his rehearsal space, which later on became Hanoi's spot to jam. We riffed on some instrumental Ventures tracks, like "Pipeline" and "Walk Don't Run." Then Andy showed me how to play E like this and then like that. I learned the bass line and we went through this song a bunch of times. Later on, I realized it was an early version of "Tragedy."

×××

We started the summer tours. There were a lot of them, festivals and other open-air concerts. Along the way, we'd make pit stops to jump in a lake and have some fun. But a lot of times there's just too much time to kill, you get some booze, get fucked up, and that's when the great ideas start flowing. On the cover of Iggy Pop's *TV EYE Live* record, he's got his legs wrapped up in gaffer tape. The great idea was to turn Tumppi into a gaffer tape mummy. We covered him up in tape all the way to the top of his head, with only his eyes and nose showing. Tumppi was supposed to come out on stage dramatically like that, and perform as a mummy, but the tape was too tight, and he couldn't move his limbs at all. He barely made it up the steps to the stage when he fell flat on his face. And then couldn't get up on his own. The show was kicking off with a song Tumppi sang, so Illi and Puosu had to rip the tape off of him in a hurry. Tumppi got a free waxing out of it—all his body hair came off with the tape. Pelle was behind the drums real amused. "What the fuck is this now…?"

At a Cherry Bombz show, Nasty Suicide had to be taped onto a column on stage. Nasse had taken a bunch of pills and his legs stopped working. So they gaffer-taped him to the pole and hung his Les Paul around his neck. Now play!

Some people are born with a mustache and a monobrow. I, on the other hand, looked like a thirteen-year-old girl when I was sixteen. Not a chance of getting into the bars after a concert for me. Illi and Puosu were big guys so they'd sometimes try to sneak me in between them, but usually the door guy would figure out what was going on and block me with a hand to my face. So I'd hang out in the bus with Bootsy, Illi's dog, listening to music on the ghetto blaster, drinking a six-pack of beer and waiting for my friends to come back shitfaced. Bootsy became my buddy. Every now and then someone would smoke a joint, but wouldn't give me a drag no matter how much I begged. Gotta watch out for the kid. Not yet, son!

After one gig, there was something wrong with the hotel booking. We were deep in the countryside and were told to go and look for this house that rented out rooms like a motel. An old lady opened the door. There was a woman, well over six feet tall, creeping behind her, speechless, just staring intensely. When the old lady noticed her, she yelled, "Liisa, go back to your room!" The woman turned and lumbered away. We heard the door to her room shut.

Everyone else got a real room, but I got a cot in the attic. I was just about to drift off when I got the feeling that there was someone else in the room. I opened my eyes and saw Liisa standing in the dark above my bed, staring at me. I jumped up and ran out like a jackrabbit, all the way down the three flights of stairs from the attic to the yard screaming my head off! It was straight out of a horror movie!

Our bus driver often drank while driving. When he ran out of booze, he'd start on the bug spray. Unbelievably, the guy is still kicking around. It's a fucking miracle that the rest of us made it out of that tour alive.

One time, a tire blew on the bus while we were going about fifty miles per hour. The driver handled it well, and we didn't end up flying into the forest. Everyone stumbled off the bus to stretch their legs and help change the tire. Everyone except Andy. He sat on his guitar case and played something that sounded like the Soviet national hymn on his Gibson Explorer, warbling about how accidents happen about every day. That's when it hit me that Andy really was writing songs and could take inspiration from a situation to write something about it. The Hanoi Rocks song "11th Street Kids" came to be because the bus busted a tire.

That tour around Finland helped me understand Mr. Hulkko's genius, as well as his growing frustration.

I could get into Elmupoli and have a beer there, even if I was underage. Everyone was cool with it. Puosu and Illi sat at a table with Dave Lindholm, and along with him Albert Järvinen, formerly of the Hurriganes. I'd already met Dave, Tuomari Nurmio, Ralf Örni, Affe Forsman, Kojo—that Finnish crème de la crème of musicians and legends. Now I got to meet my big guitar idol. *Roadrunner* is still the baddest-ass of Finnish rock albums. Hands down; it just is. I went to stand between Puosu and Albert, said hi, and Puosu introduced me. Albert looked at the buttons on my leather jacket and said, "What kind of fucking button-wearing punk kid are you?" Out of nowhere this hero of mine, Albert, clenched his hand into a fist and punched me hard in the stomach. Knocked the wind right out of me. What a dick. Then Albert turned around and kept drinking. I was still such a youngin, it totally devastated me. I walked away with tears welling up in my eyes.

Remu Aaltonen, drummer from the Hurriganes, was not into Pelle or Hanoi Rocks either. Remu thought that Hanoi Rocks used guitars like machine guns. He meant it as an insult, but we took it as a compliment. Right on!

Albert Järvinen got a lot of offers to tour internationally—with Nick Lowe, Albert Lee, Lemmy, Elvis Costello—but he decided to stay and keep getting wasted in Helsinki. Just your typical Finnish bad self-esteem and fear of the unknown. No will to leave your comfort zone and go see what's out there. The few rare chances wasted on booze. Andy was a rare, different kind of person. He wasn't afraid of anything.

In July, we started to practice at Lepakko for the Pelle Miljoona Oy fall tour. During a break, Andy pulled me aside in the Lepakko kitchen and asked if I'd move to Stockholm with him. We could start Hanoi Rocks for real.

Moottoritie on kuuma ended up selling really well. The single went to number one. Every weekend, I pocketed a thousand marks, a lot for a sixteen-year-old. We had August off, and in September, we were supposed to leave with Pelle Miljoona Oy for a three-week tour. By that time I'd played every city in Finland at least a couple of times and every venue at least once.

I thought about Andy's suggestion for a couple of seconds before agreeing. Sounds like a plan; I was in. Of course I liked all the Pelle guys, but the idea was to get out of Finland.

All the trips abroad I'd taken as a kid had left a big impression; I liked to travel more than anything. One time, Dad and I went to Gotland, Sweden. When my parents' divorce was finalized, my mom took me to Italy and Greece. I seriously wanted to move there. I talked to the hotel owner in Italy with my twelve-year-old's English and got myself a job, a room, the whole deal. Momsy ruined everything by making me get on the plane back to Finland.

Those childhood trips were only from a few years before. I was curious about the whole world. Stockholm seemed like a good place to start, and nothing was keeping me at home. Mom and I lived by ourselves. She'd go to work and I'd play shows when I didn't have school. It's not like we were attached at the hip. And when I kept thinking about it...I'd grown up listening to my brother and sister and their views about how the army or a normal job weren't for them, no fucking way. I dug Andy. I dug Michael and Nasty. Jeppe seemed like a good guy. Hanoi Rocks had to get started in Stockholm because it was bigger, more cosmopolitan, more tolerant than Helsinki in 1980. Stockholm had racial diversity. Finland was a bleak, narrow-minded corner of Europe, jealous of everyone who had it better. There was this mentality to tear down anyone who found any success. *Who do you think you are?* Bands didn't tour outside of Finland. They played in Stockholm and would turn back around. Stockholm was pretty much the edge of the Western world.

Pelle and Tumppi spent August vacationing and traveling Europe by train. During that time, Michael, Nasty, Andy, and I recorded the *I Want You / Kill City Kills* single—a first for Hanoi Rocks. The cover says *Hanoi Rocks featuring Andy McCoy* for a couple reasons. Andy was still a member of Pelle. Andy had already made a name for himself, whereas Hanoi hadn't. And Atte had promised Andy the possibility to record a solo single of his own. The recording was like a tryout—Andy asked me to play bass. A studio cat named Keimo Hirvonen was on drums. Måns Groundstroem and Namilo were engineering it. Atte sat at the mixing board with a burger in one hand saying, "Let's turn that crash up a bit." I watched thinking, okay, so this is how you mix a record.

Ralf Örn and Jaana Rinne, Måsse Kullman, Jimi Sumén, and Maria bounced around the studio for whatever reason. The drinking had already begun while recording the basic tracks for "I Want You." A bottle of Four Roses whisky and beers appeared out of nowhere. How's a kid supposed to say no to that?

The B-side "Kill City Kills" is about a punk squat in Helsinki that almost nobody knew about back then. It became a legend after it was gone. Michael and Andy were actually from Helsinki so they knew all about it. The building had just been or was being torn down. There's now a municipal building in that spot. Kill City got its name from the record Iggy Pop and James Williamson released in '77.

"Kill City Kills" was Ralf Örn and Andy's song. "I Want You" Andy straight up stole from some Swedish band. I mean, the whole song. Even the name was literally the translation from Swedish, "Jag vill ha dig." That ended up as a lawsuit. So neither side of the *Hanoi Rocks featuring Andy McCoy* single was Andy's song. It's strange to think that within half a year after that, Andy had written "Tragedy," "Village Girl," and "Pretender" and the rest of the first album.

I saw Michael, Nasty, and Andy off on their Viking Line ferry to Stockholm. They had their guitars, a few bags of clothes, a couple of amps, one of which was apparently Stefan Piesnack's Fender Combo Reverb. Someone, I don't know who, had grabbed it from the rehearsal space because Nasty didn't have his own. I hereby put an end to this long-running rumor that I'm the sticky-fingered culprit.

I said I'd be joining them a few weeks later. First, I was going on a trip to London with my girlfriend at the time, Johku. We had a slightly different idea of what we were going to see and do on our trip. I went to the 100 Club to catch some punk shows. I saw The Exploited, Anti-Pasti, and a bunch of other HC punk bands. I had to go to Marquee too. It didn't matter who was playing. That club was legendary. Marquee had a poster on the door: Rockabilly from New York! I was so sick of the assholes from that scene in Helsinki that the last thing I wanted to see was a rockabilly band. But whatever, it was worth having a couple beers there. The band playing was the Stray Cats, the show blew my mind!

On the other hand, Johku and her friend wanted to hang out in Greek discos full of hairy mustachioed macho men. Turns out she'd balled Andy in June after the trip to Stockholm. We broke up when we got back home.

At the beginning of September, I turned seventeen and told my mom I was going to Stockholm for vacation, saying I'd be gone for a week or two. Mom wasn't worried because I'd just been there over the summer. I didn't tell anyone about leaving Pelle or joining Hanoi.

All I had in my pocket was my ticket and eight hundred marks, with no idea how I was going to get any more money. But there was a big apartment waiting in Stockholm.

×××

On September 7, 1980, I hopped onto the overnight Viking Line ferry from Helsinki to Stockholm. I slammed a couple beers and passed out on a deck bench with my bag and my bass under my feet. The next morning, I walked through border control and here I was, at the Stockholm Terminal. The welcoming committee was waiting for me: Hulkko, Fagerholm, Stenfors, aka McCoy, Monroe, Suicide. I was still Takamäki back then. Andy was trying to get me to go by Sam Sodomy. I didn't even know what the English word sodomy meant yet.

"Well, let's go to the apartment" I said. The guys just stared at their feet and someone mumbled, "Yeah, well, there's no apartment." What? Where were we going to sleep then? No clue. We went to the Karlaplan shopping center. Jeppe was working at a youth center there and was able to store my stuff. We could go to the rehearsal space as soon as Jeppe got off of work.

Andy took off for Nacka, where his girlfriend Anna's family had a house. He was going to take a steam bath. Andy had a nice setup for himself. The rest of us were out of luck, so we wandered around the streets of Östermalm to T-Centralen and then finally to Hötorget. Michael and Nasty didn't have any money. We exchanged my eight hundred marks for krona, and Nasty went to buy some beers, because he never got carded, he looked old already then. We cracked open the beers as we walked around a park in Hötorget. Welcome to Stockholm! Life was good.

Around one in the afternoon, a couple of big dudes and a stout woman appeared in front of us. They started to speak and gesture to pour the beers out on the ground. I didn't understand what was going on. I barely spoke Swedish then. Nasty, knowing the language, translated for us. They were cops and they wanted to search us.

Michael was carrying brass knuckles. Now the cops got interested. Why was he carrying brass knuckles? Michael explained that they were a family heirloom, and they used to be his grandpa's. The cops confiscated them under pretense of being a weapon and charged us with drinking in public. They asked our ages and addresses. We gave them Jeppe's neighbor's address and they let us go.

That evening, we went to Jeppe's rehearsal space by the Universitetet metro stop. Everything was set up there, except for my Ampeg amp which was still in the Pelle rehearsal space in Helsinki. I'd probably never get it back.

We played through "Tragedy" first and then some of the songs Andy and Michael had written for their band, Nymphomaniac, like "Problem Child" and "It's Too Late." Nymphomaniac was together in 1979 during Michael's first trip to Stockholm.

Andy and Nasty had been in the same class. Nasty's dad was the school principal. Andy and Nasty were the worst students in school, the guitar-playing bad boys. They found each other and Nasty ended up playing with Briard. Nasty and Andy had been playing together since they were fourteen and their guitar duties were clear. Nasty loved to play rhythm; he was a real natural. Nasty could play lead beautifully if he wanted, but he really dug pumpin' out the rhythm. Nasty and Andy sat together and divided up the guitar parts: If you do this, I'll do this. If the song goes A-F#m-D-E, Nasse would play it his own way. Both of them looked up to the same guitar duos: Richards and Jones, Richards and Taylor, Richards and Wood, the Young brothers, Parfitt and Rossi. It's gotta be played just right, and Nasse had the right touch for it.

We slept in the rehearsal space that first night. When a flashlight went by outside on the metro platform, we had to shut up and hide behind the amps, since sleeping there wasn't allowed.

We rehearsed every day for a minimum of five or six hours at a time. Andy kept pulling out new songs, nearly one every day. The pace was so incredible that the songs had to be from before. Andy had been hiding his own songs in the Pelle days. They wouldn't have been a good fit for Pelle anyway.

Andy wasn't afraid to write outside of the rock and roll box. When Andy started getting into flamenco in 1983, he had all kinds of books on flamenco lying around his house. Andy could read music but didn't write his songs down that way—we all just basically followed his hands. By staring at Hulkko's hands, I learned the craft of reading music by following another player's hands. That skill has become very useful later on down the road. I never took notes. The song would sink into your backbone once you learned it with intensity. We rehearsed like madmen, but when things started to take off, we didn't rehearse as much anymore. We didn't have to go over the same things over and over. It became just a natural instinctive interaction.

Between rehearsals, Michael, Nasty, and I shuffled around Stockholm and made our acquaintance with other street urchins and checked out the general vibe of the city. What was left of my cash was almost gone and none of us had any means of income. We started bumming money in Gamla Stan. The first Swedish I learned was "Can you spare some change?" If we managed to get together ten kronas, we'd get a hamburger meal from a hamburger chain called Clock. We were a bunch of skinny bastards back then, still are. If I could bum five kronas together for myself, I'd go and get a roll with some cold cuts and a pint of strawberry yogurt. Nasty's old friend Angelique worked at Big Burger (another burger joint), and she could get us some more junk food a couple times a week.

Rain, waiting around, hunger, panhandling. Sleeping in stairwells, the subway, and the rehearsal space. It definitely wasn't healthy living. The bad air in the rehearsal space, the bad diet, and constant cold messed with my lungs and I started to have trouble breathing. But a seventeen or eighteen-year-old can handle it. Nothing mattered except the band, and we sounded better and better after every rehearsal. We were the best band in the world, and soon the world would be ours.

There was quite a big difference in how us three lived and the gentlemen's life Andy was living. Where he stayed was luxurious. But there was no place for us there. It was a real family home: father, mother, two children. Andy had boyfriend status; we didn't fit into this picture. So we just wandered around the city, day in and day out. I've never walked so much in my life. Michael, Nasty, and I became very close over those months through our shared misery. We became brothers.

I finally got the chance to call my mom, she'd been worried of course. I calmed her down and let her know I was going to stay in Stockholm. I told her that everything was okay and things were looking up, just wait and see.

Swedes are impressed if you're American, English, or Australian, and less impressed if you're just a Finn. Nasty's Finnish accent in Swedish was unmistakable and ruined his chances of picking up girls. We had to come up with something, so Michael became Australian. No one in Stockholm knew what an Australian accent sounded like back then, so Michael could make up his own accent, which was funny as hell. Michael would pick up a girl at a nightclub, while Nasty and I waited around the corner. We'd pretend to run into each other—Hey man!! Long time no see!—and just like that, we all had a place to sleep. A lot of times, these girls still lived at home, so we had to be very quiet. We'd usually first raid the fridge and then go after Dad's bar cart for a glass of Johnny Walker Red.

Some of these girls ended up becoming our good friends and later on let us stay at their own places. A Finnish girl named Tuittu who lived in St. Eriksplan let us sleep on her floor. Then she went to Berlin but wouldn't give us her keys. We knew she had a big plastic bag full of weed and we definitely needed it more than she did. We knew the code to the front door of the building, so we decided to break in at two in the morning. One of us stayed outside of the building by the door, to keep watch, while the rest of us broke in through the back window and took her stash. Now we had something good to smoke for a few weeks.

The weather was getting colder and bumming money wasn't cutting it. We got some jobs, which thankfully didn't last very long. Nasty and I were cleaning the Göta Banks bathrooms at T-Central. Michael found a job cleaning some other bank somewhere else.

×××

Sitting on the steps of Hötorget, we made friends with some Middle Eastern refugees: Ali-Baba, Bobby from Malta, Arab Punk, Chinese Arab, Hassan. Those guys became our blood brothers as soon as they got used to the fact that we looked like women who wore too much makeup. It was eye-opening to hear their stories about fleeing Afghanistan, Palestine, Ethiopia, Morocco, Malta. They had to flee to Scandinavia to find safety or at least food, but the locals didn't accept them. Sweden was supposedly a cosmopolitan and tolerant country, but they got nothing but insults and dirty looks on the street. *Svartskalle, finnjävel.* The better off sure are good at being dicks.

We became a part of this refugee group's life. We smoked weed and played Space Invaders at Café Avenue. Afghan Ali's rallying cry was "Kill the Russians." Hanging out together meant communicating across language, race, faith, and all other boundaries: Arabic, Moroccan Arabic, English, Farsi. We accepted each other as we were and were all in the same boat.

Ali and Bobby liked to frequent Club 88. Some of the door guys let us in, some of them didn't. Club 88's DJ played Marley, Bowie, the Stones, Peter Tosh. When our favorite Peter Tosh song "Stepping Razor" blasted from the speakers, we would all rush to the dance floor. "I'm like a stepping razor, don't you watch my size. I'm dangerous, so dangerous..."

Leaving 88 one night, we were walking through the deserted center of town when some Swedish nationalists came round a corner and attacked us. They wanted to jump us for being foreigners. There were seven of us, so we got right into it. I pulled the studded belt from my pants and whipped one of the guys in the face with it. That'll leave a mark. Pretty quickly, the tables turned and the Nazis-in-training were getting their asses handed to them. They ran away.

We did a lot of speed. The Muslim guys didn't drink, but they added amphetamines to their coffee. I'd drink a cup of super-joe and next thing I knew, it was morning and we'd been out to ten different places, everything buzzed by super fast, it had been a good time all the time, and now we were heading to some other afterparty.

The speed started to have an effect on Hanoi's sound. It brought in just the right touch of aggression. I turned it up to eleven. We were already mostly influenced by punk. Hanoi was a punk-hard rock band, not glam at all. More like the Clash than Sweet. AC/DC was a big deal for all of us. Dead Boys' first album. I often felt like we were already doomed because our favorite bands, like MC5 and the Stooges, never made it. Now their music is in car commercials, go figure.

Speed was great...then. Now just the thought of it is nauseating. Back in Helsinki, it was just maybe a little weed, but you could easily get your hands on anything in Stockholm. I've never been the type to say no to anything. I'd rather try anything once and make my own conclusions.

Speed gives you a shitload of energy. It also has the social aspect to keep you running from club to club. I could spend days in that state, play music or draw, get into any of that detailed kind of stuff. Your mind is flying all over the place but you're still able to focus and be totally alert. Hyperactive kids get speed in their medication so they can focus and calm down.

There were sleepless nights after sleepless nights, so things got a little out of hand. Partying wasn't really partying anymore.

×××

Jeppe's punk friends hung out at the Galleria shopping center. Kim Lövdahl aka Grillmaster, Murder-Johnny, Grippa. Kim Kuusisto became my closest friend of this band of punks. Kim lived with his girlfriend Mona in Rinkeby, which was a neighborhood with a bad reputation. It was a poor suburb with a lot of immigrants. With poverty comes crime. For a meal we shoplifted sausages and powdered mashed potatoes from the grocery store. We'd run away with half-eaten meals from outdoor restaurants. You would wait until somebody finishes his meal and pays, then grab the plate that still has some good stuff on it and run off with it. People would often leave entire meatballs uneaten. People are strange.

One time we were out with this punk and we took some tools with us, walked a couple miles to a car park, detached the front and back bumper from a car, and carried them to a chop shop where the punk had a friend working. "Hey, man! Got some bumpers!" Dude gave us a few hundred, so we bought some more speed, weed, sausages, and powdered mashed potatoes. Back then the car bumpers were made out of metal.

There was this one guy, a dealer, who sold speed from a hollow walking stick. He'd pull the speed out from the bottom and stuff the money in through the top. If the cops stopped and searched him, the speed and money would be safely tucked into the walking stick leaning against the wall.

One morning, I was hungover and beat, sitting around the Karlaplan shopping center with Nasty and Michael. Through the window, we saw Benny Andersson, the piano player from ABBA, pushing his shopping cart. It was a surreal sight to see him walking around in his long mink coat tossing prime cuts of meat and other treats into his cart, while here we were starving and awake for days on end. I got it in my head that we should follow him to the parking lot, whack him over the head, and steal his food and coat. We started to tail him, while looking for something to hit him with. But of course, Benny Andersson had someone from the store waiting on him hand and foot, helping him bring his shopping back to the car. The plan fell apart. But it could have been a good story: *Hanoi Rocks mugs Benny Andersson*.

A familiar face appeared on the Hötorget metro escalator: Stefan Piesnack. I was excited at first. I'd always liked Stefan and I was about to yell HEY, MAN!, but the guys pulled me back down to hide behind the escalator. "Are you fucking crazy? Don't you remember we nicked Stefan's amp?" It was a close call. I'd totally forgotten about the whole thing. We heard later that Stefu was in Stockholm looking for us with a gun in his pocket.

I was walking along Drottninggatan one afternoon and saw a guy passed out in the park. He was dressed neat and had a wallet peeking out from his back pocket. I crept up close and quietly slid the wallet from his pocket and went around the corner to investigate what it held in it. Two hundred kronas, a deck ticket on the ferry to Turku, and a Finnish ID. I took a hundred, went back to where he was lying, and tried to put the wallet back into his pocket when he suddenly woke up.

Of course the guy thought I was trying to steal his wallet and he grabbed my hand while shouting like hell. It was too late to explain, so I twisted free and took off running.

We were walking around Gamla Stan with a few punks. A drunk tourist turned down a narrow alley for a piss. We followed him and one of us showed him a knife. Give us your money. The tourist was Finnish. He pissed himself with fear and gave us his money.

Afterward I got to thinking that robbing people was not something I'd continue with. It's a slippery slope.

×××

The single "I Want You" came out in November, but it came out without fanfare. At the end of 1980, Hanoi Rocks only played two shows, both of them in Stockholm. One of the gigs was in Djurgården, the other wherever it was that the Sex Pistols had played, maybe Kvarnet.

While I'm playing, I'm always also listening to the vocal melody. It's important for the bass. Sometimes I'll throw something from the melody into the lick. Andy usually had all the lyrics ready to go. But he would still change the words at the last moment. Hanoi, like the New York Dolls later on or pretty much any other band I have been in, didn't have a predetermined thought process where everything had to be played just so. Not even close. Playing as a band means feeling the song out, finding what's in it, or on the other hand, it can be like an explosion, everything materializes on the spot, just pure magic. Andy would be riffing on his guitar for weeks, let's say it's the song "Nothing New." Everyone follows what's going on and jams the riff, feeling where it might lead next. Then the riff was tossed aside, until it came back a couple months later as a complete song. When we started to play it again, we were already used to playing it a certain way and that gave it the song's personality. "Café Avenue" is kind of a rip-off of Iggy Pop's "The Passenger," but it all just depends on how you play the chords.

The way Hanoi Rocks dressed wasn't part of some bigger plan. If someone was wearing some cool clothes, it'd get noticed. Michael had his own thing going on altogether. Naturally, we were influenced by each other; we were together all the time and all of us were really into thrifting and flea markets. There was no plan for having to look a certain way, but everyone had the same conception, idea, sensibility about clothes. Good bands looked good: the Stones, the Clash, the Dolls.

You couldn't find any cool stuff in Finnish clothing shops. Maybe you could find an old bus driver hat at the flea market. I bought an old fifties leather jacket from the flea market at Lepakko. It was so big that I had to sew it on the inside to make it fit. I had learned to stitch and sew in school, instead of going for the woodshop class I hung out with the girls and learned to stitch. I knew how to take in pants and I knew how to do alterations. What I didn't know was that you need a special needle to sew leather, so I ruined all my mom's needles before I found out. Andy was good at sewing as well and made his own jackets and pants. These days, I'm learning how to make hats. I got started on the hats because of the Clash. Even before Pelle Miljoona, I'd wear wide-brimmed hats and pinstripe suits.

Not that there's anything wrong with T-shirts and jeans. Everything depends on HOW you wear them. The Ramones were the perfect example of a T-shirt and jeans band. But dem hippies with their long-ass hair and T-shirts and jeans who gazed at their own feet while playing, those guys I can't stand.

Michael and I went back to Helsinki on the ferry in December to spend time with our families. When we got there, I heard the new Pelle Miljoona Oy had a show at the convention center. That meant the rehearsal space in Herttoniemi would be empty. Stefan Piesnack and TB Window were playing in the new lineup; the guys had come to the rescue last minute when Andy and I left for Stockholm before the fall tour.

I told my dad that I had to pick up my amp from the old rehearsal space. He kindly gave us a ride in his orange Renault. When we got close to the school, I asked him to turn off the headlights so we wouldn't draw any attention. This is when it dawned on my dad that we were planning a break-in. We got in with a screwdriver and a knife and went straight to Stefan's space. I unscrewed a plywood plank from the wall and squeezed through. I found my amp with the help of my flashlight and handed it to Michael, came back, and screwed the panel back into place. There was no trace of the break-in, not on either the front door nor Stefan's wall. I heard later that Stefan had flipped out when he saw that everything was exactly as it had been, but only my V-4 Ampeg had disappeared into thin air.

We got the amp to the car and pulled out. After about a hundred yards, we were stopped by a cop car. Pops had forgotten to turn his headlights back on after turning them off in the yard. He got off with a warning.

Unfortunately for Stefu, he never got his own amp back.

I met Seppo Vesterinen for the first time over that Christmas break. Michael had said that Seppo wanted to manage Hanoi. Seppo was one of the few people in Finland who worked internationally. He'd brought lots of artists to Finland, like Keith Jarrett and other high profile jazz concerts. Seppo had seen and dug the original lineup of Hanoi at Tavastia, but he didn't think the band had reached its potential yet.

Seppo paid tens of thousands of marks out of his own pocket so we'd have enough to eat, and more importantly, would have a permanent roof over our heads. Our new headquarters was a two-bedroom apartment on the twelfth floor of a building on Hagalundsgatan in one of the blue high-rise buildings in Solna, just outside of Stockholm. No more begging, robbing, dealing, or cheating. Now we could hop on the bus into town and buy our own beers, but we'd still bum them off our friends. We had enough money to buy pancake mix, bread, and liverwurst. Liverwurst because it has lots of iron and makes you strong, I heard. It was a mainstay of the Finnish diet back in those not-so-healthy days. Everyone had liverwurst and Emmental cheese in their fridge in the seventies.

I sat around the apartment in Solna, sucking on a roach and reading Agent XY9 comics, which had a fat mob boss character named Yaffa. It sounded good. I started practicing my signature: Sam Yaffa.

It looked good. From there on out, I've been Sam Yaffa.

I found out later on that "Yaffa" means "beautiful woman" in Hebrew, but hey, even that fits, since I looked like a beautiful woman as a young man. Like a Puerto Rican lady.

1981

Bangkok Shocks, Saigon Shakes, Hanoi Rocks

Seppo Vesterinen had gotten the ball rolling and negotiated a record deal with Atte Blom. The first Hanoi Rocks record was recorded in January at Park Studios in the outskirts of Stockholm. We had to take two buses just to get there.

My studio experience was the two singles and the LP with Pelle. We'd practiced enough that the songs were pretty tight, but maybe not totally buffed and polished; "Lost in the City" didn't fully come together until we were in the studio. Halfway through the solo, I kept strumming the E string even though I was supposed to play the bass line. My guess is I was too caught up staring at Andy's hands, watching where they'd go next on the guitar neck. The band asked me if I wanted to give it another go. Fuck it, it worked. That's the take that ended up on the record.

"This is going to be so the shit"—that's how we felt right from the very beginning. We're the best band in the world, period. No one else could even come close. All the Swedish bands were shit. We'd seen bands in Finland, they were all shit too. Even most of the new English bands were shit. The Stones were already old news.

Okay, when you're young and inexperienced and you're making one of your first records...Michael agonized over his vocals on some of the songs because Andy had written in the key for himself, too high for Michael. The bass line in "First Timer" is such a pain in the ass that it was obviously written by a guitarist; guitars are much lighter instruments to play. "First Timer" was rough on the drummer and rough on me; we also played it at an insanely fast tempo, noses stuffed up with amphetamines. The song ended up being worse off for recording it so fast. We didn't have a proper, experienced producer either, just some sound guy from Stockholm who had a suspiciously close relationship with his dog Bamse, it made us very uncomfortable.

I would never consider "Tragedy" a disco song—even with its four-on-the-floor beat—because it's missing bass octaves. "Don't Ever Leave Me" is better than "Don't You Ever Leave Me," even though Michael had learned to sing it really well by the second version. I personally dig the part we ended up dropping for the second version on the last album at the producers' behest: "I start living in the memory of you." Apparently it messed with the vibe. The final version is just a normal ballad.

Mr. McCoy was a very important teacher to me: musically, instrumentally, and in attitude. Unbelievable musician. Every part for the songs on the first Hanoi record was in his head: all the guitar parts, the drums, the bass. Andy had already figured out the general idea behind the bass lines. The main riff from "Motorvatin'" was Andy's; everything in between was mine. The bass line in "11th Street Kids" was Andy's, note for note. It usually took me about twenty seconds to figure out how Andy wanted me to finish off the song.

It was obvious that "Tragedy" would be the lead track. We thought about the songs in batches, five and five, A and B. The first and last songs of each side were specifically picked because those are the important spots. We checked out the mixes in the car because the record had to sound good in a car, right? We crammed in and argued in a freezing cold Volvo about the sound levels of instruments.

Because we're Hanoi Rocks, Jim Pembroke from Wigwam fame had written us a song called "Saigon Shakes," which we eventually turned down. Andy then added "Bangkok Shocks" in front of the song's name and voila! There was our first album's title.

Bangkok Shocks, Saigon Shakes, Hanoi Rocks was created with manic excitement and eat-shit attitude. Michael doesn't like the record because of his own performance, even though he fearlessly yodeled his way through it. Nasty charged through with his natural touch, like Billy Gibbons or Chuck Berry. I'd learned to keep up with Gyp. And Andy was on fire. He'd been waiting for this opportunity for the whole of his brief-up-until-then life and finally got to record his own songs.

And there it was. Some of the bass lines were rough in places, the tempos were like a rollercoaster ride, but the songs were cookin' and there's a lot on the record that feels good and unique. We had our own sound. It's my favorite of the Hanoi records.

But I never dug the cover. To me, it was a boring, pretentious art photo. And all that gray; I HATE gray. Colors are important....fuck. Gray! Okay, the photo was stylish and artsy I guess, but not in keeping with my understanding of the band's visuals or what was inside the album. I didn't like it at all. I'm sorry, Stefan Bremer.

Bangkok Shocks came out in February/March, at the same time in both Finland and Sweden. Michael had met a Swedish-Indian named Sanji Tandan who had a label, Tandan Records, that wanted to put out the album in Sweden. Sanji hasn't forgotten us and still writes me on social media from time to time.

We went to say hi to Atte Blom at Johanna, now more as a friend than a bossman. Atte was his same old good-natured, jovial self; I've never seen Atte in a bad mood. We hung out in the office with beers. Seppo was there, too. It felt like family. We talked about the release date for the single and all the marketing and press stuff. Andy and I did a lot of interviews. I did some interviews on my own as well. I've never been particularly interested in the attention; playing was enough for me.

We started a big Finnish tour: forty-one gigs in thirty-nine days or something crazy like that. We got an allowance of fifty Finnish marks a day. A bottle of Four Roses whisky cost forty-five marks, so that left only a fiver for food. Nasty especially put all his money into the whisky, so he just ate what the rest of us had left over. Andy figured out he could make money this way and he started to sell leftovers to Nasty. "Looks like you've got a couple meatballs there." "Yeah, they're a mark and a half a piece."

I traded my Fender Precision '64 for a Gibson EB3L, which was the stupidest fucking trade I've ever made, somebody must have talked me into that. Then I got myself a Gibson Thunderbird '76 reissue. We also got a new rehearsal space in Central Stockholm in the basement of a club called Studion in St. Eriksplan.

We played a bunch of shows in Finland and then came back to Stockholm for a long break. We started to play shows there and around the Stockholm area. We played at a rock club in T-Centralen with an English New Wave band called Au Pairs. They didn't take it too kindly that when they went on after us, the stage was covered in broken beer bottles, slippery as hell from the spilled beer, and covered in tiny splinters of glass because Andy had smashed the overhead lights with his guitar during the last song. Au Pairs were wearing clean, little, neat New Wave clothes and were pretty annoyed that we'd left the stage in such a disarray. The roadies had to try to put everything back in place; there was no afterparty with them.

We didn't do an official tour of Sweden until later on. We pretty much only played Finland in 1981. Hanoi Rocks played every last music and dance venue in Finland. We were a real barn band. Hanoi Rocks playing in a barn, usually with a condom ad behind us. One show was canceled when the wiring looked so dangerous that the whole band could have fried. Our bus broke down on the way to Nivala in Northwestern Finland. Of course it had to happen in the middle of nowhere. We got out to stand on the side of the road and flag down the next car that passed by. It was below zero, and we were all in teddy boy jackets (drapes), leather pants, and sneakers. After what seemed like an eternity we saw some headlights in the distance, getting closer. There was a yellow light on top. A taxi! A miracle!! We all stood in the middle of the road to get the taxi to stop. The driver called another taxi, we grabbed our guitars and made it to Nivala on time for our set. We ended up having to borrow amps and the drum kit from the opening band.

Barn shows almost never had a backstage area, so the bus would have to do. Some of them, like Lallintalo, a venue in Köyliö, did have a dressing room, but Nivala just had a cement hovel, obviously without a bathroom, with a bad chill pulling through the outside door. Trembling, we pulled on as many clothes as possible. By showtime our fingers were so frozen we could barely play. There was no backstage booze, just a couple bottles of orange soda. We did meet a farmer named Pertsa in Nivala who brought us a bottle of moonshine every time we came through there.

We played the show at Lallintalo with the famous Finnish band Popeda. The crowd circled around and around this giant pole in the middle of the dance floor and got more and more hammered as the night wore on. I watched Popeda play and was already into the singer Pate Mustajärvi back then. The man could handle his booze as well as any of us, but thank God he's quit now, I hear. Pate is a gem.

Out in the boonies, people loved to fuck with Andy. And Andy liked to give it back. This was going on already back in the Pelle days, but even more so with Hanoi. Andy was just different—even more out there than the rest of us—and he has this real McCoy way of speaking. Swedish is his first language, not Finnish. His Finnish accent comes fully from Swedish. It's not like Andy's putting it on as a shtick. That's just the way he's always talked. It's definitely a weird one. He didn't speak a word of Finnish when he was thirteen and started at Nasty's school.

It was always the same thing up in the north: the big boys from the village would come to punch Andy's face in. The rednecks had been getting wasted around the corner and now, full of liquid courage, were ready to stir up some shit. Andy has never taken shit from anyone. Andy smashed some guys' heads together and sent the neck of his guitar into someone's eyeball. It was a pretty fucked-up scene—there was blood everywhere. The guy was screaming "I can't see anything!" We had to get out of there. Straight to the bus and start the engine. That kind of thing happened a lot.

The backstage areas in England are still as shit as they were in 1982. They don't care about musicians much. What is it? Jealousy? Or just plain assholism? Do we musicians irritate them so much that we've got to be punished for it? Let's get the musicians into a bad vibe. Let's not be nice and let's not give them anything nice. The "artist menu" always means something shittier than the normal menu.

Around the May Day holiday, we played four shows with UK Subs. The show in Tampere sticks in my mind. The crowd was mainly skinhead and hardcore punks with mohawks who had decided to put this makeup-wearing band from Helsinki in their place. As soon as the first song started, so too did the shower of spit. Then came the bottles. And then the darts. FUCKING DARTS! WHAT!? They whizzed past my head, one got stuck in my bass. Michael got hit between the eyes with a spark plug from a motorcycle.

One skinhead in the front row had decided to focus on targeting Gyp with his spit shower. From song to song, the spit splattered on him, but Gyp patiently kept playing. Until he'd finally had enough. Gyp stopped playing, grabbed a fistful of drumsticks, and walked up to the offender, who couldn't escape back into the packed crowd. Gyp smacked the spitter on the head with the bundle of drumsticks; the Red Sea parted. Blood gushed down over his stunned face. Gyp just walked back to his kit and counted out the next song: 1-2-3-4!

I hadn't suffered any injuries and was having a laugh. The bass player from UK Subs, the great Alvin Gibbs, was sitting in the wings serving me Jack Daniels through the whole set. By the end I was pretty hammered and forgot to crouch under the PA scaffolding when I was running to get backstage and smashed my nose right into it. I fell down the stairs right in front of the singer from UK Subs, Charlie Harper. "You all right, mate?" Well, so what if the cartilage in my nose grew a little bit? With these blackened eyes, I wouldn't need the eyeliner for a while.

That was the first time we saw how powerful a live band could be. UK Subs were explosive. It was almost like performance art, never seen anything like it! The guitarist Nicky Garratt climbed up fifteen feet to the top of the PA and then jumped down. Of course, he had it down and never got hurt.

Charlie Harper told a guy named Richard Bishop about us when he got back to London. He was curious and started to facilitate things already around the end of 1981, when Seppo got in touch with him regarding the recording of the new album. Who knows if we'd have made it to England without UK Subs. We wouldn't have made it there that fast, in any case.

Life was a little more balanced with the apartment and the allowance from Seppo. Michael was careful with his money and always gave us advice: gotta save! Nasty and I always wondered what for. Michael moved from

Solna pretty quickly. He found himself a nice space in Mariatorget with a girl. I remember a beautiful spring day in that apartment. We opened up all the windows to let the sunshine in after a long winter. There were already buds on the trees outside. We smoked a joint, had a little speed, and some ice-cold white wine. Faces' *Ooh La La* was blasting on the stereo. We talked about how we should get our asses to England.

Andy and Anna moved into the Solna apartment in Michael's place. I had my own room and our family Lenco record player and Telefunken Concertino radio (a new one) as a speaker. We cranked Dead Boys and Motörhead on that setup. It sounded beautiful, like it should. Above us, on the thirteenth floor, lived an old Greek dude who'd bang on the window from above with a broomstick, shouting for us to shut up.

The Solna apartment was pretty much only outfitted with mattresses and records until we finally found a sofa and a table somewhere. I lived on the floor of my room. I owned a Stones photobook the size of an LP called *63-73*. I cut out the pages and used them for wallpaper.

A seventeen, eighteen-year-old has so much energy that they don't really want to sit around at home. Gotta go out and see what everyone else is up to.

Seppo Vesterinen somehow managed to get us booked at a drug-free festival in Karlshamn, Skåne in southern Sweden. A couple Swedish newspapers had already written a couple things about us, about how maybe we weren't exactly a perfect fit to be spreading such a message. Some of us had been tripping on LSD that afternoon. We were sitting on the bus, everyone with their own mirror on the table, when the festival organizer, Göran, came to say "Hi" and "Welcome to the drug free festival," while we were doing lines. "Oh hey, how's it going?"

The sound at the festival was pitiful. There were no lights to talk about, and we played way too fast. My amp started to cut in and out. My natural reaction was to tip it over and get revenge by kicking it—the amp started to screech and buzz in its death knell. In my crazed state, I tripped over it, but kept playing anyway, the notes mixed in with the death sounds of the Ampeg. There was stuff flying all over, drums rolling here and there; the band looked manic and the audience afraid.

×××

The album didn't sell that well, but our fan base was growing and we started to have a bit more scratch from ticket sales than just pocket change. Which meant we had money for better drugs. We went to Umeå from the Karlshamn drug-free festival. We had a ten-hour drive to northern Sweden ahead of us. So me and a few others in our entourage took LSD on the bus ride. One of us disappeared to the back of the bus, where the bunks were, and tried to balance his head with the movement of the bus. He thought his head was wide open from the top and his brains would slip out if he held his head too far to the side.

We stopped to eat in central Sweden. It was hot and the acid had kicked in for real. Ice cream was in order. Everything was elastic and the colors were bright. Andy and I spotted a real, live ice cream stand in the distance. I managed to order a chocolate ice cream from the big woman dressed in a white ice cream seller outfit with a little round hat on top of her head without busting into hysterical laughter and paid her duly with my change. I successfully took my cone, licked it. It tasted like metal. Andy also got his cone, but he couldn't find his money. He was cursing and frantically tried to find his cash to pay the agitated, now a giant woman inside the shrinking ice cream stand. A pair of huge chubby pink arms shot out from the tiny window of the kiosk and started pulling Andy inside. The woman started to go through his pockets. Andy was halfway into the stand; only his scrawny ass and stick legs were dangling out, kicking in panic. "Help," he cried out in Swedish, "what the fuck are you doing to me? Let me GO!" I was dying with laughter and trying to keep my cone upright.

The gig in Umeå wasn't until the next day. We had some acid left and some of us decided to tune in and drop out before going on stage. The LSD kicked in twenty minutes later. The neck of my bass was a giant earthworm that ate my fingers. We played "Problem Child," a very short punk song of ours. It felt so good that we played it again right after. We finished up the first set, took a little break, and came back to play for another forty-five minutes. We played "Problem Child" first, "Problem Child" second, and when the crowd actually asked for an encore, it was "Problem Child" again, making a total of five times that night.

Steve Roberts, a writer for the UK *Sounds* magazine, had heard of Hanoi during a trip to Finland. Roberts flew to Finland to see us play at one of our random barn shows. The curly-haired Brit was confused. Why were we playing for a bunch of hicks instead of playing at Madison Square Garden? Roberts wrote a page and a half about us in *Sounds*, that was our first write-up in the UK press.

"Motorvatin'" from our second record came out of that tour, and "Oriental Beat" and "Sweet Home Suburbia" followed after. "Lightning Bar Blues" was a Hoyt Axton cover. All the songs came together little by little during the summer, and we'd go to our rehearsal space in St. Eriksplan to fine-tune them. We recorded "Desperados" and "Devil Woman" as a fall single.

At the end of summer, we played a show in Turku. Some of us had been downing handfuls of these Spanish diet pills called Bustai. Drug enforcement agents were in the crowd and watching us in the front row. You didn't have to watch long to notice that we wired to the max. Gyp threw up while he played.

The cops kicked down the backstage door after the show and asked where Sami Takamäki was. I slowly raised my hand. They slapped handcuffs on me. After fifteen minutes, Michael was brought out to join me in the back of the police car. The cops found a tiny piece of hash in his pocket. When the cops had brought Michael out the back door of the club, he'd managed to grab a six-pack that had four beers in it to take with him.

Michael asked if there was a tape deck in the car. "Yeah, you got music or something?" Michael asked them to take out the Pat Benatar cassette he had in his pocket. The cop was nice enough to play it. The tape was, funny enough, queued up to "Hell Is For Children."

At the station, we had to leave our shoes, belts, everything we could harm ourselves with or use to break out. We'd get them back when we were let go. That is, if we were let go; they were putting on a whole tough guy act. I didn't yet know why I'd been picked out. I was put on the second floor in cell number thirteen. I heard them laughing behind the door in the hallway. "There's some chick in cell thirteen."

The walls of the cell were almost like that back room of the Helsinki rock venue Tavastia, or CBGB—full of witty insights. I read the scrawlings on the wall to pass the time; I was still so high on speed I couldn't sleep anyway. Suddenly I stumbled upon NASSE scratched into the wall. The date was 1979. No way.

They brought us oatmeal in the morning. Then we were brought to questioning. I was coming down from the speed and feeling like a ten-pound shit in a five-pound bag. The cop, Pentti something or other, took out his gun and put it on the table in front of me. C'mon, what kind of bad movie is this? "No need to beat around the bush, Fagerholm has already told us everything!" That same old story. What did he say? That "Tragedy" goes in E?

Turns out someone had sung a nice little tune; an old friend of mine had gotten picked up for dealing weed and hash. He'd dealt to so many people that he'd been threatened with a serious sentence, which he was saved from by giving up about forty people around Helsinki. We'd taken his band to open for a few shows in Finland; we'd just come in from Stockholm and had speed on us, nothing to smoke. We'd been sniffin' for days and now we wanted to come down a bit, chill out, and get some sleep. I was the middleman facilitating the trade. So the friend had told the cops about that too.

They let us go in the afternoon, and we got our belts and stuff back. Michael even got his beers back.

Cheers, you old con!

Everyone in the hotel was in a panic mode! Nasty and Andy had flushed all our leftover stash down the toilet. I asked about the graffiti in cell thirteen. Nasty was a bit embarrassed. "Yeah, I was coming back from the festival in Roskilde, Denmark, some shit happened…"

I was seventeen when I was arrested but had turned eighteen by the court case, which was good, as my family wouldn't get notified. I was seated next to the rat during the trial. I elbowed him in the ribs: What the F…???

There were some pretty hard-looking guys sitting behind me. I thought about how my friend was going to die. He ended up getting a serious death threat and fled from Finland for a few years.

I got a year of parole and a couple hundred in fines. Because the "smuggling and dealing" I was charged with happened while I was still underage, the charges aren't on my permanent record.

I didn't really think about needing to act a certain way on parole. I just didn't bring anything to Finland and was careful about what was in my pockets. In Sweden, though, it was business as usual.

When we got back to Sweden, our roadie Spede broke the news that our beloved Finnish roadie Helge had committed suicide. The news hit me real hard. Helge had become a close friend. Helge had been a roadie for the Hurriganes and Wigwam and was the cousin of Remu from the Hurriganes. The first rehearsal after hearing the bad news brought "Dead By Xmas" and "Nothing New," which we recorded as singles at Decibel Studios in Slussen. I played my Gibson EB3L, and we finished the recording in two sessions. The single came out before Christmas.

×××

In October/November of 1981, Hanoi went to London for the first time. Thanks to the article in *Sounds*, people already knew who we were, and we were booked for six UK shows. We also met Richard Bishop for the first time.

We took the ferry from Gothenburg, Sweden, to Felixstowe, UK. I had a couple hundred on me, and I bought a boom box on the ship for 185 pounds. Always gotta have music. To this day, I usually need a guitar or bass with me while traveling. Dem fingers get itchy.

We were put up in the Townhouse Studios in Shepherd's Bush on Goldhawk Road. Two to a room, and a pub called the Wheatsheaf across the way where we spent our free time. I ended up playing pool there with a short, half-bald guy wearing a sweat-stained dark green T-shirt. I beat the guy and came back to the table. Someone said, "You beat Phil, then. Had a good time with Phil?" What Phil? "Why, didn't you recognize him? It's Phil Collins you were playing with."

We had new, long, shiny guitar cables for the big stages we were expecting to play, but our first show was at a little hole called the Moonlight Club. The stage wasn't even a foot and a half high. The bar was straight across and behind the dance floor. At the start of the show, there were maybe only fifteen people in the crowd. Despite the sparse audience, we put on a show like it was a packed stadium. Those fifteen audience members backed toward the bar. We jumped down from the stage and, thanks to the long cables, followed the crowd and started to kick everyone back on the bar. Come on MFs!! Wake up! Dance! Do something!

Steve Prost, a guy from Elektra Records, was there watching; later on, he became my A&R guy in the beginning of my LA years. This show at the Moonlight Club stayed with Steve. He'd never seen a band kick their own crowd before.

The few people who were actually at the show spread the word: you gotta see this band that looks like the New York Dolls, plays like the Clash, and abuses their audience.

Our manager Seppo had gotten us a little tour opening for a hippie band from the seventies, Wishbone Ash. The guys from Wishbone Ash were chill middle-aged Brits who had a fanatical following. To us their music was a boring wank. Their bass player was fucking Trevor Bolder! Him and his sideburns were amazing. It's worth checking out his playing on Bowie's classic early seventies records.

Plymouth University. We got up on stage, the lights were low, and the sound of three thousand people shouting was like music to our ears. The lights came up, and there we were on stage. The room went dead quiet. Not a single word or a single hand clapping. They hated us at first sight. We ran around like hyenas on speed and played fast punk rock. I broke a string right at the beginning of the set. It was like pearls before swine. Our attitude was that we were the best band you'd ever see. They started to boo us. But we kept playing and winning over more and more of the crowd because the real shit always shines through. Some of the crowd even came to see us play again later on.

We were the headliner at the Marquee Club. The opener was a flamenco metal band from Spain called Baron Rojo, a bunch of guys with masses of curly hair and leather jackets. I checked them out from the back bar with Nasty, pondering the combination of flamenco and metal.

After these shows, we started to record the second album. Peter Wooliscroft was supposed to produce, but ended up fucking it up. He had been the assistant engineer on some Slade record. We were recording in the same studio as Slade, too. This is why we went to the UK and wanted to get the album there. We wanted that big, nasty Slade sound. The expectations were high.

We lived above the Shepherd's Bush Townhouse studios, it would have been more convenient to record the album there, but instead, we went into the center of town to record. The studios cost about the same and were just as good. But we went through the trouble because Slade had recorded at the studio downtown. Maybe there was some magic there, some Slade fairy dust?

We were having a party in the Townhouse apartment when Nasse had a fit and punched a big hole into the wall. Then he picked up the boom box I'd bought on the ship, lifted it over his head, and smashed it to the floor. Little pieces scattered everywhere. I was sure that the whole thing was broken, goddammit!! It was our only way of playing music. Fucking Nasty!

Somehow it kept working, even if it was a bit stripped down. Apparently all the parts that had gone flying off were just extra.

Hanoi's first überfan hung out around the Wheatsheaf pub. Simon looked exactly like Simon Templar, the actor Roger Moore in *The Saint and James Bond*. He had one leg a few inches shorter than the other and would wear a single platform boot, so we called him Simon the Half-Glam. He was bipolar and was on prescription speed. He was also gay—which definitely did not make his life any easier at the time in the UK—and he had been in an accident, which is why one of his legs had been shortened, which of course made him depressed. Simon got antidepressant amphetamines—called "blues," because they were blue pills—and shared them with us willingly. They were so strong you couldn't open your bloody mouth. Teeth always clenched. "Shhammy, you wanna haff another line of schpeed?"

The Hanoi roadies, Timppa Kaltio and Spede always in style, looked the same as us. There in the front row, dancing in his nice clean brown suit, neat hairdo and cane in hand, was the Roger Moore lookalike superfan, speedgrinning from ear to ear. I liked that Simon guy, may he rest in peace.

Michael and Andy started to let things go to their heads in the studio. They didn't exactly join forces, because they always had that competition thing going between them, but all of a sudden, they decided they were the real producers of the record. Nasty, Gyp, and I got locked out of the studio control room so we wouldn't interfere with our opinions. That was a big mistake. Arguing in a freezing Volvo over the first record was much better than getting shut out entirely. Michael and Andy had decided they were Jagger and Richards. They had started calling themselves the Muddy Twins on the first album. Which was actually pretty fitting now because they made a fucking muddy production that no one could make any sense of. You couldn't get any further from Slade's sound than *Oriental Beat*. I don't even think the cymbals were miked, because when you can actually hear them, they sound like water hissing on the rocks in a sauna. I can't listen to that record, which is a huge shame since there are some great songs on there: "Motorvatin'," "Don't Follow Me," "Sweet Home Suburbia." With decent production and mixing, it would have been the best Hanoi record. If that weren't enough, the masters were lost, so the record can't even be mixed again.

It wasn't for us to think about how to set up the mics because that's what the producers were paid to know and take care of. Over the years, I've learned that a producer's big name doesn't necessarily mean a thing. You have to stay alert all the time and see what the F the producers and sound engineers are really doing. Otherwise, basic mistakes are going to pop up during mixing, like maybe the bottom of the snare drum didn't get miked, which was the case with *Oriental Beat*. These days, producers often only record one hit of the snare and use it as a trigger, instead of using the actual snare sound.

A couple weeks later we went back to Solna with the rough mix in our hands. Our friends in Stockholm wanted to come by and hear the new Hanoi record. I pressed play on the cassette without much excitement, but everyone dug it a lot. What? They all thought it sounded like the New York Dolls' second LP, the one Shadow Morton produced and has such a small, thin sound. Rock records should not have a small and thin sound, right? Anyway, that was the rough mix that sounded pretty okay before Mr. Wolliscroft ruined it for good in the final mix.

In any case, the market value of recording in England is priceless. The mentality was that it had to be good because it was recorded in England!

I decided not to go back to Finland for Christmas. I was eighteen, I wanted a break from the societal normalcy, Christmas seemed like a bunch of bullshit. So there I sat, alone on the twelfth floor of the Solna blue tower building, eating liver sausage sandwiches and drinking my way through a case of Budweiser. Hurray, I'm independent! On Christmas Eve, I started to regret that I hadn't gone home.

1982

Oriental Beat & Self Destruction Blues

***Oriental Beat* came out right at the beginning of the year. The album cover** and three videos—"Tragedy," "Motorvatin'," and "Oriental Beat"—were shot all in one night at Lepakko. They were Hanoi's first videos ever and very high tech; the moving shots were done when someone pushed the camera guy sitting in a wheelchair. The main difference between the three videos is that Andy changed his clothes.

Then we must have played a ridiculous amount of shows again, through all the little venues in Finland and in Sweden too. But it didn't bother me, I loved it. I was gung-ho—let's do this. I got to tour with my best friends around me, every night in a different setting, got to meet new people, the music was loud and fast every night, and we never stuck around anywhere too long—move on.

Within a year, Hanoi had released two full-length albums and had a foothold in England. It was all quick, determined movement—or at least that's what it seems like looking back now, that everything was for a reason. Our plans for the year and tour schedule came down from Seppo, and Atte came up with our recording schedule. We'd get told that we'd have three days booked for recording here and we needed to have four songs ready to go. That's how we worked. If we didn't have the songs, they'd get squeezed out of us, or more like, out of Andy.

Seppo and Richard were on the lookout for big, international record deals. They set up their own shop, Lick Records. All the money coming in went to cost-of-living expenses, travel, and gear. Hats off to Seppo for getting so much going on such a little budget. Without Seppo and Atte's support in the beginning, our time in Stockholm would have come crashing to a halt, and we would have had to come back to Finland.

Atte showed up unannounced to one of our London gigs. Out of nowhere, there was just this big guy standing there in his long coat, plastic bag in hand. That eternal, legendary plastic bag, the contents of which were a mystery to everyone. In honor of the reunion, we sat down to shoot some shit.

Finland's mandatory military service loomed ahead of me as a possible nightmare. Michael and Andy had already managed to get released, which was no easy feat in the early eighties.

I found a private psychiatrist in Helsinki and told him that I made my living in Stockholm by prostituting myself, that I used heroin every day and all that jazz. It just so happened that the psychiatrist was a friend of my dad's, but my dad never told me any of this until twenty years later. The psychiatrist had broken his confidentiality oath and immediately called my dad to say that he needed to check in on me because I clearly wasn't doing too well. I'm pretty sure my dad figured out I was just trying to get out of mandatory service.

The local call-up brought out a bunch of familiar faces from Tapiola and other school friends who were enthusiastically asking, "Where are you going to go?" I'd been doing speed and had been up the past two nights. I had on a full face of makeup, a yellow beret, a silver bolero jacket, and pink leather pants.

We were shown artillery and air force videos. I passed out against the wall. Someone shook me awake: TAKAMÄKI! Then it was time to talk to the army psychiatrist. I handed him the document my psychiatrist had written, he read the statement, and pulled out a green card. I knew what the green card meant, but couldn't really show that I was a wee bit excited about it. After that, I went to stand in front of four serious-looking uniformed military men. "Do you know what this means?" No. "It means you're released from peacetime service. If war breaks out, we're calling you in." I left and called my mom, who worked nearby at the lottery commission. We went out for coffee; Mom was very happy about it.

In the spring we recorded an EP at Farmhouse Studios out in the English countryside. We didn't have any songs when we started recording and no objective beyond recording five songs. "Problem Child" and "In the Year '79" were back from the Nymphomaniac days. "Problem Child" was written by Rickhard, a punk dude from Stockholm who had played with Andy for a while. Andy took Rickhard's riff, added his own lyrics, and put his own name on it.

Andy also had a riff that sounded like the Batman theme slowed down. Gyp played just the groove on the hi-hat, it felt like your everyday blues song. I'd been listening to the Cramps a lot and especially their song "Human Fly," which didn't use the hi-hat at all, just the ride and crash as hard as possible. I suggested Gyp skip the hi-hat altogether and stay up on the cymbals throughout the entire song. Now it REALLY worked and the song got its identity, the crashing, out-of-control cymbals had this sick, chaotic energy.

After laying down the basic track, Gyp, Nasty, and I went down to the pub for a few pints. By the time we came back, Michael and Andy had finalized the song brilliantly, wrote the lyrics, and put that little spooky-ass intro on the keyboard at the beginning. That's how "Taxi Driver" was born, one of my all-time Hanoi favorites, and one that we play with Michael Monroe Band to this day. In the same session we recorded "Beer and a Cigarette" and "Whispers in the Dark," which Andy had written with his brother, Ikke. Ikke did actually got a songwriting credit. The EP came out in May. It started to get called the Venue EP because of the back cover photo of our show poster for the Venue gig.

In June, we opened up for Lords of the New Church at the Zigzag Club in London. They were a new punk supergroup with Stiv Bators from Dead Boys, Brian James from the Damned, and Dave Tregunna from Sham 69. At the end of the show, Stiv hung himself, by the neck, on the lighting rig twenty feet above stage, quite a finale. I was by nature a bit shy, but went up to say hi and tell them how much I dug the show and how honored I was to meet them. Stiv and Brian said the same thing about us, and a connection was made.

An odd-looking guy with a big nose was talking Michael's and Andy's ears off after the show, going on and on about how he just had to play drums for Hanoi. Otherwise he'd break Gyp's legs.

Gyp had a great time in the beginning, but he had started to complain about everything. He was complaining about the bad showers in England because they only had cold water, whereas the rest of us couldn't give a shit if water even came out of the showers because we were in London playing music, for fuck's sake.

But most of all, Gyp complained about himself. "Fuck, I can't play!" was the phrase heard a lot after the recording of *Oriental Beat*. That bastard of a producer had taken Gyp's self-confidence. Gyp put down his own playing, even though I and others thought he played great! Sure, drummers can't practice in a tour bus the way a guitarist can, which might give you the impression that you're not improving the way everyone else is; that's not going to help with bad self-esteem. It was a problem.

Gyp's complaining and other stuff was bringing the band down. Sometimes the shows felt like an obligation. All the fun and initial feeling of brotherhood had disappeared.

We were playing a show at an open-air festival in Central Finland, maybe Alavus. A fan climbed up on stage, and security started to push the guy down. Andy took it as an invasion of his personal space and kicked the security guy in the face. Gyp saw this, got pissed off, jumped out from behind the drums, and hit Andy. I wasn't surprised at Gyp at all. Andy hit back. We had to play the show to the end so the crowd wouldn't get pissed and start rioting.

The security guards were big burly country boys and gave Andy dirty looks from the side of the stage while whispering with each other. It was a bad scene. After the last song, we made a run for backstage and locked the door. The security guards started to kick the door down. They wanted Andy. We didn't open the door, and finally the cops showed up. We made it out without incident, but Gyp's days were numbered.

×××

During the summer break, Andy and Anna flew to London. I was a couple days behind them, by train and boat. I spent a night in Copenhagen, then continued to Hoek van Holland, where I'd take the ferry to Harwich and finally to London. The train was late and kept running later and later as the trip went on. At the harbor in Hoek van Holland, I saw the lights of the ferry in the distance disappearing into the darkness. Now what? It was eleven at night, I was wearing my gray suit and carrying a little suitcase. At least the night was warm. I looked for a park and went to lie down under a tree.

An old lady walked past and asked in a thick Dutch accent if I had a place to sleep. I admitted that I didn't "except right here, under this tree." The old lady said that she had a sofa, she could cook me something to eat and breakfast too, and would only ask twenty-five guilders.

We made small talk while we ate, and she even gave me a little bit of sherry before going to sleep. She made me eggs and tea in the morning, and I ran to catch the ferry for England.

On my first trip to England, I'd met Sophie Chery, the French bass player for a Goth band called Sex Beat. Sophie had promised to put me up if I ever needed a place to stay. Which I did now. Sophie lived on King's Road with an Australian couple, Martin and Liz, or "Tex & Max" as they called themselves. Martin was a writer and a total junkie. He'd shoot up a huge fix in the afternoon, write one sentence on his typewriter, and nod off at his desk. After an hour, he'd wake up and write another couple sentences, take another fix, write one more sentence, and then nod off all over again.

Michael and Andy had been in touch with that big-nosed drummer. Razzle was three years older than me, older than all of us. Andy's main objective in taking this London trip was to figure out what Razzle's deal was; Andy and Anna were staying with Razzle in Muswell Hill.

Razzle got the number for Sophie's place from Andy. He called me up, and we agreed to meet up at a pub on King's Road. I was able to pick out the guy from far away: that big nozz, a Ronnie Wood mane of hair, platform shoes, and a leopard jacket. Razzle radiated positivity, I felt close to him right away, even if I didn't speak much English yet. Our interaction boiled down to "The Damned is best," "Punk rock is good," and "You want another beer?" Razzle was a Damned fanatic, he'd seen them play two or three hundred times, followed them for years, even slept under their stage. "Plan 9 Channel 7" and the entirety of *Machine Gun Etiquette* were like nirvana to me. Razzle loved *The Birthday Party*, which he introduced to me, along with lots and lots of other great bands and albums. I found in him a kindred spirit—both of us listened to all kinds of music without any kind of preconceived notions.

But was Razzle good enough to be the new drummer for Hanoi Rocks?

After the week or so in London, we came back to play some gigs in Finland and Sweden. We had a mini UK tour in July. In London, we stayed in Bayswater at a hotel filled with prostitutes called the Julius Caesar. Andy found some junkie guy who got legal drugs from the state. Late one night this geezer knocked on my door to ask if he could sleep there since Andy wasn't in his room. I didn't sleep a wink since this poor bastard just groaned and scratched himself all through the night.

"Let's go find out if Big Nose can play," Michael said. Okay. We had to do the audition in secret from both Gyp and Nasty, who was really close with Gyp. The secrecy was all because there were still shows left to play in England.

We first downed some pints at the Wheatsheaf pub. There was Razzle and Simon Half-Glam and Phil Collins's pool buddies. Ten or fifteen people followed us, bottle in hand, to the Townhouse Studios rehearsal room we had rented for Razzle's audition.

We played "Tragedy" and oh boy, did it sound like shit. The tempo was all over the place. Razzle didn't really know how to play the hi-hat. His defense was that Rat Scabies and Keith Moon didn't much touch the hi-hat, they'd ride the cymbals instead. In his previous band, the Dark, he didn't use a hi-hat at all.

The second run-through, maybe because of a joint and another beer, it sounded a bit better. We played "Tragedy" one more time and now it started to sound all right. I was able to jump onto Razzle's unique way of playing pretty easily. After the audition, Michael and Andy were thinking that maybe we could find a better drummer, but he had such a good vibe that fuck it, he's in. He'd get better with time, and it was more important that he fit in with the group. Razzle already looked like a member of Hanoi Rocks. We were pretty worn out, but Razzle brought in some new energy.

I think Gyp was better off leaving Hanoi in the end. Gyp ended up playing with Conny Bloom in a power pop group after that, then worked at a record store in Karlaplan, and later on got together his own merch business.

×××

Razzle came out to Stockholm. We practiced for hours upon hours, just like we had at the beginning. Being in the band felt right and exciting again.

Razzle's first gigs were in Finland, in Nivala and Saarijärvi. We were sitting at the stoop of the venue in Saarijärvi, beers in hand, waiting for soundcheck. The venue was literally in the middle of nowhere. You had to drive through some small roads in the middle of the forest, drive down a huge sandpit and up again and continue on the forest road. It was completely deserted, no human beings in sight except the bartender inside setting up. Razzle was starting to wonder. "Fuck, mate, where do the people come from? We drove for fucking hours to get here and didn't see any houses!"

I pointed out to the forest. "From there."

After the soundcheck, we got more beers and went back to the same spots to sit. Two zombies stumbled drunkenly out of the woods. From another direction, two more concertgoers stumbled out. Soon they were appearing in the dozens. *Night of the Living Dead*. Razzle stared in horror and choked on his beer and ran to the bus for safety. "I can't fucking take this, mate!"

The Finnish avant-garde jazz legend Edward Vesala from Lepakko had come to watch a soundcheck in Helsinki. Seppo said that Edward wanted to play drums for Hanoi...

Self Destruction Blues came out at the beginning of the fall. It was Gyp's last record, even though Razzle was on the cover. It wasn't exactly a real LP since all the songs had been put out as singles or on an EP, except for "Beer and a Cigarette," which we'd recorded at the end of the "Taxi Driver" session. After getting "Taxi Driver," "In the Year Of '79," and "Problem

Child" recorded, we still had some studio time left, and Andy had that simple twelve-bar blues that we played but didn't decide to release it right away.

We chose a new group photo for the cover because it didn't make sense to promote an image of a lineup that didn't exist anymore. We were looking toward the future, even if the recordings were from Gyp's days. Kari Riipinen took the picture, it was Razzle's first photoshoot with us. Riipinen was already a freak back then. Manic, but a nice guy and great photographer. Later Riipinen got into Polaroid art and started ripping off Warhol for a bit. He was a pretty bad drunk. When he was wasted, Riipinen turned into a little jerk, always ready to throw his little fists around. Sometimes he'd swing at the wrong person and get beat up.

Seppo got us a place to live in Tooting Bec in South London in the fall. The move was a big gamble. I had started to like London a lot. Stockholm had been good to us, and English weather is what it is: depressing, even shittier than in Finland. Gray drizzle most of the time. But I liked the Brits and the Scots and the Irish and the Welsh. Good, own kind of people.

Michael and I took over the first room, downstairs on the left, with Andy, Anna, and Nasty upstairs. The place turned into the house from *The Young Ones*. Cleanliness wasn't anyone's strong suit.

The single "Love's an Injection" went to number one in Finland in October. We'd recorded it in the spring at Wessex Studios in London with Martin Freegard as the engineer. I'd been up again for days on end and had asked Andy for some more speed to pick myself up. The bastard gave me a downer instead, and everything just turned into soft, floating agony. It took two hours just to get that simple descending bass line down. And Gyp all of a sudden couldn't manage a four on the floor beat. We got Terry Hall and Neville Staple, formerly from the Specials but now from Fun Boy Three, from the next studio for help. Neville came to pump the bass drum pedal while Gyp got the rest, a weird scene. I was nodding off in my chair. Did I really have to do it again?

"Love's an Injection!" In Finland, they wrote a lot about drinking and it was glorified, but it's taboo to talk about drugs. Andy had this kind of junkie romanticism. And a huge imagination. Andy created his own storybook, a kind of comic book world. Some people write about what they see and some about what they imagine. "I'm a collector of words," as Tom Waits once said. Good lines, lyrical hooks are important. Andy always understood that. Andy listened to a lot of REO Speedwagon and Foreigner. Specifically for songwriting purposes. Andy thought they knew how to put a song together. Before that, Andy had of course studied T. Rex, the Pistols, the Clash, Stooges, Stones, and so on…

Stiv Bators once showed me how to write a song, or another way to write a song in any case. Stiv took the riff from "Don't Shoot Me Down" from the garage band The Brogues and turned it on its head. "You just turn it around and do it in exactly the same length as they do it. And when the vocals come in, do exactly what they do. Just change the melody a bit, get some new lyrics, and you have a whole song. And it's *yours*!"

Steve Conte has done the same thing sometimes; for example, take the chords from Tom Waits's "I Don't Wanna Grow Up," speed the fucker up, and add his own melody and lyrics on top. It's not out of the ordinary. Andy borrowed things for his own use all the time: from magazines, things people said, commercials, anything that caught his eye. We started to hear "I'm a living wreck, and I live in Tooting Bec!" coming from the upstairs in Tooting Bec. Then Andy would come downstairs and see me in a T-shirt that said I'm a Cosmic Ted and I'm spaced outta my head. Andy would go back upstairs and soon would be singing the words from the T-shirt worked into the song.

Michael suggested we record a rock version of our calypso song "Malibu Nightmare." Writing the next album was now in motion.

Razzle lived in the North London neighborhood of Muswell Hill while the rest of us lived down in South London, in Tooting Bec. London is built low to the ground, meaning it's really spread out, so it was a trek and a half to Muswell Hill or Portobello, where Michael and I had started to hang out with Stiv Bators. Stiv's posse was bassist Dave Tregunna and his wife, Brian James and his then girlfriend, a couple of speed dealers, and Stiv's wife Stacey, who later on became Michael's girlfriend, and later still, Andy's wife. The girlfriend thing was a bit of a mess.

Michael came home after staying up for days with Stiv. Razzle and I had filled a gray sock with toilet paper, tied thread to one end, put the sock under Michael's nightstand, and went into the other room with the thread in hand. When Michael sat down on his bed, frazzled and spaced, Razzle started to pull on the thread gently and then gave it a good tug. Michael screamed in horror of the sock rat, jumped up, and ran out the house, slamming the door.

I started to stretch my mental, physical, and spiritual limits by staying up for days on end on speed. I was sitting in my friend Grippa's printing studio in Stockholm, sipping on white wine after weeks of being wide awake on speed. I was on another planet. All of a sudden, I saw Sami, me, myself, crawling into the room on his knees and ask me in my own voice "How's it going man? Gimme a swig" What the F!!? Of course you can have a swig since you are me. Grippa walked into the kitchen and saw me talking to someone who wasn't there. Not good. This guy's gotta get some sleep. Grippa brought me home. I was out for a day and a half.

Word of mouth spread fast, especially in London and Birmingham. Nasty, Razzle, and I were always out nightclubbin'. The three of us equaled chaos and good times, we hung out a lot and made friends with like-minded people. Metalheads, skinheads, Dolls fans, punks. We didn't believe in boundaries between an artist and the fans. There weren't too many bands that would go drink beers in the pub with the crowd after the soundcheck, or go upstairs to the venue bar with the fans to drink until it was time to get up on stage. We'd barely even see the backstage before the gig.

Street level buzz grew, and a scene was born out of it. A bunch of bands started to pop up around London that were clearly influenced by Hanoi Rocks: Dogs D'Amour, Gunslingers, Marionettes, Babysitters. They all became good friends.

I brought Razzle to Finland for Christmas. We went out to my sister's house in Kerava, where we listened to the Coasters and Eskimo music and went sledding in the woods while sniffing poppers. Sledding found a whole new dimension. Back in the seventies, you'd become a local hero if you came down a ski jumping ramp on a moped or a motorcycle. One of the ways Finns liked to relieve their boredom.

Grandma dug Razzle most of all. We sat at her living room table and Grandma brought out the sherry at the end of lunch. Grandma's sherry glasses were small and narrow, as sherry glasses usually are. Razzle looked at his glass with a puzzled look on his face and whispered, "Should I pull my nose above the rim or push it in the glass?" With his giant gonk there was no alternative. Grandma wondered in her Norwegian's Finnish about what my big-nosed friend was saying when Razzle pulled up his nose above the glass rim to get to the sherry.

1983

Back to Mystery City

Our January tour started in the Netherlands. In Amsterdam, we hung out with the tattoo artist, Hanky Panky, and his wife, Patricia. There was a lot of blow around, and that's why I played like an asshole when we played the Paradiso Club. The backstage at Paradiso was something of a maze, room after room, a winding hallway after winding hallway, or at least that's how it seemed at the time. Some guy flashed me a big bag of coke, we found an empty room, shut the door, put a six-foot-long mirror on the table, and commenced with hoovering. I had completely lost track of time. I heard our manager Seppo's voice in the distance, or it seemed like in a distance. "Goddammit, Sami, where the fuck are you, we're late to the show!"

I jumped up, tore through the hallways, found the green room, and ran through it to the stage. It was like wading in the mud; my fingers just wouldn't do the job. The rest of the band were shooting daggers. My playing was a complete mess. I was fucking embarrassed. That whole day we'd gone through the trouble of setting up the gear and doing the soundcheck. After all that, there's just that one hour in the day when I should be on the top of my game, and I wasn't, I fucked it up. My nose stuffing ruined the gig for everyone and made the trip a waste. Although it was forgotten in an instant by the band, it taught me a lesson.

The first tour of Japan was all set when Seppo came up with the idea to tack on a couple of stops to the trip. "How'd you like to go to India,

Hong Kong, and Thailand?" Seppo let us know that we wouldn't be playing those shows for the money, it'd just be for fun, the expenses would be covered. No one said no.

When the contracts for the tour started to come in, the Mumbai show was scheduled to last for six hours. We were flummoxed. But it wasn't a typo. We were able to talk the set time down to three hours. That was still way too long of a set, so we started to practice a bunch of Chuck Berry songs. We stretched out "I Feel Alright" into something like a twenty-minute jam. That was new kinda for us. We'd never played a lot of covers. "I Feel All right (1970)," "Train Kept A Rollin'," "Lightnin' Bar Blues," "Under My Wheels," and "Pipeline," that was about it.

I've always played in bands that performed their own music. I never really saw the point in learning endless amounts of cover songs. A lot of my New York muso buddies came up in bar bands, they know every fucking classic rock song. I know very few, the ones mentioned above and a couple more.

No rock bands from the Western Hemisphere had come to Delhi before us. Boomtown Rats, the Police, and the Clash had been to Mumbai. *Sounds* magazine sent a journalist, Garry Bushell, and a photographer, Justin Thomas, along with us. Mick Staplehurst came as the front of house and Spede as our guitar tech and stagehand. The Indian Airlines plane looked like a flying tent from the inside, and the crew was nice enough to let us know that all the drinks were free. Big mistake. After a while of tanking up on free booze, Nasty got into a fight, which ended with the captain threatening detainment and an emergency landing to kick us off the plane.

When the plane doors opened in Mumbai, we were greeted with the smell of damp heat and raw sewage. It took hours to get our luggage and go through customs. When Razzle complained, "Jesus, what a stink," the local promoter standing next to him said, "Don't worry, we'll soon get used to you."

We drove to the hotel in the morning dusk through the endless cardboard shanties, junk, and poverty. It was miserable to realize that there are people who are born, live, and die in those slums without ever getting the chance to leave.

Those thoughts were pushed to the back of my mind once we got to the hotel. Michael wanted his own room, Andy and I shared one, Nasty and Razzle were together in the last one down the hall. Jet lag made the thought of sleeping impossible. We'd gotten our hands on some tax-free booze, and once our things made it up to our rooms, we headed out to sit on the beach wall across the street from the hotel. We passed the bottle around while we watched the sun come up over Mumbai.

There were huge piles of trash on the roadside every hundred feet or so. People with missing arms, legs, someone dragging their body on a piece of a board with wheels on it started to emerge from the garbage like zombies. The whole thing became completely surreal fueled by the jet lag and booze. They surrounded us and started begging. This was a whole other level of human suffering. I shut down; my head started spinning. When I got back to my room, I kept thinking about this fucked-up world we live in while trying to get some sleep.

Snake charmers, street urchins, guys that put scorpions in their mouths, and all kinds of beggars gathered out front of the hotel. The promoters had told us that if we gave anyone money, the word would spread and in half an hour the hotel entrance would be chaos.

Andy, Justin, and I got into a taxi and went to check out the city. We jumped onto a boat at Mumbai Harbor next to Gateway of India. We stretched out in the back and because it was a hot day, I thought I'd cool off by dipping my hand in the water. The captain left the helm and came running: "HANDS UP, HANDS UP!" I wondered why I had to put my hands up. Was this a holdup? "SHARKS!" I pulled my arm right out of the water. Five or so shark fins rose out of the water just a few yards away. That could have been the end of my music career.

When we got back to the harbor, we continued our drive with the same driver. He asked if we wanted some drugs. He proceeded to inform us that he could get us opium, heroin, and hashish. Okay, we'll take five grams of each.

The taxi driver turned onto Falkland Road from the center. Falkland Road is a leftover jail road from English colonial times, with cells on both sides. The jails had been converted into a nearly mile-long bordello, with the prostitutes stuck behind the bars. The driver turned down an alley from this miserable place and asked us to get down. "It's better if no one saw you, or else…" and he dragged his finger across his neck.

We ducked down in the car. How much money had we given him? Fifteen pounds? The driver would probably come back with a little piece of hash. But he came back with five grams of everything, just like we'd talked about. Looking at all the little bundles in our hands, it made me think to ask how much the driver earned in a day. We paid him double that and asked him to take us around the whole day. That way, we wouldn't have to hunt down another taxi.

Andy, Nasty, Razzle, and I started in on the opium. It was my first time. The ceiling fan creaked in the hot room, Indian music played softly on the radio, the sun scattered through the wooden blinds onto the dark green walls.

A knocking sound broke through all that fog. Garry Bushell, who had appeared in the room at some point, went to open the door. There was a guy standing at the door with a sign in Hindi around his neck. He opened his mouth wide open; he didn't have a tongue.

Garry freaked out and slammed the door in the guy's face. We scolded Garry—how rude—and told him to open the door and ask what he wants.

The guy turned his sign around and it read: "I'm terribly sorry, my parents cut my tongue when I was 2 years old, can you please give me some money or food?" We invited him in and offered him a hit of opium.

In the morning, I woke up to the beautiful sound of a child singing. The sun was shining through the half-open balcony doors. A little maybe four-year-old girl was floating in the air on the other side of the balcony railing. Come on…the opium yesterday was strong, but this hallucination was a little too real. The little girl was singing right to me, and she reached out her little hand. I got up and walked to the balcony. The little girl was tied to a long stick that her mother was balancing on her shoulders from the ground floor. They were panhandling this way from balcony to balcony.

Promoting a record in the West means running from radio stations to TV stations to interviews to photoshoots. Promotion in India was a little different. We got into a four-horse-drawn carriage in front of our hotel. The promoter dropped a huge ghetto blaster into my lap and hit play. *Back to Mystery City* blasted out. A sheet flew behind the horse-drawn carriage: "Hanoi Rocks Live at Rang Bhavan." People started to run alongside the carriage. We waved to the crowd like we were fucking royalty and caused a few traffic jams.

Our turbaned driver stopped in front of the University of Mumbai. We told the students about our gig the following day, which started at nine at Rang Bhavan Amphitheater. If all those pretty Indian girls showed up, it would be a pretty good gig.

The outdoor amphitheater had a capacity of three thousand. The equipment was nothing to write home about—some old combo amps, random drum parts, a little PA system. There was not enough juice. No one would hear a bloody thing. We somehow managed to wrangle a halfway decent sound and went to get some food. By the time we got back to Rang Bhavan, it was packed.

Jam-packed: 2,997 dudes and three girls.

We had negotiated our set down from six hours, but three was still a lot to fill. Chuck Berry and some other easy covers, a longtime jam on "Village Girl." Then the power went out. The promoters asked us to do something, anything, otherwise all hell would break loose.

Razzle! He'd never been one for drum solos, but he rose to the occasion. Two bass drumbeats and then he put his hands up. The crowd caught on: aha! After the two drumbeats, they had to put their hands up and shout. Hands went up like in a Jane Fonda video. This went on and on until the power came back on. That was no doubt the best drum solo I've ever seen.

The vibe was great, and by the end of the show, the crowd was going bananas. One young kid jumped on the stage and tried to kiss Michael. Michael ran away backstage in horror. More and more people got up on stage and started to rip off equipment left and right: the mike stand, cables, the bass amp…then the riot cops showed up wielding long sticks called lathis and started to beat people up. It was a bloodbath. Cracked heads everywhere. I had to kick a guy in the balls who tried to steal my bass from my neck. From a tiny window in the back room, we watched how Indian cops handle crowd control. Sticks whistling. More blood.

The headline of the *Bombay Times* the next day was "Cops Ran Amok at Rang Bhavan Rock Concert."

We went shopping for Indian clothes. I picked out a lime-green outfit, Andy and Nasty went for red, and Razzle, baby blue. Razzle also bought a big chunky wooden necklace. People on the street pointed and laughed. We were used to being stared at in Finland and Sweden, but now we were dressed in local finery and thought we were looking really good—so what the hell?

One guy stopped laughing long enough to explain to us that we were wearing women's clothing and the necklace Razzle had picked out meant that he was "a widow, but on the market."

Fair enough, laugh away. I dug those clothes so much that I wore them all the time when we got back to Europe. When the seams started to split, I tried feverishly to stitch them back together again.

The three-thousand-person dome venue in New Delhi had an even wimpier backline. I was given a fifty-watt Yamaha bass combo; Nasse and Andy got Fender combos. The drum kit looked homemade. The electrical system was taped together with duct tape and hanging on the side of the wall. Our sound guy, Mick Staplehurst, checked the microphones with a gauge. Each one came up red, meaning life-threatening. If your mouth touched the mike while playing guitar, you'd get stuck and would be fried like a French fry. Okay. Not going to touch the mike then, I'll keep a few inches' distance.

The crowd was sitting cross-legged on the floor at the beginning of the show. We were the first rock band to ever play New Delhi, and the audience had no idea what to do at a rock concert. No reaction, no applause, just dumbfounded expressions. Toward the end of the third song, a guy in a turban in the back got up and started jumping around in place. The people sitting next to him looked at him, got up, and followed his example. The vibe spread throughout the crowd, and people sprang into a pogo like they were mushrooms popping up from the ground. The communal energy, smiles, and sincerity made it one of my best concert memories.

After the gig we crammed into the van and were about to leave when one of the spectators came running up to me. The guy stuck his head in through the car window—eyes wide and blazing!—and asked in a thick Indian accent, "Excuse me, sir, but which planet are we on?" "You are on Mars, man," I answered. He thanked me and went off into the New Delhi night. Sometimes it feels like there's more than one planet on this one.

The trip continued to Hong Kong. It was hands down the most terrifying landing. The airport runway is built on the water, and you come in for a landing between the mountains and skyscrapers. We stayed at the Hilton, and my room was on the thirty-fourth floor of the skyscraper. I went up to the rooftop bar and ordered a Heineken. The check came: twenty-five dollars. That was the last drink at the Hong Kong Hilton.

I wanted to see as much of Hong Kong as possible, so I toured the bay in a boat, climbed up to a Buddhist temple at the top of a mountain, and ate squid in the harbor before the show at a club with a two-hundred-person capacity. Andy had found hash in that short time we'd been in the city. It cheered us all up, and this venue had decent gear and good sound. The audience sat on the ground here, too. Michael asked the crowd to come closer, and everyone started to crawl toward the stage. Since I was a little high, the sight made me crack up. Someone turned on the smoke machine in the middle of a song but didn't know how to turn it off. We kept playing in the growing, impenetrable fog. Our guitars headstocks banged into each other and started to go out of tune. WHERE ARE YOU? OW! We had to stop playing and open all the doors to the club to let the smoke out.

Next up was Japan, which was the original destination of the trip. I didn't know what to expect, but my expectations were high. I loved Kurosawa's movies, and I wanted to see kabuki theatre.

Getting to Hong Kong, the sunrise above Vietnam had been purple, pink, orange, and golden. We got to Japan early on a gray morning. The border control agent at the Narita airport said, "Mr. Takamäki, welcome back to your mother country!" *Que?* I tried my best to explain that Takamäki was a Finnish name, specifically from western Finland.

I chucked my bags and bass into the corner as soon as we had checked in at the hotel and collapsed in exhaustion on the bed. The closet door started to open slowly. A small Japanese girl in a miniskirt stepped out of the closet. "Hello Mr. Yaffa, can I do something for you?" I jumped up in fright, said no, and chased her out. This pissed me off as much as it startled me. I wondered how long the girl sat in that closet.

And then the circus began. Lobby call, 7:02. Breakfast, 7:05. Van, 7:34. Arrive at the radio station, 8:00. Van, 8:17. Arrive at the radio station, 8:45. Van, 9:04. Arrive at the TV station, 9:15…

The Japanese label had decided to market Hanoi Rocks as a teenybopper band and had reissued *Back to Mystery City* with a new cover using a nice glossy portrait of Michael. None of us were too thrilled about it, to say the least

We played at a hall that held up to 1,500 people. The stagehands were professionals, and everything worked like clockwork. Tokyo, Nagoya, Osaka, Fukuoka. The hysteria was something like Beatlemania. We got followed everywhere, leaving a press conference, going to a bar. If we took the bullet train, so did the fans. We called Nasty's hotel room in Tokyo "Nasty Suicide Lonely Hearts Club" because there were always girls hanging around, waiting and hoping to get his attention.

Me, Razzle, and Nasty ended up in a club full of geishas in Osaka. It was the only spot open after four in the morning. We were having a great time, dancing with the geishas and drinking shots. The promoter tried to yell something across the dance floor—"The geishas…"—but the music was too loud. "The geishas are…" "What?" "THE GEISHAS ARE GUYS!"

Oh, so it was that kind of disco. Got it! We kept on having fun, girls or not, who cares. We bowed politely to the guy geishas as we left and walked into the rising sun in the land of the rising sun.

Japan is a magical, traditional country that lives in the space age. It's a truly unique corner of the Earth, and I fell in love with it. The tour was a success and our morale was high. I got so many piles of kimonos and other presents that I ended up having to buy another suitcase.

The last stop of this dream tour was Bangkok, Thailand, after which we had some time off. Bangkok had traffic lights but no lanes. Rickshaws, cars, mopeds, bicycles, and motorcycles lined up at the red lights waiting for the race to start. *Death Race*: pedal to the metal! Somehow everyone seemed to know how to navigate the chaos without loss of life or limb. The metal hornets would swarm at the intersection, missing each other by an inch, and the ritual would repeat over again at the next intersection. The strangest thing about it all was how soon you got used to it.

The Dusit Thani Hotel had a tennis court, swimming pool, and spa on the rooftop. We relaxed in the hot tub, Singha beers in hand. In the morning, I woke up to a knock at the door; a uniformed police officer was standing outside. He handed me a thick envelope. "Your sticks, sir."

Thai sticks are really strong weed. I freaked out, threw the envelope back at the police officer, and slammed the door shut. In my paranoia, I thought they were trying to frame me and send me to jail. I made a couple of calls and was calmed down. The weed came from the promoter, who also happens to be the chief of police. They had thought this would be far safer than if the band tried to score in Patpong.

The bar prostitutes had numbers on their bikinis. Andy and Nasty both fell in love with an early 1960s Vox Teardrop guitar hanging on the wall in one bar. Andy offered a pretty big chunk of change to the German owner, but no sale. Nasty got drunk with the guy until the wee hours of the morning.

A couple days before our only gig in Bangkok, I got hit with a stomach bug. I was running a high fever and the room looked like a surrealist vision of hell. On top of that, a Thai dub of *Dallas* was playing on TV. A doctor came to administer an injection and charcoal pills, but I was still feeling weak on the day of the show. Behind my amp was a bucket I could puke in between songs. The only thing I remember from the show was the Thai national hymn sung before we got on stage and that blue slop bucket.

After the show, the German bar owner showed up backstage to give the Vox Teardrop to Nasty. Andy was pissed.

Weed showed up every day. It was impossible to smoke everything that showed up every day in those envelopes. I built up quite the stash, which wasn't a bad problem to have. We bounced around Bangkok, went to the Rama IX Park, and took a day trip to the bridge on the River Kwai.

To get to the River Kwai, we had to drive a couple hours through jungles and rice fields. Naturally, we had to whistle the song from *The Bridge on the River Kwai* once we got to the bridge. We stepped onto a boat; a couple big white birds took off, monkeys were screaming, and the band was grinning.

After twenty or so minutes, we arrived at a small dock. We followed the guide out of the boat up a jungle trail until we saw a big thirty-foot statue of Buddha. We were awestruck by the statue and the view from the top of the hill.

The guide took us another direction, deeper into the jungle. The narrow path twisted through thick overgrowth. I was getting some serious *Apocalypse Now* vibes. After a half hour, we arrived at a market in a clearing. People, animals, tents, the smell of food and spices, music. The clearing also had a little amusement park and the tiniest toy-like roller coaster.

We sipped on Singha beer and pet water buffaloes; we mused that a water buffalo would make a great stage prop.

We took off for Pattaya with open return tickets. We didn't have any work obligations coming up and we had time to take a couple of weeks off.

Pattaya was still a tiny, two-street town back in 1983. We spent the days at the beach and the nights at bars. I watched a couple of Muay Thai fights, which all start with a beautiful musical ceremony. Then two twelve-year-old girls stepped into the ring. It was a bit tough to watch them kick and beat each other to a pulp.

Razzle, Nasty, and I rented a boat and went snorkeling for a day. We floated in the turquoise water, smoked Thai weed, drank beers and whisky; every now and then we'd dive down to trip through a rainbow of fish.

Razzle claimed to be a windsurfing pro since he'd grown up on the Isle of Wight. The guy couldn't even get onto the board. He'd fall, curse, and then fall again.

I stepped into a dimly lit, ramshackle bar made out of bamboo. I was hoping to get a cold beer to my lips as soon as possible. Before I could order, a ping-pong ball hit me in the head. I didn't remember seeing a ping-pong table when I walked in. I turned around and saw a girl sitting on the sofa a few feet away, her legs spread, loading another rocket into her chamber. The power and aim was ruthless—another ball went flying by.

These girls sure had a way of picking up men. I declined and ordered a beer. This was in the beginning of the heinous porno tourism, which should be criminalized and banned everywhere. Later in the evening, I was walking along the beach road and stopped at another bar. "Singha beer and

Thai whisky, please." There was a beautiful Thai woman sitting next to me, maybe in her thirties, so for me at the time, a mature woman. We started chatting and introduced ourselves. She said she was Porn. "It's Ravaporn, but my friends call me Porn." I thought she was also a prostitute, but she convinced me she wasn't. We talked until late.

We met up again the next day. Porn told me about a beach that tourists didn't know about and asked if I wanted to go there for a picnic. Twist my arm! Next, Porn asked what food, drinks, and drugs I wanted for the secret beach. Uhh…just improvise. We left in a pickup toward the beach. Ravaporn had brought Thai weed, beers, whisky, speed, and downers. You could get uppers and downers over the counter at Thai pharmacies; just show your thumb up or down, and you'd get the best.

It was easy being with her. I ended up at her place that night, which was a little studio apartment, not fancy but homey. From then on, I was with Porn morning and night. She showed me all around Pattaya, not just the nightlife. She also never asked for money and wouldn't let me pay for anything.

We were sitting in the bar where we'd met when we heard the loud roar of a motorcycle behind us. "Hop on, Yaffa! Let's go for a ride!"

I turned around. Razzle was sitting on a 750 cc Kawasaki. I jumped up behind him. Razzle sped down a dark gravel path. Shacks and shadows of dogs flashed by. Razzle had a good handle on the motorcycle.

The guy at reception had told him about a "silver beach" about twenty miles away from Pattaya and had drawn him a map. We'd drive there tomorrow.

In the morning, we packed the saddlebags with food and beer and stuffed weed into our pockets. I read the map, and Razzle drove. Razzle put pedal to the metal once we were on the highway. My bandana started to fall back and flew off into the wind. I yelled for him to go back to get it, but Razzle didn't give a shit. His headscarf flew off next.

According to the map, we needed to turn right next. The road got smaller after the bend and turned into gravel. It felt like we were on the right path. But then around the bend, a bunch of soldiers appeared with machine guns raised.

Razzzle killed the engine. The soldiers were yelling and getting aggressive. And of course, we didn't understand a word. No understand, no comprende, nicht verstehen. Looking at the signs, it dawned on us that we had driven into a military zone. I slowly took the hotel receptionist's map drawing out of my pocket and stretched it toward the leader. I also showed him the hotel matches and hoped they didn't ask me to turn out my pockets.

The commander turned the map around and then it hit him; a smile spread over his face. He understood that we weren't terrorists, just lost tourists. He showed us the right way.

The gravel road twisted through the jungle until we saw a village. People started to come out of the little huts. Razzle turned off the engine, and we got off the bike. Little kids ran all around us and pulled on our legs. The adults gathered closer. We smiled and nodded every which way. I didn't notice right away that the crowd was leading us in a particular direction. We ended up at a bamboo hut. They gestured for us to sit down.

We were served water, beer, and some small bites. There we sat, Ray-Bans on our foreheads, cross-legged, surrounded by thirty curious, smiling villagers. There was the smell of sweet smoke and the murmur of an unknown language in the air. I showed them the map while we smoked from a water pipe. Someone understood what we were looking for, and we were shown back to the motorcycle and down a new gravel path. They waved goodbye.

Finally, we caught sight of a silver strand of beach and the turquoise sea behind it. Not a soul in sight. We parked the bike, unpacked the bags, and got to walking. We spread our towels out on the hot silver sand, took our shirts off, and ran into the open arms of the waiting water. We rolled joints when we came back to the shore and cracked open some beers. The thought of going back to gray London was unappealing. Let's enjoy this while we can.

I woke up from a nap and looked down the curving stretch of beach. There was something shimmering and shining in the hot horizon. I let Razzle sleep and got up to see where the shimmer originated. I saw human shapes a few hundred feet away. There were three Thai guys fixing homemade jet skis: the handlebars and saddle from a motorcycle, a fiberglass body and

Johnson 50HP outboard motor. The guys spoke a little bit of English and showed me their creations. They pulled them into the water and took off. I ran to wake up Razzle. We came back to the guys to ask if they'd rent us the jet skis for an hour. No problem.

Razzle and I sped along the waters of the paradise beach, grinning from ear to ear. The sea started to get choppy, and the waves started to get bigger. We pushed the gas and bounced on the cresting waves. I heard someone cry out "Heee-haaaw"; a shadow rushed over my head, and I heard the sound of a propeller. Fucking Razzle had decided to pull off a stunt and had jumped from a big wave over me.

We made our way back to Pattaya, and I met up with Ravaporn in the evening. She refused to come to our hotel, so we spent the nights at her place.

We both knew my departure was coming up, but we didn't want to think about it. We were sitting side by side on the beach when we saw a pickup truck taxi pull up. Suicide was sitting in the back; he was the only one who knew where I was hanging out. I knew I had to leave. I took off running, and Nasty ran after me. I latched onto a palm tree and declared that I'd be staying in Pattaya. I wouldn't go back to London; I probably wouldn't come back at all, they could call me when the next tour started.

Nasty talked some sense through my haze of speed/weed/booze/love. I put my black wide-brimmed hat on Ravaporn and kissed away her tears. I dragged my feet into the back of the taxi. Ravaporn's shape slowly disappeared from sight. I knew I'd never see her again.

Everyone had the same problem while packing: too much leftover weed. We held a funeral for the leftovers. We rolled a proper Cheech and Chong–size joint and passed it around while we flushed down the toilet another bag of Thai weed.

My eyes welled up with tears. The trip to Asia had been an unbelievably enriching experience. I had just turned nineteen; the future was bright, and it belonged to us.

Andy got into trouble on the flight home. He'd bought a wooden sculpture of an old man bathing in a barrel; when you raised the barrel around the bathing guy, a huge wooden dick jumped out at you. There was a family sitting behind us. The parents were sleeping, and Andy was showing the dick sculpture to the kids. The laughter woke the dad up, who saw what was going on. The flight attendants threatened an emergency landing in Malaysia, where they'd kick Andy off the flight.

These kinds of threats seemed to be becoming a part of daily life.

Everyone had had a great time in Pattaya except for Michael. He hadn't really liked being out in the sun. Michael was like a prisoner in the hotel because whenever this blonde creature stepped out onto the street in Asia, traffic stopped, car horns would honk, and everyone would start bugging him. Total drag. I could see where he was coming from.

Nowadays Michael loves laying out in the sun.

×××

We had recording sessions for the new album in March.

Back to Mystery City was the first and only album we recorded in a residential studio. Park Gates was an old farm from the 1700s converted into a recording studio in the middle of nowhere, on a field in Hastings, England; the closest pub was a half-hour walk away. Seppo probably thought it would be better if we were cut off from the world, that kind of setup was also possibly much cheaper. We went through the cabin fever together recording and hanging out. Of course everyone brought along their own stash of speed and weed. And some shrooms too.

The producers for the record were the bassist and drummer from Mott the Hoople, Peter "Overend" Watts and Dale "Buffin" Griffin. This was a noticeable improvement over the choice of producer from the last time around.

The studio's cook made all kinds of amazing culinary creations for dinner every night. There was a TV room, a dart room, and the studio itself was top-notch. We pulled long days: wake up, have a sniff, record some backing tracks, lunch, sniff, back to the studio, dinner, sniff, studio, and at the end of the day, late at night, we'd hang out in the TV room watching music videos, drinking beers, and smoking weed.

The Fairlight synthesizer had just come out; it was a big and unwieldy instrument that cost something like £25,000. The first time you get to fool around on one of those things, your good taste goes flying right out the window. We found the chicken and rooster sounds on it. When you're high on drugs, of course it's a great idea to add them into the mix of the new record. Take some bubbling stream sounds and a Medieval flute while Andy is playing Segovia-style Spanish guitar and voilà: Weird Boys Play Strange Openings.

When the weed and speed ran out, we pulled straws to see who had to go to London to get some more. I got stuck with the short straw. A couple of hours later, I was at Waterloo Station with everyone's money and a list of what and how much to buy. I hadn't really thought about it on the trip down, but coming back with my pockets full of drugs, I started to sweat and get paranoid.

Everyone was in a creative place and *Back to Mystery City* turned out to be a diverse album, although we'd done all kinds of strange stuff before too. Our single "Desperados" had been a Clash-style reggae. *Self Destruction Blues* was full of all kinds of different musical styles, a little bit of this, a little bit of that, definitely not just rock.

Michael and I had moved to Holland Park together, right next to the Shepherd's Bush roundabout. We hung out more and more with Stiv Bators and his wife, Anastasia. We'd go to SoHo clubs like the Pipeline and Fouberts, but especially the pub downstairs from *Melody Maker* magazine, the Oporto. The so-called "Rock 'n' Roll Table" was where the great writer, Carol Clerk, would drink men under the table. There were members from Anti-Nowhere League, Cockney Rejects, the Babysitters, the Marionettes, and the UK Subs at the table.

One card-carrying member of the Oporto was a pipe-smoking, whisky-drinking gentleman with a giant gray mustache who was called the Major. He had been in the Second World War as a squadron leader bombing Germany flat. Later on, the Major poured gasoline over himself, set himself on fire, and threw himself down an elevator shaft. No one else died, but all that was left of the building was smoky ruins.

The Midget was another regular, who was a really nice little guy, but only up to a certain point. After one drink too many, he'd get mean as a rattler and would start fights. He'd usually fist you on the balls and then do the Frank Cannon on the neck. When a couple weeks went by and nobody had seen the Midget at Oporto, we started to wonder. He had gotten drunk, stabbed someone, and was sitting in a prison cell.

One morning, there was a bearded, middle-aged dude sitting at the Oporto Rock 'n' Roll Table. I went over, pint in hand, to say hi. We got to talking and the old guy seemed pretty cool. A little drunk Englishman who you could tell, from his face and his gut, liked his beer.

A couple hours and many pints later, the gentleman took off and said, "Nice to meet you, Sami, take care." I'd been wondering why the bartender and the guys at the bar kept giving me the thumbs up. Once the old man had disappeared into the street, they ran over to ask, "So, how was it, man? Talking with Syd, man?"

"Syd who?"

"SYD BARRETT, YOU IDIOT!"

Syd had figured out pretty quickly that I had no idea that he was the original guitarist of Pink Floyd. So I, of course, didn't start asking him about stuff that he probably didn't wanna talk about. None of that asking about old stuff, I wasn't a journalist or a fan. I can't remember what we talked about, but we definitely didn't say a word about music. That's probably why I made for good company.

I ended up at some house party with Razzle. There was a band playing in the backyard, there was space to drink downstairs, and upstairs was a closed room of hippies smoking hash. We went up there, and someone handed me a giant joint. That's where my memory ends.

Razzle came by the next day and started in with "Nice one, Yaffa!" Apparently, I had gotten up after smoking the joint and walked along the wall until I got to the next wall, looking for the door. A record player got in the way. I'd stopped in front of it, lifted the cover, unzipped my fly, and pissed on the spinning record. I put the cover back down like it was a toilet seat and came back to sit next to Razzle. The hippies had flipped out. "You pissed on *DARK SIDE OF THE MOON*!"

Up until this time, the band's recreational aids had been alcohol, hash, and amphetamines. Downers started to join the mix. Heroin reared its ugly head. It was just as easy to get heroin as weed in London, which was almost as easy to get as a beer. Heroin was just another thing to get high on, people were shooting up so casually. It quickly became a problem for some friends, like Martin the writer. I went along with him one time when Martin went to score some scag. There was this guy with a boxer's nose working at this one store. The modus operandi was that you'd casually browse for things, pick something, and give it to the shopkeeper with a ten-pound note. You'd chat about this or that and maybe buy the item but would trade off a little bag of Turkish heroin in the handshake.

I didn't start doing heroin thinking that I wanted to be a junkie. At first, I thought you'd get hooked after the first time. And when that doesn't happen, it's easier to do it again. It takes months to become an addict.

I'd always been scared of needles, but I knew you could also smoke it. I started chasing the dragon once a week at first, then twice. The dealer's store had gotten a bit too popular, and it was better not to go there too often. I found another dealer. Bernie, a hood from Canada who had fled from the law. There was also an Anna, our nice go-to dealer who hooked us up day or night.

Heroin is the best physical feeling in the world. Orgasmic stuff. It's like there's your own personal movie happening in your head, a meditative one that you can direct yourself. Heroin makes you passive; I must have spent hours watching snooker on TV. Hurricane Higgins, Steve Davis, and Jimmy White were the kings of snooker at the time. The colorful balls gently touched each other on the green surface while the announcer whispered the score. Snooker and heroin go together because they're both slow and relaxing. I'd nod off from time to time, and my own movie would start, then I would get back to the whispering world. I didn't care about or want anything.

We had a couple months to relax before our shows in Israel. The biggest enemy of Hanoi Rocks was too much free time on our hands. The amounts of drugs grew. We became dangers to ourselves.

×××

Then it was April and time for our six-day trip to Israel. Carol Clerk from *Melody Maker* and the photographer Justin Thomas came along.

We were playing the Kolnoa Dan club downstairs from our hotel in Tel Aviv. The promoter understood who he was dealing with because he let us know that booze was included night or day for the whole five days that we were playing at Kolnoa Dan.

These shows were a good opportunity to check out our new songs. It was also pretty nice to be able to go straight from the show up to our rooms in an elevator. The crowd was a bit uptight and used earplugs, even though they were wearing AC/DC and Motörhead shirts.

The Penguin club had bunch of freaks to hang out with, like Boaz, who wore a full-body catsuit, and a British lady with a nearly ten-inch bright red mohawk. The Penguin's house band was so bad that we kicked them offstage and went up to play ourselves. We smoked Lebanese hash at the afterparty from a thing called a Stuka, built out of a children's steam engine machine.

Armed soldiers in Jerusalem chased us away from the Wailing Wall, apparently because they thought we were all women. The Arab men in the Casbah market got all worked up because they had never seen fully made-up men in pink leather pants before. Justin Thomas took pictures of us out in the desert until diamond-backed spiders the size of ashtrays started to crawl out of the holes in the ground.

The days and nights bled together. A Yemeni prostitute joined the merry troupe. Andy walked into the sea fully dressed until you couldn't see anything but his head. Andy had bolted down the stairs to see if he could fly before he went to float in the Dead Sea. Razzle floated around like a cork.

Razzle quit playing in the middle of the song at our last gig because of the crowd's indifference. The shows were all sold out, but the crowd was like the walking dead. Razzle decided to heckle the crowd and let them know that whoever guessed who he was impersonating would win a pair of drumsticks.

Razzle marched across the stage with his right arm up in a salute and his left index finger under his nose. Someone yelled, "Hitler." The crowd broke out into a fight. We finished the set understandably in bad vibes and then fled the stage to Nasty's and Razzle's room. The tape deck was blasting, bottles smashing, and people hanging out.

The night manager ran into the room screaming; this guy was an aspiring model. This surprised and freaked Nasty out, and he hit the male model in the head with a crutch. Nasty was on crutches from hurting his ankle. His cast was dangling loose around his ankle because he'd tried to cut it off with a butter knife.

The stunned night manager noticed that he'd run barefoot into a room with broken glass on the floor. He ran out of the room screaming and slamming the door while we continued where we'd left off.

At some point, I dragged myself to my own room, collapsed into my bed, and passed out.

The hotel staff was acting strange the next morning. They didn't offer me any food or even tea. The night manager with a bump on his head appeared next to me with some cops in tow who wanted to grill me about the previous night's events. Someone had pushed the balcony table over the railing. The metal table had sailed down six stories onto the roof of a waiting taxi. The roof of the taxi had caved in and the driver had taken a blow to the head. We were being charged with attempted murder, which could be a sentence of a minimum of two years in prison.

Seppo and Richard tried to sort out what had happened, but it wasn't easy. We got a notice in the afternoon to pack our bags and keep our mouths shut because we were going to make a run for the airport at six in the morning. We heard later on that Seppo Vesterinen and Richard Bishop had made a deal with the driver: a bottle of whisky and thirty pounds.

We made it safely back from Israel to the heroin haze of London.

The legend started to spread when Carol Clerk's article came out in *Melody Maker*: "Havoc in the Holy Land." Justin Thomas's pictures were on the cover and in the centerfold.

After going to Asia and Israel, it felt like we were just on an endless tour of the UK. Here we go again, playing in Sheffield, Newcastle, Coventry. It was like Finland all over again; the Leeds Warehouse, we'd been there, done that. At the same time, I understood that it had to be done, this is what we'd signed up for. The band was tighter than ever, and each time there were more people in the audience. Our audience was a mix of youth cultures: punk, glam, skinhead, even the nine-to-fivers. And lots of girls. The British press started to write about us: *Sounds*, *Kerrang*, *Melody Maker*.

The London Cowboys opened for us for part of a tour, as did Turkey Bones and the Wild Dogs, crazy Scots that were Razzle's old friends. Before a show in Dundee, I went to the pub and across from me was a guy about my size wearing a nice jacket. He happened to like my shirt, so we swapped clothes. "Nice pants, wanna swap?" We walked out wearing each other's clothes. I put the whole table on the guest list.

A fight broke out between the crowd and the band during the Dundee gig. Some wasted soccer hooligans in the front row were ogling us, spitting and giving the finger. The stage was so low to the ground that all one of the hooligans had to do was take a step forward and he was on the stage. Sure enough, one guy stepped on the stage and took a swing at Michael. Razzle jumped out from behind the drums like a Doberman and knocked the guy to the ground. More people got up to crowd the stage. Chaos ensued. I started kicking, Nasty was punching, and Andy swung his guitar around. The roadies jumped in. It was an all-out melee, which ended with the hooligans being dragged out of the building. After a while the show went on.

We had gigs just about every day. Heroin wasn't a pastime anymore, and now it came along on tour. Our mini tour with Johnny Thunders was a great example of how things were. We were sitting at the hotel pub in Manchester, each band at its own table. Our dealer came in and both tables got up to greet him. What a tour.

Every night ended with "Pills" and "Gloria" with both bands on stage. Johnny Thunders seemed like a really nice guy. When we ran out of heroin in Edinburgh, Andy found some somehow five minutes before the show. Me, Andy, and Nasty got high without even thinking about how strong the gear might be.

I fell to my knees on stage; I tried to keep it together for the song though. All you could hear from Andy was feedback, and Nasty, who was next to me, was completely checked out. The gear kicked in for us all at the same time. Somehow, we regained our senses, and the show went on. Maybe not the best show ever or in the best shape, but we got the job done.

I also got the job done when hanging out with Algy Ward from the Damned at a party. We found a bass and a bottle of gin and made a bet over how drunk you could be and still be able to play the Damned's "Love Song." We went back and forth...I emerged victorious.

We went on a half-assed European tour. Our hippie driver realized in the Dutch port that he'd forgotten the ATA Carnet, the customs documents for all our gear, on his kitchen table. He had to go back to London to get it, and we missed the Amsterdam show waiting for him to make it back. We had six shows booked in Germany, but ended up playing just Munich and Frankfurt, thanks to the stony driver.

The only tape with us in the van was *The Best of Creedence Clearwater Revival*. That's all we listened to for the four days on the road. Later on, we were in the studio and running out of songs, when someone remembered this tour and suggested we cover "Up Around the Bend."

Once we got back to London, we weren't feeling too good and headed straight to the dealer's from the train station. I couldn't be bothered to prepare a smoke so I just snorted a big line of smack. I realized right away that it had been too much. Everything went dark.

I woke up alone in a dark room. I walked around the room trying to find the door. The dealer appeared out of nowhere and was pissed. "Don't come here to fucking OD. You turned blue and almost stopped breathing. We walked you around for almost two hours!"

I quietly thanked her and made my way to the subway. It was the shittiest I'd ever felt, and that feeling lasted for two days. It was time to quit.

It was weird to sit in the pub with my sunglasses on and a mineral water in my hand, but beer would just have made me puke. Smack and booze were a horrible cocktail, and I kept doing it every now and then. All my friends who didn't use were worried, like Carol Clerk. One morning I woke up to my legs hurting, I had a sticky fever, and my stomach was messed up. My head was foggy, I was sweaty and had goosebumps. I called René Berg to let him know I couldn't meet up with him and let him know why not. René came over; he knew what was up. He hooked me up. The fever and all the other symptoms went away like that. The addiction wasn't out of hand yet, but that witch came a-knocking.

Andy and Anna had been on the rocks for a long time now. Anna was a manager at Hastings Park Gate studios and was away from London half the week. She'd stay the night at Nasty's or Razzle's or my place when she came back to London. I spent a lot of time with Anna, and we'd gotten really close. Anna suggested one day not to get high and just watch the people around me get high. The next time I was at Andy's, I declined. Half an hour later, the guys were nodding off, getting up to puke, and scratching themselves. Every now and then someone would wake up to mumble something and would fall asleep before they could finish their thought. I hadn't realized we had gotten to that point. The sight was pathetic.

Andy had started to pull away from the group, just like Monroe had done earlier. Michael's relationship with Stiv's wife was totally a negative one and was slowly killing him. Anna and I had to keep our relationship secret because of Andy. It was heavy. I tried to break things off a bunch of times.

In April, Nasty mixed booze with painkillers and ended up both in the intensive care unit in Kajaani and in the headlines. The hospital wouldn't allow anyone outside the family to visit, but before the reception clerk could finish talking, I introduced myself as a Stenfors brother. It worked.

Nasty was gray and hooked up to a dialysis machine and a whole bunch of other tubes. He looked pretty awful. His sense of humor was the same though, even at the death's door. We agreed that the four of us would finish off the rest of the tour.

Our good old friend Kauppinen—rest in peace—was with us for the remaining shows. He was well over four hundred pounds, a Middle Eastern–looking guy, half blind, and an incurable wise guy. In Tampere, he ripped off all his clothes and flailed around the stage. That weekend was the semi-religious Kirkastusjuhlat festival. There was no backstage so we had to hang out in the bus surrounded by fans, pissing in bottles out of necessity. After hours of waiting, the bus was filled with piss bottles.

Nasty's amp was hooked up to Andy's. The guitar power was suddenly Motörhead level. Andy's face lit up with a happy grin. We played Iggy and the Stooges's "1970 (Feel Alright)" as the encore; Kauppinen was flailing around, stripped again and bellowed "feel all right" into the mic. Four hundred pounds of hairy squiggly flesh was a sight to behold. At the end of the song, Kauppinen collapsed, spreading his legs so that he was showing his ass to the audience. That apparently wasn't enough. Kauppinen shoved the mike up his ass so that only the trembling cable could still be seen. The front row was mostly thirteen, fourteen-year-old girls. The poor little fluffy-headed fans were stuck witnessing a Finnish rendition of Antonin Artaud's *Théâtre de la Cruauté.*

×××

Seppo Vesterinen and Richard Bishop had succeeded in securing Hanoi Rocks a record deal with CBS Epic Records. Everything looked really good now. Seppo had played his cards to move his international plans forward. He was no idiot who wanted to do it all on his own. He realized that he didn't know the English market well enough, so he got himself a business partner in Richard Bishop.

My biggest shortcoming was that I couldn't care less about business and contracts. My indifference went so far that my name wasn't even on this, Hanoi Rocks' biggest deal. Timppa Kaltio forged my name on it. I was high at home, or hungover, and I forgot about the whole signing to-do.

The Reading Festival on the twenty-sixth of August was our first really big show in the UK. How many people were there? Someone talked about hundreds of thousands. The trip there was in a baking hot van through the slowest traffic imaginable. There was a strange energy in the air when we got the site. When we got up on stage, the front rows were really into it and digging the show, but behind them was a sea of people who *hated* us. English crowds drink a lot of beer and would piss back into the bottle. A rain of plastic two-liter beer bottles filled with piss started to fly onto the stage. One guy chucked a cheeseburger at me; I picked it up, took aim—he couldn't get away because he was trapped between a fence and a ton of people—and threw the cheeseburger right back into his face. I went back to playing with both hands.

The Reading gig turned into a war. We'd already learned how to protect ourselves from projectiles during the UK Subs show, where the crowd had thrown darts at us.

After the show, I grabbed some beers from backstage, threw them into a big garbage bag, and tossed the bag into the trunk of a car. I got a ride back to London with Carol Clerk and Buttz from the Babysitters. We drove in the heat for three hours and pulled up to the front of the St. Moritz Club; everyone was in the mood for a drink. The only little problem was Mr. Sweety, the bald Austrian who owned the club; he couldn't stand us or our behavior. He couldn't really ban Hanoi Rocks from coming in because we brought in too much money, but every now and then, Sweety would lose it and tell the doormen we couldn't come in.

We parked in front of the club. Sweety was standing in front of the club's front door as usual. For some reason, I grabbed the bag of beer from the trunk and threw it over my shoulder. Sloshing from the ride, warmed from the sun, the cans started to explode. I dropped the bag, and a shower of foam started to shoot out from it. Sweety saw the whole thing.

I decided I was coming inside. Sweety was shutting the door, but I wedged my foot in. Sweety cracked the door and punched me in the face. "You're not coming in!" I kicked him in the balls. "Yes, we are!" I jumped over his doubled-over body and ran down the stairs to the bar. I'd get a beer in my hand before Sweety was able to drag me out.

"Get out of my club!"

With my cheek still red from his punch, I started to beg. "Sweety, come on, Sweety, just one beer, one beer, one nice little beer…"

Sweety exploded into laughter and let us order drinks. "But don't come back for a while!"

Carol wrote about the Reading set, and it was a big step up for us.

We started demo sessions in September. We'd thought about Eddie Kramer and Martin Birch at first to produce our first CBS record, but when Bob Ezrin said yes, we definitely were not disappointed. Ezrin had produced some pretty big albums: Lou Reed's *Berlin*, Peter Gabriel's first record, Pink Floyd's *The Wall*, all of the Alice Cooper's important records from the seventies.

All the hard work Seppo and Richard had put in was finally paying off. We had a big international deal and one of the best producers in the world.

But the band was completely on another planet, definitely not in the place to be recording a masterpiece. The most worrisome part was that it looked like the well of Andy's songs was starting to dry out. The ideas came now in bits and pieces. A riff here, another there, a lone chorus without a bridge to anywhere.

1984

Fallen Angels, All Those Wasted Years & Two Steps from the Move

We were in a couple week preproduction period in London at the beginning of the year. Andy was showing some riffs to Bob Ezrin. There was just the up and down intro riff of "Underwater World;" we wrote the verses all together, but the chorus was missing. All the lyrics too, except for a line here and there. The song came out in bits and pieces and only under a lot of pressure.

At the end of January, Andy went ahead to Toronto with Ezrin to continue preproduction. The writing sessions took a while. There were no lyrics and they just weren't flying out of Andy like they used to. A small sense of panic started to creep in. There was a lot riding on this album, this was the make-it-or-break-it moment.

Nothing stronger than booze or weed was allowed in the recording sessions. This was included in the contract with Bob Ezrin. If even one member was caught dabblin', Ezrin could walk away from the project with the full advance in his pockets.

Being forced to go clean made the band of course a lot healthier. This group of junkie hermits started to be a real band again. There were writing sessions every day, and they'd last for hours on end. We managed to get the music together but still didn't have all the lyrics. Ezrin suggested Andy collaborate with some lyric writers. Ezrin brought a couple of lyricists to the studio. One, Pete Brown, had written Cream's "Sunshine of Your Love." Brown only wrote the lyric "I smoked a lot of sky, drank a lot of rain" for us. No one seemed to be good enough for Andy. You had to understand our attitude to write our words.

I was browsing through the Toronto phone book in my hotel room for fun, and I stumbled across a Takamäki. I called the number, introduced myself, and explained, "You don't know me, but I'm a Finnish musician in town to record an album. Do you speak Finnish?" "Well, I don't really, but my grandmother does. Hold on a second." A feeble voice said "haloo" on the other end, and I chatted with this grandma for a while. She had come to Canada at seventeen. My dad was from a small town in western Finland, Kauhajoki; he was born in the nearby city of Vaasa, but he'd grown up in Kauhajoki.

At the end of our stay in Toronto, we had ten songs in good enough shape to move over to New York for recording. Ezrin used his super producer muscle to secure us Ian Hunter to come visit us at Record Plant East Studios. Ian was ultimately good enough for Andy; Mott the Hoople had been a big deal to Andy when he was a kid. Hunter carefully listened to our recordings, went home, and came back two days later with several completed lyrics.

I was getting ready to do my basses when Ezrin brought in fucking Jack Bruce! We were working on the track "High School," which wasn't exactly the easiest one to get through. Jack Bruce gave the thumbs up behind the glass of the control room. I thought about my brother, because Cream had been Jone's favorite when he was a teenager. I pushed Jack and Cream and Jone out of my mind and focused on the composition of "High School." I asked Bob to press record.

I nailed the fecker in one take, no mistakes, that was that. Put that in your pipe and smoke it, Jack and Bob! I went to check it out, and Jack Bruce shook my hand and praised my work with a crooked grin on his face. I was sure Bob had brought Jack in for the bass overdub day on purpose, either for support or intimidation. Either way, it worked.

At the end of a long day, I went to the nearby bar called Smith's on the corner of Forty-Third and Eighth Avenue. I got my drink and took a seat at the end of the bar next to the door. I heard a drunken skirmish coming from the back. "Ay, ya motherfucker…ya cocksucker…" Then I saw one of the old winos stick a knife in the other one's stomach, and the guy who got stabbed fell to the floor cursing. I froze and stared at the surreal scene with beer in hand. The bartender, who looked deceptively like the waiter from *The Shining*, appeared in front of me. "Hey, kid, take a hike! What the hell are you still doing here?" I jumped off my barstool and ran to the hotel. Times Square wasn't exactly a safe area back then.

Another night, I went to knock on Razzle's door to see if the good lord was still up and down for a nightcap. There was a girl, who I wasn't exactly happy to see, sitting on his bed. This religious fanatic had been following us from show to show for years and always stood right in front of me. She'd even written letters to my mom. "Sami and I are getting married. Jesus made us for each other." There had been some crazy-ass photo collages in the letters too, with angel wings glued to my shoulders.

I told Razzle the whole story and said we had to kick her out now. Razzle laughed, pulled out the Bible from the nightstand, and began to read from the Book of Genesis. I pushed the stalker out the door with both hands while Razzle continued his sermon.

Now I really needed that nightcap.

We went back to Toronto to record the overdubs and vocals. Once my work was done, I spent most of my time at the Hard Rock Café playing the hockey game with Razzle. I'd go check things out at the studio from time to time, and while sitting in on one session, there was a call from reception. Ezrin answered the phone, mumbled something, and said to me, "Sami, your wife is there. I never knew you were married."

No fucking way. I crept down the hall to peek around the corner at reception. There she was, the nutty religious girl from Razzle's room, sitting at the reception of Toronto's Phase One Studios.

I went back to the control room and told Bob and the sound engineer, Rob O'Brian, what was going on. They went to reception to tell the girl that Sami wasn't around and that Sami didn't have a wife so could she please get lost. She grabbed onto the chair and started screaming that she wasn't going anywhere until she saw her husband. Rob and Bob dragged the girl outside and locked the door.

We went back to the Holiday Inn that evening. I was getting into the elevator when I saw this psychopath running toward me. I started to press the door button in a panic, but I pressed the wrong one, the doors opened. I was now panic-pressing the close the door button. The elevator doors closed and went up seconds before the psycho could make it in. I called downstairs to security to please kick her out of the hotel.

I tried not to go outside for the next few days. When I wanted to go to the studio, I called a taxi to come down to the hotel's parking lot. The fanatic had managed to get a hold of both Andy and Nasty, who'd told her I'd gone to Florida on vacation now that I'd finished recording my part. The girl must have flown off to Florida to look for me because I never saw her again. Hopefully she found something else and something healthier to focus on.

We ended up at a biker gang's party. I was pretty intoxicated, so I wanted to do some coke to perk myself up. I was told there was some in the kitchen.

There were three bikers sitting at the table. There was a proper mountain of white powder in the middle of the table. I had just seen *Scarface*, so I plunged my face into the mountain of cocaine and took a big snort. At first, it looked like I was going to get punched. Then they said it was all good as long as I paid for what I had used.

Late that evening, I was upstairs with my back to the stairs. I was talking to some lady when I lost my footing and crashed backward down the staircase. Numbed from the coke, I didn't feel a thing, and I didn't break my neck probably thanks to the booze. The next morning, I couldn't really turn myself around or even breathe properly. I dragged myself to the bathroom and looked in the mirror. There was a bruise the size of a hockey mitt on the right side of my back. The doctor said I'd broken three ribs. All I could do was take some painkillers and wait for it to heal.

I got used to the pain in a couple of weeks, but it took a long time to fully recover.

After we finished recording in March, we played a couple of shows at a place called Danceteria in New York. Those were Hanoi's first shows in the States. Then we played Boston, Pennsylvania, and Toronto over on the Canadian side. Our driver was a big Russian guy who liked to sing folk songs; he'd only been in America for a couple of weeks, and he kept getting lost.

The truck drivers at the Pennsylvania shows mumbled "fucking faggots" until they realized from the enthusiasm of our Glam and Goth support that this was actually rock 'n' roll, so they started to bob their trucker hats along.

Andy and I gave an interview at a New York college radio station. Actually, Andy just cursed on air and sent his greetings to the NYC cabbies. For my part, I was choppin' lines on the mixing board and was so high that I couldn't get out more than some wheezing. Any attempt at promotion was just tossed out the window.

A publicist from Epic brought us to Andy Warhol's Factory, which had recently moved to a new place in Union Square at the corner of Broadway and Seventeenth Street.

The elevator doors opened to a Black bodybuilder dressed as a Roman gladiator singing opera and holding a tray of champagne flutes. Then we heard, "Hi, I'm Andy..." and got a limp handshake from the great artist.

The Factory was an entire floor of a loft space. At the entrance were columns and windows, and on the left, different rooms for different parts of the creative process: a sketching room, a painting room, a darkroom, a framing room. Warhol took some Polaroids and showed us four paintings that were currently under construction and the room where the paintings were being finished.

Andy Warhol had founded *Interview* magazine, which was known for its wide-ranging interviews. *Interview* had extended to a TV show on New York public access. There was interest in interviewing Hanoi Rocks for this local cable program. We did the interviews separately, one at a time. The setup was a table with a box of pizza on it. The camera started rolling and then came the question, "So, what do you think when people say that bass players are the sexiest members of the band?" And I was supposed to answer that, oy vey.

Razzle's *Interview* interview was mostly about his previous band. Razzle said the band was called Fuck Pigs, which was true. Razzle went on: "I went onstage with the wrong band once. I had eaten so many mushrooms and acid trips, I thought the band onstage was my band. I suddenly realized I don't have any flute or violin players in my band, and there was nothing but flutes and violins—and a red drum kit. As a finale, I threw the big, red bass drum to the audience—it looked like a meteorite!" That's quite an achievement, to get on stage behind the drum kit and realize after playing a while that you weren't with the right band.

We returned to London. The label didn't hear a single from the New York and Toronto sessions. We remembered CCR's "Up Around the Bend" that we'd listened to on the unfortunate tour of the Continent. We recorded our version at Wessex Studios.

We made a video for "Up Around the Bend" at a country manor in Essex. The helicopter aerial shots almost killed the band. The director hadn't realized that a helicopter flying sixty feet over the stage would create a hell of a wind. Fortunately, we were set up around Razzle's drums and Makke at the edge of the stage, because the heavy lighting rig fell on stage and missed us by a few feet.

Then Nasse was put into a harness, because somebody had the great idea to dangle him from ropes and fly him from the rooftop of the building to the stage. An assistant tested out the harness and everything was okay. Nasty was bigger than the assistant, though, and also had a heavy Les Paul around his neck. His flight came to a halt halfway down; he hung from the ropes like poorly washed laundry. A broom was used to try to get Nasty moving again. It was all a big waste of time; Nasty was finally brought down and the whole setup was adjusted to the right weight. It all turned out great in the end, and we got a great shot of Nasty swooshing backward toward the stage. The flight almost crushed his spine, though, since he still came in too low.

The owner of the Finnish music magazine *Suosikki*, Jyrki Hämäläinen, appeared in the fancy ballroom that we used as a green room with the newly crowned Miss Finland. Andy's reaction was to throw a cognac bottle at them.

We went back to Japan in May. The tour was sold out; the venues were bigger, and so was the hysteria. Big glass windows at the hotel shattered because the girls went wild trying to get closer to their idols. There was too much commotion in the hotels, and I preferred to hang out at a French dancer named Annie's place, where there'd be a bath, coq au vin, and champagne waiting for me after the show.

Before the Tokyo concerts, we took promo shots and photos for the cover of the *Two Steps from the Move* LP. The legendary photographer Hiro, who also shot the cover of the Rollings Stones' *Black and Blue*, took the pictures. There is some resemblance between the two covers.

After Japan was yet another UK tour. We had August and September off, which was always bad news for the band. Anna and I had taken a break, but now we were back on, which meant feeling guilty and mixed emotions for me. I didn't know how to quit either the relationship or heroin; I'd just turned twenty-one. Everything was racing toward a natural conclusion. I finally understood, and so did Anna. She told me, "You're addicted to heroin. All three of you are."

I went to see my sister in Spain and started thinking about moving there. I could get away from it all: the band, heroin. Theoretically, everything was going great; the record had turned out well, and we had a big-budget music video making the rounds on TV. But I was sick of it, and the band had a shitty, junkie vibe. Everyone had started to pull away from each other and gotten really passive. Andy's egomania was exploring new depths. Michael had turned into a complete hermit, holing up in his new place in Hammersmith. Michael was working out, taking vitamins, and was on a real health kick. But he wasn't eating.

We had UK shows and the record release in October, a couple shows in Sweden in November, and then a little US tour.

I'd talked with Razzle about leaving the band. Razzle had been thinking the same thing. He came by my place one morning and convinced me to do the US tour. Razzle was pretty over it, over Hanoi, but he wanted to see Los Angeles, where he'd dreamed of going as a kid. "Let's see how the record sells. Who knows?" he'd said to encourage me.

Everyone cleaned up and pulled it together before the tour. We'd only drink and smoke weed on tour. We'd only really brought heroin along hardcore on the Johnny Thunders tour. I decided to take care of myself and do these shows right. In September, I got my hands on some sleeping pills, hash, and booze, dimmed the lights in my apartment, and kicked the habit. I spent four days sweating, puking, and in pain.

I was ready.

The gigs in England and Sweden were crazed and manic. I spent the last night before leaving for the US with Anna. The band got onto a bus in front of a hotel in Slussen, Stockholm. Anna waved goodbye to me from the lobby.

Suddenly Razzle jumped off the bus, ran to the lobby to hug Anna one more time, and ran back to the bus. "Let's go."

×××

We toured the US in a luxury bus decked out with bunks, a fridge, and a television. We had a decent amount of people show up for our East Coast shows. MTV had started to put the video for "Up Around the Bend" in heavy rotation. There were a lot of curious onlookers at the Ritz club in New York, like Paul Stanley and Gene Simmons from Kiss. The afterparty backstage was spent in a coke and weed haze.

I took a hit off a joint and a camera flashed. The next week, the picture was on the front page of the *Iltalehti* tabloid in Finland: "Hanoi Rocks in the midst of marijuana smoke in NYC." This was not the kind of news that my family liked to hear. My beloved grandma went to church to pray for me. Finland was so innocent.

The crowds in DC, Baltimore, and Philadelphia were all the same: they loved Aerosmith and the Stones, and they couldn't stand Boy George or Duran Duran. That crowd took us in as one of their own.

In Chicago, Andy accidentally jumped from the drum riser onto Michael's ankle. And broke it. Michael gamely tried to wrap up the show with his foot bandaged up, but it didn't really work and didn't look too good. Hanoi Rocks' last show in the States was at Peabody's in Cleveland. Andy and I smoked weed on stage, the gig wasn't the best we'd played. How did it end up like this?

Michael's broken ankle felt fated, and so it was in the end. We suddenly had time off in the middle of the tour. Way too much time. Which wasn't a good thing. We drove to Atlanta to decide what to do next and to party with go-go dancers for three days. Then we decided to go to Los Angeles to see if Michael's ankle could handle playing the show in Los Angeles at the Palace on December 14. With all the canceled shows, we wouldn't be playing the Palace for another ten days.

Two Steps from the Move had taken off in America but wasn't making a lot of noise. In fact, CBS was doing its best to keep the record from taking off. It's normal in the American music business that the marketing dollars only go toward a small handful of new releases. The label is ready to keep their other artists down to make a big hit for one or two others. Nothing can take away attention from the chosen ones—not even the other artists on the label.

The big boss at Epic, Dick Asher, had shown up for a production meeting where *Two Steps from the Move* was playing. He said, "I hope this shit is not on our label" After hearing that it was, Asher said, "Kill it."

That's what the American label animals are like. They decide to make one record a big hit and fade away everything else. There were all kinds of stories going around about the CBS boss, Walter Yetnikoff, but I never met him.

Los Angeles was warm at that time of year. Razzle said he had talked to Vince Neil, the singer from Mötley Crüe. We'd met the Crüe in the spring when they'd played London. Vince was coming in the morning to pick Razzle up and show him around LA. I said I'd come along. Vince came to our place at the Franklin Plaza Suites in a two-seater sports car. When I pointed out that a third wouldn't fit in there, Razzle told me to sit in his lap—let's go.

The three of us drove around sunny LA. Vince showed us Malibu, Sunset Boulevard, Santa Monica. The tour lasted for hours. Vince was happy-go-lucky, a nice guy. Nikki Sixx was the brains of the band and that says a lot. But they were good dudes. I hung out with Tommy Lee a few times after everything.

Vince suggested we get some beers and go hang out at his place. He lived in a condo in Redondo Beach right on the beach. Vince's pregnant wife made us some food, and we sat on the balcony with Coronas in hand, passing around a joint and talking. It felt good, the vibe was chill, and there was a lot of laughter.

Razzle and I decided to stay in the band. There just wasn't anybody better than the Hanoi guys, and this was the good life, everything would sort itself out.

At sunset, more of Vince's friends showed up and so did Andy with Tommy Lee. We kept drinking and smoking weed, but the Coronas were starting to run out. I stretched out in front of the TV and thought about taking a little nap.

Razzle came to ask if I'd tag along to pick up some more beer. I said I wasn't up for it and that they should go. Vince and Razzle went to the store.

I fell asleep.

×××

Someone was shaking me. I woke up to the Mötley Crüe guitarist Mick Mars' face. What's up?

There had been an accident.

Vince's place was empty. I was groggy and didn't really understand what was going on, but I went to the hospital since I'd been asked to.

At the hospital, a doctor came to ask. "Did you know Nicholas Dingley?"

"What do you mean, *did* I know?"

Andy pulled me aside and told me that Razzle had died in a car accident. Vince had lost control of the car and crashed, passenger side first, into an oncoming car.

I sat in the dark hotel room alone. I kept thinking about the car accident and the last moments leading up to it. I missed my dear friend. I blamed myself for letting Razzle talk me into the tour. If I had said no, maybe he'd...

I called Anna in Stockholm and told her the news. In the same call, Anna told me she was pregnant. The pregnancy was from the last night we'd spent together before I'd left for America. Back when Razzle had run back to hug Anna one last time before jumping onto the bus.

Within the next day, others came by my room. I was grief-stricken, messed up from the accident, and all of a sudden, some members of the group already had their plans for the future ready to go. I heard that of course the band would be more famous because a member had died.

I thought it was horrid to even think about this kind of shit while Razzle was still in a body bag. Razzle, who had brought life back to the band when we had been so in need of it. I just wanted to go back to London, to leave the band and let the others do what they wanted. I just wasn't interested in the band anymore after this.

The next days were a hopeless haze of hard hours. All I knew was that there was a kid on the way; I was going to be a dad; I had to make a change.

I came back to London from LA. I had a strong urge to go back to smack to numb the pain. But I decided to stay clean and make it to Razzle's funeral. The whole band and Razzle's friends took the train to Southampton and then the ferry to the Isle of Wight. Except Andy, who missed both the train and the funeral.

I couldn't protect myself from my own head and heart. When our roadie, Helge, had died, I took his suicide really hard. But Razzle was *family*; I'd spent Christmas with him, my mom, sis, and grandma.

I kept it together all the way to the Isle of Wight, where we had a drink at a pub and drove to Razzle's home village of Binsted. I finally lost it in the church. I couldn't hold back my tears anymore; I don't remember a thing from the end of the ceremony.

After the funeral, we had a meeting regarding the future. We were supposed to play the Culture House Theatre in Helsinki on the third and fourth of January. The latter gig was going to be televised for the program *Europe A Go-Go*, for a TV audience of thirty million. Okay, we'd do 'em as a memorial for Razzle. The gigs would be my last with Hanoi Rocks.

Our manager duo tried to keep things going, but I knew deep down that it was over.

Before Christmas, we had three practice sessions with Terry Chimes. Terry is a sober, pedantic, and tight drummer who had played on the first Clash record. He had a good, dry British sense of humor, straight out of *Fawlty Towers*. Terry ended up in Cherry Bombz with Andy and Nasty in the fall of 1985.

I packed my meager possessions in a bag, left London, and went to Finland for Christmas with Anna. We decided to start a new life together with a kid on the way. We'd get settled in Stockholm as soon as the Helsinki shows were over and done with.

The band had a few backstage rooms at our disposal at the Helsinki Kulttuuritalo Culture House. I hung out with Nasty for those couple of days. I didn't have to talk or be in the same room with Andy, who was floating around like a big dark cloud. I'd kicked heroin, but Andy hadn't. He had blinders on, pointed fingers at others but couldn't look at himself in the mirror. He was extremely pissed that I was leaving the band.

Michael was completely crushed, and I didn't see him until we were on stage.

Europe A Go-Go almost felt like a normal show, until the thought sunk in that, oh yeah, this is the last time. When I looked behind me, there was someone there other than my...brother. Despite the outbursts of emotion, I looked calm on the outside. I also couldn't wait until it was the next day and everything was over. I was really done. Completely.

Anna and I went straight to my mom's house in Kerava from the Culture House. My good friend had been buried a couple weeks earlier. In me was a horrible, dark empty place.

It was the fourth of January 1985.

1985–1990

Stockholm—Los Angeles

"Touring is waiting around.
Traveling and waiting.
Musicians turn into alcoholics
from all the waiting,
not the backstage service."

1985

Nicholas Samuel

I slept for two days at my mom's in Kerava. When I finally got up, I felt lighter. Something heavy had been lifted from my shoulders. I was free from my previous obligations, and I was free to do what I wanted. And what I didn't want to do was play music and tour.

Anna and I went to Stockholm to her parents' house, the same place where Andy had been taking baths while the rest of us lived on the street. We relaxed for a couple of weeks and then flew to Mallorca to my sister's. Maybe I could find a job there. Richard Bishop had given me 4,000 Finnish marks, not even pounds, so barely fuck all, and had said that it was a "golden handshake." I didn't even know what a golden handshake meant, but I thanked him and expected that I'd see the normal royalties from the work I'd done with the band. That cash would be enough for a little while. After that, I had no idea how to get by.

The time in Mallorca was spent getting my head together and improving my physical condition. I felt strange, really strange. I'd been working for five years straight and had nothing to show for it. Exhaustion came only after everything stopped. And it was a heavy exhaustion. I was twenty-one, but I felt like I was an old man.

The whole Hanoi experience had been very special. The chemistry between the five of us had been so natural. My time in Hanoi had been a musical crash course, so intense and tough, that one year was like ten.

That's what it felt like, in any case. I hadn't taken a break in years, or if there had been a break, it had been spent on drugs. We'd wrap up a tour, during which we drank a ton, and then when we finally would have some downtime, the smart idea would be to go get some uppers or downers… those seemed to be the only alternatives. WTF?

You can play high if you've been using long enough and your body and brain are used to it. There's a point where using is just part of keeping you, well, normal.

Heroin had been part of my downtime. Before the US tour, I'd gone through withdrawal at home, and all the climbing up the walls that comes with it. I got clean from heroin, and I quit for good because what happened on the tour happened; I just wasn't drawn to that life anymore. I had only been addicted for a year. I've seen people get really hooked, thank God I never got that far gone. When you get really seriously hooked, years can just disappear without doing shit. It's hard to climb back from that. I was going through my phonebook in the nineties, and it hit me that half my friends had died. From drugs, booze, AIDS, suicide, pills. Rock 'n' roll, let's party—wake up in the morning dead. An endless list of young, sensitive, vulnerable human beings. What a waste.

There'd hardly been time for girls with Hanoi. Sure, I'd go on dates once in a while here and there before Anna, but I wasn't really interested in anything other than playing music or drugs. Not even Andy did; well, he usually had someone at the side. But it was definitely not the same scene as the US groupie bands like Van Halen and Mötley Crüe. When I saw those hard rock bands in LA with ample-breasted, scantily clad ladies all around them, I realized that Hanoi was…well, we were more interested in drugs.

When I left, René Berg joined Hanoi on the bass, and Terry Chimes, who'd played the last Helsinki shows, stayed on the drums. That lineup lasted for four or five months, and then Hanoi Rocks was finally finished.

My parents had always supported me, but now they were worried. I was rail thin, 113 pounds and six feet tall. When I said that I was going to be a dad, my mom was on top of the world. My dad, however, hung up the phone after a "Goddammit!"

Truth be told, it saved my life. This was the end of my drug use and maniacal drinking. Clearing my head unearthed new questions. I had no interest in playing music, but I didn't know how to do anything else. I had to think of something to earn a living. We spent a couple of months in Mallorca, where I noticed that work and family are closely linked and you don't get hired just like that. Anna and I didn't really speak much Spanish either, so we kind of had to think of a future somewhere other than Mallorca. It was time to go back to Stockholm, where we had family, friends, and both spoke the language. I knew Stockholm like the back of my hand, because I'd spent months walking all over the city when I'd been homeless. No one walks as much as the homeless.

Anna got a job at the Östermalmshallen market hall, and I got a job at a car repair shop close to St. Eriksplan, where used cars were fixed up to look like new. The cars would get washed with a high-pressure hose, the inside would get scrubbed clean, the spots and stains would get cleaned off the seats, the tires would get changed out to new ones, the paint job would get touched up and all the rust repaired. I'd bring my own tapes along and play them in the cars' cassette players.

Work started at six in the morning and ended at three or four in the afternoon. It was hard work, and the pay didn't exactly make me jump for joy either. But a little bit goes a long way when you're not on drugs.

Life was calm and healthy. I was learning how to cook. I spent the evenings at home drawing, painting, reading, and listening to music. Anna's belly grew. We'd go to Anna's parents' to eat on Sundays. We'd have wine and cocktails with dinner, but that was about all the drinking I was doing. Every now and then I'd go to the pub with Gyp or other friends. A Hard Rock Café opened up close to home, and I saw some good shows there. My old, close-knit friend group, which included people big in the Stockholm nightlife like Susanne and Lotte, would hang out there. One of them got married to Johnny Thunders, and the other one to Jerry Nolan.

I rode by bike to work one morning. My back tire had gone flat, and I had to push my bike the last mile. I was already pissed off, and I wasn't in the mood to scrub car seats with turpentine or change tires. There was a rule at the shop that everything that didn't belong in the car was thrown out. All the random stuff from the glove compartment, from under the seats or the trunk was tossed into a junk pile.

I was there with my ass up, vacuuming under the driver's seat, when the vacuum got stuck on a small men's handbag. I squeezed it, and it felt soft inside. I put the bag in my overalls pocket.

I went to the bathroom during my coffee break and opened the bag. There was a bundle of bills a couple inches thick inside. Hundreds, thousands. I started counting: 20,000, 30,000…altogether it ended up being 60,000 krona, which at the time was about 10,000 pounds.

The guy from the used car company came by later and checked my work from top to bottom, thanked me for my careful work, and tipped me twenty krona. I called Anna to let her know I had a surprise for her when I came home.

I tossed the pile of money on the kitchen table. Anna stared at the money and then at me and asked what in the hell had I done. I told her and promised to return the money if anyone came looking for it anytime soon.

A month went by, then two, then three. I was at the shop scrubbing a car as usual, and someone tapped me on the back. There was a toughie with a boxer's nose standing behind me. A greasy-haired guy was standing behind him. I straightened up. The ogre started to poke his fingers into my chest with his stocky fingers. "You can have ten percent."

Anna was due any day now. Shit, I'd found that money three months ago. These guys were just guessing that I'm the one who found it; in all probability, the money was under the table. I asked, "Ten percent of what?"

My coworkers gathered around out of curiosity. The old guy started pushing, and my friends shouted and pushed back; someone said they were calling the cops. Hearing that, the ogre and the greasy-haired guy beat it.

I was pretty jumpy the next few weeks and slept with a fifteen-inch machete under my pillow. But no one ever came again.

×××

Anna announced that her water had broken in the middle of the night. It was August 6, 1985. We went to the hospital, and seven hours later, at 10:30 a.m., my son was born.

The birth of your child is a different kind of joy altogether. Children really turn you into an adult. Birth instigates all these eternal questions about how the world works. All the big things suddenly seem so simple.

We called our boy Nicholas, which was Razzle's real name. I didn't even think about any other options; if we had a boy, he would be Nicholas. Anna didn't like Sami as a middle name, so the kid was Nicholas Samuel.

There was a couple at Anna's work that had also just had a baby, and they wanted to move back to the center of Stockholm. I had gotten a little studio with the money I'd found. We swapped places; they moved into the studio, and we moved to their place a little farther out in the burbs, to Midsommarkransen.

I stopped working at the auto shop. I had thought about advertising, which was how my dad had made his career. I went to art classes to draw models and fruit baskets using different media from pencil to acrylic. "Draw some shoes." Okay, I drew some shoes. I hadn't really figured out which direction I'd go in that field. I was pretty unemployable, since I'd quit school in the ninth grade, but because of the kid, I had to at least try. I ended up spending a couple of months cleaning public bathrooms until my old friend, Jamlo Sarisalmi, got me a job at Studio Råttan doing silk screening. Hanoi had taken some pictures at Råttan for a single cover in 1981. I silk-screened everything you could possibly print, a logo or a picture at Råttan. We'd be silk screening tens of thousands of lighters all night, Miles Davis's *Bitches Brew* playing on loop. Jamlo and I had a lot to talk about. The lighters were attached at the bottom. I'd put the frame in place, spread the ink, take the frame off, and put them below to dry. Next batch.

One night in the fall, the phone rang. Michael was calling from New York. He, Stiv Bators, and Johnny Thunders had decided to form a new band… the New New York Dolls. They'd already put together the lineup: Stiv and Michael on vocals, Johnny and Nasty on guitar, Jerry Nolan on drums, and me on the bass. I could tell that he was serious.

There was a baby sleeping next to me. I was in a different place with other thoughts on my mind. "No."

But the bass sitting in the corner of the apartment had started to stare at me. C'mon, we ain't done yet! Taking a half-year break had done me good; the thought of playing again was finally possible. I played a gig or two with Stevie Klasson and Neon Leon in Södertälje. Neon Leon was the former guitarist of a Philly punk band called Pure Hell, and Stevie Klasson was a seventeen-year-old guitarist who ended up playing with Johnny Thunders's band when Thunders moved to Stockholm and played with him until Thunders's death.

I did a tour of Spain in April of 2016 with Stevie Klasson and Sylvain Sylvain. Old friendships never die.

When I was ready to start making music again, I got in touch with Gyp, but he wasn't interested in joining a band; he had a steady job at a record store. Gyp suggested I get in touch with Pelle Almgren. "He's not bad at writing songs and seems to be in need of a bass player."

And so he was. I started hanging out with Pelle Almgren, and it wasn't long before we pulled the guitars out. Pelle had some good song ideas, and we started putting them together. The early lineup was Dave Zanoni on drums and Adam Seipel on guitar, who were more into metal, which was a bit of a problem for me. If music doesn't have a bite, what's the point? Zanoni and Seipel fell off, but the two of us kept on playing together.

I thought that maybe with my contacts, we could get a record out for Pelle Almgren. Seppo Vesterinen had founded Yahoo! Records, which later turned into Polarvox. After Hanoi broke up, Seppo's and Richard's focus had turned to Cherry Bombz, Andy, Nasty and Terry's new band. Cherry Bombz was supposed to be the next big thing. Their first song was "Hot Girls in Love," a cover of a song by a band called Loverboy. I thought that McCoy had finally lost his mind.

Seppo offered us a four-song EP, nothing more. We thought about it like an introductory thing; Pelle didn't even have enough songs for a full-length album anyway. That being said, if Seppo had said that we were making an LP, Pelle would have figured out the rest of the songs in time.

1986

Sam Yaffa—Pelle Almgren

In January, Pelle and I recorded the basic tracks at Marcus Music in Solna in Stockholm and the overdubs at Finnvox in Helsinki. The recording engineer was T. T. Oksala, who was one the biggest guys in the field in the eighties. Conny Bloom was on guitar, I can't remember the name of the drummer. I was looking for a Tom Petersson kinda sound with my eight-string bass. My brother came to play the saxophone, it was the first time we'd recorded together in six years. Jone had been to New York and had brought some gifts from Michael, a tube that had glow-in-the-dark stars and other little magical things. Seppo was listening to the new Cherry Bombz recordings in the studio, which would become the *The House of Ecstasy* EP.

The *Sam Yaffa — Pelle Almgren* EP came out fast, in February. It was a sweet little thing that we hoped would sell some units. There was a Monkees cover, "Last Train to Clarksville," but all the other songs were Pelle's own. "Lonely in Love" seemed like an obvious hit. It wasn't.

Cherry Bombz played a show in Stockholm in February. I brought Nicholas to say hi to the guys at the hotel. I had a couple of beers with Andy, and we shot the shit like nothing bad had ever happened.

People think, or at least want to think, that Andy and I have hated each other all this time. That's not true. The bad blood was just around the end of 1984, beginning of 1985. It was already a high-drama time, but those weren't thorns that stayed in the side for the rest of our lives.

We let bygones be bygones, got over all the bad shit, and Andy and I have been good ever since.

Cherry Bombz didn't really hit me. All talk, no walk. The full-length album never came out, a couple of EPs and then a live record when the band was already on its way out. Andy was going downhill fast, and his creative arc was falling. When I was moving to LA later on, I went to London and saw Andy there. He was in real bad shape. His big dreams were broken. We all handled the trauma of Hanoi in different ways.

Andy's fade out was also probably stress related. He was the only songwriter for Hanoi Rocks, and every twelve months, a new LP had to come out with singles on top of it all. Around *Back to Mystery City* was when there started to be a shortage of the good stuff, because all the other stuff was getting in the way. There was an obvious song drought by *Two Steps from the Move*, but everything went okay in the studio, thanks to Bob Ezrin's preproduction efforts.

Andy had known what was up from early on and knew that holding the publishing rights was key. Andy didn't give up the rights to the record label, but made a deal with Zomba Music Publishing, if I remember right, and got a big advance.

And in a way, Andy deserved it. He did the most work. Andy wrote a ton of stuff. Really prolific. He just pulled songs out of his hat for two, three years nonstop. Andy didn't even want to hear anyone else's ideas, didn't want to include or help anyone else with writing. And in all honesty, none of the rest of us were good enough songwriters. I understood music and form, why some things worked and what to do with the lower end, but I couldn't figure out how to put an entire song together. That kind of skill was unattainable magic to me.

×××

That summer, Almgren and I played some shows in Finland with Jone on sax, Dan Lagerstedt and Conny Bloom on guitar. The drummer was the guy whose name continues to escape me…let's call him Thomas Wassberg. Our setlist included all the songs from the EP, plus Cheap Trick's "He's a Whore" and Billy Squier's "Everybody Wants You." I'd never even heard of Billy Squier until Pelle told me listen up, we're adding him into the set.

It was summer, everything was good, and I got to play again. The tour was short; we played some small stages in and around Helsinki, but that was it; there was no making a living from it. And while it had been fun to scrape together some songs with Almgren, my heart wasn't totally in it. There was something holding me back. Unfortunately, Pelle and I got into a squabble, and our collaboration ended at the end of the summer.

I kept on with odd jobs at the silkscreening shop with Jamlo. Anna had gotten a good job at the Elmkvist fish market at the Östermalmhallen market hall. I was a stay-in daddy-o, mostly around the house until Jamlo would ring up again to say let's screen two thousand T-shirts. I'd go take care of the job, and then I'd come back home to childcare.

Johnny Thunders had gotten married to Susanne, and Jerry Nolan to Lotte, and they lived in Stockholm just a couple of stops away on the subway. Johnny called me up and asked in a raspy voice, "Sammy, wanna make a thousand krones?" I had to show up at an address with bass in hand; the venue was a speakeasy in Södermalm. "What are we playing, John?" "Well, you know!"

Jerry Nolan and Peter Criss had grown up together in Brooklyn, and both of them idolized Gene Krupa as a drummer. There's a picture of them both all dressed up posing with Krupa. Fan boys. Krupa was one hell of a drum idol. Drummers these days only know how to bang it out, but don't really know how to swing. They only know how to rock, but not how to roll. It's not good if a rock musician hasn't played anything other than rock. You have to know what else is behind rock. The musicians on Little Richard's first record were guys from the New Orleans jazz and rhythm and blues scene. Jerry Nolan also had a jazz background, and that's why he was such a ridiculously badass rock drummer. Jerry was the oldest of the New York Dolls, maybe that's why Sylvain once remarked that "Jerry was never a *Doll*." What he probably meant was that Jerry had a different look and outlook altogether, and that being a few years older made him belong to a whole different musical world.

I heard later on that Jerry hadn't liked my bass playing at the Södermalm speakeasy show. Not one bit. I started to think about why he hadn't dug it. I like to bang it out, punk style, play really hard. That wasn't really Jerry's thing. I figured out how I should play with Jerry and at the shows that I did with him after that, Jerry was like aha, now the kid is playing.

Later, at Marquee in NYC, at the Johnny Thunders memorial concert, Jerry and I backed up three or four other artists, we were the rhythm, and he admitted to me: "Man, at the beginning, I thought you couldn't play at all." Thanks a lot…but what are you going to do? Back in the early Tapiola days, I had such flimsy equipment that I had to learn to pound the bass in order to be heard.

I hung out with Thunders in Stockholm, we watched gangster movies at his place and jammed without any bigger plans. The New New York Dolls didn't make their comeback. Michael had a new band in New York, Secret Chiefs, and Nasty and Andy had Cherry Bombz and Suicide Twins.

But we had our own stay-at-home Thunders, who cooked killer pasta and played cars with one-year-old Nicke.

Nicke got sick at the end of the year. He got a fever that lasted for days. Nicke was under a year and a half and couldn't say what or where it hurt; he just cried and was obviously suffering. Kids go through all kinds of illnesses as a normal part of getting stronger, but this fever got out of control. Nicke was sitting in his highchair when all of a sudden his eyes rolled back and his body went stiff—he was having a seizure. We called the doctor, who told us to take the baby's clothes off and bring him in front of the window because the cold would help hold off the convulsions. An ambulance was on the way.

They did all kinds of tests on Nicke while he was unconscious at the Karolinska Hospital. He was hooked up to an IV and placed in sterile isolation. The doctor asked which one of the parents wanted to go inside. I went inside and couldn't come back out until he got better; the isolation room had three doors and an airlock.

Nicke withered into skin and bones in two, three days. His eyes sunk back into their sockets, and I was positive he would die. He had a virus but was getting antibiotics for treatment. The boy didn't make noise or cry; he just shriveled up silently next to me, it was horrid.

On the fourth day, Nicke made a sound. I let the nurses know he was awake. I handed him a bottle, and he drank. He was soon able to get down solid foods. His fever broke. All in all, we were in the hospital for around ten days, but Nicke got better and we were able to go home. It was the most hellish experience of my whole life.

1987
Los Angeles

Anna started coming home later and later. Things weren't going very well. I heard that Anna had a thing going on with her boss's son. She told me she wanted to break up and move in with this guy.

Having a kid changes a relationship anyway, and we were also very young. I kept running into problems finding work. Anna wanted Nicholas to have a more balanced, regular environment, and that's not something a musician can offer. Not even when there's gigs and money. The relationship was doomed.

I went to London in February to catch up with friends and see what was going on playing-wise. René Berg had promised to let me stay with him. London was in the midst of a heroin epidemic. Andy was in a really bad way, and Nasty wasn't exactly fresh either.

I took two trains, a bus, and a taxi to get to the airport for my return trip. When I got there, I found out that my flight had actually been the previous day. It's the only time I've ever missed a flight by a whole day. I made the same trek back to René's and asked if I could crash for a couple nights more.

I went to visit Richard Bishop at his office. There were no bad feelings, we had a long history together in any case. Richard had something to tell me. A San Francisco band called Jetboy had just fired their bassist and had asked Richard for my info. The band had a big deal with Elektra Records and was an up-and-coming name in the LA club scene, and they wanted me on bass. Okay, I'll think about it. I put Jetboy's demo tape in my pocket and went back to Stockholm.

Anna had moved out with Nicholas while I was in London, but didn't tell me the new address right away. Quite a trick. In the end, I found them in the Östermalm neighborhood on Jungfrugatan. I tried to get Anna to change her mind and reconsider.

But that demo. I listened to it and could tell that the band was young, not that great, but there was heart and potential there. There was promise in the music. I wanted to get back in the biz and see what was going on in LA. I made an international phone call to Jetboy's manager, Brigitte Wright. Brigitte promised to pay for my trip to LA and fix me a place to stay as well as a monthly allowance if I accepted the band's offer.

I hadn't wanted to join another band for a long time, because I didn't want to be in any band that wasn't as good as Hanoi. That's why I couldn't really tie myself to Pelle Almgren—I was comparing it to what I'd had before. That being said, I'd figured out that there's more to life than just one band.

I looked outside. It was March and winter had come back full force in Stockholm; a snowstorm had covered all the houses. Everything was a mess at home, I had no work, and I'd gotten that offer from Jetboy. I called Brigitte and told her I'd come to Los Angeles at the end of April to check things out.

The last weeks with Anna were really rough—devastating. It's a miracle I didn't start using again. I convinced myself that I'd get my family back once I was back on my feet again.

My friendship with Jamlo from Studio Råttan ended up lasting, and we saw each other every time I came back to Stockholm from LA. I brought Jamlo's daughter Sofi a witch doll, which I thought was cool, but was apparently terrifying to a four-year-old. The little girls were damn scared of it, and Jamlo had to hide the witch on the top shelf of the closet. A couple times a year, the girls would ask Jamlo to open the closet doors. The evil witch would be sitting on the shelf staring at the girls, who'd run off shrieking. The closet door would close again.

I kissed Nicho goodbye on the day of my departure, flew over the Atlantic, and landed at LAX. It was April 27, 1987.

×××

Brigitte Wright was waiting for me at the gate and drove me to my new place in the Hollywood Hills, just a few blocks from the Franklin Plaza; Hanoi Rocks had stayed there just two and a half years before. It was a weird feeling to go back to the same spot. The memories were still raw in my mind.

I sat on the balcony and listened to the birds chirping while I sipped a Corona. It felt like a new chapter was beginning. The bass was in command again, and life followed.

I met the Jetboy guys at the practice space. We started playing straight off, because it seemed like a better way of getting to know each other than talking. There was definitely something there. Billy Rowe, Mickey Finn, Fernie Rodriguez, and Ron Tostenson were a good group. What they said sounded legit and their influences were the same—the name Jetboy even came from a New York Dolls song. New songs needed to be written for the new album, and the guys expected me to take part too, which was a new thing. This was refreshing; back with Hanoi, I was definitely not welcome to take part in the songwriting process.

Brigitte Wright seemed like a capable manager, and Elektra's budget was big. A week after the jam session, I decided to join the band. I called Anna; she was happy to hear the news. She knew playing music was my thing, not polishing bathrooms or cleaning cars. We agreed to be in touch every week. I let the manager know that one of my conditions for joining was that I had to be able to go back to Sweden as often as possible to see my son. I also made it clear that I wouldn't stay in a band if anything harder than booze or weed came into play. This was cool with all the guys since the previous bassist, Todd Crew, had gotten the boot for just that reason.

We shook hands on the deal and celebrated at Zuma Beach.

While I'd been busy as a stay-at-home dad and silk screener in Stockholm, I hadn't noticed that a whole scene in LA had grown out of our little band.

Like, entirely. The scene was the same as London from 1983–1984, just much bigger and more American. On my first night, I ran into about fifteen Sam Yaffas, twenty-ish Andy McCoys, and at least thirty Michael Monroes. Hanoi Rocks was surprisingly well-known. CBS had released just the last record in America, but the superfans had ordered all the rest of the catalog as imports from abroad.

The end of the eighties was both weird and innocent. The new generation did things their own way, and LA was the epicenter. There was a ton of bands on the scene who had gotten signed and were making a stink but didn't musically move me much—Poison, LA Guns, Faster Pussycat—they seemed to be a dime a dozen. There were actually two scenes going on at the same time in LA: the glittery Sunset Strip scene and the underground scene, with the club Scream at its heart. The two camps were pretty different from one another. Perry Farrell was hardly a fan of Warrant or Pretty Boy Floyd.

Thelonious Monster and Jane's Addiction's shows made a big impression; both had their first albums coming out in the fall. Jane's Addiction defies description; the music is beyond all genres. I fell for the big, rolling effects and bass lines that reminded me a lot of Alice Cooper. I haven't heard anything else like it until when I've more recently listened to Indonesian prog from the seventies. I felt threatened by them at first and didn't want to like them, but they were an insanely great band.

I saw the Red Hot Chili Peppers play a show before *Uplift Mofo Party Plan* and Guns N' Roses before *Appetite for Destruction*. They both played in little clubs with okay attendance. Slash was one of the first people I met in LA. He was hammered beyond belief doing cartwheels in a bar, no shirt, no shoes, just leather pants and a top hat. "I'm Slaaaasshh." I'd see Slash around at bars, but Izzy Stradlin and I would hang out outside of clubs too. Hanoi's old guitar tech Timo Kaltio was living in LA and was buddies with Iz.

Izzy told me about hitching from Lafayette to Boston in 1984 to a Hanoi Rocks show. I remembered that we had gotten fan mail from America before the tour. Razzle and I had talked about the letter; it seemed so unusual. It was Izzy who had sent the letter.

Duff McKagan and Todd Crew were good friends, so kicking Todd out of the band had started some shit between Guns N' Roses and Jetboy.

I fell between the two camps; I had no beef with Todd. I'd have been more than happy to step aside from Jetboy for Todd, if he'd gotten a handle on his drug problem. I sat down with Todd a few times and tried to talk some sense into him, tell him what we'd been through. I could tell Jane's Addiction was doing the same shit that Hanoi Rocks had done a few years earlier. Not musically, I mean, but all the drug stuff. They had a really heavy junkie vibe. I could see it in their eyes and hear it in the way they talked; there was no mistaking it. I was too freaked out to be anywhere around heroin and people who used it, so I stepped out of those circles.

Mötley Crüe had a release party for *Girls, Girls, Girls* in May. I went and saw the band for the first time since the accident. I talked with Vince Neil for a long time. Vince was still in tears two and a half years later, completely broken up about the whole thing. He had developed a serious drinking problem.

It's strange that you can pay your way out of anything in the US. A normal person would have gone straight to jail. Vince paid millions here and there, like to Razzle's dad, Henry, who Razzle had never liked. Razzle had been adopted, so Henry and his wife were his adoptive parents. They once had gone on vacation and left sixteen-year-old Razzle all by his lonesome for a month. They had an old parrot that knew how to talk. Razzle set a picture of Henry in front of the parrot and said, "Fuck you, Henry," to it over and over again for the whole month. When his parents came back from their vacation, the parrot shouted, "FUCK YOU, HENRY!" any time his dad walked into the room.

That's the kind of prankster Razzle was.

The whole operation around Jetboy was way more professional than anything Hanoi had ever seen. There were managers, co-managers, lawyers, PR reps. When the merchandising and publishing companies made a deal, the advances to the band were massive. We got $200,000 from the T-shirts and $200,000 from copyrights. The MCA/Elektra deal was worth two million. All of this before we even went to the studio. The downside was that everything had to be calculated and there was a lot of caution. The head of the label thought that our singer Mickey's big, beautiful mohawk would hurt us succeeding…in the Midwest. Really?

Our monthly pay was not a lot to live on. But fortunately it was cheap to live in LA back then. I moved into the same room with Billy, Mickey, and Mickey's three iguanas, who roamed freely around the apartment. Ron and Fernie lived on the other side of the wall.

We had to get songs out of the riffs ASAP in the writing sessions, and the whole process had taken way too long because of the mess with Todd. I did the best I could with the arrangements, and we picked the best of the old material. The main pressure was to write new songs, and the guys were hungry to do it.

The final rehearsals for the album, meaning our preproduction, happened at SIR, Sound Instrument Rentals at Santa Monica Boulevard; there's two SIRs, one in New York and the one in LA, where Neil Young's *Tonight's the Night* was recorded. It's a pretty sterile practice space. The rooms are spacious, the sound is good, and the gear is top-notch. Nothing special, but it costs a fortune.

Tom Allom had been picked out to produce. The man had produced some Judas Priest records and been engineer on the very first Black Sabbath album. His credentials were impressive, but I didn't totally see what this metal dude had to do with an AC/DC-style band.

I dug some of the Jetboy songs musically. I couldn't really get over the lyrics, though. Oh boy. I tried to relax into the vibe and do my best and keep my mouth shut. Let's put this record together with what we've got and start writing the next one right away. And maybe the lyrics would get there, little by little.

We laid the basic tracks in May and June at Record Plant West on Santa Monica Boulevard. Tom Allom didn't want to use a room specially designed for drums or any other high-tech spaces; he just stuffed the whole band into the concrete storeroom behind Record Plant. The cables from the control room were brought all the way out there. Allom wanted the drums to get a cannon sound. Big drums, big hair, this was the point in the eighties when Tony Thompson, the drummer from the Power Station and Chic, came up with that massive KOSSHH snare drum sound. Suddenly *everyone* wanted that same stadium-ready snare drum. Help, here we go…

Record Plant has a lot of studios, recording lots of records at the same time. I was making tea in the studio's cafe when Morris Day and Jerome from the Time and the *Purple Rain* movie came to ask for sugar. The studio's owner told us stories from the seventies about the Eagles' *Hotel California* sessions, Fleetwood Mac, the Rolling Stones...this guy had huffed Peru's entire cocaine export up his nose, all while recording hit records.

A little guy with a New York accent showed up in the control room looking for a bong. Of course we had a bong on us. We went to sit in his studio, where a few other guys were sitting around. We rolled a joint and listened to what they were up to. It was rap and the dudes were named Adam, Adam, and Mike and they were the Beastie Boys. *Licensed to Ill* had been a big hit, and now they were recording a demo between tours that would end up becoming *Paul's Boutique*.

Back in the control room, I saw somebody trying to peek in through a tinted glass door out of the corner of my eye. I went to open the door, and fecking Rod Stewart was standing there. He asked if we had a corkscrew. Of course we did. "I just heard some rock 'n' roll coming from here," Rod said and sat down to listen in on our recording. "Sounds fucking good!" Then Rod asked us to listen to the songs he was making.

Rod the Mod's control room had sushi catering, a ridiculous spread: sushi, lobster, caviar, fruit, cheese, crackers, champagne on ice, vodka, wine, candles, the whole thing. Rod knew how to enjoy life. We opened a bottle of Pouilly-Fuissé and shot the shit about music: Al Green, Frank Sinatra, Don Covay, the Stones, Faces...he was really a cool guy. We hung out for a couple of hours and drank Rod's wine. We didn't exchange numbers or anything, it was just a really nice moment in time.

After three weeks, we had the record in the can. We had a two-week break ahead of us, and then we were going to mix it at Criteria Studios in Miami. I flew back to Stockholm to see my little Nicholas.

It was amazing to see Nicke, but dealing with Anna was rough. I told her that I was making okay money and I'd be able to find her work in LA too. Anna refused to listen, and she didn't want to be with me. Things had really changed.

I planned to be a part of my son's life in any case, one way or another.

×××

I flew from Stockholm to Miami on July 20. A heartbroken Jetboy was waiting for me at the hotel. What happened?

Todd Crew had OD'd on heroin two days earlier in New York and had died in Slash's hotel room.

The news hit me hard, even though I barely knew Todd. He was only twenty-one when he died.

It was good that we had a hectic work schedule the next two weeks, so we kept our minds busy through the shock. We did some overdubs and got started mixing. I thought that I wasn't really needed for the mixing, too many cooks, not enough chefs, so I spent my time by the pool with a piña colada. Every day, I went to listen to what had been done at the studio.

One day, the guitarist Billy gushed, "Jaco just left!" Jaco Pastorius had shown up to the studio in quite the state, in sandals and swim trunks, with a swim ring around his waist. Jaco had no reason for being there, just came to hang out. He walked over to the pool table—where there was a game going—grabbed the eight ball, and walked out with it.

If only I'd come an hour earlier. There went my chance to meet Jaco Pastorious, because he died a couple of months later.

Rob Halford showed up on a massive Harley. There was a young beautiful Cuban man wearing shorts and a pink shirt sitting behind the leather-clad Turbo Lover. Rob didn't have any reason to be there either, other than to say hi to Tom Allom.

We'd spent a month and a half in the studio. We came back to LA from Miami at the end of the summer. We went to the *Psycho* house to take the album cover. We got to use it for free because Universal Studios owned both it and MCA the record label.

It all sounds better than it looked. The infamous house isn't recognizable on the cover, it could be any old barn; it's just a film set with four walls. No partitions, just a hallway with columns holding up the roof above, maybe a ladder behind the window where "Norman Bates" lurks behind the curtain. Absolutely nothing special. The photographer just wanted an open inside space that had nice light coming in from outside, and it was a tasty tidbit for the magazines to say that we took the picture at the house from *Psycho*.

We played a couple of shows to break the monotony. We practiced three, four times a week, but was there any point to practicing the same songs over and over again? The waiting started to go on for a little too long. I spent my free time hanging out at the Cat Club, The Whisky a Go Go, The Roxy, The Cat & Fiddle. Familiar names, legendary clubs. The Roxy can hold about four hundred, and The Whisky isn't all that big either. Those historical spots have their own feel and energy though, there's no denying that.

We played some big shows in October. The promoter Bill Graham got us into the one-day Day on the Green festival at the Oakland Stadium that holds a crowd of 60,000. Mötley Crüe, Whitesnake, Jetboy, and Poison were all performing.

Fernie and Ron were already up north. Billy, Mickey, and I went up the morning before the show in a rental car. We barreled down the Grapevine until the 5 flattened out again. Billy drove, I was sitting shotgun, and Mickey was passed out on the back seat. We stopped at a truck stop outside of Fresno for breakfast. I went to the bathroom and read the stupid graffiti. The right-side wall had familiar words scratched into it.

Oh Tragedy, life reminds me 'bout a symphony on the radio
First a little bit too fast and then a little bit much too slow.
Oh Tragedy, life reminds me 'bout a symphony I heard today
First a little bit too fast and then a little bit much too slow for me.

The chorus from "Tragedy." Hanoi Rocks. That was far out. Billy laughed when I told him.

There's no median separating the north and south traffic on the 5, just a several-foot grass trench. We were going about seventy-five miles per hour. I saw from far off that an oncoming car was driving strangely. It was jerking from side to side, then it plunged through the shallow ditch right into our lane, coming right at us. Everything after that happened in slow motion. I put my head between my legs. The car hit us head-on to the left front and sent us spinning around and around five or ten times. Now I was going to die.

The car finally came to a stop on a field facing where we came from. I lifted my head up. An eighteen-wheeler came straight toward us, missed us by a few feet, and fell to its side with a sound of a dying metal animal in a cloud of dust. Two huge containers had scattered onto the side of the road.

We were all wearing our seatbelts. I had had time to lower my head, so I didn't get glass in my face, but Mickey had been sleeping in the back and now his mohawk and face were covered in blood. All the car windows had shattered.

Billy's right arm had twisted into an L shape. Billy was in so much shock that he didn't even scream, despite his arm very clearly being broken. It was a miracle that I only had a bump on my head.

The car that hit us didn't have an engine anymore; the whole front half of the car was missing. There was an old man inside who was at least conscious, but the driver was definitely dead because his chest had split wide open. The steering wheel had broken all his ribs.

The helicopter ambulance picked up the old men first and then us. Billy was brought straight to emergency surgery. The cuts on Mickey's face weren't deep, there were just a lot of them. The two of us didn't need to stay the night, but Billy's arm was getting plates and screws. He had to stay in the hospital for at least a week.

The promoter Bill Graham was concerned and asked if he could do anything. If we wanted to back out of the show, it would be totally understandable. We called up our manager, and we called Billy. This was Jetboy's big hometown show, and we had to do it. Billy agreed: don't cancel. Fernie could play the guitar parts on his own.

Mickey and I were still shaky when we were doing the soundcheck at the stadium. Mötley had already done their soundcheck and had gone back to the hotel, except for Tommy Lee, who had decided to wait for us once he heard about the accident. I went to the Crüe's backstage area to get a bottle of cognac. I downed half the bottle in one gulp and told Tommy, "There's some bad mojo going on here." I told him about seeing the lyrics to "Tragedy" in the bathroom right before the accident. This was the second time having anything to do with Mötley after Razzle's death, and I had almost just died too. "This is not a good combo. This is the last time I'm in any kind of contact with you guys." Tommy got it.

I was still feeling pretty shaky the next day; I hadn't been able to sleep or eat. The stadium backstage had a full-blown party going on. Big hair everywhere: Whitesnake, Mötley Crüe, Poison. Lars Ulrich from Metallica was walking around all coked up and yakking incessantly. A loudmouth talking nonstop. Run away, Lars is coming! He had the nerve to say to me, "You have a funny accent!" The guy is from Denmark, and he's telling me I have a funny accent. Funny world.

Then it was time to get on stage; there was a 500-foot ramp that led up to it from backstage. The roar of 66,000 people almost made my knees buckle. Reading in 1983 had been bigger, but that festival had more than one stage and the peeps were spread out all over the fields. This was a different thing altogether.

The promoter Bill Graham stepped up to the mike and introduced each one of us individually. He talked about the local heroes and the accident that had happened the day before. I just wanted the show to be over.

It was weird to play without Billy next to me. The sound was bad anyway. Fernie tried to fill in the space that Billy left behind. I realized at one point that I was playing chords and Billy's riffs on the bass. I was trying to patch the holes that Fernie forgot about. I didn't enjoy a second of it.

We canceled the next few shows so Billy would have time to get better. Billy was and is an unbelievably stubborn guy. As soon as his picking fingers could hold a pick, he asked our manager to book some shows. That's how we did it. Billy played with a giant cast from his shoulder to his wrist, but he somehow got the job done.

We had given a couple interviews already and were in great shape to play after all that rehearsing. We'd start touring for three months nonstop at the beginning of February. I was flying to Stockholm in the middle of December and was taking Nicholas to Finland with me for Christmas.

Jetboy's record was scheduled for worldwide release on January 28, 1988.

1988

Feel the Shake

I flew back to Los Angeles on the fourth of January. Our manager Brigitte was waiting for me at the gate. Once we got to the car, Brigitte told me she had both good and bad news.

Give me the bad news first, please.

"We got dropped."

Elektra records had dropped Jetboy. The record and the world tour were canceled.

What a nice Christmas present from Elektra. They just stone-cold took us off their roster a month before the record release. After all that work and the expense—the video alone had cost $160,000. Elektra's A&R guy had signed Faster Pussycat and got the order to choose who to do business with going forward. He chose Faster Pussycast.

We had a two-record deal with Elektra, but the threat was that if we tried to take them to court, the whole mess would keep us in court for years, and the record would never see the light of day. The good news was that Chrysalis was interested in buying the record off of Elektra. Also, Elektra was in breach of contract. They'd failed to meet the terms of our agreement when we hadn't done anything of the sort, and that was reason enough to void the terms.

Chrysalis agreed to cover some of Elektra's losses, but the negotiations dragged on and on all the same. We lost our monthly, and we were caught with our pants down. We made some money playing the clubs: Los Angeles, San Francisco, Las Vegas, Phoenix, Orange County. Things got so bad that Billy's grandma sent us a big glob of government cheese two months in a row so we could make quesadillas, which was our main source of nourishment. We got our drinks comped by nice club owners, like Scream club's Dayle Gloria or Riki Rachtman from the Cathouse.

I had a few short relationships with women, but nothing serious, just fly-by-night hangouts, two ships in the Sunset Strip.... One lady, in the middle of it all, said to me, "You know, honey, you're looking at a ten-thousand-dollar woman." I said damn that's expensive but I definitely didn't have that kind of cash. But she was no prostitute. She pointed to her nose, $2,500, her tits, $5,000, and her thighs, $2,500. Liposuction.

Timo Kaltio moved to LA in '86. He'd been a roadie for Hanoi since the early days and had even been on the way to becoming the bassist for the band toward the end in the summer of 1985, when Andy and Michael wanted to get rid of René Berg. Timppa was buddies with Billy and Mick and ended up roommates with Mickey.

It felt good that there was an old Finnish friend who I'd known for years living just a few hundred feet away on Hollywood Boulevard. Timppa lived off of his art in LA. He painted elaborate pictures on album covers and the backs of leather jackets. Lots of bands, like members of Guns N' Roses, had jackets painted by Timppa.

I saved Timppa's life once. He had passed out in bed with a cigarette in his hand and almost burned his bed down. I was spending the night at his place and woke up to the room full of smoke. There was a huge flame dancing around Timppa. I got water and threw it onto Timppa—Wake up! Timppa opened his eyes. "Oops, damn!!!"

I walked home from Timppa's and Mickey's once at three o'clock in the morning. The street was deserted. I heard a weird, faint noise. I turned and saw a pack of dogs approaching. I hid behind a palm tree and waited for the group to go by. They were coyotes. A pack of fifteen coyotes or so strutting down Hollywood Boulevard in the middle of the night. Los Angeles is so close to nature and the desert, weirdly entwined with it, even if most of the time people just think about the neon lights and the swimming pools.

Timppa taught me how to drive a car. It's hard to get anywhere in LA without a car. Timppa had a '66 Cadillac Coupe deVille, a big light-blue boat of a car that we called Betsy. Timppa tossed me the keys and told me to drive to Sunset, turn right, drive as far as you can on Sunset, and turn back. You don't have to change gears with an automatic transmission. That's how I learned to drive. Out of necessity, I borrowed friends' and girlfriends' cars and I zoomed around. I've never been into cars, even if my first word was "bus." I've lived in so many shifting situations that I didn't feel the need to drive one around myself. Not having a driver's license was also a principle, I didn't want to belong to the polluters of the world.

We drove Betsy to the beach and the mountains and found all kinds of interesting spots. WC Fields Park, Errol Flynn's estate, Malibu Beach, Big Bear Mountain.

Timppa introduced me to Jimmy Ashhurst, who was the bassist from Broken Homes. Timppa had painted the cover for their album *Straight Line Through Time*. I met a lot of new people like Marc Ford, the guitarist from Burning Tree who later joined the Black Crowes, and Craig Ross, who became Lenny Kravitz's longtime guitarist. I made the club rounds with this group of merry men, and sometimes we'd jam.

I was sitting around one night with Craig Ross; I browsed through my cassettes and put one on. Craig was a huge Hendrix fan and jumped up. "Which Hendrix bootleg is that? I don't have that!"

I cannot tell you how proud I was. "It's me and my friends at fifteen!" It was a recording of my very first gig back at the Aurinkoterassi in Tapiola. Arto Tamminen was doing Hendrix so well that Craig couldn't tell. The recording was kinda hissy too, maybe that helped. Apparently Craig thought I sounded like Billy Cox or Noel Redding, not bad.

That old troublemaker Andy McCoy moved to LA in the summer of '88. All of a sudden, Seppo and Richard appeared there too. Andy weaseled his way into other people's business, and soon he'd hooked himself up with my manager, my label, my lawyer. Unfortunately, Andy was still in a bit of a downward spiral. Talking to him on the phone was along the lines of, "Fuck man, I got twenty-eight guitars and I've written over a hundred songs that are all hits and I got a million-dollar record deal." At this point, I'd usually put the phone down, go take an unhurried leak, get another beer from the fridge, and pick the phone back up to the continued yada yada. "…I'm buying a Lamborghini next week, and I'm going to Monaco for vacation. Got an offshore bank account in Barbados…"

One time he actually called with some business. He'd gotten a gig in Iggy Pop's band and asked if I'd go on tour as the bassist. I had invested over a year into Jetboy. I wanted to stay loyal to the guys, so I had to decline. I would have gotten to play a nine-month tour with Iggy Pop, but I said no. I've regretted this decision many times afterward. Half a year after talking to Andy, I saw Iggy play in LA and cursed myself. Fucking idiot…

Michael Monroe and I talked on the phone every now and then. We saw each other for the first time in ages when Jetboy played at the Cat Club in New York. Michael jumped up and played the harmonica on a couple of songs. He promised to come out to LA for a visit. When he did come out in August, I fixed a couple shows at the Scream club and got a band together for the occasion. Craig Ross and Marc Ford were on guitar, I was on bass, and Joey DePompeis was on drums. It was amazing to share the stage with Michael again, we played a bunch of covers and threw Hanoi's "Taxi Driver" in the set.

A few months later, Michael got a deal with PolyGram and started working on an album called *Not Fakin' It.*

×××

The managers got the deal together with MCA at the end of the summer. I spent a lot of time going to the flamenco club El Cid and flew back to Sweden or Spain to see my son. Jetboy was constantly going on one of these breaks, we were constantly chasing momentum which we never reached, the whole thing was a mess. The album would finally get released in November, even though it was supposed to come out almost a year earlier. Getting dumped by Elektra had put us in a weird limbo. Guns N' Roses' *Appetite for Destruction* had gone gold. It had come out the previous summer, but it took a while to blow up. It didn't really start to get big until the spring of 1988. After listening to it the first time, I thought there were only three good songs, but the album grew on me over the years. I guess it could be considered an honor that Guns nicked the line from the chorus of Hanoi Rocks' "Underwater World" and turned it into "Welcome to the Jungle." Some of "Paradise City" was pulled from "Lost in the City."

There was nothing to get excited about on the Faster Pussycat or Poison records, but that kind of music still sold millions.

Izzy Stradlin called me after getting his first big royalty check and said hey, I bought a car, come for a drive. Not just any car, but a fecking $60,000 BMW. I got in and asked straight off if it had a good stereo. He got excited. Sure does. Had I heard of a band called Niggaz Wit Attitudes?

Izzy put on NWA's four-song tape. We drove around the Hollywood Hills listening to "Straight Outta Compton" over and over. That shit was unreal, never heard anything like it.

Guns N' Roses had started their own imprint, Uzi Suicide, under Geffen and had kindly decided to release all of Hanoi Rocks albums at the beginning of 1989, as a way of saying thanks for being an influence on their music.

Publishing our entire back catalog would mean a huge advance on the royalties. One night I was hanging around the house, penniless and watching *Sanford and Son*, when my accountant, Candace Hansen, called. The Guns N' Roses check had come in. Did I want a car to come pick me up the next day?

Don't bother, I'll walk.

The walk to Candace's office was a good three miles away, and my sneakers were in bad shape. Still, it felt important to walk and pick up the check that would do away with my money troubles for the next year or two.

First things first, I wanted to get my teeth fixed. The Japanese magazine *Music Life* had a full-page picture of me onstage where I'm laughing, my whole Shane MacGowan mouth on full display. It was high time to take care of business.

Back in the sixties, it had been common to give kids sugar water. It made your baby teeth completely black. After taking junk and speed, my whole set was in such shit shape, broken as the South Bronx, I could mostly eat soup and soft stuff like pizzas. So as soon as I got my hands on those Uzi Suicide royalties, I went straight to a dentist on Rodeo Drive and asked him to fix me up. "Okay, but it's gonna cost you a little!" For the first time in my life, I could say that money didn't matter.

I had to get ten teeth fixed. All at the same time. The doctor drilled the teeth down all the way to the root and put caps on them. The roots had to stay alive. They were exposed bare while I was lying there numb. The doctor left me to sit in the chair because we had to wait an hour for the inflammation to go down. When the anesthetic started to wear off, it was like an electric shock, then another, then the pain was turned up to full blast. I screamed, and the doctor came running to give me a shot of numbness.

I had a "monotooth" for a week. I looked like Superman; he never had separate teeth drawn, just one big tooth. I was doped up on codeine so the nerves wouldn't get out of control. The whole job cost $8,000. So, I've got Beverly Hills teeth in my mouth.

Living in a little studio with Billy and Mickey was starting to get on my nerves. I moved into a place on Melrose Avenue with the photographer Robert M, who had put a room out for rent. Robert had photographed a lot of bands in the late sixties, early seventies in the Detroit music scene. Living with him started to stress me out when I realized how much coke he did. Also, his Mexican girlfriend cried and raged every day. Drunken, coked-out fighting all day long. How was I supposed to get peace and quiet there?

My son and Anna were coming out for a two-week trip, and I had gotten $2,000 from the bank for plane tickets. I had to pay for them the next day. I hid the money in a book and put the book back on the shelf. Then I went out for a walk.

When I came back, the place was empty and my room had been turned upside down. The thieves hadn't been interested in my bass guitars; it was like there was something specific they had been looking for in my room. The whole bookshelf had been combed through and the money in the book was gone.

I had mentioned to Robert that I was picking up the money. His girlfriend happened to be in the kitchen just then and had heard the whole thing. Two grand was a bit of money back, then when my rent was $300. When Robert and his girlfriend came home, his girlfriend started screaming about how dare I try to call her a thief. Okay, fuck you both, I'm calling the cops.

The screen in the window had been busted so it would look like someone had come in that way. I went outside to look and asked the cops to come. Hey, if someone had come in this way, the dust on the windowsill would have been disturbed—my Colombo moment. But it was untouched. So the thief had come in through the door.

I thought the two of them were in deep shit, but the police didn't have enough proof against them. "I'm sorry, man." I told the cokeheads to fuck off and started to pack my stuff.

I found a really nice spot in an Art Deco–style building from the sixties at the corner of Hollywood Boulevard and El Cerrito Place. There were twenty or so units in the building and a kidney-shaped pool in the courtyard. The landlord was Lee Marvin Estate. That's the name I wrote on the rent checks, even though the actor had died years before.

It was to this new apartment that Anna and Nicholas came for vacation. Those two weeks were a really nice time. I tried one more time to get Anna back, but she was set. I had no choice but to give up. I finally understood that our relationship was over for good.

One of the other tenants in the building was Joe Chambers from the soul band the Chambers Brothers. He was a big guy that showed up at my door one morning in his robe. "What's up, man? Got any of that green?"

"Yeah, sit down, I'll roll one."

Johnny Thunders and Patti Palladin's version of "Uptown to Harlem" was playing on the record player. Joe perked up. "That's a badass tune. Who is it?"

"C'mon, Joe, you should know, you wrote it."

Two doors down lived a Vietnam veteran who hadn't come back quite right. He sometimes left his front door open, and I could see inside. The over-six-foot-tall guy sat in bed rocking himself back and forth. The TV would be on with the sound off. He had a full arsenal of hand grenades and M16s on his wall. I found him worrisome, even if all the other tenants tried to calm me down. "He's harmless. He's a sweetheart."

The infamous Tomi Rae lived above me; she was a really fun lady with a loud voice. She came from Atlanta, was missing a front tooth, and could sing like Janis Joplin. I was watching *Entertainment Tonight* in my apartment in New York some years later. Tomi Rae's mug popped up on screen and the headline was: James Brown's New Bride!

That's how Hollywood was. I stood in line for some fast food with Esai Morales from the movie *La Bamba* behind me. He was a couple of dollars short on whatever he was buying. I lent it to him.

Before *Feel the Shake* came out, we played a few shows on the West Coast. We'd played the Stone on Broadway in San Francisco. I came back on another night for a beer, and a "Blues Festival" was being advertised outside. I was waiting for a drink at the bar when the next act was introduced on stage. "Ladies and gentleman, John Lee Hooker!"

Wha wha WHAAAT!?? What a surprise. It was one of the best shows I've ever seen.

We toured around with a group called Kix, and I saw how a band could be a big deal regionally, but completely unknown elsewhere. In LA and New York, Kix could fill a smaller 500-person club at most, but 30,000 would easily show up to see them in their hometown of Baltimore. Kix was also big in Virginia, Maryland, and Washington, DC. Anywhere there, they'd play arena shows.

Washington, DC, was our last gig before taking Christmas off. Since I was already on the East Coast, I called up Kim Montenegro in Philadelphia and was invited over for Christmas. Kimmy was Timppa Kaltio's girlfriend. I sat in the dining car the whole train ride there, and Timppa was waiting for me at the train station. The Christmas festivities went up until the twenty-eighth of December, and then I went up to New York to hang out with Michael for a few days before Jetboy's New Year's gig in New York.

1989

Stronzo & Smack

Our tour with Stryper kicked off in January. Stryper was a terrible band that played Christian metal in bumblebee costumes and tossed out bibles to the audience. Jetboy and Stryper were a weird and pointless combo, but the deal was made and the tour had to be done. We lived on the bus and stopped to shower at truck stops or at the venues.

Stryper was on their In God We Trust Tour, but since the tour started in Florida and continued on through Alabama, Mississippi, Missouri, Kansas, Texas, Georgia, Kentucky—all those red states—it got nicknamed the Bible Belt Tour.

I woke up on the bus to a racket, horns honking and a bunch of people screaming. I opened the curtains and saw a crowd outside. There were a lot of signs: You're Gonna Rot in Hell, Whoremongers, Sinners, Go Back Home. The sign-holding fanatics must have read our lyrics and figured out that we weren't a Christian band.

But was Stryper? They really sucked. You could see right through them, that they were just faking it. Stryper's game had nothing to do with religion, but it sure had a lot to do with money. "To Hell with the Devil." Sure. There were fans of ours in the crowd too. They were wondering what in the hell we were doing opening for Stryper.

Jackson, Mississippi. We were playing our own gigs on our off days, and this time Jetboy was out playing in the boonies. I'd played many a barn in Finland at the beginning of the decade, but this show outside of Jackson was something else altogether.

The barn was over two hundred feet long. The stage was to the left and the bar to the right. I asked the bar lady who looked like Dolly Parton for a beer. They had Miller, Miller Lite, and Bud. Bud in hand, I took a look to my side. There were three guys, straight out of *Deliverance*, sitting at the far end. Just the banjos were missing. Big ears, narrow faces, walleyed. And if that weren't enough, they were albinos. The booker had clearly found Jetboy's target audience: Mississippi inbreds.

We set up our gear. The barn started to fill up, and hundreds of kids began to show up; the rough start had turned around. We sold a whole bunch of T-shirts, signed autographs all night, and hung out with the youth of Jackson, drinking beer and whiskey and smoking weed. Great time had by all.

We had a couple days off in Memphis. I went over to Beale Street to take in some blues. I stepped inside the promisingly named Rum Boogie Club. There was a Stax Records neon sign hanging above the stage, which was a really good sign. Mojo Buford and his band were performing. Mojo used to play the harmonica for Muddy Waters. There were only old guys in the band; the youngest, "Junior" the guitarist, was fifty-five.

This was my first time hearing real blues from the Deep South live, played with the right touch. John Lee Hooker had been legit, but Hooker's backup band had been a bunch of white guys. There's no two ways about it, there's a difference.

I went to chat with the bass player in between the sets. I wanted to know why he was playing a fucking stick bass with no headstock. Well, his wife sold his bass, amp, and car when he hadn't brought home enough money from the last tour…

Blues.

We did shots of tequila during his half-hour break and then the bass player got back up on stage. After their first song, he introduced a special guest star and called me up on stage. I was like, shit, I just wanted to enjoy watching these guys, not play myself. But he wouldn't take no for an answer, and I had to do it. He hung the stick bass around my neck and whispered into my ear. "It goes from E, you know what to do." I guess the old man wanted to get back to the bar and put me to work in his place.

I ended up playing the whole rest of the set. I had a couple hundred dollars in my pocket, and the bar was still open for another couple hours. I bought rounds for the band and their wives, sons, and the rest of the family.

I hadn't seen the time pass and had no idea how much of a tab we'd run up. I asked the owner for the check. It was $260. I asked if $200 was okay.

"Sure it's okay, if you wanna do dishes here for the next three days."

I asked if I could use the phone. I called up the hotel to wake up our tour manager, Steve. He wasn't too happy about the phone call, but he promised to come save me from doing dishes at a blues club. I needed another hundred, because I was going to do a last round and leave a tip.

I didn't end up in kitchen jail, but was sitting at a table with the old guys from the band drinking another round of tequila. At three in the morning, a taxi stopped in front of the club. Steve stepped inside in his Mickey Mouse pajamas and slippers. Even in his day clothes, Steve was a pretty weird-looking guy. Six foot four, but his head was barely bigger than a tennis ball.

Mojo Buford and the rest of the guys fell silent at the sight of him. I told them that this man in his jammies was my banker, and the table exploded into laughter. I paid the rest of the bill, and the band waved goodbye. Steve gave me his sermon in the taxi. He would not help me out again; next time, I was on my own.

I was hungover, and we went to Graceland. Our roadie Tim's little whiskey flask helped pass the time waiting in line. There were two old lady Elvis fangirls from Alabama with blue-tinted beehives and cat-eye glasses standing in line behind us. They enthusiastically told us that "Elvis was beautiful, can't wait to see the Jungle Room."

Elvis's gilded grand piano was in the first room at Graceland. We followed the roped-off path from room to room. One of the old ladies started shrieking, "Look, Mavis, it's the King's toenail!!" I glanced behind me, and the old lady was holding a piece of nail that she'd found in the wall-to-wall carpeting. She dug out a Ziploc bag from her purse and secured the holy nail.

I asked Tim for another swig.

Jackson, and Wichita, Kansas...the whole band wanted out of this pointless tour. The tensions flared; Mickey and Fernie were at each other's throats.

There was a clause in our contract that we couldn't quit the tour without getting fined, but if Stryper kicked us off the tour, we'd still get paid for the whole tour, or something like that, some insurance jargon.

We arrived in San Juan, Puerto Rico. We were playing a baseball stadium with a 20,000-person capacity. The crowd was shooting fireworks and building human pyramids that inevitably collapsed. People got carried off in a couple of ambulances, and the smell of gunpowder was hanging in the air.

Stryper had forbidden us from swearing backstage, which I found extremely difficult since every other word out of my mouth was "fuck." We also weren't allowed to drink straight out of a bottle either; we all had to use plastic cups. Smoking weed was of course a no-no.

The crowd was with us from the very first note. There was a kid in the front row who was offering a joint. Stryper's tour manager, standing on the side of the stage, caught wind and pointed: Do not, under any circumstances, take it!

It dawned on me: This was our ticket out of this religious fanatic tour!

I bent over to take the little joint, dug a lighter out of my pocket, and lit up. The crowd loved this! They started to throw joints on stage. It was a proper rainfall. Stryper's manager was beet red in the face; he slashed his finger across his throat and cried, "YOU ARE OUT! YOU ARE FUCKIN' DONE!"

Which was fine by me. I asked Tim the bass tech to pick up all the joints on stage to put into a plastic bag. We got confirmation after the show that Jetboy had been kicked off the tour. The managers and lawyers still had to square everything out, but we were on top of the world.

We went out in San Juan to celebrate. Fifteen or so purdy Puerto Rican girls came out with us. We bounced from bar to bar all night long. Tim and I were the last men standing that night. Finally, Tim had had enough and went back to the hotel. I was alone.

I was walking along the gently curving beach when the first light appeared on the horizon. The city was deserted.

Well, not completely deserted. A man appeared out of nowhere next to me; he was wearing a Panama hat, shorts, and a Hawaiian shirt. "Gimme your money." He lifted his shirt and showed me his gun.

I had a twenty in my pocket. No point starting trouble over twenty bucks. The guy took the money and took off walking. There was still a joint left in my front pocket. For some reason, I called out after him. *"Oye, espera, quieres fumar?"*

"Que?" the thief asked me. He was totally confused and stopped walking.

"Quieres fumar un porro?"

I showed him the joint. He walked back slowly and suspiciously. I lit up and offered it to the thief. We smoked it together and watched the sun rise. Out of nowhere, the thief asked if he could buy me a drink.

We walked to a bar on the beach, and the thief bought two margaritas with my twenty. Not a cent of the spoils was wasted. We drank the margaritas in peace and silence, and then went our separate ways.

MCA was still behind the album. The video was playing on repeat on MTV, where we were also giving interviews. The record sold 10,000 copies in a week, and sold altogether around 100,000 copies. A new tour was put together, this time with Cheap Trick—everyone in the band's favorite.

The tour started in Seattle and drifted toward the Midwest and the East Coast. Jetboy and Cheap Trick got along excellently.

I woke up in Denver, hungover from partying at the hotel. I had ten bucks in my pocket, my head was aching, and I was horribly hungry. I opened the windows and saw a strip joint across the street advertising ALL YOU CAN EAT PIZZA AND BEER $8!

Was this real or just a mirage? I pulled my clothes on, went across the street, paid my eight dollars, and took a seat at the bar. It was an all-nude place with not a thread of clothing on the dancers. The buffet was in the corner, and you could get pitchers at the bar. The only open seats were around the round stage. I sat down with a full paper plate of pizza slices and a pitcher of beer. A pretty girl walked up to me, and I wanted to tip her my remaining two dollars, but where was I supposed to put it when she wasn't even wearing underwear? So I threw the money on the stage. I was taking a bite of the pizza when the stripper turned around, got down on all fours, and backed up toward my face. It felt weird to eat pizza after that.

That night was the birthday of Robin Zander, the singer of Cheap Trick. Rick Nielsen asked if we knew any Cheap Trick songs and if we wanted to play with them. I raised my hand. "He's a Whore!" I knew that one! I had been practicing that song in 1980, back in the early stages of Hanoi.

Tim the roadie got some of the strippers to come from the pizza place and showed up with them on stage in the middle of "He's a Whore." The birthday lineup included Mickey on vocals with Robin Zander, Billy on rhythm guitar, and me playing Tom Petersson's twelve-string bass. The sound was like a bass orchestra, I had never heard anything like it!

Touring as an opening band is expensive. Bands that are just starting out have got to get financial support in order to open for a bigger band. Going on tour as an opening act is pretty important because the crowds are big, which hopefully will lead to more records sales. That's what happened with Jetboy. The Jetboy album made it into the eighties of the Billboard list during the tour. That wasn't a big surprise; Jetboy worked well as a live band.

But after the first or second week, the label cut off the money. MCA's new A&R guy, Michael Goldstone, saw that *Feel the Shake* had gone as far as it would go. They wanted us off the tour and back to writing new songs. We had to put out a new record ASAP, and it better be a breakthrough.

We were having a good time with Cheap Trick, though, so we decided to stay on the tour, even without financial support from the label. Our manager crunched the numbers and let us know that there'd be no more hotels from there on out; we'd be sleeping on the bus and living off twenty-seven dollars a week. But of course, roadies were getting paid as normal. We told Cheap Trick we wanted to keep touring with them, but the numbers didn't look so good. Because they were such a buncha nice guys, they let us eat from their catering every day for lunch and dinner. On top of that, they gave us wine and beer after every gig, such gentlemen are hard to find. We were on our own for the days off, though.

I asked our roadie Randy for a dollar in Las Vegas, and I put it right into a slot machine. I guess it's all the same how you make money if you're in a casino. I turned and started walking away when the machine lit up and started ringing DING DING DING…I quickly put my hat under, and the money just kept coming and coming. I won almost three hundred dollars, which was a big for my broke-ass self. Randy demanded half the winnings, because it was his seed money. C'mon, as a roadie he was getting three hundred a week, while the band was getting just twenty-seven. I gave him his dollar back. But then I decided to splurge and took everyone out to the $2.99 buffet.

Feel the Shake kept climbing the charts to sixty-eight, and it sold 150,000 to 180,000 copies in total. There was a bad vibe in the tour bus though. Mickey and Fernie still weren't getting along. We'd just missed going gold. Hanoi Rocks was a little too early to get on the gravy train, and Jetboy just a little bit too late. And in all honesty, *Feel the Shake* just wasn't a good enough record. It was missing THAT song.

We came home and sat around writing songs. I was joking about how Poison was selling millions, so maybe we should write that kind of shit too. Maybe that's not exactly how it works. So we started writing in earnest and tried to change things up a little. The band had four songwriters, but not one of them were able to write THE song. We had to bring in some other writers.

But then Mickey came up with some lyrics. It was more of the same. At a rock concert, lyrics aren't that noticeable, they're just sorta there, but the most important thing is the energy that is created. It's when you're sitting at home listening to a record that shitty lyrics jump out. The record label didn't step in over Mickey's lyrics, because Poison's "Unskinny Bop" was around as a point of reference. The label thought that if "Unskinny Bop" sold, why wouldn't this.

No one cared about quality in 1989. The whole decade was so tacky—just think of Steve Vai's double-necked heart-shaped guitar—and that tastelessness doesn't get any better thirty years later when a band makes their comeback. "You sucked then, why are you not gonna suck NOW?"

At home, the building across the street from me was full of students from the Guitar Institute of Technology. These GIT students didn't think Jimi Hendrix was shit. "Yeah, he's an okay guitar player." The trend in the eighties had moved on from more of a feel to a speed game, but it's so out of context if you hadn't lived in the time of Hendrix. Magic Johnson and Pelé would look like they're standing in place compared to the players of today, but back then, you couldn't imagine anyone being more masterful.

×××

Jetboy didn't have any gigs coming up for weeks, even months on end. That kind of free time started to get to me. I didn't want to hang out poolside forever; that's not healthy. To stave off the boredom, Mickey, Timppa, and I decided put together Stronzo, a Sex Pistols and Little Richard cover band. Marc Ford and Craig Ross joined in, and others would join in too from time to time. We wanted to get a couple guys in on brass, someone on a pedal steel guitar and another drummer. Stronzo—"turd" in Italian—played shows all over town. We'd alternate from Pistols to Little Richard every other song. And it worked. I think we threw in a Clash song and a Bob Marley tune. I don't usually like playing covers, you will always be worse than the original, but Stronzo had a clear concept. This was way fresher than just throwing out covers of the Stones' "Wild Horses" or Zeppelin's "Rock and Roll."

Stronzo swelled up to ten members over the summer, and we opened for Michael Monroe's two sold-out shows at the Whisky a Go Go. The Whisky stage isn't big, and Stronzo had to put up their equipment in front of Michael's band's gear. There was no room to move about, and even standing in place was hard because you had to make sure you didn't hit anybody else with your instrument. Seeing that kind of a band play "Lucille" followed up by "Anarchy in the UK" left quite an impression.

Stronzo opened for Bo Diddley at Coconut Teaszer. His entrance was spectacular; Bo drove up in a gold and copper 1920s Cadillac with tiny windows and gangster boards. Bo made his entrance in a sheriff's hat with a guitar case in hand; within five minutes, he was up on stage playing. Afterward, Bo asked to be called Bo-pop and told me to stay off drugs. I hid the joint behind my back. "Yes, Bo-pop, I promise."

I ran out of cigarettes around three that morning. Everything closes at two in LA, so I went to a gas station at the corner of Sunset and La Brea.

Photos courtesy of Ingrid Takamäki's collections

Mika Jussila's tenth birthday in 1973. The picture shows Antti Sajantila, Sami Takamäki, Mika Jussila, Jukka Pohjola, and Jouko Nuora.

Photo courtesy of Mika Jussila's collections

Photos by Janne Haavisto

Suopo 1979: Markojuhani "Kobo" Iron danger. Sam has an Einoj hani Rautavaara jacket.

Photos courtesy of Sami Yaffa's collections

Pelle Miljoona Oy in Kaivopuisto in 1980.
Photo by Tarina Lounasmaa

Pelle Miljoona Oy.

Photos courtesy of Tumppi Varonen's collections

Pelle Miljoona Oy.

Photos by Martti Jämsä/Ari Taskinen's collections

Pelle Miljoona Oy.

Photos by Martti Jämsä/Ari Taskinen's collections

Mom, Grandma, and Razzle.

Photos courtesy of Ingrid Takamäki's collections

Hanoi Rocks in India 1983.

Photos by Justin Thomas

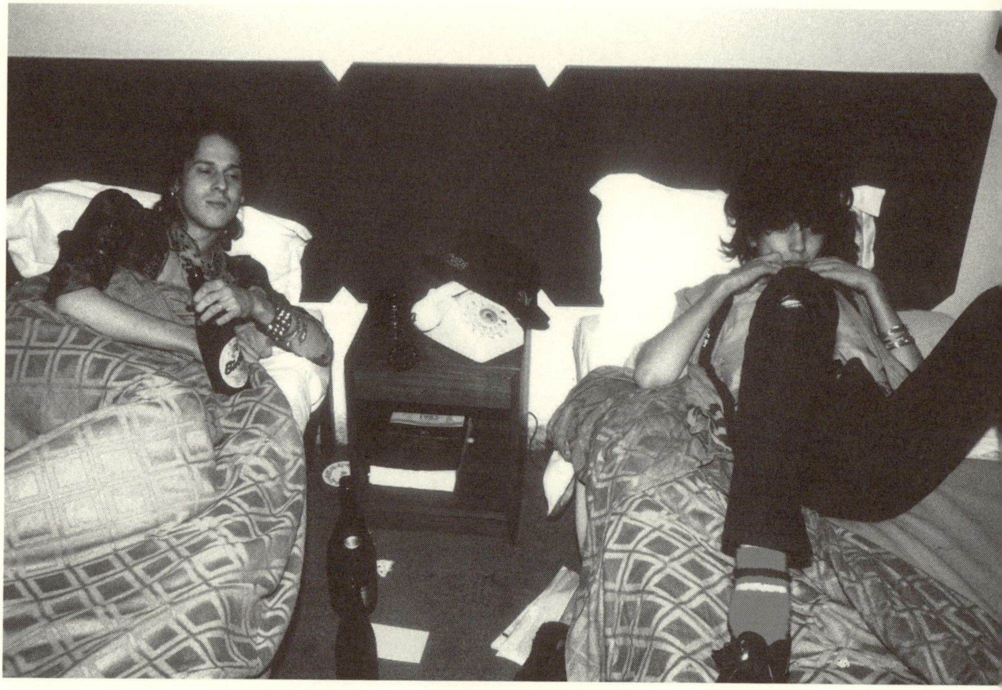

In India and the Dead Sea.

Photos by Justin Thomas

Message to sister: "Here's a picture of Japan. You can watch it on dark autumn evenings…if you want."
Photo courtesy of Ingrid Takamäki's collections

Photo by Justin Thomas

Hanoi Rocks 1983.

Photos by Justin Thomas

Photos by Justin Thomas

Mother and sister.
Photo courtesy of Sami Yaffa's collections

Andy examines the Hanoi fan's clip folder in Södertälje on June 19, 1983.
Photo courtesy of Sami Yaffa's collections

Jetboy.

Photo courtesy of Ingrid Takamäki's collections

Betsy.

Photo courtesy of Timo Kaltio's collections

Mickey Finn, Jetboy.

Photo courtesy of Sami Yaffa's collections

Smack Live at The Roxy in Los Angeles, CA: Rane Raitsikka, Sami, Timo Kaltio, Claude, Repa Kauppila.

Photo courtesy of Timo Kaltio's collections

Stronzo in Coconut Teaszer 1990.
Photos courtesy of Timo Kaltio's collections

Demolition 23.

Photos by Mark Higashino

Mad Juan's precursor in New York.
Photo by Mariano Asch

Ingrid and Nicke.
Photo courtesy of Sami Yaffa's collections

Finn in Dolls.
Photos by Hilary Hulteen

New York Dolls in Buenos Aires, backstage.
Photo by Mara Hennessey

David Johansen.
Photo by Mara Hennessey

New York Dolls.
Photo by Mara Hennessey

Steve Conte.
Photo by Mika Jussila

Dregen Himos
Midsummer 2012.
Photo by Mika Jussila

2011–2012. *Photo by Mika Jussila*

2011–2012. *Photo by Mika Jussila*

Pelle Miljoona Oy 2011.
Photos by Mika Jussila

Gyp Casino a.k.a. Jesper "Jeppe" Sporre.
Photo courtesy of Sami Yaffa's collections

Cochise Anderson.
Photo courtesy of Sami Yaffa's collections

Mad Juana, New York 2014.
Photos by Alan Rand

Mad Juana, New York 2014.
Photo by Alan Rand

Mad Juana, Helsinki 2014.
Photo by Mika Jussila

Michael Monroe today.
Photos by Mika Jussila

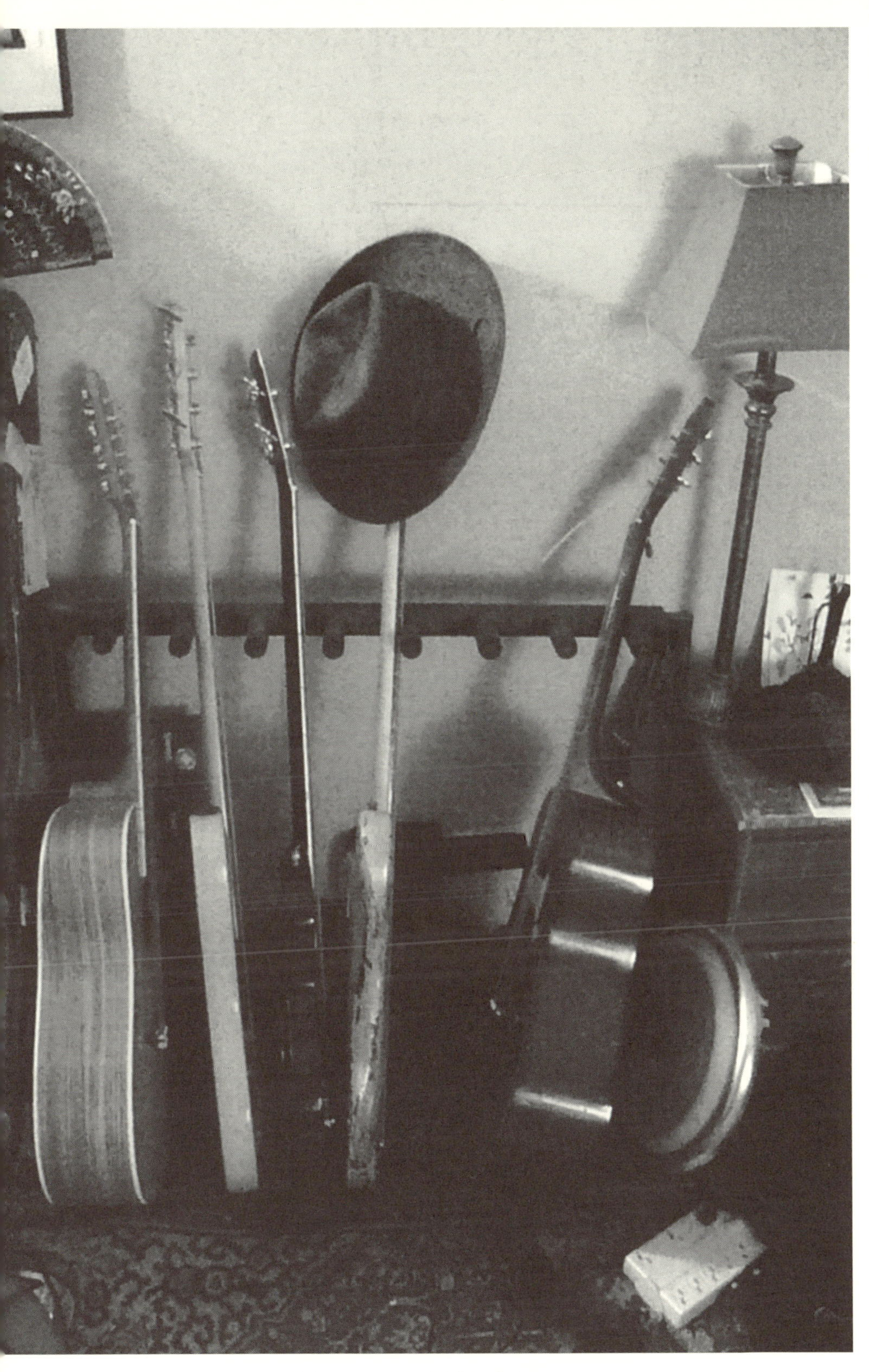

Photo courtesy of Sami Yaffa's collections

1963. Maarit, Sami, and Jone.
Photo courtesy of Ingrid Takamäki's collections

2016. Maarit, Sami, and Jone.
Photo by Meeri Koutaniemi

A busted-up station wagon, some 1982 Oldsmobile with wood panels, rolled up. Out steps Bo Diddley. I went to ask him what happened to the Caddy. "That's just for the show. It reads in my every contract, this is what I roll with!" Didn't matter how big the venue, they had to find him that kind of ride.

But that's the hidden truth. Even though Bo Diddley was a living rock and roll legend and had basically half invented the whole genre, he still was driving himself around in a beat-up station wagon with all his gear in the back. Things had not gotten any better for him over the decades.

"If you're ever in Texas, look me up," he said when we parted. "Sure, Bo-pop," I said, despite Texas's size, which is five times Finland's.

Johnny Thunders rolled into town. He called me up before getting in. "Hey Sammy, it's Johnny. Wanna make some money?" I hadn't seen him since the show at the Stockholm speakeasy.

The sax player, Jamie Heath, called up on the day of the show to let me know where the rehearsal would take place. I showed up at the spot. Heath, the drummer Bill Bateman, the guitarists Will Sexton and Frankie Infante from Blondie were there. What about Johnny? Snoring on the floor. Didn't even respond to a bit of a kick, either. So, that kind of rehearsal. We went through the set with Johnny snoring at our feet. We were playing the last song when he finally woke up. "Hey, hey man…LET'S GO THROUGH THE SET!" Listen, Johnny, we already went through it, so yeah, we'll see you at the show…

It was the day of the performance and that's the kind of shape he was already in. The set time was at ten. We waited around at the venue's backstage, hours ticking away, and the gentleman hadn't even shown up at midnight. Okay, done deal, there won't be a show.

Then Johnny busted in through the backstage door in a canary-yellow suit with a huge high pompadour and crazy eyes…GUYS! LET'S GO PLAY! Johnny had found some quality uppers and apparently had taken quite a cocktail. Two forty-five-minute sets, a twenty-minute solo set in the middle. "Wipe-out," "Pipeline," "Walk Don't Run." Fuck, almost entirely Heartbreakers songs. Playing was fluid, everyone including Johnny was on fire! One of the most unforgettable gigs I've ever played.

I was eating dinner over at Joey DePompeis and his wife Dessica's place. We were sitting at their upstairs table when Joey announced to Dessica that, "Oh yeah, Tommy is also coming, he'll be here in fifteen." Joey went to open the door when the bell rang. I almost choked on an olive when Tommy Chong walked up the stairs. Michael and I had the movie *Up in Smoke* memorized, word for word. Cheech and Chong had been Hanoi's heroes. We exchanged numbers at the end of the night.

Los Angeles started to look tempting for a lot of other Finnish musicians. Nights of Iguana came to town in 1988, but they didn't really get much work, just a couple of gigs; the band slunk back to Finland. Then Smack rolled into town. Smack lived out in Orange County with a guy called Ed who'd brought them over, and then they moved to a place a few blocks from my house. Rane Raitsikka was like my brother from all the way back in the Lepakko days, and I'd known Manchuria as a little brat when we went to that same pop and jazz camp.

The bassist from Smack had had enough and went back to Finland, so Rane asked me to fill in on some shows. Hell yeah, I'd love to play with Smack. I took Ulan Bator as a pseudonym since there was already a Manchuria in the band and MCA had barred me from using my own name. Agreements can have some pretty laughable limitations and restrictions.

I appeared as Ulan Bator on Smack's last single, too. It was the only recording I made with Smack.

Smack's shows in LA were badass, amazing shows, although some of the venues were a bit questionable. But one of them was real interesting: the campus green at a college at two in the afternoon, with students walking by in baseball caps and books under their arms. Yeah, go ahead and rock out there then.

Rane, Timppa, and I would get so-called Cadillac margaritas at a Mexican restaurant on the corner of Sunset and La Brea. We also went to the Cat and Fiddle to day drink and play darts. We'd go to the clubs to see music in the evenings or play hockey at Smack's house. They were big tournaments where we'd go through bags of weed. We'd jump into the dirty swimming pool at night. Once, Rane and I were tripping on LSD and went bowling. It was acid bowling. I'd started getting Uzi Suicide checks, and checks from Japan, and I probably wasted most of them on getting lunch, tequila rounds, and dinner with Rane and Timppa.

I missed my son and was starting to get sick of sitting around twirling my thumbs. On top of that, Andy's wife, Anastacia, pestered me with daily, even hourly with phone calls. "Is Andy there? I know he's there! Stop lying to me! Put him on the phone!" There was no getting her to believe it when I'd tell her I hadn't seen him in weeks.

I was hanging out with my manager, Brigitte, at the Cat Club, and I asked her to plan a vacation for me for a week or two. I didn't care where to, I just had to get away from my boredom and the telephone terrorism in LA. My only criteria was a beach.

I went to an afterparty after the Cat Club and got home at five in the morning. An hour later, Brigitte was pressing the buzzer. She breezed in energetically and started tossing my clothes into a suitcase. I wondered what the hell was going on, but got back into bed. Somehow, Brigitte managed to get me up, to the airport, and on the airplane.

A flight attendant woke me up. We had landed.

But where exactly were we? While waiting for my bag, I read the signs and ads on the walls. Everything was in Spanish. Okay, maybe we were in Mexico, Puerto Rico, Costa Rica, Guatemala, Belize…I'd find out soon enough.

I asked the guy at the passport check: excuse me, but where am I? The police officer gave me a suspicious look and answered, "Señor, you are in Mazatlán, Mexico."

At my request, the taxi driver brought me to a cheap but nice hotel. "Las Brisas" means haste or wind, so be it, let's go there.

I spent the next ten days with mussel divers and their families. They started work early in the morning at the beach in front of the hotel, floating all day on the tractor inner tubes, and spent the day diving for mussels that would go to restaurants or for jewelry.

I ended up jamming with a mariachi band one night. I bought the bassist a shot of tequila and asked him about his stand-up bass; it had a headstock carved as an eagle, phoenix birds and other mystical stuff painted all over it. I asked him to teach me some Mexican songs, like "La Cucaracha" and "La

Bamba." After the lesson, I got up on stage. The band was playing in mariachi clothes, I was wearing a leather jacket and leather pants. We continued to jam in the cantina until dawn.

Back at the hotel I asked the concierge where I could get some weed. He told me to go to a place called El Dorado.

I entered a dark, windowless room; the only light was coming from two faint candles in the corner of the room. A hand appeared in the darkness, and it led me by the elbow to sit down. A bottle of beer and a glass of tequila appeared in front of me. I heard a voice with a heavy Mexican accent behind me. "Gringo, looking for something?" I told him what I wanted. "How many kilos do you want?"

Uh…just a couple joints, thanks. The voice told me to get into his car; we were driving up to the mountains where there was a guy selling good shit.

I finished my drink, declined, and walked out. I had no interest in going anywhere up the mountains alone with that guy.

I wasn't drinking during those ten days as much as I would have in LA. I went jogging every day and went swimming. I was clear in the head for a change and in high spirits. All the business and all the other garbage was washed away.

I flew home, threw my suitcase on the bed, and sat down at the table for a cigarette. The phone rang.

"Hi Sami, is Andy there?"

I threw my phone out the window.

×××

I turned twenty-six at the beginning of the fall. I had planned on spending a calm birthday on my own. Then Joey DePompeis called up and told me to get ready because a car was coming to get me in fifteen minutes. I tried to get out of it, but he wouldn't take no for an answer.

A tacky white limo rolled up to my house. One of the tinted back windows rolled down, and out popped Tommy Chong's head. "Hop inside, man." I was handed a joint the size of a child's arm and a bottle of champagne. The limo started heading east.

The restaurant Cha Cha Cha was in East LA, and some consider it the most authentic Mexican restaurant in LA. Tommy, his wife Shelby, Joey and Dessica, and a few others joined me at the table. At the end of the night, the lights went down and the waiters came out of the kitchen carrying a huge cake while singing "Happy Birthday Dear Sancho."

Sancho?

The cake did, in fact, have "Sancho" written on it in big letters. Tommy explained that when they made the reservation and ordered the cake, the restaurant let them know that a birthday party for Sancho had canceled, leaving behind a cake. "Sami or Sancho, close enough, we'll take the cake!"

I had reclaimed the "i" in my name. When I was younger and had just moved to Stockholm, Sami Takamäki hadn't sounded so good. I had no problem going on in life with the name "Yaffa." But I'm Sami, not Sam.

I almost ended up as Sam Sodomy back in 1980. Andy had kept trying to see if it would work. I had admitted that yeah, it looked good. Then I found out what it meant—fuck you, Andy. Him and his warped sense of humor.

The name came back to haunt me years later when I got caught up in a lawsuit. The plaintiff had tried to get some dirt on me, and their lawyer asked me out of the blue, "Well Sami, does 'Sam Sodomy' ring a bell?" I said, "Yeah, that was my gay porn name." They thought I was being serious. I ended up having to clarify. "For the record, IT'S A JOKE. I was never in porn or gay, OKAY?"

"Well, tell me about Sam Sodomy."

C'mon, seriously…you've clearly done your research, because Sam Sodomy only ever appeared in some Finnish papers before 1981 when I came up with Yaffa.

Using an artist's name belongs to rock and roll tradition: Alice Cooper, Johnny Rotten, Sid Vicious, Joe Strummer, Iggy Pop, Johnny Thunders, Pelle Miljoona. The list goes on and on.

Stiv Bators called up and said that Dee Dee had left the Ramones. Dee Dee had apparently suggested me as a replacement. Sami Ramone… yeah, right…and New York, which had been on my mind lately? But this was too much of an acid trip to think about.

Bill Wyman and John Paul Jones are old-school bassists; they'd learned blues and Motown. That's why their playing leans back. And after that generation came Dee Dee Ramone: down strokes only. Everyone thinks original punk rock is played at a really fast tempo—the Pistols, the Clash, Dead Boys—but when you listen to their records, they're actually slow. They sound slow now because hardcore punk and speed metal came after. You get numbed to the speed. Same thing as the whiny snobs from the Guitar Institute of Technology. But you can't just keep on upping the tempo forever without losing the human touch and feel.

×××

We started preproduction for the second Jetboy album in October. John Purdell and Duane Baron were picked out to produce. They had made music with Kix and Ozzy Osbourne, among others.

We had made demos at the Capitol Records studio. The records were started in the Devonshire studio and One to One. We worked all the way up until the Christmas break.

We had stuff coming up that was better than *Feel the Shake*, but still not quite good enough. The Jetboy guys were really damn nice, but that doesn't make the band necessarily good. When I joined, I thought that maybe it would go somewhere. But now I knew that it wouldn't get better than this. My attention and interest starts to wander, if the music doesn't tear your heart out.

1990
Damned Nation

Jetboy had been with Gold Mountain Management. Our other manager, Anita Camarata, left the company to start her own thing with the former manager from Kiss, Larry Mazer. John Silva had joined Gold Mountain and was the one who was going to step in Anita's shoes to manage us. He soon signed a couple of bands, Sonic Youth and Nirvana.

Jetboy wanted to follow Anita and Larry. "Just think, the manager of Kiss. Could we maybe get on a tour with them?" I countered that we shouldn't be ridiculous. John Silva was a hot ticket, and we should stay on his roster. But the guys were stubborn about sticking with Anita and Larry. This drove a bit of a wedge between us.

We had promo pictures planned, and I showed up on location a little early. Then the other guys showed up. And all of them were wearing plaid flannels. What kind of joke was this? They started talking about Seattle and that it's the new thing...

The photographer lost it. "What the hell does this lumberjack look have to do with rock and roll? This is just nooooot going to work!" The photographer was wound up tight. When you're full up on steroids and coked out, the veins in your forehead and neck are ready to pop at any second. His jaws were flapping nonstop, and he twirled around the studio like a pinwheel.

The guys agreed to take off the grunge shirts, but it just went to show that they were ready to jump on the bandwagon and change themselves just to succeed. All the issues and business BS had made the guys insecure and ready to follow the changing winds.

Damned Nation was also a record that did not have the big hit on it. Flannel shirts couldn't help with that either. Michael Monroe's *Not Fakin' It*, on the other hand, was a damn good record—even if the guitars veered a little too much toward metal for my taste. But the lyrics actually had something to say, they had fire! I liked that the lyrics were talking about the world we lived in. Like punk. Like Little Steven's *Voice of America*. The Clash.

I was really starting to get sick of LA. The city is way more spread out than London, which is pretty big itself. There are buses there, but it takes forever to get anywhere, three hours just to go a mile. Completely useless. You have to have a car to go to the bank, to the store, to your friends'. From one bubble to another: from an air-conditioned house to an air-conditioned car. I hate breathing air-conditioned air.

I fell in love with Los Angeles at first: the sun, the palm trees, the swimming pools, the Mexican influence on the food, and the music. It takes a while to realize that it's actually one of the loneliest cities in the world.

I craved the raw truth and chaotic beauty of New York, the colorful inhabitants and the surprises that turn up out of nowhere right in front of your face. I'd been to New York lots of times to play shows and to hang out with Monroe. The reconnection was strong; I'd taken the five-hour flight whenever I could to crash on Michael's sofa for the weekend or even the whole week. We'd listen to records and talk. We had a special connection and the same understanding of what rock and roll should be. The kind of energy created on stage with Michael is unlike sharing the stage with anyone else.

One night, I was leaving the Whisky with Timppa Kaltio and a few others. We were driving along Sunset Boulevard when a big car made a dangerous turn right in front of us and cut us off. I was sitting in the front seat and I gave them the finger. We turned onto our street, and I got out of the car. The other car had followed us without their lights on. I got punched in the face and kicked in the head by a big dude. I still had a cigarette burning in my hand. I angrily flipped the cigarette at him and hit him right in the forehead. Then I laughed.

That was a mistake. The guy jumped me for real and started kicking hard with his boots. I protected my head as best I could, which fucked up my elbow, fortunately not for good. But I still have a scar on it.

I flew to my sister's in Mallorca. It must have been in March. I was talking it all out with my sister and her husband over lunch when I'd had a bottle of white wine with my fish and a carajillo for my coffee. I blurted out that I needed a change, wanted to move to New York, and wanted to play with Michael again.

My sister's husband said, "Why don't you call him now?"

I got up and went to a store that had a phone for long-distance calls. I stuffed a handful of coins into the slot. The connection was bad, and I shouted into the receiver. "Michael, I'm fucking moving to New York and you can't say anything about it! Like it or not! We're going to start playing together! Punk and roll!"

Michael laughed on the other end. "Good idea, welcome, any time!"

I put the phone down. My mood was definitely lighter.

×××

I went back to Los Angeles, and the next day, we had a meeting between Jetboy and management about a music video for the first single. Anita, Larry, and the guys were saying that we had to get bikini models for the video. It sounded really damn stupid. I couldn't stand that kind of stuff, hot girls rolling around on a car hood or spraying each other with a hose. My roots were in punk. Models in videos were a *nyet*.

I let it be known that I thought the idea was fucking stupid. Fernie's blood started to boil. "Why don't you just fucking leave the band, if you're not interested?"

I had planned on letting them know when the time was right. Apparently, this was the time. "Well, now that you've brought it up, I quit."

The guys looked at me in shock. "Are you for real?"

We went to the Jet Mansion and talked about it. In the end, the band understood. I said that I'd do whatever was needed for the band up until April.

It turns out that there wasn't a whole lot needed. Jetboy got their video that had a spider and woman and all that, a really tasteful feast. I play on the track, but there's some blond dude in the video in my place. The video director was Ralph Ziman, who also made the video for Faith No More's "Epic."

Stronzo played its farewell show at Coconut Teaszer. I planned a big party for my friends on the Hollywood Tower rooftop. It had been a beautiful three years, I'd made a lot of close friends, but it was time for me to move on.

At the beginning of the eighties, my brother had had a little vacation fling with a Colombian girl from New York, Piedad Palencia; I got to know her too during the recording of *Two Steps from the Move*, and we'd kept in touch. I called Piedad up now and asked if she knew a place I could stay while I was looking for my own spot. Piedad was nice enough to say I could crash on her couch. Her apartment was on Greenwich Street, right next to the World Trade Center.

I knew a Native dude from Texas, a big metalhead, from the LA club scene who was a truck driver. I told him I was moving to New York, and he told me he drove cross-country pretty often delivering vegetables. We agreed that I'd pay him a couple hundred for the trouble, and we could put my stuff in the back with the lettuce. So that's what we did. My stuff didn't end up smelling like salad or anything, but I don't know if that lettuce ended up smelling like my stuff.

My contrabass also went in the back. I had recently bought myself an upright bass and had been playing it at home. It requires stamina, it's such a physical instrument, and you lose your touch for it if you don't play it regularly. If you leave for a month-long tour, when you come back, it's like starting all over again.

1990–1995

New York City

*"You have to listen to the song, to hear what it's trying to say.
Not necessarily even what the songwriter is saying.
Or if the tempo is going up or down.
As a musician, you can tell
when a song clicks into place."*

1990

Twenty-Seventh Street, NY

I read the apartment listings in the *Village Voice* and went to look at apartments. After three weeks, I found the right place on the corner of Twenty-Seventh and Broadway. There were a couple of subway stations close by, so it was quick to get to the East Village, where everything was happening. It was a roomy apartment with high ceilings, but there was very little natural light since it was between two other buildings. Out on the little balcony, you could only see a brick wall for as far as you could crane your neck up to the little sliver of sky.

I lived in the middle of the wholesale district, busy and lively during the day, but everything was gone by six o'clock in the evening. It was only quiet for a moment though. By eight in the evening, it was an entirely different world: two shabby rundown hotels that were used by the prostitutes and the traffic that came with it.

I'd met a Native Pawnee woman at the end of my time in LA, and our friendship had turned into romance. I got married quickly in part for residency reasons. I was in danger of losing my work permit since I'd left Jetboy, and the record deal no longer covered me. I would have needed to find guarantors every six months and just hope I'd be able to keep my work permit. So she was my Green Card wife. I'll just call her S because she's doing really well these days—with kids and a family—whereas back in the nineties things weren't going so well.

When I got my own place, S moved in with me. It was all good at first; the whole first year went okay. It took a while to notice that she had some deep-seated issues going on, and I had no idea about anything that she had been through growing up on an Indian reservation.

I got used to my new normal. I was finally living in the city I'd fallen in love with six years earlier. And I wanted to start making music with Michael right away.

But it wasn't as straightforward as that. Between my phone call from Mallorca and my move to New York, a third guy had come between me and Michael: a guitarist named Steve Stevens.

Michael Monroe and Steve Stevens. I thought they were a bit of an odd match. Steve was Billy Idol's old sidekick and had written "Rebel Yell" with him. When the three of us went out to eat together, Steve stressed that if we ended up making a record together, he wanted to keep it bare bones, just one rhythm guitar, solo, and that's it. There had to be space and air for the ears.

This talk sounded all good, because why wouldn't I want to make a simple fucking punk album à la *Never Mind the Bollocks.*

We started hanging out and writing and demoing at Steve's home studio. Our writing sessions were sometimes fun, even if somewhat psychotic. I'd get stuck sitting between Michael and Steve while they were trying to show me what the fuck to play. "Play like this: da-DAANG-dada-DAANG." Michael would correct him: "No, play like this: DA-daang-da-DA-daang-da." Steve: "No, play like this: dadadada-DAANG-dada..." Diverging opinions were stuffed into each one of my ears. I'd end up erupting: "Will you both shut the fuck up and let me play what I wanna play!"

Steve was very excited over the songs and went on and on about how we were making a seminal album—raw and unpolished street rock, in yer face. I thought that was a bit of a reach for Steve, who had a huge guitar collection and was also a total control freak. Steve Stevens was technically an amazing guitarist, but a little too metal for my taste. He was always in heels and had bigger hair than Michael. He was very friendly, but one of those kinds of guys that you never really get to know.

"Let's keep it real punk like Billy Idol." Really? Hmm, Billy Idol is punk? *Whiplash Smile* is a VERY produced record. Thommy Price—who is like a drum machine come to life—wasn't a tight enough drummer for Steve Stevens and the producer, so they brought in a drum machine to do the work.

When we weren't at Steve's home studio, Michael and I talked about the arrangements and the songs over beers at the Telephone Bar & Grill. I had my suspicions about the whole thing, but didn't make a big deal out of it. After all, I had only just moved to New York. I'd jumped into the record in the middle of everything and was just trying to find my own place while these two already had something going. This was Michael's solo album, Michael and Steve's show. I tried to stick to my own business and not force my opinion anywhere other than arrangements; I kept my mouth shut about the songwriting.

We flew a drummer out from California, practiced the songs picked out for the record, and recorded a demo. It sounded good. The songs were okay. There are things on the demo that I still like to this day, and Michael recorded some of the songs later on. The music was mostly Steven's, while Michael wrote most of the lyrics with his wife Jude.

Right in the middle of it, some non-music roadblocks popped up. Michael was signed to PolyGram and Steve Stevens to Warner Brothers. This took some negotiating, which ate a lot of time. Peter Rudge came aboard to manage the project; this was the guy who managed the Rolling Stones, the Who, and Pink Floyd in the seventies, a real heavy hitter. Rudge managed to make a deal with backing from both PolyGram and Warner. To my knowledge, it was the first time two big labels struck that kind of deal.

We still had to wait for the final agreement though. I used my free time to play with other people. Mannish Boys had opened for Hanoi in London, and I was now playing with the singer, Gass Wild, doing Stones-type stuff, and in another lineup with Johnny Thunders's backup singer, Alison Gordy. I played a few songs with Alison on the stand-up bass, which I had never gotten to use in shows in Los Angeles.

1991

You always have to placate guitarists

The back cover of the first New York Dolls record has a photo of the band posing in front of a place called Gem Spa. When I got a new place on the corner of Second Avenue and St. Mark's Place, it all clicked: Gem Spa! My balcony was right above it—you can almost see it on the cover.

I still had too much free time. I would end up playing Addams Family pinball for days on end at the bar across the street. Pinball is the biggest waste of time ever. I'd like to get those hours back for a better purpose. I also played pool a lot, sometimes against this beautiful woman with one eye. It was like something straight out of a Tom Waits video: as the woman bent down to strike, her glass eye would spin wildly around, and the pupil would roll back into the socket and stay there without her noticing.

I got to know Dee Dee Ramone better. He would come over to my place, I'd make some food, we'd swap stories and drink beers. Dee Dee was good company and a street-smart guy, but he could be pretty unpredictable. One day, I was leaving my apartment to go buy some cigarettes. It had been a couple months since we'd last seen each other. Dee Dee was sitting on my stoop and staring off into the distance. I asked him how it was going. Dee Dee jumped up and started shouting in my face, "FUCK YOU, MAN! FUCK YOU!" He took off toward Third Avenue while giving me the middle finger and continuing to rage.

I was completely confused. It was like Dee Dee hadn't recognized me. I met Joey Ramone a week later at a club and told him what happened. Joey responded, "Oh, you finally MET Dee Dee."

×××

I met another Finn over Addams Family pinball. We became friends; he ended up becoming the drummer for Lewd Vagrant and Mad Juana. It turns out that Maukka Palmio and I were born at the same hospital on the same day, had lived in neighboring houses for three years, had played in the very same sandbox, and on top of all that, our mothers were friends.

Maukka was a bartender at a bar called Little Finland in the Upper East Side. Maukka lived in an apartment above the bar, and we'd go back and forth between his apartment and the bar.

I'd been to Little Finland once back in 1988. I was sitting around our hotel in Chelsea before a Jetboy concert. I suddenly remembered that my dad had told me about the bar right below Harlem on the Upper East Side. I opened up the phone book. Dad had been there in 1968, and amazingly, it looked like the place was still around. I memorized the address and jumped into a cab.

I shook the snow off my boots and stepped inside. It was small joint, and there was no one there, not even a bartender. Jukebox, pool table, and the bar. I knocked on the bar, and an old woman hobbled out from the back. She had a full-on New York accent, but I asked her if she spoke Finnish. "Of course!" Did she have Finnish liquor? The old lady looked at me for a minute. Well, for *me* she did. She pulled out two glasses and a bottle of Koskenkorva from the fridge, and she started to pour…onto the bar. She was almost completely blind and had missed the glasses. The old lady showed me some pictures of her dancing with Mauno Koivisto— the president of Finland—at the Presidential Ball.

She'd come to New York from Finland during the Prohibition in the twenties and started working at a speakeasy under the legendary mafia bosses Meyer Lansky and Charlie "Lucky" Luciano. Little by little, she started taking over bars of her own. She lived in Harlem in the thirties, where there had been a Finnish community for decades.

My wife's backstory came out little by little. She had grown up on an Indian reservation in Nebraska. The schools on reservations were crude places, and their disciplinary actions still aren't talked about. Native kids were taken from their families and brought to schools hundreds of miles away. S went to a school on a reservation in the seventies with a white teacher who didn't want the students to speak their own language; they had to speak English. If little six-year-old S spoke Pawnee, the teacher would bring out the metal ruler, hold the sharp edge against her mouth, and hit it with the butt of her hand. The ruler cut open the sides of her mouth and left permanent scars.

S's father was in the military and hardly ever home. At sixteen, S ran away from home and ended up doing all kinds of things to survive.

S had suffered abuse and other shit at a young age, and the shit had just continued up until then. The knot inside her started to unravel. Our relationship started to get more and more hellish.

Musically, things were also confusing. Was the record's producer Steve Stevens's idea? Michael Wagener had produced the German band Accept and was Udo Dirkschneider's old school buddy. He also produced one of Skid Row's records. I hadn't gotten involved with choosing the producer, and the choice was a little unusual to me.

At the end of winter, we went to Lake Geneva, Wisconsin, to record. I came down with a bad flu on the first day, and Michael got sick pretty soon after. Maybe the flu was an unconscious reaction to the whole process of making the record, because things started to take a turn for the weird and not in a good way. Steve had picked out a friend of his from LA to play drums, a guy named Greg Ellis.

We spent a week just recording the drums. Steve bossed Greg around, how the drumbeat should go and how the kick drum pattern should go. The original concept quickly disappeared when Steve decided that everything should be played to clinical perfection.

Steve ordered a bunch of Marshall amps to Wisconsin from New York and LA, and then sent them back to New York and LA. The FedEx fees from the first week were around ten thousand bucks. The bloated FedEx costs alone could have paid for the recording of a good rock 'n' roll record.

When the basic tracks had been recorded, after weeks upon weeks, Michael and I thought that we'd fly out to LA for more recording. We were available and wanted to see the production through to the end. But the managers didn't want either one of us there. There were two managers now, Steve's own manager in addition to Peter Rudge. And then there were these two labels. And the egos.

Michael flew out to LA, and I started to get increasingly worried phone calls from him. Wagener and Stevens had locked themselves into the studio to jerk each other off and wouldn't let Michael hear what they were up to. And now they tried to drive me and Michael apart. Divide and conquer.

I paid for my own ticket and flew out. As soon as we knew Wagener and Stevens were taking a night off, Michael and I sneaked into the studio and asked the assistant engineer to see the soundboards track listing.

And fuck, the track listings were unbelievable to read. Wagener had put two tape recorders together to double the tracks. There were quadrupled rhythm guitars, four on each side: eight tracks of just rhythm. The guitar solos had been doubled, note by note. There were acoustic guitars and different guitar overdubs with different amps here and there. It made no sense and sounded even worse. Every available space crammed up with something.

The basic tracks recorded in Lake Geneva had been totally fine, despite the obsessive fucking attention to detail. The whole thing could have been maybe workable if the guitars had been kept in check. Could there be a reasonably good record buried deep down beneath all that musical masturbation?

The bass parts also sounded weirdly stiff and lifeless. Wait a second—that's not me playing! Mr. Stevens had re-recorded all the bass parts himself. The original bass parts must have had too much life and feeling for his taste. In the end, I was left only on three or four tracks of the entire album.

Michael tried many times to stop the whole miserable process. Of course, the producer and Steve didn't want to hear any of it. Michael's record ended up turning into Steve's. Cutting off the funding wasn't in Peter Rudge's interest because Rudge was getting money from both labels, a management percentage off every dollar. Rudge got a pretty decent cut for himself for not doing much of anything when he should have been overseeing the creation of the record and keeping an eye on the budget.

Steve Stevens cut off all contact, spoken or otherwise. After cramming every last second of the album full of guitars, Steve disappeared. We then heard that he'd joined a band with Vince Neil. Of all the people in the world, he hooked up with Vince Neil, even though he certainly knew all about our history. Steve Stevens was evidently an all-around classy guy.

1992

Jerusalem Slim

I hung around Nightbirds on Second Avenue pretty frequently, where S had gotten a bartending gig. I was sipping whisky at the packed bar listening to Muddy Waters on the jukebox when a guy holding an Uzi stepped inside. "NOBODY MOVES, NOBODY GETS HURT!" Everyone froze right away. The guy and his Uzi walked calmly to the back of the bar where the pool table was, inspected it, and walked back immediately. "Thanks for your cooperation," he said and disappeared into the night. It only took fifteen seconds for the party to pick up like nothing had ever happened. And in a way, nothing had.

S got me to come along to an American Indian Movement meeting to hear John Trudell speak and to a bunch of happenings of the American Indian Community House on Broadway. It was interesting to hear about the experiences of the Indigenous American community from the horse's mouth, but also really, really heavy. There's still shockingly little known about the wrongs that have been done to the people.

Other Native people other than S started hanging around Nightbirds. One night, she called up and asked me to come around to the bar so she could introduce me to some friends. "There's a whole bar full of Indians." I thought why not and turned off the TV.

There were some Native guys in hats with long hair having some drinks. "Sit down." There were four guys in total: Lance, Cochise, James, and I can't remember the name of the fourth. Lance was Lakota and a descendant of Crazy Horse. Cochise was Chickasaw and Choctaw, and James was Choctaw too. I've kept in touch with Cochise all through the years, like just recently while doing the first season of my show, *Sami Yaffa: Sound Tracker,* in America. I wanted Cochise on the show because he is a musician and a keeper of Native traditions and has a unique perspective on the continent. I always thought that if I ever make a documentary about American music, there has to be someone representing Native American music. No one really talks about how blues or country music were influenced by Native music.

Cochise and I hung out at bars, went out to eat, or would go somewhere to talk or go to the American Indian Community House, which often had volunteer or cultural events going on.

One night we had an afterparty at our place. We drank Southern Comfort for hours, talking about the state of the world, spirituality, music, ladies, hockey, politics, soccer until I finally passed out on the sofa.

I woke up to a loud banging. Was the neighbor pounding on the wall? I opened my eyes, and the four Native guys were singing and dancing in a circle. They'd pushed all the furniture out into the hallway of the building. Very early that morning, we climbed onto the roof of my building at the corner of St. Marks and Second Avenue. At sunrise, Cochise raised his hand and showed the five emerging suns in the sky.

There were lots and lots and lots of live music clubs in the East Village. Jazz clubs, blues clubs, punk clubs, hardcore clubs. CBGB was still as good as ever. Trigger, the owner of Continental Divide, is the most fucking irritating guy in the world, but good people; he seemed to hate both life and himself, but his club had a vibrant scene anyway. Dee Dee Ramone would bust out a solo set, or Cheetah Chrome from Dead Boys or Walter Lure from the Heartbreakers.

A few years earlier in LA, I absolutely could not hang out around heroin addicts, but it was happening now without me even thinking about it. I was secure in the knowledge that I'd never start using again. I would never put my hands on that junk again. Spacely was part of that circle. I got Spacely an apartment and promised the landlord that this pirate with an eye patch was "an outstanding, upstanding citizen, completely trustworthy and a very great guy." And of course he was loaded—from dealing—so Spacely got the apartment.

I would buy joints from Spacely. The apartment started to show traces of his lifestyle: blood splattered on the wall like a Jackson Pollock painting. Once when Spacely was wearing shorts, I noticed that his calves were covered with infected scabs. He was so far gone that there was no coming back. A month later, Spacely was dead. Rest in peace.

×××

We had to come up with names for the record that we hated and the band that didn't exist. I dug through my old memories. When I was a kid, I had flipped through my brother's slang dictionary and had found the Harlem slang for Jesus: Jerusalem Slim. I threw it out as a suggestion, and it stuck. Michael and I were trying to stop the shit from being released entirely. The best option would have been to burn the tapes and scrap the whole project. But that kicked off a whole set of problems since PolyGram and Warner obviously wanted to get a return on their investment. *Jerusalem Slim* was written into Michael Monroe's contract as a solo record. The problems went on for months, everything was on ice, and we couldn't get a new record deal until the whole fiasco with Steve was wrapped up. Word spread around the labels, and this definitely didn't do Michael's reputation any good. It's a bad place to be as an artist when you're labeled as difficult. No one is going to want to work with you with that kind of rep.

We had to agree to the record being released at least in Japan, where Michael's name would sell probably 80,000–100,000 copies. The labels would take a loss because this cock rock drivel had ended up costing the ridiculous sum of $800,000.

Jetboy was too late to catch the LA band wave, and here I was again, on a record that was dated as soon as it came out. When *Jerusalem Slim* came out in Japan in October of 1992, grunge had spread everywhere and this kind of jerk-off guitar was old news, totally behind the times. I don't wanna even see the bloody record. It doesn't have a single song on it that I could imagine listening to.

Jerusalem Slim never played a single show. The lineup that made the record broke up a month before release. The record release tour was coming up, and we had to find new people. Our bro Nasty Suicide jumped in and played guitar on the tour in Japan. The masterful Thommy Price was the only choice for drums. Phil Grande, who had played on *Not Fakin' It* and had played and toured with Joe Cocker, also joined on guitar.

We played to crowds of three to six thousand in Japan. We played Michael's solo stuff, some Hanoi, but nothing from *Jerusalem Slim* except "Teenage Nervous Breakdown," which was a cover. We were there to promote a new record, but in a way, we didn't promote it at all. The project had had an odd start and was continuing on down the same path. Michael said not to buy the *Jerusalem Slim* record in all his interviews: Beware of that record!

Nasty had gotten his life in order, and it was really great to share the stage with him again. Playing together just fell into place naturally, even if we hadn't had any contact in the past two years.

I've probably played "Taxi Driver" ten thousand times—it's one of the easiest songs in the world to play. And yet somehow at one of the shows, I started to play it all wrong, starting from A. It was like the Batman theme but slowed down. Michael gave me a WTF? look. I got stuck on the upside-down riff and couldn't turn it around, shake it off, and move on. That "Taxi Driver" went down like a lead balloon.

The tour Nasty was the same kind of jolly gentleman as me; both of us liked to bullshit and hop from bar to bar. Mötley Crüe happened to be touring Japan at the same time. We ran into Tommy Lee at a place called Pips—one of the famous rock 'n' roll hangouts in Tokyo. We got a bottle of absinthe. We had a blast but after an hour and a half, Tommy, Nasty, and I were in such a state that we couldn't even talk anymore. Absinthe is heavy stuff. The only thing that we managed at the end of the night was, "See ya later bro." I hadn't seen Tommy in five years, since Oakland Stadium.

I kept playing shows around New York with the Alison Gordy Band. The band's name changed to Blonde & Blue; the guitarist changed from Joey Pinter to Josh Brown and the drummer from Charlie Soxx to Chris Musto. We went to the studio to record *Mad As Hell* in November of 1992. I played the upright on a few tracks, just like in our live shows.

This was around the time that everything was slowly making the switch from analog to digital. Minidisc and DAT and ADAT all came and went. The *Mad As Hell* sessions were recorded in a studio that had the newest ADAT setup. The music was stored on a Super VHS tape, so the old tape setup was synced to the new digital system. I was used to the tape compression, the warm sound of tape; ADAT felt cold, the instruments didn't somehow blend together, the sound was somehow unnatural, too clean. Which is why it's sometimes a little hard for me to listen to that record, even though the songs are really good. Alison is a gem.

We did all the recording in one evening. Alison was recording the album on her own dime; she didn't have the money to spend several days recording. The quick pace wasn't a problem, since we had played the songs live lots of times. We played Tramps at least once a month, plus all the other gigs.

We also played at Cafe Au Go Go. The legendary spot apparently hadn't changed at all; the stage is in the same place. Just the sofa Hendrix had sat on was moved to the other side of the bar. It was cool to think that I was playing on the stage Hendrix had performed on only some twenty years earlier.

So little time had passed from then to the early nineties. When Tumppi Varonen asked me to join Pelle Miljoona in January 1980, it had been nine years and four months since Hendrix's death. Nine years when you're young is a looooong time, now time just speeds ahead and nine years ago seems like yesterday.

1993
Mad As Hell

Alison Gordy and Blonde & Blue's *Mad As Hell* was released as a CD on her own label. The next recording session was for the Johnny Thunders tribute album that drummer Chris Musto was putting together. We all flew to London, the Blonde & Blue band and Michael. Rat Scabies, the drummer from the Damned, was waiting for us with a van at Heathrow. We drove to the countryside studio in Surrey and got situated.

With Alison, we recorded the Thunders song "Just Another Girl" with Michael singing backup. Michael, Nasty, and I covered "Disappointed in You" and "So Alone" with Chris Musto on drums. Steve Nieve from Elvis Costello's Attractions played a Hammond organ on "So Alone." Nieve showed up to the session with his eight-year-old son, which made for a good vibe. The kind of spooky thing about "So Alone" was that it sounds like there's another, whispering voice backing up Michael on the track, but there weren't any whispering or backup vocals recorded.

The great Thunders tribute album *I Only Wrote This Song for You* came out the next year.

I took another studio trip to England in May. Michael asked if I'd be interested in playing on a song for the *Coneheads* movie soundtrack. The lineup would be Slash, Kenny Aronoff, and Dizzy Reed. Twist my fucking arm!! Back then, you got paid pretty well for movie gigs. This was Slash's deal, and he had picked out the Steppenwolf song "Magic Carpet Ride" to record.

Two days had been booked at the legendary Olympic Studios in London. The night of our arrival, we were supposed to jam with Guns N' Roses at their huge concert at Milton Keynes Stadium; Ronnie Wood from the Rolling Stones was supposed to join Michael and I as well.

A black stretch limo was waiting at the airport in London. The driver was wearing a uniform and he informed us that the car belonged Ronnie Wood. "If you need a hit of blow, Mr. Wood's old grinder is in there." I checked the car door and sure enough, there was a coke grinder with only a bit of dust left. I left it alone.

Before the flight, I'd been asked if I needed anything waiting for me at the hotel. Emphasis on the word "anything." I asked for yellow Lebanese hash and a bit of wine. There was a little nug waiting for me in my room wrapped up in a pretty little bow and a tag that read "Welcome to London." I took a shower and a jet lag nap and got up at three in the afternoon; I had to leave for Milton Keynes by seven. I rolled a spliff out of the Leb and turned on the TV. There was a live broadcast from Morocco coming through on satellite. It was a stadium concert with Morocco's crème de la crème playing, one after another. In the end, there were forty musicians on stage, playing a trance-inducing groove that just grew and grew. The whole stadium was swaying and dancing, it was fucking mesmerizing! The TV shook from the volume, and I rolled another joint. When the show ended, I looked at the clock.

It was eleven, FUCK!

I had missed the car to the GN'R show and missed the chance to play with the Guns and Ronnie Wood, oy vey…

I saw Duff McKagan, Dizzy Reed, and the GN'R roadies at breakfast. They died laughing when I told them why I hadn't shown up. "You thought it was a better idea to smoke weed and watch TV than play 'Honky Tonk Women' with Guns N' Roses and Ronnie?"

"Yeah…sorry…I got lost in space and time." The live telecast from Morocco had been unbelievably amazing. It left something simmering in my brain that finally came together in Mad Juana.

We sat in Slash's suite and went through "Magic Carpet Ride." One arrangement was close to the original version, and Michael and Little

Steven had arranged the other. Someone knocked on the door in the middle of rehearsal. I was closest and went to open the door. "'Ello mate, I'm Ronnie," Wood said as he stepped inside and plopped himself down on the couch across from me. He poured himself a pint of Smirnoff with a splash of cranberry juice. "Just for the color, mate!"

We kept going over the arrangements. I noticed that Ronnie was checking out my playing. Totally surreal—Wood himself was a badass bass player, he had played bass on the unreal Jeff Beck group album *Truth* and of course as the guitarist in the Faces and Stones. Someone else knocked on the door. Jo, Ronnie's wife, came in. Ronnie shoved the pint of vodka in front of me faster than lightning, winked, and stood up. "'Ello, darlin'!"

Ronnie was going home to Ireland in a few hours; his birthday was the next day. Apparently artists that live in Ireland only have a minimal tax rate. Ireland is one of the few countries to understand the worth and necessity of art, that art is the communal psychiatrist of society and that the people who create it should be supported.

The Guns' producer, Mike Clink, sat behind the console at Olympic Studio while we went through the arrangements. We nailed the first version by the third take. The second version went just as painlessly. Slash started to record the guitars. I parked myself on the sofa with the drummer Kenny Aronoff, he snapped open his black briefcase and pulled out a bottle of Jack Daniels. We sat back and enjoyed the music.

The studio's phone rang. Slash answered. "Yeah, he's a good guy... yes...very good player...sure, I'll tell him."

Slash hung up and told me that Ronnie Wood had called and asked for my number. "He's gonna suggest you as a new bass player for the Stones."

..........What?

Bill Wyman had just left the band. I'd caught Ronnie's inspecting eye at the rehearsal in the hotel suite.

I cursed Slash for telling me because now I wouldn't be able to sleep at night. I wanted to get the whole thing out of my head. I didn't hear a thing from the Stones or anyone, and a few months later, the Rolling Stones announced Darryl Jones as their new bassist. Apparently Charlie Watts got to make the call, which makes sense.

×××

When we got back from London, Michael and I started planning next steps for life after *Jerusalem Slim*. We couldn't afford another mistake like that one. Next, we'd make the punk record that *Jerusalem Slim* was supposed to be. A raw, scruffy record with superb songs and simple production. We'd try to forget the cursed last couple of years and go forward. Michael's good buddy, the legendary Little Steven, was ready to collaborate. We stressed that we only wanted one guitarist, one guitar in the band. We sat with Little Steven for a dinner at an Indian restaurant called Nirvana and talked about fucking Mötley Crüe, how the good die young, and how those who should really die instead live forever. "Scum lives on," I mumbled. That stuck in Michael's and Little Steven's ears, a song came out of what I'd mumbled a year or so later.

It's sometimes funny how songwriters suddenly own what other people say. "Yeah, it was me who said 'Scum Lives On.'" Listen up: no, you didn't…

I came up with the band name again. I was walking to the Eighth Street subway station on a gray and rainy day, and I passed a Barnes & Noble, then the biggest bookstore in Lower Manhattan. I could feel someone staring at me. I turned toward the bookstore and there, standing on the other side of the window display, was William S. Burroughs in a long coat. He was staring and smirking at me. I froze, but then I remembered that I had read that he would be reading at the bookstore. Even the weather was perfectly gray for the occasion. I had read a lot of Burroughs at that time, all his seminal works like *The Place of the Dead Roads*, *Junkie*, *Naked Lunch*, and *Exterminator*, which is where I had plucked out the term "Demolition 23." Michael and Little Steven thought it was good enough for a band name.

Little Steven suggested Paul Cook from the Sex Pistols as the drummer for Demolition 23. We didn't even reach out to him because I claimed to know that Cook wasn't playing anymore. We found out later on that this was not the case—my bad.

I suggested Rat Scabies from the Damned. I asked Rat to come out to New York for the week and said he could stay with me. We'd jam and see if it worked. Little Steven was filling in on guitar at this time.

We went to rehearse. We played Iggy's "1970," which the Damned had covered on their first record and Hanoi played at nearly every show. It became apparent that you can't tell Rat Scabies how to play; it's impossible. Rat's meter was Rat's meter, the same as Razzle, who idolized Rat.

The songs sounded different with Rat than we had thought. Some songs worked in their own way, but others, the straight rock songs, didn't work at all. Rat clearly had problems playing that kind of music. We were playing "Dead, Jail or Rock 'n' Roll" when Rat stopped playing in the middle to ask, "Excuse me, Michael, let me ask you a question. Did you just sing, 'I was the meanest dude on a meanest machine?'" Michael admitted, "Yes, that's the line."

"Sorry, mate." Rat let it drop. "Can't do that. I can't play with you."

Rat is also a songwriter and a lyricist. Rat-man cowrote classics like "Love Song" and seems to be one of the rare few drummers to be particular about lyrics in the songs he plays. "Meanest dude on a meanest machine" clearly did not meet the standards. It was the line that broke the camel's back, that was the end of his tryout. But no harm done, we all agreed that this was for the best, love Rat.

I spent the next couple of days walking around New York with Rat. Rat was very much into Freemasonry and its history. We spent hours walking around looking for Freemason symbols on the NYC buildings.

Rat's departure was approaching. He asked if he could stay for a few days more. Of course he could. When I woke up in the mornings, Rat was usually sitting on the sofa in the living room, already fully dressed. "Good morning, Sam. What shall we do today?" A proper English gentleman in mind and body. And so another day with Mr. Scabies would begin.

Days turned into weeks, and the man showed no signs of leaving. Rat crashed on my couch for nearly a month. Finally, I had to say: "Rat—GO HOME! Or start paying rent."

We found Jay Hening from Star Star to play guitar for Demolition 23. Jay was a nice guy from Lower Manhattan, a great rock 'n' roll guitarist, who was brought up on Steve Jones / Thunders / Mick Ronson and was in the same mindset regarding music as the rest of us. We played a benefit gig for our "office" friends, meaning the employees of the Telephone Bar & Grill.

It was Jay's first show with me and Michael, but it wasn't Demolition 23. quite yet. On that gig, Johnny Rao from David Johansen's band was on guitar and Thommy Price was on drums.

We asked Thommy to join us for good, but he was already in Joan Jett's band. Thommy suggested Jimmy Clark, a guy from Cleveland with a similar style who'd played with Debbie Harry and Scandal. Playing with Jimmy clicked right away. Now we had all the pieces together.

We rehearsed in a rundown dump on Avenue B in Alphabet City. The owner was a crossdresser, super nice guy whose name escapes me. He hung out there while we rehearsed with his thirteen-foot python snake. "By the way, if you go to the bathroom, my snake's in there, I just gave it a shower. But don't worry, it's been fed." One time, the snake didn't eat the rat it had been served, but chomped on its owner's hand and started to swallow it. It was a bit of an ordeal trying to get the arm out from the uncooperative snake's mouth.

Over the course of long days writing and practicing, it became clear that Hening was a bit of a mess, with violent mood swings, manic depression. And he seemed to have a drug problem too. Jay was taking lithium for bipolar disorder, but he complained that lithium dulled his feelings and got in the way of his musical creativity. So Jay decided to stop taking lithium and to self-medicate with heroin instead. It was just one big roller coaster from there. Jay would show up at my place in the middle of the night—"Gotta talk. Gotta talk."—and just cry…it was sad beyond belief. Jay managed to stay in more or less okay shape for practice, though.

Little Steven hooked us up with a weekly gig on Fourth Avenue at the former Cat Club, which was now known as Grand. We played covers as well as our own songs every Wednesday night, and a special guest star always joined us on stage for the end of the set. We played Ramones songs with Joey and some Mott the Hoople songs with Ian Hunter.

Had to be careful with Ian Hunter. "All the Young Dudes" and "Roll Away the Stone" both start with a descending chord change, but with one little difference: If I remember correctly, one goes from C to B, and the other from C to B flat. Everything went okay at soundcheck, but at the gig

I fucked up the half note. After the song, Ian walked over to me on stage, pushed his sunglasses down, and said, "One-nil, mate."

Other special guests at our Wednesday night shows were Kory Clarke from Warrior Soul, Bobby Steele from the Misfits, Walter Lure from the Heartbreakers, and Sebastian Bach. We did NOT play Skid Row songs with Sebastian Bach, we played Hanoi songs instead because Sebastian was a fan. The thing took on a life of its own, word spread, and Grand started to get pretty full on Wednesday nights. The Grand connection strengthened us as a band, because it was a regular gig and our repertoire grew quickly.

When I came to soundcheck for our third Wednesday night show, there was some scaffolding on stage at Grand. But it wasn't scaffolding after all. Jimmy Clark had bought this fucking weird thing for his drums, some kinda metal tubing that went around the drums that you could screw the toms and cymbals onto. It was the ugliest damn thing to hold your drums together imaginable, like the drum version of a stick bass. If that weren't bad enough, it was white.

I was horrified. Jimmy was made of a different fiber than the rest of us, after all. "Take it down, Jimmy!" Michael agreed. Little Steven showed up and saw this children's playpen. "No no no—WHAT'S THAT?" Jimmy got real upset, he had a short fuse—fuck you, everybody!—but started to tear the stuff down and set up his normal drum kit. "Are you happy now?"

The new hot thing in NYC's East Village rock 'n' roll was D Generation. They'd just signed a deal with Columbia but hadn't gotten the advance yet, so they were just hanging around at Grand, broke. I got to know the guys: Jesse Malin, Danny Sage, and Ricky Bacchus. They always came to say hi backstage before the show, and when we got up on stage, we always expected that Jesse, Danny, and Ricky would join the crowd from the backstage. But they wouldn't; they'd just stay in the back drinking our booze. This happened quite a few times. It was so shameless that it was almost funny. I ended up hanging out and playing with Jesse Malin and Ricky Bacchus in the 2000s, when D Generation had broken up and Jesse had gone solo.

There was an after-hours club on St. Mark's Place that opened at four when all the bars closed, a total cokehead hangout. People openly did lines on the tables. The speakeasy owner bribed the cops to let the place operate in peace as long as there was no trouble.

I was sitting in the club on one very early morning after staying up all night. I got up and walked downstairs to the bathroom; there were two toilets next to each other, ladies' and gents'. I pissed in peace until three shots rang out in the next toilet over. I started considering through my brain fog if I should just stay in and be completely silent. The second option was to kick the door open, leap up the stairs, and run out into the sunny street. My option was the second one. The club cleared out in seconds, and there were little baggies abandoned all over the tables and floor. Everyone had emptied their pockets while leaving, knowing that the cops would show up. Gunshots weren't exactly an uncommon event in the East Village, but it's a bit of a rude awakening when it comes from the next bathroom.

×××

My personal life was quickly going down the drain. After the honeymoon period of the first year ended, our love story turned into endless pain and insanity. I was trying to help my wife out any way I could during those years: by talking with her, supporting her, looking for a psychiatrist. She did end up in the hospital a few times from self-destructive behavior.

S came back home from the hospital and was okay until she fell back into drinking and other bad habits. Then she settled down again. It was a roller coaster. Our relationship was heading to a really dark place. I realized that I couldn't help her in any way, we were not good for each other, and that she needed professional help.

We divorced in the fall.

×××

We now had enough songs and went to the studio to record at the end of the year. The record would come out on Little Steven's Renegade Nation label, except in Japan, where it would come out on PolyGram through Michael's deal.

Demolition 23.—there's a period after the number—was recorded at Power Station in NYC with Little Steven producing. The studio was a very good, world-class joint. The main room is more or less round, but the window wall to the control room is straight. The drums were placed toward the center of the room, but not exactly in the center, and the amps were behind isolation booths. It took three or four days to record the backing tracks. We concentrated on the band performance, trying to get just THAT take. I remember clearly that when we played "Endangered Species," a super fast UK Subs song, we were very tight as a band thanks to those shows at Grand. Jimmy counted it in, we played the shit out of it, and that was it, a one-take wonder.

There are always random people hanging around during recording. The word always spreads and tempts people to show up. Michael Stipe and T.M. Stevens, who were friends with Little Steven and were working in another studio room at the Power Station, showed up to hang a bit. The pace we were recording at was so fast that we got out of Power Station pretty quickly. Michael sang everything in pretty much one day. That's how an R&R record should be done.

1994

Demolition 23.

I was single again. I wasn't up for another relationship and definitely wasn't looking. In January, I went out to say hi to a friend who was DJing at Webster Hall—it had been the Ritz ten years earlier and was where I had been spotted smoking a joint by the Finnnish tabloids.

Webster Hall was pretty tired that night. There was a fat, hairy Kiss cover band from Brooklyn swaying on the stage, butchering Kiss songs. Another friend of mine, this French guy, Patrick, was out with a couple of ladies. He asked if I wanted to join them for a drink somewhere else. I said no because I was thinking of heading home. Patrick kept bugging me and I finally relented and agreed to a beer.

Patrick's friends were Karmen Guy and her cousin Brittany, who was visiting from Iowa. I started talking with Karmen, and before long, we were talking about everything we were both interested in: music, art, literature, philosophy, the Second World War. We couldn't stop talking. The four of us walked back to Karmen's on Eleventh Street, and the conversation kept going. I fell asleep on her floor, and went home when I woke up. I couldn't get her out of my mind. I called Karmen that afternoon, and we met up again.

I felt like I'd met a kindred spirit in Karmen. She was a very interesting and smart person, curious about the world and humanity. We started sharing books and making mixed tapes for each other. Karmen started throwing poetry books at me, and I slowly got into it. Rilke's *Solitude*, his brief ruminations on loneliness, knocked me out. I made Karmen mixes with flamenco, Tom Waits, and the Velvet Underground, and she made me ones with Sonic Youth, Glenn Branca, and Napalm Death. I brought her to see Cecil Taylor and Reggie Workman at the Village Vanguard and blues on Bleecker Street.

We checked out the cultural offerings of the East Village together. You never knew what you were about to walk into. There was always some special event happening at the back of a bar, and there was always some luminary like Jim Jarmusch standing next to you.

The bums of downtown had some pretty ingenious methods to make some cash. The "woodman" tied branches to his head and body, you could see him a mile away, a walking tree waving his cup around the Lower East Side. The "photographer" had made a Polaroid camera out of water bottles; he'd aim, say "cheese" and "click," mime the photo developing, and then show off the imaginary picture. "Fifty cents, please."

One performance artist guy at Mona's had put eight tape players out onto a table. He'd press record on the first and repeat "works…works… works" for two minutes, then record "works…works…works" on the next, then go back to the first tape, rewind, and press play. The end result was a rhythm, an incredible mass of sound twirling and changing, the word "works" merged together into a mass of bouncing vowels and somersaulting consonants. Pure magic

The Gas Station was a punk bar converted from an actual gas station on the corner of Avenue B and Second Street. The façade was the joint project of made out of scrap metal by three speed freak welder artists: bicycles, bathtubs, umbrellas, reading lamps, sewage pipes, barbed wire, you name it, everything was welded together. Depending on what the owner had gotten for free or cheap, the Gas Station had either Cheese Fest or Bud Fest: "$5 All You Can Eat Cheese" or "$8 All You Can Drink Bud." There were hardcore punk matinees from one in the afternoon until eight, filled with either cheese plates or Budweiser cans, bands playing one after another.

Karmen wrote poems and sang. Or maybe more accurately, she'd bellow out her poems and improvise vocals on her dad's old Fender Tremolux amp—reverb and tremolo dialed all the way up. Her tone was amazing and hoarse with power and depth. I had gotten sick of listening to the same old music and was craving something unexpected, something new. It's no surprise that we started to write together and see where it went. There was no place for traditional song conventions in our writing. It was outside of the box, open-minded, all inspired by the world around us.

Patrick, who Karmen introduced me to, joined as our drummer, but he didn't stick around for too long because he wanted to play Red Hot Chili Pepperish style skate funk music, which didn't really mesh with our ideas. Harri Kupiainen from Piss Factory joined on guitar, and he brought along his friend Johnny Tirado. The Finnish contingent kept growing with the addition of Maukka Palmio on drums. We got some songs together and went to the studio to record a cover of Patsy Cline's "Crazy." We turned it into a droney version that ended up being closer to the Velvet Underground than country. The legendary Nite Bob was our sound engineer; he'd worked with MC5, the Stooges, Aerosmith, Kiss, you name it. He knew Michael as well from *Not Fakin' It* days.

We called the band Lewd Vagrant and played some shows around the Lower East Side when Demolition 23. wasn't busy. Karmen and I had been in love for months when she moved in with me at St. Mark's Place.

×××

It was fall and the record release was approaching. Little Steven asked me to draw a homemade logo for the cover of *Demolition 23*. He got what he asked for: the text gets smaller and smaller all the way to the edge. That's the beauty of it, that it's not perfect. After that, I drew a logo for Little Steven's Renegade Nation: a skull wearing a Southern cowboy hat with feathers. Steven still uses that logo.

I'd started to work a bit on the other side of the board too in the studio. Mercer Street had Sorcerer Sound studio, where I worked a few times as an assistant engineer. The engineer, Patrick Derivas, who'd played bass on a lot of Tom Verlaine's records, showed me the ropes around the studio, I sat in on a lot of sessions. I recorded, mixed, and produced the Dogtown Balladeers' first EP, *A Tale Worth Hearing*, together with Patrick, and later on their full length, *Antique Wine and Roses*, which came out in 1996. It's a great blues rock album a la Faces, but the Dogtown Balladeers weren't made to last; a follow-up never appeared.

The dark cycle seemed to be over. Life was interesting again, the tour was starting in three weeks, and *Demolition 23.* was a really solid great album that I was very proud of. I thought that finally everything was moving forward. It's still one of my favorite records, because it's grounded in simple songs that just work. Nothing unnecessary was squeezed in at the studio.

Then Michael called. Bad, bad news. Jay Hening had been run over by a van while fucked up. He'd been coming out of his dealer's place on Avenue C and had stepped into the street without looking. His femur was broken.

Now what? We were down a guitarist, our ONLY guitarist, but canceling the tour wasn't really a great idea with the record coming out on October 10. We had to get Nasty Suicide. Nasse was our first choice, because the Japan tour a couple years earlier had worked out really well. He agreed, and we flew out to London, where we had our first show, to rehearse.

Me, Nasty, and Jimmy rehearsed in London for a couple of days, just the three of us. Nasty had learned the songs ahead of time. There were some questions in some places, but things seemed to be in good enough order for us to play through the whole set twice; then we went out to the pub and closed out the night there. We repeated the whole thing the next day: run through the songs twice and then some pints.

Then Michael flew in, we went through the set twice, and Michael went to the hotel to take care of his jet lag. The three of us went out to the pub.

The London Palladium was a big space on Tottenham Court Road. It held up to a couple thousand people. Even though things had sounded good at the rehearsal, at the gig, it was like some big clam monster had shown up. We grinned and bore it to the end through the mistakes and decided to do a long soundcheck at the next venue.

It had been our habit to go to the pub first and have a few beers and then go rehearse, you know, get ready. Four or five beers later, someone was sure to ask again: Hey, are you thirsty? We had clearly now practiced drinking beers more than our set. Rehearsals are a different ball game than performances. There's no adrenaline rush at the practice studio, and you can always stop and start over. The set has to be hammered right into the spine so it stays in your physical being. And after all, it was no easy thing for Nasty to get into things. He was used to being mostly the rhythm guitarist, like Malcolm Young, now he was thrust into playing lead plus taking care of the rhythm, one-man guitar band is a whole different thing all together. It takes a different style of play, and even the slightest fuck-up sticks out like a sore big toe. I liked that there was more space than when there were two guitars playing but the sole guitarist had to be REALLY on it.

We played a couple of shows in Finland. The set started to flow, and with the good amount of gigs and rehearsals under our belts, we flew to Japan. The fans are loyal in good old Nippon, they stick with a band and its members for years, following them from lineup to lineup. The tour was a success, every night sold out. Michael locked himself in his room after each show as usual, and the rest of us would head out. Nasty was physically in fighting shape; he'd been living clean for a while now and had picked up budo. But he would still join in the merrymaking with the band.

1995

Michael moves to Finland

Demolition 23. played some shows in Finland and Sweden in February. The morale had turned bad. Nasty couldn't stand how Michael waved the mike or mike stand around on stage, it sometimes got a little too close to the guitar, missing it by an inch. It didn't bother me; I was already used to it, and I kept an eye on it, so I wouldn't end up in harm's way. Michael was usually really in control on stage anyway.

Nasty was more uptight than usual otherwise. He was not having a good time. And then, Malmö. The stand came crashing down on the guitar. It was the first and only time it happened. To make matters worse, it wasn't Nasty's own guitar, but one borrowed from Darrell Bath, an old fifties Les Paul Junior, a piece of wood worth a lot of money, and it's not really about money, you find a guitar like that it becomes your treasure.

Nasty lost it. Michael made the mistake of not taking what happened seriously. "That's what might happen when you're on the stage with me." He wouldn't apologize to Nasty.

The bad fucking vibe stuck around and obviously affected everyone else. Our last show was in Gothenburg. There was a black cloud hanging over soundcheck, but no one, definitely not Michael in any case, did anything to make the situation any better. I walked to the hotel with Nasty after soundcheck and asked him what's up. Nasty was still pissed off about the whole thing; he wanted to quit the band, quit playing entirely, and start teaching. I called Michael from the hotel room: "Hey, you gotta call and talk to Nasty, because he wants to get packing." To this day, I don't know if Michael did talk to Nasty.

We banged out the show like it was our last, which it was. The opener was a young band from Sweden called Backyard Babies. That was the first time I met young Dregen.

Nasty flew out to London the next day, and the rest of the band flew back to New York. Nasty confirmed that he would not be continuing with the band. We checked out some guitarists, but none of them were right. Michael disappeared from the face of the Earth; he stopped answering the phone and became a hermit.

Weeks later, Michael announced that he was moving back to Finland. That was a total surprise—Monroe going back to Finland. How was I supposed to respond to that? I was losing my blood brother. The news permanently ended the story of Demolition 23.

I had to start working selling tapes and CDs in St. Mark's Place for a while after Michael left NYC to have some money to live off of and pay the rent. Demolition 23. wasn't exactly a cash cow. It wasn't a real record store, just a stand on the street. Julius was something of a well-known character who only sold bootleg recordings: bootleg tapes, records, CDs, and live videos. One day Perry Farrell showed up to rifle through the crates and found a Jane's Addiction bootleg. He was pissed off. "You're making money off my music!" We had run into each other a long time before, and Perry didn't recognize me. I didn't introduce myself, I just put my hands up. "Ahh, well you know…gotta make a livin'…"

The difference between bootleg and pirated recordings is pretty clear. Bootlegs have rare stuff, often live recordings, stuff that hasn't officially been released that only the hardcore fans are interested in, whereas pirated recordings are just illegal copies of official releases. Bootleg collectors usually pick up the official releases as well but want to have a complete collection of their favorite artists. Labels have gotten wise to this nowadays and release the most in-demand rarities officially. Bootlegging the bootleggers.

Writing songs with Karmen had continued alongside Demolition 23. We had tried out all kinds of stuff, like the William Burroughs cut-up method: We wrote a three-page story and cut out words and lines from it. We experimented with noise and feedback and went to see Thurston Moore's solo shows, William Parker Jr., Rashied Ali, at this club called the Cooler in the Meatpacking District...we absorbed all these influences like sponges. I had been doing R&R for fifteen years, and I was getting bored. I loved Demolition 23., though, and was heartbroken that it fell apart.

I really wanted to learn how to write music and play new instruments. New York is wonderful and plentiful, but it's expensive, and it can wear you down. It's hard to make a living there. The rock scene in New York felt dead to me. I just wasn't interested anymore. Karmen and I started planning a move to Spain. Life was less expensive there, and it would be a chance for new ideas and new music.

Some money from the Japanese record sales showed up in my bank account. It was enough money to pay for the moving costs and settle into the new place without having to think about how we'd make ends meet for some months.

I sent my records, books, and instruments by air freight. My sister found us a place in an area called El Toro; we could stay there until we found our own house. In May, Karmen and I drove to Newark with our Dobermann Greta and a new Yamaha 8 Track cassette recorder—top of the line for portable recording.

We had to sedate Greta before the flight. We gave her a sleeping pill in a piece of ham and put the kennel in the cargo hold. We had a layover in Madrid and were able to get her from the hold to give her water, some food, and hang out with her until our flight to Palma de Mallorca. We gave her another, lighter sedative. We checked again that all the information, stickers, addresses were right, and we handed Greta over to the airline staff.

1995–1997

Spain

"A big circle formed.
I wasn't playing any songs I knew;
I was just improvising it all,
but in less than three hours,
I'd collected enough money for three months' rent."

1995

Montuïri

We waited for our luggage and Greta at the Palma de Mallorca airport. It was two in the afternoon. Our bags came, but there was no sign of the kennel. We found the lost luggage office and reported our dog missing. We were brought to another office, where there was a bureaucrat smoking cigarettes; he stopped joking around with his coworker to take down our info. But then he didn't do anything with it, no fax, no phone call, just kept bullshitting with his buddy and smoking cigarettes. I sat there for five minutes, and then I asked what was going on. "Tranquillo." I clenched my teeth and waited another five minutes. More cigarettes, more cackling.

I got up, walked around the table, and shouted that he get on the fucking phone and start sending some faxes now, because he was going to find my fucking dog.

Now the fat man got to work. In fifteen minutes, he found out that the ground crew had mixed up their Palmas. Poor Greta had ended up on a plane going to the Canary Islands, to Las Palmas instead of Palma de Mallorca. Greta wouldn't arrive until midnight. That many hours alone in a crate couldn't be good for a dog. I was told that Greta would get a walk and would be given food and water.

We waited. At midnight, we went back to the airport baggage claim, and there on the conveyor belt was the kennel. I opened the door, and Greta jumped out, in good spirits and happy to finally see us.

The apartment my sister had found was in El Toro, at the tip of the cape just outside of Palma. There was a view of the sea, and it was a two-minute walk to the beach, fifteen minutes to my sister's, and half an hour away from Palma. It was next to the pinewoods and there was a nice little bar on the ground floor of the building, where we could go for food and wine. El Toro was small and quiet and mostly shut down by midnight except for a couple of bars. Worked well for me. The air was fresh and clean. I did not miss the stench, rain, or chaos of New York.

We got started making music right away, even though we were living in an apartment building. We wanted to find our own house so we could make as much noise as we wanted. Sometimes we'd bring the acoustic guitar down to the bar and play some songs in exchange for wine or cognac for the rest of the night.

Mallorca's casino was a few miles away, in Sol de Mallorca, where my sister lived, but the casino's seasonal workers lived in El Toro. There were dancers, fire eaters, horse riders, and musicians hanging all around us. We hung out with a member of the Four Tops, Edward Butler. Three of the four Tops were touring Spain at the time. Some incarnations of the Spinners and the Temptations were also touring the world. Is any one version more original or any better than the other? At first, there were fights over name rights, but a deal was struck. Everyone would mind their own business and no one would move in on anyone else's territory. It's just a question of survival.

We found the right house in the middle of the island in the fall. It was in a village called Montuïri. When we showed up in the village for the first time, the old ladies ran inside their houses and closed their shutters.

The two-hundred-year-old house had stone walls a couple of feet thick. There was a well in the corner of the living room where there was actual groundwater. When you hauled up a bucket, you'd get the best-tasting water you ever tasted. We started to grow tomatoes, chili peppers, garlic, roses, and basil in the little garden in the backyard. And a bit of weed too. Four big plants to be precise. You could grow up to five plants legally in Mallorca. When it was time for harvest, the whole village knew. You could smell the skunk blocks away.

We bought cheese from the cheese shop, meat from the butcher, and vegetables from the farmers' market that happened twice a week. The market opened early in the morning, when Karmen got there it was packed. Some old lady with a broomstick in her hand would poke Karmen out of the way—my turn!

Silence prevailed in Montuïri…until we showed up with all our music gear. I built up our home studio and recorded ideas and bits of songs every day. We could get Algerian and Moroccan stations on the radio. Before long, we were creating our own mix of flamenco, Arabic music, rock, and Celtic music. I mixed unlikely instruments together, like a toy accordion played through a wah-wah pedal. I experimented with different kinds of guitar tunings to see what would happen. I tuned all the strings on a guitar to E and played it with a slide as accompaniment to the Algerian radio station, refreshing myself on the pentatonic scales. Karmen wrote poems and stories, which ended up becoming lyrics. Some of the texts were based on conversations we'd had. I've mostly been a co-writer; I couldn't write songs on my own yet, and I definitely was not any good with lyrics. I've always listened more to the music than lyrics. Music has a magic on its own. I do appreciate great lyricists though, they come in all shapes and colors. I have recently started to write songs on my own, better late than never.

One day, I was sitting in the home studio feedbacking my guitar through the Fender Tremolux, when I heard a banging on the front door. There was a guy in a morning robe standing outside on the street. "Por fa-vor! Si-es-ta!" "Oh, sorry, I woke you up?" "Yes, look, any other time—no problem. But NOT during the siesta!"

Siesta is from two until five in the afternoon; you make a big lunch, stuff it into your face, and then go take a nap. This heavy lunch is basically the main meal of the day. Chicken and fries, salad, bread, aioli, olives, and a couple glasses of wine. You get terrible nightmares, really psychedelic ones, going to sleep after a big meal like that. It was thanks to siesta that I gained a deeper understanding of Picasso, Joan Miró, and Dalí; you dream all kinds of stuff after eating a big lunch. It's no surprise that their work turned out the way it did.

I thought I was learning Spanish in Montuïri, but turns out I was hearing Mallorcan, which is a dialect of Catalan. Montuïris' accent is a really heavy accent. Each village has its own accents that people recognize right away. These days, regional dialects are disappearing since people move around so much, and most people have internet at home. Supposedly there was a ninety-year-old woman in Montuïri that had never even seen the sea. She'd been born around 1905 and had lived in the same village throughout the twentieth century, but she'd never been to the coast even though she lived on an island and her native village was fifteen miles from the nearest beach. Strange stuff.

There was only one other foreigner living in Montuïri besides us. Harry was born in India and had worked as Elizabeth Taylor and Richard Burton's personal chef in the seventies. He worked as a butler for a German millionaire later on. Harry was semi-retired when we met him. He invited us over for dinner. After the meal and some wine, Harry asked us if we'd like to play a game. What game? He brought out a huge sack filled with coins. The sack was full of money from all around the world, and we'd have to pull out a coin, then toss it at the right country on the huge map posted to the wall.

We took turns tossing coins—Isn't it somewhere over there?—and tried our best to aim. The night ended when Harry grabbed a handful of money and sang, "New York, New York." He raised his hand: *"If I can make it there, I can make it…ANYWHERE!"* BAM! The coins hit the floor scattered all over the room. *"IT'S UP TO YOU!"*

Harry told us that he believed he was Juana la Loca, the reincarnation of Mad Juana, the sixteenth-century Spanish queen, born again. Karmen and I looked at each other. No way. Just recently we'd found the name for our band in Patti Smith's poem in the book *Babel*: "Mad Juana."

Sometimes there'd be a knock at the door, and when we'd open it, there'd be nobody around but veggie curry on our steps. Harry would bring us food and would run away. When the moon was full, Harry ran out to the field and howled under it.

The other summer, Karmen went to Mallorca and Montuïri; Harry was still living there. Our Mad Juana is almost blind now.

1996

Vinegar Blood

I was painting a lot. I was again using colors and working on paintings for the first time in a long time. The slower pace of life gave me the chance to focus on things for days or weeks, my attention span wasn't constantly being distracted by hanging out with people or other temptations or bad living. I listened to PJ Harvey's *To Bring You My Love* and Nick Cave's *Murder Ballads* a lot.

Nasty Suicide called me up at the beginning of the year. He had gone back to being Jan Stenfors. Nasty got sick of his stage name back in the Hanoi days and tried to get us to call him Nigel at one point. "Just call me Nigel." But it didn't stick. Nigel sounds like a freckled cyclist's name. Or if he was sick of Suicide, why not Nasty Sewersmell?

Jan Stenfors had called because he was making a solo record and he wanted me to play on it. The record would come out in the spring, and there would be a Finnish tour after. Sure thing; I was more than happy to make the record and go on tour with the old chap.

Tiina Vuorinen, a friend from the Johanna label and the grande dame of the Finnish music business, came to Mallorca for vacation and stopped by to visit us. Over dinner, I put on a tape of Karmen's and my recordings, about a dozen or so songs. Tiina stopped to listen; I told her that Karmen and I had been tinkering around with this stuff for about two years now. Tiina took the tape and gave it to Riku Pääkkönen, who was getting his label, Spinefarm Records, started. Spine hadn't become the full-blooded metal label yet, and Riku was interested in releasing a Mad Juana record. We agreed to come to Finland to record in the summer.

Then it was Michael Monroe's turn to hit me up. He had made a deal with Poko Records and asked me to play on his record. All of a sudden, I was in demand again. I let him know that I'd agreed to play on Nasty's album and would be touring with him too. Michael was irritated that I was doing business with the guy who'd left us high and dry in Gothenburg. I answered that: Hey homie, I haven't heard a thing from you, not a single word in well over a year. So don't you start with me, buddy boy. Michael's wife, Jude, got on the phone and started barking at me—"Where's your loyalty…?"—that kind of thing. I hadn't gotten any signs of life from the couple for a year, but then I'm supposed to be ready to jump on board with him at a moment's notice, weird stuff. I suggested Michael cut a deal with Nasty: They could split my expenses. I'd record Nasty's album and would stay in Finland to make Michael's. Michael was offended by the suggestion.

We didn't talk for a while because of this.

×××

Jan Stenfors's *Vinegar Blood* came out. The production was good and basic, no gimmicks, no eighties snare. The record got some attention as Nasty's comeback, and he had TV interviews and all that. Nasty had been writing songs for a long time; it had only been a couple years since Cheap or Nasty, and the last Demolition 23. show was even more recent than that. Dropping his stage name was a new thing though, a tough one; everyone knew him as Nasty, not as Jan.

After the tour, Nasty got out of music, went back to school, and became a pharmacist. At first, he was going to become a large-animal veterinarian, since his big brother had been around horses his whole life. But when Nasty had to stick his arm shoulder-deep inside a cow ass and feel around which way the calf was facing, he changed his mind.

We got some money from the Finnish government for our recording, plus we got some cash from Spinefarm too. It was enough to fly to Finland for a couple of weeks in September to make the Mad Juana record. Hombre Lampinen produced it in his studio in Tikkurila, Vantaa, just outside of Helsinki. The budget was so small that we slept on my mom's couch in nearby Kerava and took the commuter train to Tikkurila.

Day after day, we dutifully paid for our train tickets, but we'd never see the ticket inspectors. We decided to go without them one day and of course that was the day the inspectors came by. I took out my New York ID and spoke Finnish badly. "Sure, I was born in Finland, but I moved away a long time ago. I thought the trains were free of charge, you guys sure are ahead of times!" The inspector answered angrily that traveling in Finland absolutely wasn't free. We got off without a ticket though.

Recording took ten days. We ended up using a lot of the home recordings from Spain. A lot of the songs originated from a specific moment, with a specific vibe, in a dark cave-like room in the middle of the night. We couldn't replicate the wah-wah toy accordion or the wah-wah bongo in the studio, the magic wasn't there. We definitely tried everything at first, but it was the wrong way of going about it. We had to take into consideration what was the most important element. Sometimes that element was already on one of the cassettes, sometimes we found it in the studio. Affe Forsman handled drums and percussion, Karmen sang, and I played all the other instruments. Jimi Sumén did the final mix, and thus, the first Mad Juana album was born.

×××

We went back to Mallorca and began putting together the actual band for Mad Juana. The first step in our plans was to tour at least Finland. Johnny Tirado and Maukka Palmio who had played in Lewd Vagrant came out from New York to Mallorca to try out, but it just didn't work out. In the end, Johnny just wanted to make straight indie rock and Maukka tagged along with him. They moved to Palma and won a band competition there.

It wasn't any better with local musicians. They weren't serious about playing; soccer and food were more important. I tried to suggest rehearsing at two o'clock, they looked at me like I was crazy: Are you kidding?

That's siesta. Four didn't work either, and soccer games would come on at six. The same thing every day. It was impossible.

We played a couple gigs around the island. It wasn't possible to make a living on that pay and the handful of shows. Our unhurried absorption of influences and artistic experiments were about to end because we were running the risk of running out of savings.

There was a direct ferry to Barcelona from Mallorca. We started to think about moving. Barcelona was a good-sized city, and it was on the mainland. We'd find more potential musicians and opportunities to play shows there.

1997

Skin of My Teeth & Live (At the Bluesville)

Spinefarm released *Skin of My Teeth* in the beginning of the year. The record only came out in Finland. I had cut my hair short and used my real name on the record, a la Jan Stenfors. No one knew who the fuck Sami Takamäki was, so the result was poor record sales. It got good reviews, though, and is still one my favorites. In any case, *Skin of My Teeth* was one of Spinefarm's first releases, and the manager of the label later said that it was the best thing they ever put out.

The figures on the inside of the record sleeve are close-ups of my dad's paintings. Dad had let me pick out what I wanted. I was really into the weird characters with big feet; maybe they were actually spirits.

Karmen and I moved to Barcelona in March. We found a cheap apartment in the Old Town, next to La Rambla. It was a touristy area, and I decided to try to make some money busking. I brought out an acoustic guitar, a slide, and a battery-powered amp, a Pignose, and sat down on my guitar case and started improvising some blues. Rushed footsteps slowed down, and coins flew into the hat at my feet. I went home with a hat full of money and brought Karmen out to eat. We could stay in Barcelona for a while, no problem.

Maukka Palmio called me in April when I happened to be in Mallorca and said, "Help, I'm panicking!" Maukka played in Pep Banyo and the Blue Devils, an old-school blues band in Mallorca. They had a live recording the next day and their bassist had disappeared, fucking over the band. I agreed to step in and had to learn forty or so songs overnight. Mostly Howlin' Wolf, Little Walter, and Muddy Waters. I stayed up until noon, took a little nap, and traveled out to Palma. We got it all together and I played on the live recording.

Pep Banyo means more or less "Bathroom Pepe." The sixty-year-old "Guru of Mallorca Blues" has a raspy voice and a strong Spanish attitude. It's a surprisingly good combination. The name of the album is *Live at the Bluesville*, or just *Live*. Bluesville was a dark and hazy club where the crowd smoked so much weed that you couldn't see your own hand through the thick smoke. You'd get a contact high just from breathing the air.

I played on the street in Barcelona almost every day, once in the afternoon and once in the evening. I was armed with the little Pignose amp and a miked acoustic guitar that was tuned to open G. I definitely wasn't playing "Hey Joe" or anything well-known, I just improvised. The money was good all the same, especially during the summer tourist season.

My improvisation and tempo depended on my mood and the conditions: if it was hot, if there were people watching, if it was day or night. I couldn't be bothered with the fast tempo stuff in the heat. Some chord progressions started to show up in the daily improvisations over and over again, they'd develop over time and eventually would turn into actual songs for Mad Juana.

Barcelona had great concerts and museums; good, cheap food; and the rents were still okay. Manu Chao's band played weekly gigs right around the corner in Raval. We still recorded at home, and the influence of our environment meant that we were getting more of a dub and groove influence.

A six-foot-plus, close to seventy-year-old crossdressing male prostitute with badly dyed blond hair hung out on our corner; cigarette dangling, bad boob job with one tit up to the shoulder, the second next to the belly button, and a prison tat peeking out through fishnet stockings. I had observed the clientele that would frequent this wonder.

One night, two Moroccan dudes walked up next to me on the street and tried to talk to me about soccer. I wasn't in the mood to talk; I could feel my wallet moving in my pocket. I was able to grab the thief by the wrist.

I yanked his nose up to my face and yelled at him to get lost in Spanish. I got my wallet back, and the guys beat it.

I would take Greta to the park, where she made friends with a little black dog. The little black dog lived with his owner in a tugboat. The guy kept to himself and didn't talk to anybody. He'd leave his dog in the park alone at sunset. Two women sat down on a park bench, and one of them put her purse on the ground. I happened to notice the little dog slowly creep toward the bench, grab the handle of the bag with its mouth, and then he took off running, disappearing into the Barcelona streets.

I saw the same thing again the next night. The man came back from his boat, and the dog a few minutes later. I went to tell him that his dog was a genius, I'd seen what he could do. The guy's face went pale. Things got a little uncomfortable when he knew I knew what was up. Then he told me that he'd trained his dog to steal because he was unemployed and had no money, but he didn't want to deal drugs. The smart dog had picked it up quickly; he would carry his spoils down the paths of Old Town to another park, where the guy had ridden his bike to wait.

I got some sad news in the spring: the original guitarist of Demolition 23., Jay Hening, had shot himself. Another wonderful human and musician lost. Jay couldn't find any relief from his bipolar condition. So, do you choose a balanced life without music, or the up and down seesaw of life while keeping the writing channels open? Jay didn't want to live without music. Self-medication with heroin didn't work for him either.

It doesn't work for anyone.

We weren't making any progress putting together the band for Mad Juana. Soccer was more important than music for the musicians in Barcelona too. One record label wanted to release *Skin of My Teeth* in Spain, but they got cold feet and bailed. It was also hard later on to find a label for Mad Juana, one that understood the band and the market, because our music doesn't fit into a neat little box. It might be a good thing for creativity to keep hitting your head against a wall, but nothing much was happening. We only got a couple weird gigs.

We'd been playing the streets of Barcelona for half a year. Our busking area was the Ramblas, Plaça del Pi, Plaça Reial. Greta was tied to the guitar case to guard the money. Karmen sang and played percussion. We had a loose set of songs and made a show of it. Different artists kept a schedule at Plaça Reial; it wasn't written down anywhere, you just had to know it.

The jugglers were first, then the fire eaters, and then it was time for the musicians. The 9–11 p.m. dinnertime slot was the most desirable. We started off playing at worse times, like eight or after midnight, until we made it to the moneymaking time slot.

After one night of playing, we went to our local bar, and I got recognized by four young dudes. I told them I was playing in Barcelona, just not a concert but on the streets, they looked baffled. I told 'em to come to Plaça Reial at nine to check it out. They were mildly surprised, but came with friends and followed us around all night.

I was playing at La Rambla one afternoon when this African guy stopped next to me. He was from Senegal, was also a street musician, and introduced himself as the Reggae Doctor. It was his first time in Barcelona, and he asked me about the ins and outs of playing on the street. I told him how it worked and the good spots to play at. I said there's plenty of room, except at Plaça Reial, it's kind of tight. I also told him that whatever you do, don't show up at Reial at nine, because that's my spot.

I was carrying my guitar to Plaça Reial the next night right before 9:00 p.m., and of course the first person I saw was Mr. Reggae Doctor. The guy was playing in front of the first bar—my spot. I tapped him on the shoulder: WTF man? "Fuck off mon," was his answer.

I punched him, and it turned into a fight that ended with other people getting involved. I was boiling with anger. Karmen dragged me away for a drink and to cool off.

Sipping on a cognac at a beach bar, I started thinking: Is this it? Is this where we've come to? These past couple of years had been eye-opening and fun, but fighting over a busking spot? Soon I'd be fighting with seagulls over a hot dog wrapper. It was time to go back to New York and put together a band with permanent members. New York knows no siesta.

We went back to Mallorca for a month. We sold all the stuff we didn't want to take back to the States at a market. The last thing to go was a chessboard made in India with elephants instead of horses. My sister's five and seven-year-olds had lost a rook, and it had been replaced with a Mr. Potato Head.

The chessboard buyer came back twenty minutes later and dug Mr. Potato Head out of the plastic bag. "Que es esto?" I answered, "Este es Señor Cabeza de Patata!"

The man disappeared into the crowd muttering obscenities.

1997–2001

New York City

"Who would have guessed
that the legendary seventies glam rock band,
the New York Dolls, would make a comeback at the beginning of the new millennium.
And that the comeback record would kick off with a Finn, Sami Takamäki's,
heavy bass line and a song he wrote."
(Jarkko Jokelainen, Helsingin Sanomat
July 8, 2006)

1997

A mattress on the street

It was the end of November when we came back to New York. We only had $400 in our pockets and no home. It was a rough landing. It was about five degrees out, colder than a well digger's ass, which just highlighted the fact that the easy sunny days were behind us. We stayed at our friend Erika Noise's place first; she was moving out at the end of the year, and there was an empty room for us. It was totally empty: no bed, not a single piece of furniture. We slept on a pile of our own clothes the first few nights until we found a mattress on the street and dragged it inside.

I looked for an apartment and spread the word with all the musicians I knew that I was back in town. Some random shows here and there came out of it, but the money didn't quite cut it. I'd gotten used to having my freedom in Mallorca, and I didn't really want to be a sideman with some band; I wanted to keep moving forward with Mad Juana. Which wasn't easy.

Karmen called through her own contacts and heard about a new restaurant opening up on Ludlow Street. Karmen is a go-getter and got the bartending gig at Torch. That would be some badly needed steady cash flowing in.

Torch was a mix of fine dining and live jazz. Their booking wasn't just normal jazz. You might see someone like Phoebe Legere there, who puts on quite a show...a very interesting artist. Harri Kupiainen hung out at Torch in his free time, since he worked slinging drinks at the next-door Motor City

Bar; he ended up being the guitarist for Mad Juana later on. We moved in with Harri for a while when we had to give up Erika's room.

Moving back to New York meant that we couldn't get by day to day just on change. We set aside money from bartending at Torch and from my royalty checks so we could save up for a down payment, which was three months' rent in New York back then.

1998

Lenny Kaye takes notice

We were crashing at Harri Kupiainen's place in January. One day, Karmen said that she saw Lenny Kaye go into the bodega. Lenny Kaye: the guitarist from Patti Smith Group! The man who compiled *Nuggets*! I happened to have some songs from *Skin of My Teeth* on me, and I took off running in the direction Karmen had pointed. I rounded the corner and bumped right into Lenny. "Uh…you don't know me—but!" I handed him the record, nervous and starstruck. Lenny was totally cool about it, though, and asked if Mad Juana was from the Patti Smith poem. "Yeah! Yeah, exactly!"

I met up with Lenny a week or so later. He said he'd listened to the record, and he'd never heard anything like it. He thought it was pretty amazing. And from there on out, Lenny was usually in the crowd during Mad Juana's Manhattan shows.

In February, Karmen and I moved out to Brooklyn, to the southern part of Williamsburg. The three-bedroom had wood floors, high ceilings, and an antique ceiling fan. The rent was cheap because of the awful stench. The last tenant had died in the apartment, and the body hadn't been found for two weeks. In that time, the man's forty cats had started to eat him out of hunger. And, of course, had shit all over the place. We made a deal with the landlord that we wouldn't pay the first month's rent in exchange for cleaning the apartment ourselves. Scrubbing and disinfecting the place took over a week. We had to paint over all the surfaces.

There were bullet holes in the windows. The neighborhood was very Dominican and Puerto Rican, and there was some gang activity back then. The second week, I woke up to a commotion in the street in the middle of the night. There were two or three hundred local youths jumping in three girls. They got the shit kicked and beaten out of them for at least five minutes. I watched the whole thing go down from between my curtains, from the window with the bullet holes.

A month later, a young guy got shot in the face just around the corner from us. The victim had just been passing by at the wrong place and wrong time and got shot. When Karmen came home in a cab from the night shift, I'd go down to meet her to make sure she'd get inside safely.

There was another Vietnam vet that lived below us; he got terrible nightmares and would scream out his torment in the middle of the night. I couldn't get away from Vietnam: The war had made its way into our Tapiola living room, my neighbor in LA had been a vet with hand grenades and guns on his wall, and now there was this shell-shocked guy who screamed in horror throughout the night.

I bought my first digital recording machine and a drum machine and started to mess around with it. Little by little, a new path was lighting up. Acoustic instruments dominated *Skin of My Teeth*, but it had its stoney moments too. We didn't want to make the next record with the same kind of vibe. If ideas take off in an unknown direction, it's best to follow them. It looked like this stuff was going to be more slowed down, groovier, and more bass heavy. I didn't listen to anything other than dub for a long while. I was also really into the Portishead record that had just come out and all that other Bristol stuff.

All the musical developments that had begun in Mallorca opened my mind and gave me self-confidence. I got to write music; I could write music; I was capable of writing music. We were starting to see exciting stuff happening in the New York scene, and Cooler, the little underground club in the Meatpacking District, came up as an important spot to hang out. Blonde Redhead was basically their house band. Thurston Moore would play improv on Monday nights, doing whatever he wanted with whoever he wanted.

1999

Bootä

Michael Monroe's former manager, Charlie Stettler, offered me some work. Charlie managed Jesse Camp, this nineteen-year-old kid who had won MTV's *Wanna Be a VJ*. Jesse had gotten a huge record deal—Gene Simmons had his hands in it somehow with a big investment—and the album was coming out in May. "This kid is the biggest Hanoi fan you'll ever find," Charles assured me. He asked me to put a band together get them rehearsing, and then head out on tour.

I agreed because I'd be getting paid a LOT per month, and the legendary Nite Bob would be coming along as the sound engineer. I met Jesse, a swan-like beanpole, and asked Todd Youth and Joe Rizzo to join the band. Jesse wanted his childhood friend Keith Robert on guitar, who thought Ace Frehley was God. The record—*Jesse & the 8th Street Kids*—was bursting with big-name busy people that were a bit out of the question for touring.

We arranged the string and keyboard parts from the record and made the songs work live with the traditional two guitar, bass, drums setup. Jesse had a lot of MTV obligations, so we rehearsed without him. And when Jesse finally did make it to practice and started singing…I mean, I've *never* met anyone as completely tone deaf as him. And he had a million-dollar record deal. Jesse's yodeling came close to bursting a blood vessel in my head, but I kept telling myself: You're getting paid, you're getting paid, you're getting paid…

Everything on the record was fixed with ProTools. Nite Bob knew he'd have to do the same tone correction live too. Nite Bob had this thing that could fix the note before the sound comes out of the PA.

One of Jesse Camp's first shows was at Hugh Hefner's place, the Playboy Mansion. There was a radio convention going on, a yearly schmooze fest, where the station bosses would hang out with the label heads. A whole lotta booze and babes. Everyone was handed a burgundy silk robe and sandals as you went through the gate. Surreal stuff.

I'd flown Karmen out, and while I was at soundcheck, she'd found her way to our hotel's rooftop where there was a wine convention going on. The owners of vineyards were tasting wines, and Karmen, already dressed up in an emerald-green cocktail dress, spent four hours helping herself to different wines before the car picked her up to take her to the Playboy Mansion.

"Your wife is down there," I was informed. I went down to the front door, and there was Karmen, a few sheets to the wind. "Lemme in, motherfuckers!" I dragged Karmen to the side and got her some coffee.

Karmen noticed that Gene Simmons was there, and she decided that now was the time to get a picture with him. Karmen handed me a disposable camera and sidled up next to the big man, who was not too happy about the drunk woman next to him. Simmons is notoriously anti-alcohol, which probably has something to do with his old bandmate, Ace.

Gene is a big guy. Karmen tried to get her arm around him and accidentally knocked him on the head. Gene's toupee tilted a wee bit to the side just as I clicked the camera. He was not amused.

×××

I was hanging around the bar at Torch with the owner, Johnny Santiago, and the restaurant's marketing guy, Brian Cunningham. We were talking about all the shitty rap that you heard everywhere all the time. I said that we should put our own fucking rap band together with Johnny as the rapper.

Johnny said no, he didn't know how to rap, but I said it didn't matter. Brian would make a logo and come up with the marketing plan. We needed a short, sweet, and idiotic name, and we landed on Bootä.

I came up with four beats and taught Johnny then and there how to rap—like I even had a clue how to myself. We wrote the rhymes together, the stupidest, most sexist possible, really juvenile, as dumb as we could come up with.

Brian came up with believable single covers and a website for Bootä. We only had these four songs, but there started to be a buzz about Bootä in Manhattan anyway: Have you heard about Bootä? The famous celebrity photographer Patrick McMullan heard from a contact that Bootä was the cool new thing and asked us to perform at his birthday party.

Fuck…now what? We had a gig coming up, and we only had four songs. Well okay, we'd just get a lot of girls up on stage. We called up all the good-looking ladies we knew to ask if they wanted in. We got about five or so girls to dance in the end. I did a little bit of Muay Thai around that time and asked one of the teachers who was built like a house and had an impressive afro to join us. All that was required was to stand there with his arms crossed the whole show. "Okay, I can do that!"

There were 1,400 or 1,500 guests at Patrick McMullan's birthday party, all kinds of celebrities, and Bootä played a kickass show for them.

We went so far with this bullshit experiment that we ended up meeting Moby's lawyer and an A&R guy from a huge label. They were on board to sign Bootä. That's how fucked up the music biz is: You can get pretty far with any old bullshit. The signing negotiations broke down in the end, not because of the poor quality of the music, but because of the lack of a manager. American labels, or pretty much any other labels, do not want to deal directly with artists, there's a reason for that. If you don't have a manager, you're not getting further than the opening negotiations.

It was all the same to us. The whole fraud born from a bar joke shriveled up and died, and so much the better for it. Mad Juana was getting busy right around then. The new record hadn't come out yet, but home recording was an ongoing thing, as were the random odd shows with the random odd lineups. Some good players got caught in the net, people who we could play and plan future gigs with. Wylie Wirth ended up on drums, Ricky Bacchus on guitar, and Jimmy "Lonesome" Goodman on the keyboards and vibraphone.

I played shows with Walter Lure and the Waldos, Ricky Bacchus's Vásquez, and Gass Wild and Android's Love Pirates in addition to Mad Juana. Before moving to Spain, I'd produced the Love Pirates EP; Michael had played harmonica on it, and Alison Gordy had sung backup vocals. Gass Wild and I had known each other back in the eighties in London when we'd trade smack and coke and do speedballs in the bathroom.

I played here, there, and fecking everywhere not just for the extra money, but because my fingers were itching. The third reason was sanity. It's dangerous to live in a city like New York if you don't have stuff to do. You'll just start drinking and go crazy, at least I would, at that time and space. So it was necessary to keep my head busy to keep it from going elsewhere. I need to know what I was doing when I got up each day, so I don't listen to the little voice in my head that pushes me into bad situations. It's all for the best if the little psychopath inside doesn't get the chance to speak.

As soon as I learned the Love Pirates setlist, it wouldn't be necessary to practice it for more than a couple hours every three months. I have a pretty big stock of songs in my head that I know how to play, but the difference between that and playing covers is that these songs were ones the band had written themselves. Those songwriters didn't usually mind that I came up with my own bass lines to their songs.

I've obviously ended up having to play covers. It's part of the business, especially as part of a house band that gets a lot of singers coming up on stage. One lady wanted to sing Van Halen's "Panama" at a big benefit concert at Irving Plaza. I shuddered thinking about it, but I had to practice. The repertoire also included some Zeppelin, dread! It's a bit hypocritical of me to judge though, since I also learned how to play by playing other people's songs. Hendrix, the Dead Boys, Weather Report, Tom Robinson Band, the Damned.

Karmen lost her job because Torch got torched to the ground. The official cause was a short circuit in the back office. The rumor mill said something different.

Ludlow Street, where Torch had been, was a prime example of the neighborhood cleanup that happened when Rudy Giuliani was mayor. Ludlow Street in 1990 versus 1999 was night and day. These days, it's full of nice restaurants. But in 1990, I was there buying coke from a ten-year-old Puerto Rican kid when some rivals started shooting at each other. I had enough time to buy my baggie and then crawl under the nearest car so I wouldn't get a bullet to the head. I climbed out when the shooting stopped and scurried away.

Rudy Giuliani made cruel use of the Rockefeller Drug Laws, which meant that if you were caught three times for even the smallest amount of drugs, you'd get a minimum eight-year sentence. All the smalltime dealers that kept their families in food and rent were wiped off the streets and sent up the river for that mandatory sentence. But of course the crime never went away, nor did the criminals. It just morphed into something different: delivery services.

We started planning an English Mad Juana tour. Keith, an old Hanoi fan, was booking it; he'd done the same for some of Monroe's UK tours. Keith volunteered himself, and we started talking back and forth on the phone or on the computer. The details took two months to iron out. We'd sometimes talk every day, and in the end, the two-week tour in early 2000 was starting to take shape. There'd be ten shows around the UK; we'd have a ten-seater van at our disposal and Keith's guarantees had taken care of all the expenses. We'd even be able to pay the band members a little bit of money.

It looked like it was going to be fun.

2000

Bowl gilder

We landed at Heathrow early in the morning. As planned, Keith was there waiting for us. Unlike how we'd planned, there was no van. He mumbled something ambiguous about not having a driver's license. Wylie was the only person in Mad Juana who had both a driver's license and a credit card. We rented a van and drove to Keith's, showered, and went to our afternoon soundcheck.

The Purple Turtle club is a chain of clubs. This one was on the outskirts of London. We walked in with our guitars under our arms. The club manager greeted us when we walked in and asked us who we were. Mad Juana. The old boy was confused and asked again. Who?

We told him that we had a gig at the club that night. The manager apologized, but he'd never heard of us and there was another band booked for the night.

Keith was trying to hide behind everyone. I grabbed him by the shoulder and took him to another room. Keith stammered that he didn't know how this was possible, he'd fixed everything and it was so weird that they didn't know Mad Juana…

I asked to see the agreement. Keith answered that there was none.

Say what?

During all the conversations in the past few months, Keith had sworn that there were agreements for all the shows, he'd read through them, and he'd send me the figures for wages, percentages, and the approximate take from merch sales.

I locked the door behind us. I calmly told him to explain what was going on immediately. Keith cracked and admitted that there was no Mad Juana UK tour, he'd made the whole thing up because he had so badly wanted to bring Mad Juana to England. Maybe he was out of his mind or something, but it was what it was.

I've seen all kinds of shit, but this has gotta be at the top. Out of his own warped selfishness, he'd gotten five people to come out from New York for a tour that didn't exist. In that moment, I wanted to kill the sniveling little asshole.

I went back to join the band and told them just as much as they needed to know for the time being, because I didn't want to rile anyone up. The club owner was confused but said we could play that night anyway. He'd make the announcement on his own radio station, and they'd do the best they could for the gig with the time they had.

So we played the Purple Turtle, and the owner paid us three hundred pounds after, which was a lot more than there were people there. He comped us food and drinks and wished us good luck. Classy guy.

I was alone in mulling over Keith's betrayal. I'd paid everyone's tickets out of my own pocket, and our return flight wasn't for another two weeks. There wasn't enough to book new tickets, and it was super expensive to book hotels in London. We had to get the band out of this mess somehow.

And then the light bulb went off in my head. We could go to Mallorca! I called up my sister and the travel agency. The tickets from London were cheap, forty pounds per person. My sister agreed to put up the whole band; there was enough space at her house. The unbelievable sense of betrayal had turned into happy enthusiasm. I knew I'd be able to arrange some shows and salvage some of the "tour."

We played shows in villages around Mallorca over the next couple of weeks. Almost seven hundred people showed up to catch our show in Palma. We ended up in the black, and we came back to New York tanned and more or less satisfied. For my part, though, I was disappointed. I hadn't wanted to go play island shows, but to get a foothold in England with Mad Juana.

But I did keep in mind that we should go back to Spain since the reception was that good. After all, a lot of Mad Juana's influences were from Spain and the Moroccan radio stations we'd listened to there.

I was burned out and sick of drinking after the tour and decided to take a break, probably a long one at that. Maybe even for good. I wanted to see what totally sober life was all about.

×××

Broke, I ended up doing some work gilding. I knew a Sandra Spannan who had a gilding business through my friend photographer Mark Higashino. She showed me how to do it. I'd do odd jobs when Sandra asked me to, maybe a thousand tiny Ganesha statues might need a gold finish, but it was mostly the mid-September to mid-November Christmas rush that was the busy time. The Macy's and Saks Fifth Avenue windows needed to have an ungodly amount of Christmas decorations.

I'd go to the Gretsch Building (the one where they did make Gretsch guitars) at one in the morning, and I'd spray the glue fix on the bowls that were to be gilded with a high-power pump. I'd have to spray seventy-five to a hundred bowls every night. I had to be in overalls and wear a gas mask to do it, but fortunately, I could get a Walkman to fit inside too. I'd have Tom Waits on full blast for the five hours I'd be there. At six, I'd go home, take a four-hour nap, then go back at eleven to start gilding. I'd gild until seven in the evening, then go home, sleep for a few hours, and do it all over again. The night shift was solitary and lonely work, whereas fifteen or so guys and women would be around the place during the day, blasting Eminem. I fixed their bowls too at night.

The 24-karat gold came in thin little strips of paper. It wasn't really physical work handling it; it was more like trying to hold air. Each sheet of the gold leaf was worth a couple hundred dollars and would easily crumble in your hands, so it was careful and precise work. The leaf would go on top of the adhesive, and none of the seams could show. If there was any overlap, the seam had to be sanded down, so the surface was smooth. Some customers didn't want it to look completely perfect though, so it was okay to leave some imperfections. The Indian statues would usually need to look aged, with darker grooves and greenish oxidation. Silver and bronze had to be taken into consideration during the adhesive stage. There were special chemicals for everything, and they were serious shit. Special protective equipment was necessary.

Sandra got cancer, got better, and got back to work. She's gilding some cathedral in Italy now. Tough cookie. When Sandra got sick, I started to ask myself if I'd always worn a face mask at work. I'd spent months in a toxic environment. Did I need to start worrying about myself now?

The gilding rush for Christmas came to an end, and I had to come up with something else to do. Sandra suggested me to a carpenter she knew, and he gave me a job. I had to sand down the long planks for a wall, sand them four times with sandpaper, and then stain them. It was a lot of sanding, staining, watching paint dry, and more sanding. It was monotonous work, hard on my neck and my elbows, and after a ten-hour day, I'd walk away with a hundred dollars. Ten dollars an hour. I was an assistant carpenter for no more than a week or two.

The landlord kicked out the Vietnam vet who lived downstairs, and a Japanese techno café moved into his place. Apparently it was a "hip" spot. The poor guy's nighttime nightmare roaring wasn't much to complain about compared to the nocturnal techno parties that happened from time to time and made sleep not worth dreaming about. Being sober made the noise even more annoying. So I threw on my robe and slippers, and Greta and I went down to the café. I walked up to the DJ booth and picked the needle off the record. That was the end of that night.

I moved my home studio system out to Fire Island to Maukka Palmio's boss's place for the month, and we got started recording the second Mad Juana record. We did some of the recordings in Jimmy "Lonesome" Goodman's Transporterraum Studio, with Gordon Raphael as the sound engineer. The music was some sort of soul/dub/reggae/space rock.

A new band called the Strokes was recording their first album at the same time at Transporterraum. There was a huge buzz around the band, and they were selling out all their Manhattan shows by this point. Gordon Raphael was producing their record, and I asked to hear what the fuss was about one night. Gordon played three or four of the mixed and final songs. It didn't make much of an impression, so I asked, "Is this it?" This is what everyone was getting so worked up over?

Maybe Gordon told the Strokes about it. When their record finally came out, it was called *Is This It*.

×××

I was sober for a total of eleven months, until Thanksgiving. We went to Karmen's mom's and stepdad's in Des Moines. They all ordered white wine at the restaurant and I thought, you know what, give me a glass too. Thanksgiving Day was the straw that broke the camel's back; wine had started to taste good again. Sobriety had been reasonable and a good detox, but in the end, it didn't seem like a solution for the rest of my life.

2001

In Your Blood

The crowd would fall for Mad Juana at live shows. Totally and completely. So it was frustrating that we couldn't get any managers interested and we couldn't find a label either. We needed a manager who could have sat at the negotiating table and taken care of all that business shit that I'm allergic to. It takes time to do everything yourself—the cover art, distribution, marketing, everything—but there was no other choice to get *In Your Blood* out. They weren't even pressed, just CD-Rs we'd burned at home, with covers we'd photocopied ourselves and mailed out to anyone who'd sent in ten dollars plus postage. The record stores in Tokyo took a hundred copies right off the bat. The record went here and there around the world in small numbers, and we sold some copies at our shows too. We got some records out in England and in the States later on, through small labels like Acetate Records and Diesel Motor.

Mad Juana and Gogol Bordello started to play some shows together. We'd gotten to know Oren Kaplan and Eugene Hütz at a place called Baby Jupiter, where Gogol Bordello had gotten their start. Oren was the house mixer at Baby Jupiter.

We came up with the idea to book a snake charmer to one of our Baby Jupiter shows. He had an albino cobra and a black cobra. How would these giant, six-foot-plus creatures react to loud music? The snake charmer was down, and a big basket was placed at each end of the stage. The stage was about twenty inches high. During the first song, the snakeman took the lids off of the baskets. A white head popped out of one basket, a black one out of the other. People started screaming and bolted right out of the club. The Mad Juana snake show cleared out Baby Jupiter in five seconds flat. Oren was still upstairs mixing, and there was exactly one person left inside the club. That was a great idea. What did we learn from this? Don't mix animals with show biz.

×××

I tried to fix a proper UK tour for Mad Juana and get the record released there as well, but it didn't happen; I couldn't get the money together or anyone to help. Then Ricky Bacchus decided to quit Mad Juana and focus on his own band, Vasquez; I would play with them for a while later on. My old buddy, Harri Kupiainen, replaced Ricky on guitar. We decided to go to Spain for the summer with this revised lineup. A friend named Senen in Barcelona booked us a cheap two-bedroom in Vallvidrera, just outside the city. We'd have anywhere from two to four gigs a week for the whole summer, which would keep the band fed and busy.

We decided to take our Doberman, Greta, with us, which meant that I'd have to fly out early in May. Airlines didn't allow animals on flights from June 1 to September 1. The rest of the band would follow a week later.

I landed in Barcelona with a Doberman, a kennel, three suitcases, two guitars, and a Fender amp. I had the howling Greta on a leash and a mountain of stuff I was slowly pushing toward customs. The customs agent was smoking a cigarette and looked at me with a mix of horror and curiosity like he should stop me, but thought better of it and waved me through, most likely because he didn't want to have to deal with a howling Doberman.

I spent the first week getting the shows together with Senen. As soon as the band arrived, we played three shows the first weekend, one in the Basque Country and two in Galicia. We were driving down the mountain to Vigo when we saw smoke and helicopters hanging over the city. We were showing up right in the middle of a protest that had turned into a riot.

We rolled past burning trash fires on the side of the road toward the riot police. Red flags were flying and a thousand people were there protesting together. The mounted police galloped by.

We got to the venue, Club Iguana, and carried our gear inside. The owner of the club came to say hi and brought us beer and cognac. We were wondering about the intense atmosphere outside, and the owner told us that the dock workers were out protesting the lowering of their already poor wages.

We watched the situation develop on TV. There was a ten o'clock curfew put into place.

Our show was supposed to start at eleven.

The owner just laughed about the whole thing. He paid us in advance and said that we could perform for him, his wife, the bartender, and the cook.

And so it went; no one else showed up. We had a nice night and left for La Coruña and the Basque Country the next morning. After those shows, we came back to Barcelona for four days. Most of the band went out clubbing, Karmen and I stayed behind to take care of business.

We stopped in Rioja during the next week's shows, which is the main wine region in Spain and where our driver, Roberto, was from; his family had a wine business. So of course we'd stop by the winery Roberto knew so we could buy a twenty-liter barrel of wine that barely cost a thing. We stuffed it in with all the other stuff, and suddenly we had a mobile wine bar, just reach back from the back seat and fill up your glass.

We started to get some cancelations in July. We had to get money from somewhere. Senen had a day job as a TV producer on this Spanish kids' show, *Los Trilocos*. Senen got an idea: Would I make an appearance on an episode of *Trilocos*? I'd get paid 50,000 pesetas, which was about then about $500. I agreed, even though I was no actor by any means and my Spanish was still basically at a Tarzan level. The money would cover the band's food and gas expenses; Spain was still unbelievably cheap back then, until the euro came along a few years later and doubled the cost of everything.

Senen gave me the Spanish script. I tried to memorize my lines without totally understanding what I was actually saying. Of course I forgot everything completely when I got to the studio. I went to makeup and put on a Motörhead jean jacket and sunglasses because the role was, wait for it…a rocker. The scene took place on a boat deck where I was supposed to be napping in the sun. I said that I could probably do this demanding role justice.

The shooting began. I stretched out on the chair. Tri Locos shuffled past and woke me up. I forgot my line. I jumped up and said the first thing that came to mind: "OYE, QUE PASAR?" The director looked at the script confused, raised his head, and smiled. "Bravo!"

I got a round of applause from the crew and the 50,000 pesetas in hand. My work at the service of Spanish TV was done.

The plan was to go to Mallorca from Barcelona in August. We had gigs coming up after some quiet weeks. But the band morale had dropped. Harri had started to complain about the lack of money and plans, and he dragged Wylie and Jimmy into his nega vibe with him. I thought we'd left for the tour in the spirit of adventure. I hadn't made any promises about making money, but I'd said that we'd spend a fun summer together without ending up in the red. If you wanna hang out in clubs and drink all your money, go ahead.

The whole summer had been a one big ball of stress for me, except for the first week I was there alone before the band showed up. I had taken care of all the stuff tour managers do: hotels, gas, mapping, phone calls, wake-up calls. I had promised to cover the expenses, which I did, but that wasn't enough for the guys. They wanted more money so it turned into a clash, and the whining didn't stop there. I told the three of them that if they didn't feel like going to Mallorca, I could exchange the plane tickets for a sooner date, and they could head home.

They feebly answered that yeah, they'd tag along.

But the vibe was still off. I should have sent the guys back to New York right then and there. The complaining kept on going when I hooked Harri, Wylie, and Jimmy up with a house in Sineu. It's a beautiful old village, but apparently unrelentingly boring without clubs or parties.

We played some shows in Mallorca, and things came to a head on the last night. It was the same old question of money and circumstances. It was a relief when I saw them off to the ferry back to Barcelona the next morning and said that was the end of us playing together.

Karmen and I stayed with my sister until the end of the month. We got back to New York on September 2, as soon as it was possible to fly again with a dog. I celebrated my thirty-eighth birthday two days later. The gilding and the Macy's Christmas decoration work would start again in a couple of weeks. It paid so well, I'd be free from money troubles for the rest of the year.

×××

I woke up to the sound of Karmen's mom's voice. It was coming through the answering machine, quietly drifting in from the kitchen. "…a plane has hit the Twin Towers…please pick up." Karmen ran to the phone and motioned for me to turn on the TV.

There was a massive hole in the side of the World Trade Center. The reporter didn't know yet how big the plane that hit it had been. The first guess was a Cessna or a tourist helicopter. The news was speculating that it was a small private aircraft. We climbed up to the roof, which had a clear view of the East River and over Lower Manhattan. It was a clear, warm, and sunny morning. We stared at the smoking tower when another small flying dot sped toward the towers. We saw the explosion before we heard it.

We ran down from the roof back to our apartment. The phone wasn't working anymore. We started watching the TV news. People were running around in panic. No one knew what was going on. The news came in that a third plane had crashed into part of the Pentagon, and a fourth had fallen into a field in Pennsylvania.

When I saw both the towers crumble, I knew that the whole world had changed.

The wind blew our way over the Williamsburg Bridge, and that's when the darkness rolled in with the burnt rubber fumes and the sickly smell of burnt hair. And dust. Lots of dust. The awful stench hung in the air for a whole month. The fire smoldered so deep that it took a long time to get put out.

The bridges were closed and you couldn't go south of Fourteenth Street. You couldn't go to Lower Manhattan without an ID. There were tanks in Union Square. The Go America bros drove around waving American flags chanting U-S-A! U-S-A! It was all surreal. A Pakistani-owned shop on our block was destroyed, and the owners were beaten up.

Our personal circumstances also changed. Karmen couldn't get down to work in Lower Manhattan for a couple weeks. My well-paying gilding job for Macy's got canceled. Our landlord informed us that he'd be raising rent by $400. I thought he was pulling my leg, but the asshole was serious.

We had to move. I made dozens of phone calls and looked at places in the *Village Voice*. It didn't look too good; rents in New York had gone stratospheric.

I left a message for an apartment on Tenth Street in the East Village. The phone rang a quarter of an hour later. The caller had a familiar voice and accent. "Hwat iz your name?" "Sami, yours?" "Konstantino." And then it clicked. "Konstantino, the crazy Greek?" "Yes! IS THIS SAMI, THE FINNISH BASTARD?"

What a coincidence. I knew Konstantino as a photographer, but he also managed a bunch of his family's buildings around town.

The next Friday, Konstantino picked us up from Williamsburg to look at the apartment. A Wall Street character also came to the viewing who was ready to pay in cash on the spot, name the price. Konsta pulled us aside: I fucking hate those yuppies, so the apartment is yours if you want it. We signed the lease there and then and moved back to Manhattan from Brooklyn on Monday. Thanks, Konsta.

Current Mad Juana had a lot of dub as well as some electro influences. At the end of the year, there was this feeling to ditch all the synths and drum triggers. We'd get back to our original idea: acoustic music. Horns, violins, accordions, instruments you could make explosive, up-tempo music with. I wanted sweat and foot-banging ecstasy.

Mad Juana's first acoustic lineup practiced for hours on end in our living room. Tony Mann on bass drum and congas, Amalia Daskalakis on viola, Jimmy Bushart on trumpet, Xavier Becerra on saxophone. If the neighbors complained, Konstantino told them to leave Sami and Karmen alone.

Xavier Becerra was from Mexico City; he'd never properly learned how to play the saxophone, he blew it free. He didn't play in Mad Juana for long, but he left his mark on the band.

We gave an interview to a Japanese TV station. There was a lighting guy, a cameraman, and an interviewer besides the band. We took maybe one tequila shot during the interview. Except for Xavier, who'd been sipping on, or actually pouring tequila down his throat the whole day. During the interview Xavi got up and started calmly undressing himself. Shirt, shoes, socks, pants, all of it. The Japanese TV crew wasn't sure if they should stop, but they kept on filming. There he was in all his birth glory. This great Azteca guy from Mexico sat there naked for the rest of the interview without saying a thing.

Mad Juana was able to win the crowd over in any situation, whether it was a trans gallery opening or Joey Ramone's birthday bash. The latter was a yearly event that started off when Joey was still alive, and his brother has kept it going. Maybe eight hundred to a thousand people showed up at Irving Plaza with the Dictators, Ronnie Spector, Sylvain Sylvain playing—the crème de la crème of New York.

And Mad Juana. We lined up six chairs in a row and banged out an acoustic set in the midst of all the loud amped-up R&R—it was a blast.

We ended up as something of the house band for this little bar on Avenue C called Micky's Blue Room right around the corner from us. We'd play there about every weekend. The nights were sweaty and smoky, full of whiskey and vodka, the backroom full of East Village nutcases. One night, Lenny Kaye walked up from the crowd and asked, "Do you mind if I play a song?" From then on, we'd play the Patti Smith Group's "Ain't It Strange" and finish the night off with "Gloria." Depending on the lineup, Lenny Kaye became Mad Juana's seventh, eight, or ninth player, unofficially. His support was really important to us, and he helped spread the word.

I'd gone back to work at Seth's record store, Norman's Sound and Vision, as soon as the dust had settled in the city and the worst of the 9/11 shock was behind us. I would have hung out there anyway to listen to records and shoot the shit. Now I was hanging out there, listening to records, shooting the shit, and getting paid. Not a whole lot since I got into a bad habit; I started to take my pay in records. Karmen wasn't too happy when I brought home a hundred dub CDs instead of grocery money.

Norman's was on St. Mark's Place, across the street from the apartment we'd left a few years ago to move to Mallorca. It was funny and very humbling to sell people Hanoi Rocks records. Almost no one ever recognized me. "That's $28.50, please." But what are you gonna do, it's survival.

After a month or two standing behind the register, I started to get itchy and bored. I wanted to start earning my living by playing music again. But like I've said, being a hired hand wasn't really my thing and neither was settling down into a cover band. What could be more gruesome than ending up doing Led Zeppelin covers in a Bleecker Street tourist bar? I think I'd rather sell records.

I played with Walter Lure, sometimes with Ricky Bacchus's Vasquez band. I played on Vasquez's third EP and Ricky's brilliant Luckiest Girls album, *Jet Black and Beautiful*. But I wanted something more permanent. An active, touring band, one that would pay the rent and play some raw, loud rock 'n' roll to balance out the acoustic Mad Juana sound.

I'm aware how this all sounds: rock…acoustic…rock…New York…escape from New York…New York… Fuck, I'm restless, I've always been restless. I can't stand sticking around in a situation that's stagnant. I get bored and change directions maybe a little too easily. You have to fight against the urge to battle boredom and change directions because it's part of life to have those downtimes too. But when you've spent your whole life on the move, things start to feel stagnant real quick, and that's when I have to change the situation.

2002

Acoustic Voodoo

The third Mad Juana record, *Acoustic Voodoo,* was recorded in our shoebox living room in the East Village. I used my laptop to layer the acoustic guitars and bass over the drum machine. Tony Mann fixed the drum machine with hand drums, then we recorded the accordion, viola, and saxophone. Little by little, we got it done. Lenny Kaye made a guest appearance on "Ghost Riddim." It was fun to pass a joint around and watch this legend play his twanger on a song I wrote with Karmen.

By this point, the saxophone player had switched from Xavier to Danny Ray, Marni Rice joined on accordion, and the lineup was finalized.

Ricky Bacchus had joined Murphy's Law, a legendary New York hardcore band. Ricky let me know that there was an opening for a bass player in the band. Would I be interested in joining for the near future, at least for the tour of Japan?

I got the setlist. It was full of ska, punk, reggae, and rock and roll. Why not? I'd get the chance to play all the stuff I'd been playing my whole life, even before Pelle Miljoona. Hardcore is just really fast rock, nothing more. It comes natural to me. Murphy's Law wasn't traditional hardcore anyway. There was no sign of speed or trash metal, no metal influence at all, thank God. It was more like rock and old-school punk, but just sped up.

We started practicing in February in the singer, Jimmy Gestapo's, basement in Queens. Jimmy had grown up in a rough neighborhood next to the Triborough Bridge in Queens and he'd learned how to use his fists. My predecessor had left the band because Jimmy punched him in the face.

Murphy's Law kicked off the hardcore scene in New York in 1982 and 1983, along with Agnostic Front and Cro-Mags. These bands' home base was the Lower East Side, which was in apocalyptic ruins and plagued with drugs in the early eighties. Cabs wouldn't drive down to Alphabet City; the avenues had their own nicknames. A=assault, B=battery, C=cocaine, D=death.

Despite his air of potential violence, Jimmy Gestapo was insanely funny, had a great sense of humor, and was great drinking company.

We practiced in Jimmy's basement for a couple of weeks and then left for the two-week tour of Japan. The tour was a traveling hardcore punk festival, we moved from city to city by train. Murphy's Law was the headliner, the Japanese band Aggressive Dogs was opening, and there were ten or so other bands playing too.

The tour kicked off in Osaka. As soon as we got to the hotel, Jimmy Gestapo announced that there'd be a band meeting in his room in an hour. I took a shower and headed over to Jimmy's room when it was time for the meeting. There was a muffled thud, and the wall in the hallway shook. Then some grunting and another thud. The door to room number 411 was cracked. I looked inside. Jimmy was smashing guitarist Sean's head with five wood hangers; there was blood. It was a pretty gruesome sight. If this was just another band meeting, what happens if there's an actual disagreement?

"Hey, how's it going?" Both looked up and stopped fighting. "Yeah, all good here, just havin' some fun. Wanna beer?"

We sat down and went through the setlist, the tour schedule, and the travel plans. We all had to wake up on time because we couldn't miss the trains. The first band would start playing at three in the afternoon, then one punk band after another, until we finally went on at nine.

There was a crowd of about eight hundred in Osaka. The whole place exploded into a mosh pit as soon as we played the first note. Everyone was bouncing around in circles with their fists up, kicking and pushing each other. This went on for the whole hour and a half set. I noticed how much I'd missed this adrenaline kick.

With Hanoi, Jetboy, and Demolition 23., the Japanese tours had all been about weeklong sojourns and had concentrated on the same cities: Tokyo, Osaka, Fukuoka, Nagoya. With Murphy's Law, we also went to Kyoto, Tokushima, Matsue, Yokohama, and Hiroshima. This time around, there was more time to see all the temples, samurai castles, and cities.

We came back to New York from Japan. I'd passed the trial period because Jimmy let me know that in a couple of weeks there'd be a tour of the Midwest.

Pittsburg, Cleveland, Detroit, Chicago. We took a van, doubled as our own roadies, and shared hotel rooms. Back to square one. The tour was full of drinking and fighting. Fighting in the day and punk rock at night. But there weren't enough shows, and we didn't earn shit from them. And Jimmy was a bit of a loose cannon.

My last show with Murphy's Law was when we played some party of Björk's at a big industrial space in the Meatpacking District in NYC. There was all kinds of performance art going on that evening. Most of the guests were in the fashion industry: designers and models. Not really the target audience for Murphy's Law.

Before us on stage was a woman that used fake blood in her performance. She left behind a big Jack Daniel's bottle filled with fake blood on the drum riser. During the show, the trendy designer boys started to giggle and point at Jimmy. They had no idea what they were doing, the volcano was about to erupt: It ain't gonna be pretty. Hopefully Jimmy wouldn't notice that bottle of blood.

Jimmy kept his cool, but muttered, "Those motherfuckers." The designers kept teasing and giggling way in the back of the loft, and Jimmy just kept getting more and more drunk during the show until he finally went "fuck it," stopped singing, dropped the mike to the ground, yanked his shirt off, grabbed the bottle of Jack—which he'd apparently noticed right away—and spilled the blood all over himself, from the head down. Jimmy was staring at the trendies covered in blood, jumped off the stage, and charged at them with his arms flailing. Ffuh, ffuh, ffuh.

I'll never forget the look of terror on those faces. The guys screeched and took off running down all four flights of stairs with a big bloody skinhead on their tail. I went to the window and saw the boys crying in panic, stumbling on the cobblestones and running off into different directions. Jimmy's voice echoed in the alley. "YOU MOTHERFUCKEEEEERS."

This was the funniest shit I'd ever seen. I had tears in my eyes.

That's how my brief but memorable tenure ended. Murphy's Law has apparently had something like two hundred members. I was told I'm the only one that Jimmy never punched in the nose.

×××

Mad Juana took off for England. This time we had a reliable booker, but some of the shows canceled through no fault of his own. We had to improvise replacement gigs after the flight so we wouldn't take hell for it. I loved the band, but did not love the feeling of constantly hitting my head against a wall.

In the summer after the UK tour, I was sitting in the noisy and packed Don Hills in New York when Thommy Price came to say hi. He was the drummer who did the Monroe Japan tour in 1992. "Hey man," Thommy said. "We are looking for a bass player for Joan Jett, do you know any?"

I looked Thommy right in the eye and kept mum. It suddenly clicked. "Oh shit, stupid me, kick this ass! YOU play bass!"

Thommy set up a tryout and sent me a CD-R of the setlist. Most of the songs were eighties mega hits: "I Love Rock 'n' Roll," "Bad Reputation," "I Hate Myself For Loving You," "Crimson and Clover," "Cherry Bomb"... and a cover of Sly and the Family Stone's "Everyday People."

I have nothing but huge respect for Joan Jett. She started Blackheart Records in the early eighties and was the first woman to own an independent label. I'd met Joan the first time at Record Plant in 1984 while Hanoi had been making *Two Steps from the Move*. Joan was recording in the next studio, and we ended up hanging out and talking.

I went to the SIR practice space on Fifty-Second Street. Joan and the band were already there, as was Joan's longtime manager Kenny Laguna, the Svengali who had worked on the sixties Tin Pan Alley hits and had written "Yummy Yummy."

I turned up the amp as loud as I usually did when playing, and Kenny came up to me right away complaining about the level. "If it's too loud, you're too old."

Joan was a tough lady and a very tight guitarist; her right hand was insane. She wasn't too technical, but a great rhythm player, tough, and laid-back, super tight. And Thommy Price, whose roster was nuts, Billy Idol, Mink DeVille, etc., had been playing with Joan since 1986. Thommy was a machine. He'd hit at the last possible second. The perfect drummer for Joan. It was hard for me to find the pocket at first because I was used to drummers playing in front of the beat. It's a bad habit, which is why I jam over Motown and reggae records at home.

"11th Street Kids" speeds up toward the end, actually the tempo speeds up in all early Hanoi recordings, no click track anywhere near the imagination yet.

If you play the New York Dolls, well the Bo Diddley song "Pills" too perfectly, it just sounds lame. Keeping it loose is the only way to get music to swing in just the right way. It sounds like things could collapse at any second when you listen to a Stones record. "Honky Tonk Women" goes twice as fast at the end. It's normal when you're young to play in front of the beat. Songs can speed up, but they can slow down too if you have a bad drummer. It's awful, the worst really, if the tempo is dragging in a rock band. You're only as good as your drummer.

After the tryout, everyone was all smiles: I'd gotten the gig. Kenny Laguna was totally serious about me playing quieter though. On top of that, I had to start learning to sing backup. Up until then, I'd just yodeled out some ohhs and ahhs in bands, but now I was supposed to sing entire lines, three and even four-part harmonies. Joan Jett and the guys were Beach Boys fans and were real serious about hitting the right notes. There was no room for error. We'd practice singing with a piano. It was so bare naked that I actually properly learned to sing with Joan and Kenny, thanks for that.

The first show with Joan Jett and the Blackhearts was at a private event in the China Club in New York. Big NYPD guys were there as security. A New York Irish captain introduced himself and gave me his business card. "Hey man, I'm Mark. Welcome to the family. This is your get-out-of-jail-free card. Any problems short of murder, don't hesitate to use it." Mark was the head of security whenever Joan played New York. That's how it had been since the seventies, when Joan started doing benefit shows for NYPD orphans and widows. The first benefit earned $200, and later on a LOT more. Having a good relationship with the police meant that Joan never had any trouble. She always had a number to call.

I'd wanted to be in a regularly touring band. And now I was. The whole circus started a month after the China Club show. Every week, shows from Wednesday to Saturday. The bartenders at the La Guardia bar got to know me and my drink order. "The usual?" Whisky and a beer. Home Sunday morning and back to work on Wednesday morning.

The attacks on the World Trade Center ruined plane travel. But not for everyone, of course. You can't bring a knife on a plane, but they still let you cut your steak in first class with metal utensils, go fucking figure.

We played the same setlist the same way every night. The band was tighter than a duck's asshole, but after a few months, I started to go numb and asked if they ever switched things up a little bit. Well, every now and then they'd throw a new song into the mix, but Joan Jett also wanted to give the crowd what they wanted, and what they wanted was the big hits. They didn't want new songs or B-sides. Or that's at least how Joan laid it out, and that's how we did it.

Meanwhile Michael and Andy had played some shows together in Finland under the name of Hanoi Rocks Revisited. They hadn't asked me, Nasty, or Gyp to join in. Andy and Michael had apparently decided that in the end, the band was the two of them. But Hanoi was the sum of its members, you've got to be pretty lost to not understand that. My thought was that the two of them just wanted to make some money.

Now the duo were putting a band together under the Hanoi Rocks name. They didn't ask me or the other guys anything about this either. I left Andy and Michael to their hustle; I had my own thing going anyway. But all the same I wondered what would come of it.

2003

Casinos, State Fairs, and USO Shows

There are a lot of "Findians," the descendants of Finnish immigrants and US Natives, living in Upper Michigan, in Sault Ste. Marie. I hung out with a bunch of them after a concert at a casino and listened to the peculiar Finnish that had morphed over generations. It sometimes took a minute to understand what word they were trying to say. I tried to teach them proper pronunciation, but it didn't sink in, just a lot of laughter. When the casino was closing, a seventy-five-year-old woman waddled in to pick up her kid and some of the other Michigan Finns. I greeted her by asking her how she was doing in Finnish, saying that it was nice to meet her. The old gal perked right up. "Well thank you! I'm good, thanks. So nice to hear proper Finnish!" We sat down for a few minutes to chat, and then I went to sleep, the clinking of hundreds of slot machines ringing in my ears.

The Blackhearts went to the studio to record four or five new songs. The manager, Kenny Laguna, underscored that these were just demos and they would not end up on a record. The demo rate was $150–200, whereas an album recording rate would be much higher. Kenny Laguna's modus operandi was to pay musicians as little as possible, and low and behold, these recordings ended up on a proper release. First *Naked* in Japan in 2004, then *Sinner* worldwide. I'm credited on *Naked*, but Enzo Penizzotto, the Blackhearts' bass tech and later bass player, was credited on *Sinner*. Oy vey.

We did some sessions at Revolver studios on Attorney Street. The short-lived studio was owned by a coke dealer who was officially in construction, but his illegal income had to be laundered somehow. He was a rock fan, so he built a studio. I hooked him up with a forty-two-track console when a friend of mine was shutting down his studio. A console worth a hundred grand, just like that. You'd find recording gear sitting out on the street when everything was switching from analog to digital. The thought at the time was that all this old stuff was now junk, until it was understood that you've got to get the signal to go through some analog equipment and not just straight into a computer.

We toured every small town, every state fair, every casino in the US. It was weird that Joan never seemed to play big venues in big cities. We always played the out-of-the-way markets. A hell of a lot of casinos in the winter and state fairs in the summer. Every state has a weeklong state fair in the summer: the Nebraska state fair, Michigan state fair, and so on. We'd catch the rodeos, ride the roller coasters, eat a ton of food, and drink lots of beer. The local trades are always on display at the state fair. We saw the world's biggest pig and the world's biggest cow at the Iowa state fair. The pig was the size of a balcony and the cow, the size of a patio. I don't know what kind of genetically modified feed they were given, but they weren't even able to stand. Then Little Richard performed at the speedway, picked up a young skinny guy right there on stage, walked to the limo that was parked behind the stage in plain view with him at the end of the gig, and drove off.

We hung out with Rick Derringer at the Montana state fair. Joan's old friends from the Runaways, Cherie Currie and Lita Ford, popped up at some of the shows.

Lita and I had had the same weed dealer in LA back in the eighties, a curly-haired metal dude named Head. Head asked me once, "Dude, do you wanna be a part of the Bong Hall of Fame?" He had a photo album bursting with Polaroids of rock stars who had sat down on Head's sofa for a hit off his bong. The album had everybody in it.

We had to play two seventy-five-minute sets in the ninety-degree heat at Sequoia National Park. During the twenty-minute break between the sets, I was parched and chugged almost a gallon of water and a couple beers without thinking about the consequences. Then we heard the announcement from the stage: "Ladies and gentlemen, JOAN JETT!"

I hadn't thought to go take a piss, and now I was up shit's creek. I had to go so bad by the second song. I knew that during the fourth song, Joan would go over to the monitor mixing board on the side of the stage to adjust her monitors. That was my window of opportunity.

As soon as Joan walked over to the mixer, I ran behind my big Ampeg amp. Thommy had a half-full bucket of KFC next to the drums. I just said "Sorry!" to Thommy and started pissing in it. Joan turned around and saw me behind the amp. "What the fuck is going on?" I asked because there was some trouble with the amp...I pretended I was fixing something with my other hand. I let it flow while the five-thousand-person crowd waited for the concert to continue. I zipped my fly. I turned around and saw Joan's parents sitting there on my side of the stage. They had witnessed the whole thing. They smiled and lifted their fingers to their lips.

Bob Dylan also performed at Sequoia National Park. I didn't meet the guy backstage, but did run into an old acquaintance, Charlie Sexton.

Being a musician is social; you're around people all the time, both new faces and familiar faces. Booze is like a protective shield that gives you the energy to hang with people and be able to deal with it all. It sure as hell is not the best medicine long term, so I took another few months off drinking while working with Joan Jett. When I stepped on the stage sober in front of three thousand people, I wasn't sure if it was a good idea at first. But as soon as I started playing, I forgot about dem nerves. Playing felt exactly the same. Except I enjoyed it maybe even more, I was more present.

Playing in my first band at fourteen, we had a couple of beers after the gig. This kicked up a notch when I joined Pelle Miljoona. Suddenly, I was playing shows from Wednesday to Saturday. The couple of beers turned into a little bottle of rum. The rum was warm and calming after the adrenaline rush of the show. It started off as just havin' a drink when the gig was over, then it became havin' a drink before the gig as well, and on the way to the gig. It became a habit.

When you want to experiment with everything, it's hard to have boundaries. Boundaries only came out of necessity, when I backed myself into a corner that made it absolutely necessary. I don't think I had a single day straight during my four years playing in Hanoi Rocks. Every single day, I was on something. I took as much speed as I could get my hands on in Stockholm, constant boozing, then came the smack. After Nicke was born, I was pretty calm and clearheaded for a long while. But then it started up again in LA after our breakup. I wasn't doing anything hard anymore thank God, but I drank and smoked weed.

×××

Bob Hope started a tradition during the Second World War that Joan Jett diligently carried on: entertain the troops. We'd play the US military bases in different countries. In Europe, they're around the NATO countries. The highest mountain in Mallorca is topped with a big American radar station. Big Brother.

We played for paratroopers in Arizona, for the Air Force in New Mexico. After the show for the Air Force in New Mexico, we flew to the next base in Phoenix. But not on any old plane—on one of those massive military transport aircrafts they use to fly around tanks. There were only ten seats on the plane, the rest of the space was for cargo. Once we'd lifted off, the pilot flying the plane asked, "Hey, boys, anybody wanna fly this thang?" I got up, walked over to the cockpit, and the pilot started to show me the ropes. "You do like THIS, it goes like THAT." "Yeah, yeah." "You steady? It's all yours!"

I was terrified. Don't move, don't touch anything. "C'mon guy, do something! Just twist it to the right a little bit." I turned it, and the whole plane turned in the air. Terrible and cool at the same time. I was flying.

"You know I'm not an American citizen," I said pointedly, and the pilot's face twisted. Whatthefuckareyoutalkingabout? "I'm a Finn."

You had to get military clearance for every base, since the locations are secret. I always got the green light. There was nothing suspicious about me in any registry, or maybe Joan's NYPD contacts were good enough.

There was barely a break between the weekly shows. On the off chance we did have a weekend off, I'd book a Mad Juana show. I liked to sit at the

Luna Lounge bar on Ludlow Street on my nights off. Elliott Smith was a drinking buddy. He clearly had some problems, but was a sweet guy and an interesting conversation companion. When I came back to the Luna Lounge after a long break, his seat was empty. I asked why Elliott wasn't around anymore, and if he'd moved to another stomping ground. Someone told me that Elliott had stabbed himself in the heart.

Another beautiful man gone, but scum lives on.

We had concerts in Japan in October. We played for the US Marines in Okinawa. Okinawa is the southernmost island in Japan, on the open sea with a tropical climate. It has palm trees and turquoise water. There were five thousand bald-headed soldiers on the Marine base, and they'd been given permission to let loose on the day of the show with an open bar. Some of the Marines got into it and started crowd surfing. There'd be all these Marines riding back and forth on their backs over the sea of bald heads. Another totally surreal scene seen from the stage.

I got a $300 fine from the US Army a couple of months later. I'd smoked a cigarette out the window of my room in Okinawa and had flushed the butt down the toilet, but someone had apparently smelled the remnants of smoke.

When we got to Budokan, the promoters told me my former band was playing there the next day. And so it was. How funny. On top of that, the revamped Hanoi Rocks was staying in the same hotel. The Blackhearts were free on the day of the Hanoi show, so I went to check out the gig and say hi to Michael, Andy, and the new members, Lacu, Timppa, and Costello. Lacu is a nice dude and a sickass drummer, even if he's more of a metal drummer. Gyp and Razzle loved Topper Headon and Jerry Nolan's style amongst other drummers; that was the world they came from, and it came through in Hanoi.

I joined on stage for "Up Around the Bend." I noticed right away that the band's sound was foreign to me. I didn't hear any punk or the Clash aggression in the band's new songs, just pop and metal. I didn't think it really fit with the Hanoi Rocks legacy that we'd left behind.

2004

Naked

In February, we had another USO show, this time outside of Venice, Italy. It was cold, dark, and rainy, and all the restaurants were closed the night we got in. Except for one. I had the best penne marinara of my life there. It's the simplest thing in the world to make, and it's hardly ever made right.

The crowd was a couple thousand soldiers that had served in Iraq and were now on their way home. Some of them had done two tours and they'd probably seen enough to require psychiatric help for the rest of their lives. I walked around the crowd and told them about my home country of Finland, because no one knew a thing about it or even its location. I talked about the Northern Lights and clean air, the dark winters, the long days in the summer, hockey heroes, the war against the Soviet Union, and about gin Long Drink and Koskenkorva.

One conversation with a couple really left an impression on me. They had met and gotten married in Iraq. After a couple of whiskeys, the stories started pouring out. They'd seen the kinds of things no one should have to. Like a bomb blowing a child up into twisted rags. They were basically children themselves, in their twenties, and both of them were completely broken.

When you're poor and from Alabama or Mississippi without a job, your options are military or poverty. The GI Bill program tempts young men into enlisting. If you join the Army, you get to go to college for free. A lot of people think okay, three years of military service and then I get to go to college. But then there's a war and the big powers sacrifice their pawns in the game. Even if you live, something inside you is dead.

The crowd's trauma was forgotten for a second when the Dallas Cowboys cheerleaders got up on stage to jump around. The next acid trip on this extravaganza was this Italian all-girl country and western band. Five ladies in Daisy Dukes, cowboy boots, and flannel shirts knotted up, like five Sophia Lorens singing country in heavy Italian accents, beautiful. A U2 cover band had been flown out from Las Vegas. Fake Bono and Fake Edge were mimicking their heroes the best they could.

×××

Joan Jett's manager, Kenny Laguna, was a bit of a downer. He always found something to criticize and mostly wore a frown while traveling. If I sang even the slightest bit offkey during a show, I'd be sure to hear about it afterward. The problem was that he was on my side of the stage blasting his keyboards and singing offkey himself, didn't really make my job easier. The band and crew had stayed the same for years, which was surprising considering that everyone seemed to have a word to say about Laguna, and especially about the tour manager, Elliott. I would get paid out monthly, the wage was so measly that I wasn't really able to put anything aside, hand to mouth as usual. The amount of travel alone was pretty incredible. I spent about three days a week at home, and most of that went into recovery: sleeping and watching movies. Kamen and I pretty much only had Mondays and Tuesdays together.

I've played concerts with a hundred-plus-degree fever, sitting on the drum riser, barely able to hold my bass, I don't cancel shows over nothing. But I was feeling really bad in April. We were supposed to go to Niagara Falls for a gig and then fly out on three flights to California for two weeks. On top of my fever, I felt dizzy, I was having chest pains, and I was wheezing when breathing. I played the show in Niagara without remembering much of it afterward and went to sleep. I got much worse overnight. I was coughing up blood, had the chills, and was fever hallucinating.

I called the tour manager to let him know it might not end well if I flew out to California like this. Elliott didn't listen to a word I said and told me he'd go get Advil from the pharmacy. No, there's something off here, way past that, Advil won't fix this. I'm not going on the tour to die. I suggested that Enzo Penizzotto, the bass tech, could take over. Enzo had been there every step of the way for ten years and knew every last song. He was a badass bass player and had his own band, REO Speedealer.

There were daggers flying from Kenny, Elliott, and Joan's eyes the next morning. They didn't say a word. I didn't really give an F because I just needed to go to the hospital. I was diagnosed with atypical also known as walking pneumonia, I know, and the boogie woogie flu. The doc put me on some heavy-duty antibiotics called Ciprofloxacin and ordered bed rest until it was gone. I wasn't supposed to sit up or get up for anything more than a piss.

The whole time I was in the bottom of the bed, no one from Joan's camp so much as asked me how I was doing. When I got better, I went to pick up my paycheck; I was on a monthly retainer. The accountant refused to give it to me and explained, "Kenny has told me to hold your wages until further discussion." To me there was nothing more to discuss at that point. The bad vibe the manager had been spreading for a long time had poisoned even the good moments. There was always the whining, and now no one even gave a shit that I'd gotten infernally sick. The trip to the hospital had cost me a lot, because I didn't have insurance. Without insurance, an ambulance ride in Manhattan back then could cost you over a grand. And now Kenny was telling me I wouldn't be paid this month, that I was on probation.

Probation? After two years and hundreds of concerts?

I told the old sourpuss to eat shit and wished the Blackhearts good luck.

Playing the same setlist one concert after another was not creative work, it had started to get stale the year before. On one hand, it was a luxury to earn a living playing the instrument I love and to play with a legend like Joan Jett. On the other hand, I started to feel like I was a factory worker: every day the same thing. Rock and roll should be freedom, open to the moment and to change. It's gotta be a joy to play. If I sang a single note flat in the Blackhearts gig, Kenny would come with his frown and finger-pointing within the hour.

×××

The phone rang in July. It was Donna, my friend and a former member of Cycle Sluts from Hell, who was now playing in SheWolf, which often played as Sylvain Sylvain's backup band. Donna let me know that Sylvain had asked for my number.

I'd run into Sylvain the first time in an airport sometime in 1983 or 1984. It was just a fast hello; he was touring with Johnny Thunders and Jerry Nolan. Our proper meeting didn't happen until the 2000s, in the fall of 2003, to be precise. We had a long, nice night at my local bar on Tenth Street. My dog, Elvi, a Doberman, was with me, just a five-month-old puppy then. I was so immersed in our conversation about clothes—both of us are a bit of clotheshorses—that the teething Elvi had eaten almost half of the wooden table.

The situation now was that the living members of the New York Dolls, Sylvain Sylvain, David Johansen, and Arthur "Killer" Kane, had played a comeback show in June 2004, a few weeks before in London at the Meltdown Festival that Morrissey had curated. Morrissey had been a mega fan of the Dolls since he was thirteen and had written a book about the band in the early eighties, a little fan book. Curating the Royal Festival Hall, Morrissey begged David Johansen to put the band back together at least for a couple of shows.

After the reunion shows in London, Arthur got sick. He thought it was the flu, but he was diagnosed with late-stage leukemia. Arthur passed away a short time after checking himself into hospital, on the thirteenth of July.

A few days after Donna called, Sylvain called and told me that before Arthur had died, the New York Dolls agreed to play a show in New York, a couple in the UK, and a Japanese tour. They needed to honor the agreement. Would I be up for playing the shows with them?

I managed to get out the words to say that it would be an honor. I'd played some gigs with the late Johnny Thunders and Jerry Nolan in the eighties, and I was pretty confident that I knew how the Dolls' music should be played. David Johansen wanted to set up an audition all the same because he didn't know a thing about me. I knew all the Dolls songs inside out from listening to them thousands of times, I just needed to refresh my memory of which key they were in. The tryout would be in two days.

The New York Dolls had a massive influence on rock and roll. The band made two records from 1973 to 1974. The hard and dirty street rock 'n' roll, the over-the-top image was a huge influence on the Ramones, the Sex Pistols, the Clash, and countless more bands. Hanoi Rocks took a lot from the Dolls and that carried on to Guns N' Roses and so on from there. I had just happened to live above Gem Spa, which could be seen on the back cover of their first album. That wasn't the only coincidence related to Dolls mythology. And now this.

It was of course weird that Thunders, Nolan, and now Kane weren't in the band. Their sound was inimitable, totally unique. And even if you could try and copy their sound, only the originals could make it sound like the original Dolls did. Goes without saying.

I took a cab up to Midtown to the guitarist Steve Conte's studio. Steve, who I hadn't met before, had stepped into the late Johnny Thunders's giant shoes and had played the Dolls reunion shows. A guy named Brian Delaney was sitting in Jerry Nolan's place.

A bearded guy in shorts and a Megadeth T-shirt walked out of the audience before I went in. I thought that if this was my competition, the gig was mine.

Sylvain had told me to learn the songs "Jet Boy," "Personality Crisis," and "Who Are the Mystery Girls." When I walked in, David's first words were, "You're from Finland? Aren't you all alcoholics up there?" Well, hah, yeah, more or less. "And you carry fuckin' knives, don't you? You guys are the Puerto Ricans of Scandinavia!"

I told them why I'd left the Blackhearts, and then we started to play. After three songs, David asked if I knew any others. "Yeah, I got them all." We played through the whole of the *New York Dolls* first LP. I was grinning from ear to ear because the experience alone was enough for me. David was singing right in front of my face with that huge voice of his, and I got to play the entire first album with him and Sylvain, a record I had blasted a long time ago when I was a kid in Tapiola…that was it, I can die happy now! I don't even care if I get the fuckin' gig or not!

I went home. Sylvain called me up. "Jackson, you're in!" He called everyone Jackson. I went out to Micky's Blue Room to celebrate the news.

Sylvain Sylvain let me know that the first show was on the fourteenth of August on Randall's Island at Little Steven's Underground Garage Festival. The date rang a bell: Did I have something planned for that day? I looked in my calendar. Oh shit! My wedding!

I told Sylvain that that was the worst day possible, because I happened to be getting married that very day. My mom had bought plane tickets, the venue was booked, and so was the catering, ice, everything. "C'mon, Jackson, you can figure it out."

Show time was at nine. We were getting married at a West Side Highway art gallery at five. I talked to Karmen, and we decided to move up the ceremony. Dinner would be from three to six, then we'd head over to Randall's Island, where the wedding afterparty would be a New York Dolls show.

On my wedding day, we sat down in the car at six, Karmen in her wedding dress and me in a white tux. We were at the festival grounds at seven thirty. We got congratulations on our wedding from no less than Iggy Pop and Bo "Bo-pa" Diddley.

Little Steven had rustled up a legit sixties rotating stage. One side could tear down the previous show and set up the next set while there was a performance going on in the front. After the last song, the stage spun around and the next band could start playing right away. It was a pretty smart setup, because forty bands would fit into a twelve-hour event. Most of them only played four songs. The headliners—the Strokes, Bo Diddley, the Dolls, and Iggy and the Stooges—would play longer sets.

The stage had broken down halfway through the afternoon, right after the first band. The motor got stuck, and the stage couldn't even be turned by hand. Rescheduling was madness, and the decision was made to have everyone play with the same backline. A few of the smaller bands had to be dropped off the program so that the schedule wouldn't be totally fucked.

The performers were chauffeured around in golf carts. We drove past Bo Diddley and Sylvain yelled out, "Hey Bo, we're doin' 'Pills!'" Bo answered, "Good, 'cause I ain't."

Sylvain saw my quizzical look and explained. In 1972, the Dolls caught a Bo Diddley show. Johnny Thunders yelled out that they played a cover of Diddley's "Pills." "Bo, we got a band. We do 'Pills!'" But Bo apparently, or supposedly, thought that Thunders meant they were talking about drug use, and quipped, "Good for you, 'cause I ain't."

We'd prepared in exactly two rehearsals. This was the first New York show the New York Dolls had played since 1975. It was a far out and trippy-ass feeling when the orange sun set behind the Manhattan skyline and David Johansen growled, "When I say I'm in love, you best believe I'm in love, L-U-V..." in front of 30,000 screaming, clapping, and whistling hometown fans.

The show was the good kind of chaos: an amp blew out, there were fuck-ups, the tempos were up and down, somebody forgot that part, someone this part, but it all rolled out ferociously. It was real. The setlist was chock full of songs that I've loved since I was a kid. The last rays of the sun were still shimmering behind the East River when the last chord of "Personality Crisis" hung howling in the air and we exited the stage. It was an unforgettable moment and a wedding day.

We left for a festival tour of Ireland and England ten days later, four big, 40,000-person concerts with the White Stripes and Peaches. I had become a fan of Peaches in the beginning of the 2000s after hearing "Fuck the Pain Away." I hadn't been much of a White Stripes fan before, but the duo absolutely killed live. Every night after our set, I grabbed a bottle of wine from the backstage and sat with Peaches behind Jack White's amp to watch the show. It was mind-bogglingly fun and great.

At Marlay Park in Dublin, I heard that Shane MacGowan from the Pogues was eating catering backstage. I absolutely had to go say hi; I'd never met him before. Sitting there at the plank table in catering was one of my all-time favorite lyricists with a big red drink in one hand and a half-eaten cheeseburger in the other, and he was puking. I backed off. Maybe I'll wait a minute...

Shane MacGowan then followed David Johansen around for the whole night. David was horrified. Here comes that toothless guy again. Run away!

We played at the Azkena Rock Festival in Spain in September. Our show time was at two in the morning. It started to pour in the evening, and the power went out. The organizers went looking for a generator, and let us know that we'd be on at three. We weren't. The show was moved into a huge tent. It was 4:30 in the morning by the time we got on stage to the sound of the crowd singing soccer anthems. The tent was full of smoke from cigarettes and joints, wine bottles were being passed around. Great vibe and great show, as is usual when playing in Spain.

It was easy to travel with the New York Dolls. David had quit drinking years earlier, and the rest of us weren't going out of control either. There were no negative vibes on the tour bus, no bloated egos, no one bossing anyone around or fighting, just laughter, lots of it, it was all very light with tons of great stories floating around. That's how being in a band is supposed to be.

The three of us younger guys were like school boys when David and Syl, the walking musical encyclopedias, got going. Ask them about any late fifties/early sixties known or unknown single, and they'd give you the catalog number, release date, ranking on the charts, songwriter, producer, players, studio, recording date. David originally has a theater background; he worked at some freak theatre in Lower Manhattan before the Dolls. I put a record on in the bus, and David was surprised. "Oh! You don't just listen to rock?" I answered that I rarely listen to rock. David for his part listened to whatever, from Emil Zrihan to Numidian wedding polka. He burned me a mixed CD full of obscure blues from the thirties: "It's Cold in China," "I Live in the Alley," etc. Still a treasure of mine.

It was great putting the setlist together, especially when everyone wanted to play the Shangri-Las' song "Out in the Streets." Live, with this band? I was at first skeptical. But it worked. The Dolls stood out from other seventies bands in how big a deal the early sixties girl groups were to them. The Shangri-Las, the Ronettes, the Crystals. Way more important than the Rolling Stones. Which is...strange and beautiful.

As far as fashion sense, the guys had been influenced by each other, and also by Alice Cooper, Marc Bolan, Andy Warhol's Factory gang (like Candy Darling and the other trans performers), and, of course, Max's Kansas City, which was where Sylvain's favorite band, the Velvet Underground, had played regularly, and the Dolls ended up playing too. Bowie started to get big in New York in 1971.

The first drummer for the Dolls, Billy Murcia, had died during their first tour of England. The guys were opening for Faces in London, and Billy took an accidental overdose at the afterparty. The band almost broke up from the heavy blow. Jerry Nolan's drumming lit a new fire in the band and they decided to continue.

The New York Dolls is the only band I've ever been in that had other members aside from me that didn't particularly like Kiss. I was the only one in Hanoi who couldn't get down with Kiss. Usually everyone in rock bands, especially American ones, dug Kiss. I was into Alice Cooper's theater, not Kiss's. On the other hand, Kiss's first record is so bad, it's actually great. Totally dry, no reverb in sight. Before Kiss, Gene and Paul had been in a band called Wicked Lester, about which Sylvain had this to say: "A really weird band, country and western with flutes!"

Sylvain Sylvain's story was like something straight out of a novel. He was born to a Jewish family in Cairo. His dad was a banker, they lived in a nice penthouse with help and everything. But when Gamal Abdel Nasser became the president in 1956, he expelled all the Jews with very little warning. Sylvain's family fled the country in the middle of the night, with only one fucking suitcase each, and they ended up in Paris via Italy for several years. Sylvain was a teenager when his family applied for US residency and got it. They were only given two options, though: Lawrence, Nebraska, or Buffalo, New York. His dad said that well, New York, obviously. Without understanding that Buffalo was hundreds of miles away from New York City. The family arrived in Buffalo in January. Sylvain had a thin suit and little French shoes; the family landed amid huge piles of snow everywhere. Buffalo is known for its snowy winters and for being in the so-called snow belt. Sylvain remembered how his mother had cried and cried. His mother cried for the whole first winter. The poor lady was from Egypt after all, and she had thought Buffalo was covered in a thick crust of snow all year round.

His dad, a former banker, ended up doing handyman work back in Paris and was learning to become a tailor. But as Sylvain said, "He was a tailor who couldn't stitch a straight line."

In the mid-sixties, after a couple years in Buffalo, the family was able to move to New York City, where his dad's family had also landed. And one of them was a proper tailor. Sylvain went to work for him and later on got a job at a clothing store.

One day, Brigitte Bardot stepped inside the store. Sylvain told his boss that he'd handle it. Syl spent the next hour, hour and a half picking out clothes for B.B. He said that the best of it was standing outside her fitting room and knowing that right at that moment, on the other side of that curtain, there was Bridgitte Bardot undressed. Just knowing that was enough, maybe too much.

Sylvain's first home in the city was LeFrak City, an enormous redbrick building area in Queens, which became a ghetto in the eighties. Sylvain, Billy Murcia, and Johnny Thunders went to the same school and ended up in the same class, and they soon started playing together. Syl was always wearing the best-cut suits, Beatles boots with Cuban heels, trimmed hair, very suave.

Sylvain came to check out a Mad Juana gig at Micky's Blue Room and sometimes joined on stage too. "Jackson, that's your ticket to stardom—not us!"

David hadn't gone back to Japan since the Buster Poindexter years and was somewhat nervous. The decision was made to rehearse for the tour, a LOT. We rehearsed every day for three weeks. And as a result, Syl started coming up with new riffs. Steve, Delaney, and I naturally jumped on board and jammed to them. We kept it very instinctive; it doesn't do any good to think too hard about that kind of music, at least at first. We realized that there was maybe a future here. We didn't put any songs together yet, but the jamming indicated that it was possible to make new music together. If we really got into it, there really would be songs.

The first gig in Japan was in Osaka for an audience of a couple thousand. In true Japanese fashion, the venue had the backline, PA, and lights to perfection, everything worked like a well-oiled machine. And the band was on fire. So I got confused when David walked up to me in the middle of a song and growled, "This ain't working."

I got worried. What was not working? My bass playing?

After the show, David called a band meeting. "Guys, way too tight! Way too tight. Can you get back to being sloppy? No more rehearsals—EVER!"

It was the first time I'd heard of a band being tight being a bad thing. But the natural loose, sloppy swing, the roll in the rock was part of the New York Dolls' thing. We'd over-rehearsed, and now we had to fix it and get sloppy again. We never rehearsed again in the following six years.

At the end of the year, we got some new requests for some well-paying shows. When Los Angeles offered a good-paying gig, why say no? And the crowd gave us one hell of a warm welcome. There were obviously people grumbling about playing without the three late members. But fuck that—we played the stuff the right way and the music came from the right place, from the heart.

The same question came to mind when right around then I got a phone call asking if I wanted to join the new Hanoi Rocks. I said no, because I had already said yes to the New York Dolls. But if Nasty and Gyp had been asked—and Gyp had been in shape to play—there would have at least been a discussion about what we'd do with it from then on. If it was the same guys, meaning the same sound, and all the egos stayed in check so we could actually work together as a band, that would have been worth the effort.

The springtime case of pneumonia had put my smoking days on hold. I kept smoking during my recovery, until one day in the fall, my morning cigarette made me feel awful. It tasted like absolute shit. I quit right then and there, threw my cigarettes in the trash, and haven't smoked since.

2005

Hurricane Katrina

Our manager came up with the plan to play SXSW in Austin in March with this idea that the New York Dolls were back.

Austin's a progressive city. Sixth Street is full of bars with live music, with blues, jazz, rock, mariachi, country, you name it playing every night. Austin has been home, by birth or otherwise, to Willie Nelson, Janis Joplin, Jimmie and Stevie Ray Vaughan, Alejandro Escovedo, Joe Ely, Roky Erickson, Townes Van Zandt, Doug Sahm. There really is something special in the water in that town. I'd spent a couple weeks in Austin in the eighties and hung out so much at this one bar that the bartender let me create my own drink. I jumped behind the bar and mixed together rum, orange juice, pineapple juice, cognac, and absinthe. The cocktail stayed on the menu for a few years: the "Yaffa Zombie," a real liquor bomb the color of swamp water.

I ran into David Bason, an A&R man I had met at Dave Novik's Christmas party in the beginning of the 2000s. Dave Novik had been Hanoi's A&R guy at CBS in 1984. Bason had worked as Novik's assistant and was now doing A&R at Roadrunner Records. He was at SXSW scouting new bands. Roadrunner had started off as a metal label, but they wanted to scale out to rock and roll.

We went out for lunch and talked about what a positive reception the Dolls reunion had gotten. David Bason asked when the new album was coming out.

No idea, there's no deal, I told him.

Bason choked on his bun. "Do you really mean that the Dolls are still unsigned?" Everyone in the music business had thought that of course someone had already scooped us up for their roster, but it was still a secret. "Wait a second!" Bason called someone, got off the phone, and asked me for the Dolls' manager's info. "We're going to make this happen."

In a few weeks, the New York Dolls had a record deal with Roadrunner Records. We'd be their first band on the rock side, and there'd be proper marketing behind the release.

The first songs we wrote together were "We're All in Love," "Plenty of Music," and "Punishing World." "Plenty of Music" was a girl group–inspired number with some castanets and plenty of backing vocals. Very Dollsy stuff.

I wrote the music to "We're All in Love" at home and sent the demo to David. There are plenty of overtones ringing throughout the entire chorus. David thought they sounded like words "ee-aa-oo-ee-aa, we are all in love." "Sami, you're a genius. There's no vocals, and you already put the words to the chorus." He wrote the verses in ten minutes.

The song is about us. We were absolutely in love with each other. The new beginning for the New York Dolls was a total love affair.

We took these three songs to the demo studio. It turned out okay but wasn't exactly right. We'd all write at home, and once a week we'd meet and show each other what we had.

David Johansen is a very charismatic character, but he's also one of the most fun musicians I know. We were driving home from Washington, DC, one night after a show. We were in a van, not a tour bus, and David sat shotgun telling jokes in the dark about Tom Selleck and Diana Ross the whole ride, from 1:00 to 4:30 a.m. For over three hours, he told the joke about Diana Ross doing her last tour before moving to Norway with the oil magnate Arne Næss. "And then Diana said…" This endless stream of baritone chatter from the front seat had us laughing to tears and pissing our pants. "And then came the lampshade, and the fire extinguisher…I don't know what happened with that, but…you know, Tom knows."

When the silhouette of Manhattan appeared before us, David finally dropped the punch line. It was so bad we couldn't believe it. We started to throw stuff at David. "Fuck, we listened THREE HOURS for THAT?" Another lesson on "It's not the result that matters, it's how you get there."

×××

Karmen's and my apartment on Tenth Street between Avenue B and C was starting to feel way too small. We got an offer from this guy John Stavros who owned three floors of commercial lofts in Hell's Kitchen. This new apartment was a former photo studio, with over ten-foot ceilings and around 1500 square feet. On Thirty-Seventh Street, between Eighth and Ninth Avenue, and just around the corner from the apartment we'd lived in while recording *Two Steps from the Move*. The first thing I did when we moved in was to go to Smith's bar for a glass, where I had seen the stabbing back in 1984. The bar itself hadn't changed much in over twenty years, but the outside was a whole new world. Times Square had become Disney Square.

Stavros asked if we wanted to tear down the backdrop that had been built in for the photo studio. I asked him to leave the backdrops up because it would be a good spot to project movies on. I bought a projector to project movies on VHS and DVD. I knew a guy who collected rare concert footage and got a concert recording of Patti Smith playing CBGB in fucking 1974 from him as a gift. It had never been released, and on top of that, the sound was great. I organized a Patti Smith party. I hooked up the music to play loud through a PA system and pulled the projector back until Patti was life-size. I turned out the lights, and the video started rolling. Everyone was almost in tears, it felt like the band was there in the room with us. A time machine back to CBGB in '74.

Nile Rodgers, the guitarist from Chic, had an office in the building, as was the hip-hop producer DJ Premier studio, and next to me was Erez Sabag, an Israeli fashion photographer. The walls between Erez and I were really thin, but everything was okay until one night when I put dub on through the PA system at full blast late at night. Erez got pissed off, but he had a PA system too. So he turned the speakers to the wall and put on

Never Mind the Bollocks even louder. Which would win? I turned my speakers to the wall too, and we were locked in a standoff until four or five in the morning. "Turn it off." "No, you turn it off." "Okay, let's go to bed."

Stavros the landlord was quite the character himself. He saw Andy Warhol's *Body Parts* in a window display. It was a whole series of little books where Warhol had collected Polaroids of body parts. Looking at one cover of those little books, Stavros exploded. "FUCK! THAT'S MY ASS!" Stavros had been a part of Andy Warhol's Factory circle in the sixties and seventies. "WITHOUT PERMISSION!" He brought a huge lawsuit against the Warhol Estate for using a picture of his ass on the cover of the book without his permission. And he could absolutely recognize that it was his, John Stavros's ass. He was incredibly vain, especially about his body, and did five hundred pull-ups every morning. He was very fit and a completely mad, very lovable Greek.

×××

We did a one-off gig at the Notodden Blues Festival in Norway that August. A lot of the performers were on our plane from JFK: Pinetop Perkins, Guitar Shorty, Hubert Sumlin, and Bettye LaVette. Bettye didn't sleep a wink on the flight, just walked around the cabin drink in hand telling jokes and stories, even singing a bit. Me, Conte, and Sylvain kept up with Bettye and used the airplane like a flying bar.

We got on the bus in Oslo and took off for Notodden. The party continued thanks to the bottles picked up from duty-free. The older guys nodded off, but sixty-something Betty just kept on going without getting tired.

We ended up in a hotel in the middle of the forest, which is apparently a ski resort in the wintertime. We went to get ready for dinner. Guitar Shorty sat himself down behind the piano in the dining room, and Bettye started to sing. I started to get sleepy after a cognac and went upstairs to crash.

I woke up at three in the morning, jetlagged and hungry. I went down to reception. From the elevator, I could already hear Guitar Shorty on the piano and Bettye's incredible voice. Everyone else had taken off ages ago, but these two were still up and jamming. I ordered a beer and sat down to listen. At some point, Bettye disappeared for a couple of hours, and then showed up for breakfast fresh as a daisy.

It was the same performance all over again on the flight back to New York. Outside arrivals at JFK, Bettye gave me a kiss on the cheek and slipped into a black car. I was exhausted.

We'd been booked to play a show in New Orleans, but it was canceled due to Hurricane Katrina. The festival in question had been pushed back and moved from New Orleans to St. Louis. We agreed to do a benefit concert for the volunteers cleaning up New Orleans, the firefighters and nurses. We went to New Orleans a month and a half after Katrina, and it was like an atomic bomb had gone off in the city. The walls were salt-bleached where the water from the burst dam had risen up to depths of six feet. Some areas had been completely evacuated, and the houses were uninhabitable. I saw only one person walking in the deserted streets, an old Black woman dressed in a big garbage sack.

The benefit show was on a small stage, basically someone's backyard, in a neighborhood that had escaped the worst of the destruction. The city's mayor, Ray Nagin, MC'd. The crowd was full of very tired-looking nurses and workers.

The French Quarter had been spared from water damage but had been looted and was full of trash. The windows to the restaurants were busted, and the doors had been chopped down with axes. I walked around the city that night and found a small, old theater where there was live music playing. I sat down at the bar and ordered a beer. After a while, an older woman who had sat down by me turned around and started to tell me about the night of the hurricane. She was a nurse in the neonatal intensive care unit. The power had gone out, and the hospital was running on its generator. Finally, the water got into the generator, and the hospital had to keep going without electricity. The ventilators shut down, and in the dark, premature babies started to die in their ICU cribs. The doctors administered the premature babies Valium so they wouldn't suffer in their last moments.

The woman cried and cried and ordered one drink after another. I tried to comfort her, but the words got caught in my throat.

2006

One Day It Will Please Us To Remember Even This

It was time for a slightly more unusual concert in February. Jesse Malin asked me to play bass in the house band for the Carnegie Hall tribute to Joni Mitchell. The drummer, Paul Garisto, and I would be on stage backing five artists. Paul Garisto had played in the Psychedelic Furs and with Iggy Pop as a tour drummer in the 1988 tour Andy had asked me to join.

You can't just master Joni Mitchell's songs in a couple of hours, because she uses unusual guitar tunings that also affect the bass lines. Some of the songs had friggin' Jaco on the recordings, oy vey. I don't read sheet music effortlessly, so I had to map everything out on cheat charts and memorize the rest.

The legendary Tin Pan Alley tunesmith Neil Sedaka was one of the performers. I went to a real Broadway rehearsal space with wood paneling like in some old gentlemen's club, and of course, a big Steinway. Neil sat behind it and plonked away as we went through the songs. Neil Sedaka was a little, super polite, flamboyant guy in a camel-hair coat.

On the night of the sold-out tribute, I walked onto the dark stage and picked up my bass. The first performer was announced: Neil Sedaka! The lone spotlight for some reason shone down on me. All of Carnegie Hall started cheering. I realized it was because I was standing center stage, the lighting guy must have thought that the main guy would of course be center stage. I pointed with my thumb to the right direction—that way!—to stage right. The crowd cracked up. The light slowly moved over to the right spot on the stage where Mr. Sedaka was sitting at his piano.

Every artist performed two songs. The next one I accompanied was Amy Grant, a mainstream star who's always been very vocal about her Christian faith. After that were folk queen Judy Collins, Michelle Williams from Destiny's Child, and of course Jesse Malin.

Right before Judy Collins, I took a little break while someone else was performing. That's when Judy's musical director came to say that Judy doesn't want to sing from E, so the song was moving to F#.

Oh man, not now! This was not a twelve-bar blues but a rather complicated piece of work. I'd figured out all the fingering, which notes needed to be played from the lower octave, which from higher octaves, this was no root note song. I only had five minutes to go through the new arrangement on my own. Playing the song was just a one giant focusing session, I barely noticed what anyone else was doing, much less the audience, but the Queen of Folk was satisfied.

Arto Tamminen told me back in the seventies that one day he'd perform at Carnegie Hall. But you can't play loud at Carnegie Hall, the sound gets mushy. The theater is built for chamber music and violin concerts, that's why it's so fucking weird that the fucking Who played there.

×××

We had to find a producer for the Dolls record. Mike Ness from Social Distortion made his interest known, and David Johansen met up with him. Afterward, David said, "I don't know if I can make a record with a guy with a neck tattoo." Mike Ness hadn't once looked him in the eyes either. That's totally foreign to someone who was born and grew up in New York.

The producer of the New York Dolls' first 1973 record is listed as Todd Rundgren. But Todd got tired of watching the partying after a few hours: the Dolls had shown up to the studio with thirty friends. Todd thought this was no way to make a record and left. The sound engineer, Jack Douglas, was the one who really produced the record. For this reason, Douglas's name came up, and it turned out he was still working. Jack produced Aerosmith's records from the seventies, Patti Smith's *Radio Ethiopia*, Cheap Trick, and John Lennon and Yoko Ono's *Double Fantasy*. Jack was also the tape editor on *Imagine*. He was given the task of editing the radio version of "Imagine," cutting and taping the tape. Jack recalled that it was "probably the first time I got real sweaty while working."

We did the preproduction in two weeks at Anthony Esposito's Schoolhouse studio on the corner of Twenty-Seventh Street and Seventh Avenue. We honed songs together every day and worked on new ones as they popped up. David brought home CD-Rs of the new songs of the day and scratched together lyrics overnight.

Roadrunner Records' A&R man, David Bason, had suggested "Ain't Got Nothing" for the record, which was a lesser-known song from one of David Johansen's solo albums. Sylvain refused to play on the song because it didn't sound "Dolls enough" to him. He didn't want "Maimed Happiness" on the record either for the same reason.

"Dance Like a Monkey" is credited to Johansen-Sylvain, but it should read Yaffa too. The chorus was missing from the song when I finally came up with the idea to keep the same chords from the verse, but change the drumbeat to straight R&R and the bass line from "Lust for Life" to a walking bass. The song was done.

A lot of people think that's just song arrangement and not songwriting. It's not songwriting unless there are chord changes. That's a load of hogwash. I've had to open my mouth lots of times to ask, "How about my writing efforts?" because lots of songs have only taken shape after some years and after this kind of suggestion, which might seem like a little thing but it makes the whole thing. And especially in a situation where everyone is putting in a lot of effort working on the song.

×××

We took a weeklong break after preproduction and started the real sessions at Shelter Island Sound studios, also on Twenty-Seventh Street, but at the corner of Third Avenue. Jack Douglas showed up to the studio on the first day of recording in a long parka and on his knees, that old trick where you walk around with your knees in the shoes. "Hello, I'm mini Jack!" He was holding hands with the legendary engineer, Jay Messina.

"Gotta Get Away from Tommy" was done in the first take. And the only take. Jack Douglas said right off, "That's IT! It's there. No need to do a second take." We listened, and Jack was right. We didn't play a single one of the songs more than four times; we got most of them in two, maybe three takes. Jack knew from preproduction what the songs sounded like and he could hear when the songs clicked. He had the ear and the balls to say there it is, no need to keep grinding.

We used a click track, but only into Brian Delaney's headphones. I could have gotten it for myself, but I'd rather play listening to the drums. Brian's got a good swing; he doesn't try to play too far behind the beat. Gyp and Razzle were good drummers, but not like this; they were still young and hadn't had the time yet to become *drummers*.

We stepped out from the studio room for a minute while Steve Conte banged out the solo immediately after the take, still riding on the song's adrenaline. That's it. Done. Let's move on. This way of working is just beautiful and worked well for us. We had the basics and solos done for the album in less than a week.

I'm not saying this to put down any of the amazing singers that I'd had the honor to play with, but David Johansen's presence when singing is one of a kind. It was mind-blowing to be so close to watch as that strong voice—that tone, that phrasing, that feeling—rings out; he is so completely in control of it all. I went to see the Who at Madison Square Garden sometime in 2003. I didn't know who the opening act was, but I recognized David Johansen's voice immediately when stepping inside the doors of Madison Square Garden, it boomed all the way to the halls. I had thought David didn't sing rock anymore.

All kinds of guests dropped by the studio. Bo Diddley, Iggy Pop, Michael Stipe, and the Rolling Stone magazine's legendary writer David Fricke, with that permanent grin on his face.

David Johansen asked for all the album cover stuff to be left to him to take care of. On the day of the photoshoot, we got the address, the time, and a command: "Bring a change of clothes." That was it.

I went to borrow a suit from my friend, Craig Robinson, for the album cover. He'd stopped playing music and was now making suits. I picked out a blue suit, the one that's on the cover. I left my loft and passed by my landlord, John Stavros. I told him where I was going, and he gave me a switchblade. "Here. For good luck." If you look at the cover carefully, you can see I'm digging under my fingernails with the knife.

I knew the photographer from before. John Scarpati had done the album cover for Michael Monroe's *Not Fakin' It*. My jaw dropped when I stepped onto set. Everything was painted, floor to ceiling, pink. Like a stripper's dressing room. Great one, David…could you get some more pink?

I brought John backstage after a show at Irving Plaza. Sylvain just glared at Stavros: That guy? Turns out Stavros had gone to same school with Johnny Thunders and Sylvain, but was two grades ahead of them and their bully. Stavros used to beat up the little guitarists. They started talking, and suddenly I was thrown back to their fifty-year-old schoolyard antics and all the weird shit between the two of them, just two sixty-year-old boys like they'd never left the playground.

We played the Olympia in Paris. Everyone has played there. There were framed posters from past concerts hanging backstage: Edith Piaf, Yves Montand, Ella Fitzgerald, Louis Armstrong, Frank Sinatra. The legends looked down from above as if to ask what have *you* got to give? The green room had its own bar, and its waiters were full of Parisian attitude, with little mustaches, red and white striped shirts, and black vests. There was a very elegant older lady sitting at the upstairs green room lobby wearing cat-eye glasses, a Chanel suit, and a cigarette in an old-fashioned holder. We got a cold but professional welcome from her. Olympia was like a time machine to decades-old etiquette. At the same time, the stage was technically modern, and there was a TV monitor backstage with a fixed picture that showed what was happening onstage.

Both the New York Dolls and Hanoi Rocks were performing at the Peace & Love Festival in Sweden. This was the time when a Swedish newspaper reported on Andy forgetting his teeth on the bus: "Rockstar's teeth found on the bus." My son, Nicholas, came along, and we headed off early for the hotel. It was a hot night so we had to keep the window open. We could hear some metal band playing from outside. Then I realized that the band was playing "I Can't Get It."

I asked Andy in the morning what kind of a Polish pop metal band they'd become, and he flew off the handle. To Michael's credit, he's actually good at taking criticism, he just shrugs it off. I've always been able to be straight with him.

The Dolls' new record came out in July. After the Ruisrock Festival in Finland, we flew to New York to tape *Late Night with Conan O'Brien.*

Conan had been making fun of Finland for a year and a half, especially about how he looked like the woman president then, Tarja Halonen. I was getting a bit annoyed that Conan had been mocking us Finns like that. It was funny enough at first, but then it just kept going and going. Before the taping, I called up my old pal Rane Raitsikka in LA who was making T-shirts then. I had seen one of the shirts Rane was making and asked him to send an XL since Conan's a big guy. The black T-shirt had PERSEENREIKÄ written on it in white letters. It means "ASSHOLE" in Finnish. Just to be sure, I asked Jimmy Vivino, the guitarist in Conan's house band, if Conan could take this kind of a joke or if I was just burning bridges. Jimmy assured me that Conan could, and I should give it to him.

We played "Dance Like a Monkey" on the show, and Conan shook our hands at the end. He's even bigger than he looks on TV, especially his huge head. I told him, "I'm from Finland," and handed him the shirt. Conan said, "Oh, great. I love your country," and he asked me what the shirt said. I told him that it was an old Finnish saying.

A couple months later, I saw Jimmy Vivino at a club and asked him how Conan had liked the shirt. Apparently, Conan had loved it so much that he'd been walking in it all around the hallways of NBC with ASSHOLE emblazoned on his chest. An NBC employee who had a Finnish partner saw the shirt and exploded into laughter. "Do you know what that says, Conan?" "No, but I guess it's some old Finnish saying." Conan had flipped out when he got the whole truth. Best fucking gift one can get!

The end of the year was spent mostly sitting in buses. A one-month tour of Europe and then a one-month US tour right after that. We played on *The Late Late Show with Craig Ferguson* and *The Henry Rollins Show* in LA.

It was a surprise to find out that Henry's manager was the former Hanoi manager, Richard Bishop. We found out while playing England's biggest talk show, *The Jonathan Ross Show*, that Jonathan was an old Hanoi fan and had seen us live in 1983 or 1984.

The Dolls' comeback record didn't sell that well, only about 50,000 copies worldwide. There were about half a million illegal downloads, though. The business had already gone in the direction that records were pretty much just calling cards, signs of life, and to earn a living, bands have to tour endlessly or do other work. My royalties started to dry up by the late nineties with Napster and all the other file-sharing services that showed up. People were starting to think more and more that listening to music should be free. That's a hard mentality to change, and in the near future being a musician or working in music will stop being a profession because it doesn't pay anything.

2007

Glitter in the Gutter

Jesse Malin has come a long way from when he and the rest of D Generation drank Demolition 23.'s backstage dry. He began his solo career in the 2000s, and these days, he's basically the mayor of New York. He's the kind of friend you can really count on, which is a rarity in New York. If a friend is short on cash, Jesse will try to set him up with a job at one of the bars he owns in Lower Manhattan or something. A true blue, very loyal, steadfast guy.

Jesse asked me to play on his third solo album. It wasn't hard to accept; Jesse's songs are great. We had sporadic rehearsals for a couple of months. "I've got a couple of new songs. Can you make it Wednesday?" Jesse is really particular, but I'm very okay with analyzing every last note and weighing the options on what to play. You don't always have to stick to your first instinct.

Jesse had a big suitcase full of diaries and notebooks from the last twenty years. Different colors, sizes, completely busted-up notebooks. Only he knows what's in them and where. They look like a complete mess. "You got some lyrics in there, man!"

We went to a studio out in the middle of nowhere for the week, an old barn with accommodations. We got started on the basic tracks. And that's when the vibe changed. I was expecting it to be tough work, but this was tough work that was far from any sort of creativity. The production duo, strange Beavis and Butthead types, were metal dudes, and if you ask me, were totally wrong for the job, in both style and attitude. I tried to get through with humor, but it didn't work; there was no humor involved.

Their method was to play forty takes of each song. No joke. We spent seven days in the studio, thirteen hours a day, playing the same song over and over again without hearing any difference between the take we'd done eight hours earlier. I played my fingers to the bone along with the drummer, Paul Garisto, Christine Smith on keyboards, and Jesse singing guide vox. Was there any reason to wear out Christine and Jesse too on the drum and bass takes?

Okay, playing music is a nice way to spend my time, it doesn't bother me, I actually love it you know. But overplaying something that already works is just a waste of time. Maybe that's how metal records are made, precise to the last nanosecond. Jesse's music isn't like that at all though, and the endless takes didn't make any difference to the final product.

I had been under the impression that the metal twins had been listening to my bass too and how it worked with the drums, but turns out they had just been listening to the drums, for a week. Which is absurd when you're talking about a drummer of Paul Garisto's caliber. A few takes would have probably been more than enough.

I had given everyone the date I had to leave for a Dolls tour well in advance. But on the last night I was meant to be there, as Paul was packing up his drums, "Beavis" let me know that we were now going to get started recording the bass.

I looked at him like he was nuts. What in the hell had I been doing in the booth for hundreds of hours, then? Sorry, man, you got the bass already, and good luck to you. I've gotta go.

On one or two of the songs, there's someone else playing the bass, using all of my bass lines though. And only because of the bass tone, not my playing. Jesse's friend, Bruce Springsteen, sang on "Broken Radio." So I played bass on a song with the Boss, cool stuff. But Bruce didn't show up to the studio until after I had left for the Dolls tour.

The music nowadays is missing its raw power and unexpectedness, because there's the calculated power, not the unleashed energy bursts. This is not to criticize Jesse, but Jesse's producers. When Andy showed a

Hanoi song at a specific tempo, it changed only if it obviously felt better at a different tempo...but that and the Dolls experience of making music were two completely different things. There was a click track banging away the whole time with making the album. Then the producers needed to try what it would sound like with one BPM more, then half BPM less... like splitting hairs, or as we say in Finland, fucking the dots. The only Hanoi record we made with any kind of click track was *Two Steps from the Move*. Bob Ezrin tried to have us use a mechanical click, but we couldn't manage to play with it, so Ezrin put together a cardboard box, stuck a 58 mic inside, and beat the box with a drumstick. Voila, a click track a la Bobo Earzone.

Kids these days hear the Eagles as offkey, but they were at the top of human harmonizing back in their day; kids are used to hearing everything with the cursed autotune. And the beat can't falter at all either, it's not allowed anymore, everyone is mesmerized by the grid, they are looking at music instead of listening to it. You can find isolated tracks for the Rolling Stones on YouTube: just the drums, just the bass, just the guitar. When you listen to one stem at a time it's unbelievably sloppy, all over the place. But when you put it all together, oh fuck, there it is! Keith Richards was asked what drives him in the studio regarding takes. It's the feeling that they've all been in the studio for fourteen hours already, everyone's tired, pissed off, and maybe a little drunk, and THAT'S the take. A song doesn't really fly until everyone's finally stopped trying.

Maybe that's what was driving Jesse Malin's sessions; Beavis and Butthead were trying to wear out the musicians. But I just don't think that was the case.

Another D Generation member's album came out at the end of the summer, Richard Bacchus and the Luckiest Girls' *Jet Black and Beautiful*, which I produced and on which I also played the bass. Christine Smith from Jesse Malin's band played keyboard. Ricky's record was an example of how some musicians end up working together over and over. It's rarely a problem to know a lot of people. The word spreads, and you get interesting job offers. Working on Ricky's LP didn't earn me a dime, but working on it as a producer and engineer taught me a lot.

2007–2009

San Diego

"Nothing had changed even though I moved to California because the Dolls never rehearsed. Sylvain Sylvain had already lived in Georgia for ages."

2007

Bei jing Pop Festival

The apartment we were renting from John Stavros was starting to get a little expensive now that Karmen was out of work. We'd lived in New York for the past ten years, and I've got a love-hate relationship with the city. Sometimes I just get fed up with New York. And before long, I keep coming back.

Okay, let's make a change and move somewhere else. We'd spent some time in San Diego with friends, and it came to mind as an option. The pace of life there was more chill, and the populous was interesting. The mild California climate would be a nice change from New York's pollution, long winters, and unbearably hot summers.

We brought our dog, Elvi, with us and moved to Ocean Beach for its bikers, surfers, punks, and hippies community. Since San Diego is right on the border with Mexico, you could take a bus from right outside our place and get over the border to Tijuana for a dollar fifty in under an hour. We went down to Tijuana a lot since the place was completely nuts, food was good, drinks cheap, and the music scene was diverse and interesting. It can be a dangerous town, though, and you definitely have to pay attention to where you're going. It entered my mind to start fusing mariachi music with other styles of music. I was thinking about that as a good direction for the new Mad Juana album.

San Diego has the same downside as Los Angeles: There's just no getting around without a car. We bought a 1983 Mercedes-Benz diesel station wagon. A friend of a friend converted the engine so it could run on waste vegetable oil. Once a month, we'd collect barrels of used cooking oil from local restaurants, filter it on our balcony, and fill the tank. The whole time we lived in San Diego, we didn't spend a cent on fossil fuel, plus we weren't polluting the environment. The local TV station even did a story on us and our veggie Benz.

×××

The Dolls were asked to play in China in the fall. Did it pay well? Yep. The other performers at the Beijing Pop Festival included Public Enemy, Marky Ramone, and Brett Anderson, the guy from Suede.

I thought that my commute to China would be shorter now that I was already on the West Coast. China is just there on the other side of the ocean: San Diego-San Francisco-Beijing, boom, I'm there.

I woke up at three in the morning to get on the six o'clock flight. San Diego sometimes gets a lot of fog, and that was one of those days. I called the airport, and they said all flights were postponed until the fog cleared up. I got on the plane three hours late, so all of my connections had to change. I had a long layover in San Francisco and was now flying to Osaka from there, and then I'd have an eight-hour wait for my flight to Beijing.

I sent the manager an email to say I'd be late, but I never got a reply. The message didn't go through, and no one in Beijing knew when I'd be landing. I just had the name of the hotel.

I got to Beijing a day late. When I got in a taxi, I gave the name of the hotel to the driver. She looked at me and smiled. She didn't understand. I showed her the paper with the address, but it was all written in English, so it wasn't ringing any bells. The driver just shook her head.

Well this was just a nightmare. What do I do? As a last attempt to get out of the mess, I put on a fake Chinese accent, how I thought Chinese sounded, and said: "ZONK-HAATSIKUKOTHOOKANTHA Hotel."

Okay! The driver's face brightened, and she took off driving.

The taxi stopped in front of a building that looked like more of a convention center than a hotel. Was this the right place? And that's when David Johansen and his wife Mara walked out the front door.

After twenty-eight hours of travel, my back was toast. I found the Institute of Massage and went inside. There were people dressed in white lab coats looking like doctors, and I got my back fixed up. They asked me at the end of the session if I was interested in cupping. Why not? The glass cups had really big openings, the size of a drinking glass. It felt like an eagle was grabbing me by the back and lifting me up in the air by its talons. Chinese cupping is dry, they don't break the skin, unlike Finnish cupping, where the clots of blood end up slithering down the drain.

We had a press day the next day and were driven all around Beijing. I wondered aloud why all the walls alongside the freeways were painted green. They looked freshly painted, and the green went on for miles. The translator lady answered with a little embarrassment that the Olympics were coming to Beijing the following year, and when the Olympic committee had shown up to inspect the locations and the air quality, they concluded, "You need more green." What they had meant was trees and plant life for more oxygen, to combat pollution, and to generally improve the environment. But the city had misunderstood and had painted everything green.

The Beijing Pop Festival took place in the massive Chaoyang Park. We ran into Brett Anderson backstage. His entourage was pretty, how should I put it nicely, insufferably English and licking Brett's bum with vigor. "Well, BRETT thinks…BRETT says…BRETT this and that." That kind of idolatry drivel flowed constantly from the tour manager. Uh, please don't say the word Brett again!

Marky Ramone walked around cradling his Rock and Roll Hall of Fame statue. He didn't let go of it for a second, sitting or standing.

Our set time was nice and early, at four in the afternoon. The crowd was split into two sections, each one with about three thousand people. There was a walkway between the two sections with the mixing booth looming at the end. There were armed soldiers standing every few feet watching the crowd. That was the festival's security. There was a VIP gated area in the front with chairs, mostly Beijing and China's top military personnel in military finery, plus business moguls and their wives.

The sections seemed to be divided into Chinese and non-Chinese. The Westerners danced and jumped around without problem, the soldiers didn't really know what to do with them anyway other than asking them to stop and sit down. The event was supposed to be a light, good-vibe rock and roll festival, but it was full of soldiers. While we were playing "Dance Like a Monkey," I saw something happening some ways out in the park out of the corner of my eye. A line of soldiers shouted and marched two by two right up to the stage. It was the change of guards.

I changed into a fresh shirt after the show and ran to catch Chuck D getting on stage. It was quite the experience to see Public Enemy performing in Beijing. Of course, their first song was "Fight the Power."

Steve Conte ordered from the menu "the best cup of coffee" at the hotel breakfast. Everyone else's coffee came right up, but Steve's was nowhere to be seen. Finally, an entire laboratory rolled out from the kitchen. Test tubes siphoned up into a glass ball with a small reservoir underneath and a little tap the waiter used to pour a cup of coffee for Steve. Steve took a taste: Yeah, it's good, thanks. When the bills came, everyone's coffees were two dollars each, but Steve's "best cup of coffee in the house" was twenty-seven bucks.

2008

Bru ja on the Corner

We got a burst of inspiration in San Diego and began to write new songs that were a mix of our ideas with Balkan Romani music, dub, and Mexican music. If Mad Juana's first record had opened up to North Africa, Romani music, and Ireland, then this one was open to Mexico and the Caribbean as well. I laid down all the backing tracks with the master drummer Paul Garisto, just the two of us. When it was time to put a touring band together, Steve Rodriguez joined on bass, Dustin Luna on drums, and Nico Camargo on trumpet in addition to Danny and Marni. Nico also played trumpet on the record.

It was an amazing sight when the mariachi bands finished their shift at two in the morning and gathered on a plaza near Avenida Revolución in Tijuana: a couple hundred mariachis in their badass suits and sombreros passing around a bottle of tequila in the moonlight.

I went over to a guitarrón player and asked if I could give it a try. The guitarrón is a big acoustic Mexican bass tuned to octave strings. It's not something you can pick up just like that. I handed the guitarrón back to him and asked him to show me how it's done. He asked me what I wanted to hear. Whatever he played at home was my response. The guitarrónista flashed me a gold-toothed smile and started in on John Coltrane's "A Love Supreme."

We got Mad Juana a record deal with Azra Records in San Diego thanks to our demos. Greg, the head of the label, let us use his house for the duration of recording the backing tracks with Paul; it was outside San Diego and in the middle of the desert. When going outside, you'd have to check your shoes to make sure you weren't taking a scorpion along for the ride, and if you went a little farther out, you'd have to look out for rattlesnakes. In the middle of recording, we would hear explosions in the distance followed by machine gun fire. Just over the hills was the Black Water Security training center.

Paul Garisto and I got the basics done in five days, and we flew out Danny Ray and Marni Rice. Danny's raw and urban saxophone screaming was an interesting complement to Nico Camargo's mariachi trumpet.

Derek Plank, a friend from San Diego, came out to shoot the cover. Karmen brought some fake roses to the photo session, and I brought a shotgun and a toy gun. For some reason, I wanted weapons on the cover. We took a promo photo where I'm aiming the shotgun at the camera. Then we took some more, in different positions and with different props, but it didn't feel like we were getting close to the shot we were looking for. I asked Derek for the camera. I made a crown of roses on Karmen's head sort of reminiscent of Day of the Dead. I asked Karmen to open her mouth as if screaming and point the guns at me, I squatted down and snapped the picture. Close, but now quite there. Derek saw the vision and took one shot. There was the cover.

Azra Records ran out of money in the middle of it all. Greg had to sell the masters to Acetate Records, who finally got *Bruja on the Corner* released.

Mad Juana left on tour. A musician friend named Mario Escovedo took care of all the booking. Mario wasn't officially our manager but was helping us out with a lot of the day-to-day things. And sorry, God knows I'm no manager, I'm a musician. I managed to use my connections though to book some one-off shows, and since Gogol Bordello was coming out to California, I asked Eugene if Mad Juana could open for them a couple times. We played San Diego and Las Vegas with Gogol Bordello and a Serbian band called KAL. That's how I got to know Dragan Ristić from KAL, who I got as the fixer when we went to Serbia for an episode of *Sami Yaffa: Sound Tracker* five years later.

We made our way down south from Seattle, via Portland, Reno, San Francisco, Las Vegas, LA, Anaheim, San Diego. The van broke down in Death Valley on the way to Vegas. It was well over a hundred degrees outside, the cell phone service was spotty. We were sweaty and tried to get someone to stop on the side of the freeway, but no one would. I started walking off into the desert to see if I could get a signal, and finally got some bars and was able to call for a tow truck from Vegas. An hour later, the tow truck showed up and a big woman jumped out of it. Like, really big. Her name was Bertha, or she looked like a Bertha in any case. She hooked up the van and ordered us to sit up front with her. We were running late, but Bertha told us not to worry, she'd drop us off right at the venue, and we could deal with the van later.

The audience was hanging out in the parking lot in front of the club when we showed up in the tow truck. The show must go on.

Rick let us know that Acetate was a small label, and the tour support would pretty much be that we'd get four hundred CDs to sell at the shows. The venues were all so small that we had to scrape the extra money together. So we made voodoo dolls in the van; one person would make the body, another the eyes, someone else the hair. Someone would sew the Mad Juana tag on the doll by hand. We'd easily sell twenty of the voodoo dolls in a night at twenty dollars a head. It was good enough for extra income, and making the dolls in the car was a good way to kill time. It would have been too easy to suck on the Serbian pacifier and start drinking, because it's the easiest, and also the most destructive, way to pass time.

×××

The New York Dolls went on tour in South America. A couple shows in Buenos Aires, one in São Paolo, and one in Recife.

We were sitting down to dinner in Brazil with the local promoter and his team when the conversation turned to cocaine and how nice and pure it was in South America. I said that I hadn't done any in years. After the show and the afterparty, I headed back to the hotel. I woke up to a knock, and I went to look through the peephole. The promoter's assistant was standing in the hallway, so I opened the door.

"Here's your coke, man," he said with eyes like coffee saucers and opened his hand that had a tennis ball's worth of coke inside. I let him know that I was sleeping and hadn't asked for anything. The assistant wouldn't let it go though and insisted I take it and give him the money. I told him more sternly that I hadn't asked for anything and I hated the stuff. The guy started to get aggressive. I had to get rid of him somehow.

"Listen, there's a guy right below on the next floor who will almost definitely take it off your hands," I told him and showed him the guitar tech, Duncan's, room. This was good enough for the hothead, who turned around and headed toward the elevator.

Duncan was holding onto the breakfast table with his knuckles white, teeth clenched, and his eyes bugging. He managed to say, "Thanks a lot, Mr. Yaffa! Thanks a FUCKING lot! You know what I've been doing all night? Polishing your fucking guitars, over and over again!"

It was still unclear whether we were playing the São Paolo gig or not. We'd agreed to be paid upfront in cash. The promoter showed up with the money, but a grand was missing. Our tour manager said we wouldn't be playing until he had the missing money in his hands. The promoter was horrified; there'd be a riot if we didn't get on stage. Sorry, but that's your problem, not ours, a deal's a deal.

The guy was gone for about an hour and came back with a mixed bundle of bills. Euros, dollars, yen... The tour manager calmly pulled out a calculator to do the conversions. The money was exactly a grand. So we played the show.

The venue had been sold over capacity, over a thousand people in an eight-hundred-person venue. The stage was high up, there was barely any oxygen. I squatted down gasping for air between songs. I have no idea how David Johansen was able to get enough air in his lungs to belt through the songs, or how the crowd was able to sing their soccer chants between songs.

In Recife, in the Pernambuco state of Northeast Brazil, there was a festival that the Dolls were headlining with Bad Brains. Whoever came up with this lineup idea had to be a genius. Our hotel was right on the ocean boardwalk. There was a view of the beach from my room. The balcony door curtains were lazily dancing in the sea breeze. I took a power nap after the long trip and the couple of caipirinhas that were offered at the check-in.

I woke up to loud banging. A whole lot of drummers and horn players walked in a line from hotel to hotel on the boardwalk with dancers surrounding the band. Busking Brazilian style.

It was an hour's drive into the jungle to get to the festival. When we got there, we found the Bad Brains enjoying some herb in their dressing room. They were just as surprised to be on the same bill.

The festival organizer, Paulo André Pires, owned a record label in Recife. He gave us a huge pile of CDs as a welcome gift.

The crowd was just as crazy as in Buenos Aires or São Paolo. I was kicking on the beach the next day with Steve Conte. We got to chatting with a guy named Clayton who owned the fish fry next to us. We ate some delish fish from his joint and took in the view of the beach. A toothless guy showed up who played Beatles songs bossa nova style in Portuguese for a couple of bucks. He only had three strings on his guitar, but it was absolutely amazing.

Clayton asked us in the evening if we wanted to go out, and if so, if we wanted to party at the beach clubs or if we wanted to go to his hood. His hood, obviously. We drove through the jungle and arrived at the village of Muribeca; its main drag was full of open-air bars. Each bar had its own PA system blasting! One bar was bumping samba and maracatu, another one reggae, a third metal, the fourth techno. There was definitely a competition going on, mostly on volume. There were horses walking around, people were dancing around with liter bottles of beer in their hands.

We partied in Muribeca until seven in the morning. We found out later on that we were in one of the most dangerous neighborhoods in Recife. But we found no bad vibe there at all, just smiles. The only ones with long faces were the horses.

On the trip home, I listened to the CDs Paulo André had given us and I fell in love with the amazing music of Pernambuco.

The interest in New York Dolls shows started to dwindle. We probably played too often in the same places and maybe not enough of the old stuff. Most people just want the nostalgia trip and the familiar songs.

David Johansen was against turning into a jukebox of old stuff. If you're not making anything new, there's no point in being a musician. Truth in that.

It didn't help that the Dolls had overpriced all the shows. The shows needed to sell out for the promoters to make their money back. And we didn't. Olympia in Paris was at eighty percent capacity, so the promoter took a big hit. This happened at a lot of places, so the next time around, we played smaller venues. And next time around, they weren't sold out either. In 2008, there was less demand. Steve, Brian and I got paid less than the two originals. It wasn't enough to live off of anymore. "We're All in Love" ended up in the movie *Kick-Ass*, so fortunately, some cash came out of that.

When things turned the way they did, Roadrunner Records didn't want to continue the agreement, so the Dolls had to look for a new deal. The managers landed on Sanctuary Records, or Sanctuary Records landed on the Dolls.

We agreed that Todd Rundgren would produce the next record. And that we'd make it at Rundgren's place in Hawaii.

Sylvain hadn't exactly been happy and satisfied with the previous record. Sylvain had a very clear idea of what the Dolls are and are not. We told him that maybe he should be the musical director for this record since he knew better, and we'd follow his vision.

The songs were slow in coming. We kicked around some riffs and ideas, but the vibe was off. There was something going on between Syl and David. And most of the songs were missing lyrics. David just said, "Don't worry. I got the lyrics."

2009

Divorced in Hawaii

Things weren't going too well between me and Karmen in San Diego. By the last days in New York, we were already living more like sister and brother, and moving didn't fix things. We just kept fighting and poisoning the air for one another. I was depressed and no longer in love, but still cared tremendously about Karmen. We'd lived together for fourteen years after all, and we had a band together. For ages, I hadn't known what to do, and then I realized that I needed room to breathe. I hoped that after the divorce, we'd still have a good enough relationship to be able to work together and keep Mad Juana going.

I started to mull over the idea of moving back to New York.

But I had to go to Hawaii first.

The Dolls hadn't done any kind of preproduction before going to Hawaii. "Don't worry. I got the lyrics." The whole thing was just kind of together, and we almost canceled the whole thing three days before leaving. What's the point of going to blow all this money if we don't go home with a record? Or would we just end up with a fucking expensive demo?

But a month-long trip was on the table, so fuck it, let's go. We assured each other that we'd get a record out of this.

We got to Kauai and went to Todd Rundgren's ridiculously great *Scarface*-style pagoda of a house. Steve Conte and I settled into Todd's house, the rest of the band was a little ways away in the guest house by the golf court. There was a living room in the middle of the main house, and since we were in Hawaii, it was outdoors with a Japanese koi pond. The four surrounding rooms had been built out of black wood. There was a little studio on one end, where we ended up recording the vocals.

The day we arrived, Todd went to talk to David and Syl to go through all the songs while Brian, Steve, and I hung out in the living room. After a long wait, the three of them came back and Todd said, "You guys have a great holiday. You are off for a week. These two, they gotta write the lyrics and pull the songs together!"

I started every morning of my week off by jogging down the gravel path to the beach. I'd swim and run and mull over my divorce with Karmen because it was heavily on my mind. I started eating properly and only had a couple of glasses of wine tops in the evening. In the evenings, after the preproduction, Todd would sit himself down in front of the TV, turn on some political program, and yell at it.

One morning I walked into the kitchen, and Liv Tyler was standing there cooking. It took me a second until I remembered that Todd was her stepfather and had raised her. "How would you like your eggs?" Liv asked.

After a week, we moved our gear to a rented house in the hills of Kauai. The living room was the drum room and where we all played. We put the amps into separate bedrooms. Todd set up his mixing board in the office and we officially started recording. One of the walls in the main room was a floor-to-ceiling window overlooking the ocean. It was whale migration season, and we could see the big breaching backs and water fountains off in the distance while playing.

The mood on this album was taking a more chill turn than the previous one. Maybe it was the setting. It was further away from OG Dolls and closer to Tamla Motown, blues, and soul. The song David, I, and Steve wrote, "Temptation to Exist," could have been a Mad Juana song. I wrote "Muddy Bones" like a country and western song at first. The chord progression worked, but the attitude didn't. Then David made a suggestion in the studio: play it like the Who would. And that was it. Every now and then, you gotta stop and take a look at the song from a different perspective. We captured the songs very quickly once we found the style that spoke to the lyrics and the singer. It only took a week to lay down the basics, so I ended up with another week off. I got asked to come sing backup or play maracas or melodica every now and then, a little spice that was needed for the record.

I went running every day on the beach in Kauai. It cleared my head and my thoughts, and I started to feel a lot better. I knew I had made the right choice. If Karmen and I hadn't split up, it would have ended badly, and I wanted to keep Karmen in my life as a friend.

2009–2014

New York City

"We were nearing the end of this rock band's lifespan;
You make a couple of albums and then it starts to fizzle away.
Almost as if it were some kind of law of the universe."

2009

Kumpanía & Cause I Sez So

I packed my stuff myself, and I moved from San Diego to New York. I got an apartment on Thirty-Seventh Street in Hell's Kitchen in John Stavros's house. All of Stavros's lofts were too pricey for me, but a hatmaker named Orlando Palacios owned a smaller loft in the building and agreed to sublet it for a thousand a month. Karmen and I had been commissioned to write music for an off-Broadway musical called *Kumpanía* about Romanis in New York. The producer of this, Andrew Kriss, had grown up in a Romani community and had gotten to know us by listening to Mad Juana. The musical was about a relationship between a Romani guy and a white girl, kind of like *West Side Story.*

The new start in New York was both good and heavy at the same time. Breaking up with a long-term partner is no small thing. It wasn't easy on Karmen either, who was still mad at me and writing lyrics for the songs from the script.

I hauled a drum kit over from a friend's place and set it up in my loft. When we started recording the songs for the musical, I realized that all of Karmen's lyrics were personal and were about US. "Is this still the PLAY?" The pencil was on fire as Karmen unburdened herself and then sang the songs next to me while I was engineering. First it was a bit comical, then it got annoying, until I realized this was going to be really good. There was a spark, so let it burn.

Then we needed horns for the songs, specifically Balkan-style horns. Marni suggested Frank London from the Klezmatics; he'd produced stuff for Ljiljana Buttler and other Romani artists. The musical's budget was so small; most of it had gone into a new computer and some other recording equipment. I called Frank London anyway and told him about the project, and how we needed a full Balkan horn section for it. I explained the script to him and what I was aiming at; I didn't want it to be traditional all the way, I also wanted the New York vibe to it too.

I told him that what comes next would probably sound like an insult, there was only $200 in it. "Yes, that *is* an insult." Frank asked to hear the songs anyway, no matter what shape they were in.

Two days later, Frank called back: "Don't worry about the two hundred. It's a cool project and the songs are good." He was in.

This stout guy who had the aroma of music, garlic, and cigarettes showed up with six trumpets dangling from his shoulders. Frank pulled the whole arrangement together himself. He had something written down on the sheet music, but really he did everything on the spot, totally on the fly. He listened to the songs, what was there a couple of times, and said, "Press record." I got a perfect horn section for all the songs in one afternoon. Heart and soul, taste, knowledge, and virtuosity; that's Frank London for you.

Frank got another two hundred from me later on when he played trumpet in Brooklyn with Mad Juana. We played a huge party in an industrial space for Mexican Independence Day, organized by Pedro from Gogol Bordello and his friends.

We got all the musical's songs together by summer, but the writer, Andrew Kriss, ran out of money. The Romani subject matter was too much for some investors and theatres, and that's where the project came to a screeching halt. Andrew was extraordinarily fair and let us use the music whichever way we wanted.

I couldn't get a publisher for the songs, so they were shelved. I said something about the project years later to Michael Monroe's manager at the time. She wanted to help out and got *Kumpanía* onto iTunes. Nothing bigger came out of it, but at least the songs were available for anyone to listen. They have since been taken down.

×××

The Dolls' second comeback record got the name *Cause I Sez So*. It came out in the summer. But Sanctuary Records didn't really publicize it, so no one really even knew when it came out. It was a non-event. Todd Rundgren was the producer; on that basis alone, there should have been some press around it. Just a few write-ups and that was it.

It wasn't easy to book shows when even the promoters didn't know that we had a new album out. We did a tour of the US and random gigs here and there. My bank account was doing a disappearing act and the boat was starting to go under again.

My son Nicholas caught our show in Stockholm. There had been some radio silence during his teen years; we had lost contact. When Nicke turned seventeen, I managed to keep in better contact with him, and he came out to New York for a longer stint. From then on, we've kept in touch better and have built our relationship over again.

The Dolls performed at the Down by the Laituri festival in Turku that July. We asked Michael Monroe to come up on stage and jam; he played the sax and sang on "Personality Crisis" and "Pills / Hey Bo Diddley!" After the show, Michael and I went for a drink at a boat restaurant on the bank of the Aura River. We started catching up and going through unsolved things. And we talked for a long time. Demolition 23. hadn't lasted for as long as it should have, and that bothered both of us. We both wanted to continue with that vision in mind if we ever played together again. I had missed Michael, and the idea of playing together again felt really good. The New Hanoi Rocks had fallen apart in the spring, so Michael was free to do whatever.

Michael's manager, Virpi Immonen, came to New York in the fall. I'd been through so much shit that I wanted to hear from Virpi directly what she had in mind as a manager. The Dolls' first manager had taken care of everything alone and that was enough up to a certain point. Then the Dolls operations got bigger, and we made an agreement with Gold Mountain Entertainment. The company's head, Ron Stone, had managed a bunch of big names in the seventies and eighties, and he had also been somewhat involved with Jetboy. But Mr. Stone had gotten somewhat stuck in the past and didn't seem to get the importance of the internet or social media. The shape of publicity had radically changed in a short time. You've gotta share news and videos on social media, be your own marketing person. The slow demise of the New York Dolls was partly on the management too, me finks.

This was 2009. Virpi wanted for the whole band to work together and to use the net and street teams. This all sounded good and dandy, and I was ready to move forward. Virpi went looking for money and a record deal and to think about how to launch this new band.

The whole industry was in the grips of change and in the middle of the biggest robbery ever committed in the recording industry, the robbery committed against the musicians and songwriters. Streaming was on its way.

Michael had already started writing songs with Ginger Wildheart. Ginger wanted to take a break from his band, the Wildhearts, and specifically from being the front of a band. Richard Fortus, who played with the new Guns N' Roses, and with whom I had played and recorded in NYC, was another possible guitarist. I also thought about Todd Youth, my friend from the early nineties, who'd been the original guitarist for Murphy's Law and had played with Danzig, Motörhead, and D Generation. Todd has played with *everyone*. He was interested, and so was Jimmy Clark, our drummer from Demolition 23. Michael flew out to LA to meet Todd and Richard Fortus.

It turned out that Richard's schedule was too packed to join the band, so he had to drop out of the picture.

2010

Another Night In the Sun: Live in Helsinki

We announced the new project in January, which was just called Michael Monroe. We knew from past experience how hard it was to launch a new project with an unfamiliar name, like Demolition 23. for example. You had to tell everyone that well, both Michael Monroe and Sami Yaffa are in Demolition 23. It would take a year or two to pound the information into the heads of the old fans. It's easier just to stick with the brand.

The tour was set to start in March. We rehearsed for a couple of weeks, and then Jimmy Clark announced that he couldn't commit to the band. Okay. There had been a bit of a problem with Jimmy in practice anyway. After living and playing in Nashville for years, he'd lost a little bit of his touch for punk rock. Todd Youth introduced us to Karl Rockfist, who was just the right kind of drummer and guy. I'd met Karl some years before when Chelsea Smiles had opened for the Dolls.

But Todd was the next to leave, just a couple weeks before the tour. Todd didn't call Michael or the management, or even me, even though I'd known him for a decade. Todd just sent Michael and Virpi a short, two-line email. Todd pretty much fucked us over and took off with Ace Frehley. His decision didn't even make sense, because while Ace might have paid better, he only toured a few months out of the year.

What guitarist would be able to pick up the whole set with only ten days' notice? My bro from the Dolls, Steve Conte, of course. I knew things were a little slow for him at the moment as well, since the Dolls' next show wasn't until June, although Stevie is never completely unemployed.

Michael agreed to Steve for the tour, but we'd see how it all played out. I predicted that Michael would fall in love with Steve as soon as he started to play. And that's exactly what happened. Steve also sings like an angel, so it was a done deal; Steve was in the band.

Me, Michael, Karl, Ginger, and Steve were the lineup that went to tour the West Coast. We noticed right off that the chemistry was all there. The shows had a good turnout, and the crowd was into it. It felt like they'd been waiting for us; Michael wasn't in the States that often. Our new songs, "You're Next," "Another Night in the Sun," and "Motorheaded for a Fall," quickly made the set. The other songs in the setlist were more from the punk end: Hanoi Rocks, Demolition 23., Michael's solo stuff, and a careful selection of covers.

We played two or three shows in a day at South by Southwest. First at a little bar in Austin at two in the afternoon, then a different bar at four. Some of the crowd followed us from one show to the other. SXSW officially ended on Saturday, but everyone in the know knew to wait for the closing party on Sunday that Alejandro Escovedo hosted at the Continental Club. We played there too. The Austin crowd didn't really know much about us, and they probably thought Michael was some eighties hair metal relic, but they went completely nuts for us like all the other crowds did that spring.

We made demos out at Seawolf Studios in Helsinki. We learned the new songs and recorded them right away; it didn't take long. We kept punk and the melody close to heart, but there were some heavier riffs brought by Ginger and even some country rock, like "Gone Baby Gone," which music I wrote and could have been a Flying Burrito Brothers song. Ginger's and Steve's songwriting gifts were put to use, and everyone took an active part in writing. Only two songs on the album weren't a joint effort, so it was pretty amusing later on when Ginger said in some interview: "When I wrote the album."

Some of Ginger's riffs were heavier than Michael was used to doing, but I urged him to give it a chance, even if it felt off at first. Michael has his own comfort zone, and it's sometimes hard for him to take the leap out of it. Conte wrote the music to "Got Blood?" and Ginger wrote Little Richard style machine gun lyrics for it with some assistance from Michael. It's reminiscent of "Thrill Me" from *Not Fakin' It*, I knew it would work.

The new material felt fresh as a daisy, the band was in good spirits, and the live show was explosive. The next step was translating this kind of energy onto a record.

The New York Dolls had shows lined up at clubs in Ireland, England, Belgium, Holland, Germany, Denmark, and Norway. We also performed on Jools Holland's TV show. The only festival we had for the summer was in France. In six years, we'd gone from playing on big stages to little clubs holding only a couple hundred people and the Le Mans motorcycle race.

It felt like the Dolls were on the way out and Monroe on the way up. We played Tavastia in Helsinki in July, and we used the money from ticket sales to record the gig. We wanted to get a release out as soon as possible, maybe even a live one, to show off how good the band was live.

A few days later, Virpi, Michael, and I were at the Ruisrock festival in Turku, Finland, when a bottle of champagne was brought to our table. We hadn't ordered one, but we were told that it was compliments of the next table. We turned around, and Jarkko Nordlund, the head of Universal Finland, waved at us. He wanted to sign Michael Monroe to Universal's Spinefarm imprint. The offer was name your price.

The manager negotiated the contract with the aim of recording in the fall. The live album *Another Night In the Sun* would be released in early October, the first on Universal / Spinefarm. I sent a message to the New York Dolls manager and to David right away that please whatever you do, don't book anything for the first three weeks of September. And of course, I got a message from the Dolls' management a few weeks later letting me know, "We're going to make a record in September!" What? Did you not read my emails? Then the manager started to piss me off. "You have to choose. You have to choose." As much as I hated to make my decision, I had to do it and called Syl and David: I couldn't keep going with them. But there was no bad blood in my leaving, it was just that the Monroe sessions had been agreed upon first and I was made to choose. I don't think the Dolls' managers were trying to test my commitment by deliberately booking the studio at the same time, I hope. They had just spaced out.

We started looking for a producer and were throwing names around. Steve and I suggested Jack Douglas, who had done really great work on the new Dolls album. It also was definitely not a problem for the band that he'd produced Cheap Trick. We were all huge fans.

Jack managed to haggle a little on his rate, and we flew out to LA to record. We stayed at a place far enough away from the studio that Ginger—the only one with a driver's license—got thoroughly sick of driving us around every day in LA traffic. Which is very understandable.

Karl and I got the basic tracks done for sixteen songs in four days, it was a doddle. Lemmy came to sing on "Motorheaded for a Fall." I sat on the couch with a view through the window of the booth—notes, reading light, cigarette smoke, and Jack Daniel's—that unmistakable growl coming out of the booth. It was the highlight of the session.

I'd gotten to know Lemmy in 1983 when Razzle, Nasty, and I were hanging out at the St. Moritz club in SoHo, London. Lemmy basically lived at the St. Moritz, pulling the lever on the one-arm bandit all night long. We started to say hi when we saw each other. I was high on heroin one night, and Lemmy noticed right away. He lifted me by the neck up to the wall. I thought I was gonna die, but then again, if I was to die, at least I'd have been killed by Lemmy. He gave me a lecture in a quiet and threatening tone about using heroin: You have no idea how fucking stupid you are. Quit that shit. It stayed with me. I had no idea that the love of Lemmy's life had died of heroin in the early seventies.

In the early nineties, Lemmy played at a Toys for Tots benefit organized by the Hell's Angels in NYC. I'd done a lot of coke and was wandering around with a drink in my hand. Lemmy recognized me, it had been some time since I'd last seen him. "Sammy, how are you doing nowadays then?" I assured him, "I'm good. I'm good." Lemmy brushed the hair out of my eyes and looked into them to see if they were pinned from heroin. Quite the contrary, my eyes were big black saucers from the coke. Lemmy was delighted and let me go. "Oh, you're doin' all right!"

I don't understand anymore why I did coke at all, because it was just insufferable. Well, I was able to drink more and for longer. But coke on its own is just terrible. I'd get tense and nervous and would want to kill myself before I died of the heart attack that'd be coming any moment.

Cocaine takes away your ability to the hear high frequencies. "I can't hear the treble, gotta add more." That's why all of Motörhead's records are so trebly. The Stooges' *Raw Power* too, produced by none other than the Thin White Duke himself, David Bowie. Cocaine is also particularly dangerous for musicians because it creates mindless, out-of-control self-confidence.

The problems started after recording. Long-distance mixing is never easy, and Michael likes to be in control; he wants to be a part of everything. And with good reason. He had a vision for what he wanted and a shitty track record of experiences. Don't trust other people, just do it yourself if you know what you want.

We were expecting greatness, since Jack Douglas and Jay Messina are legends. But the mixes weren't working. The songs hadn't sounded that small even during recording. No, they were supposed to be more present, in your face, blasting out of your speaker. But Jack had already moved on to his next project, so now we had to focus on plan B.

Over Christmas, Michael went back in to Seawolf Studios in Helsinki, where we'd recorded the demos over the summer, and started mixing the record with Petri Majuri.

All kinds of weird stuff was discovered in what we'd recorded in LA. For example, on some of the songs, the bottom snare hadn't been miked, Petri had to use a trigger to get out the sound. There was some other cleaning up due to carelessness.

×××

I'd moved in with my new girlfriend Mina in Brooklyn. I came home one day to find both Mina and Karmen in the kitchen. Shit, this can't be good... but there was no problem, they were just talking. I'd kept writing songs with Karmen and Mad Juana was still somewhat in motion. I was lucky that

I didn't lose a person who I respected as a person, friend, and artist from my life.

One night, Mina walked into the bedroom with a gun in her hand.

Uh…what's going on?

Mina had found a gun in the spare bedroom closet but had forgotten to tell me about it. There was a trapdoor that Mina had opened with a knife, there was the previous tenant's 9mm and a clip hidden in the floor.

New York had a "No Questions Asked" policy. There were signs about it all over town. The police wanted guns off the streets, and you could bring them in, no questions…Mina brought the gun into the police station and was promptly dragged into questioning. She really got grilled, not exactly no questions asked. This goes against your campaign, Mina protested. They weren't going to let Mina go, but she had a cop friend she'd met through work. Mina got to call her Brooklyn detective friend, John, who guaranteed that Mina was certainly innocent. Mina was released from questioning, but as she left, she said that this was bullshit and the campaign was a lie.

2011

Sensory Overdrive

Michael had left the album cover design to me. Same for coming up with a name for the album. Doing all the gigs had left me feeling with a bit of a sensory overload. I changed "overload" to "overdrive"—it felt more rock and roll—and *Sensory Overdrive* was good enough for everyone.

The graphic designer, Kii Arens, sent me ideas for the cover that maybe would work with the name. An Asian chick with wires coming out of her helmet? Well, maybe not that. But I did a double take when I saw a leftover draft Kii had made for Marilyn Manson: a big zippered eye. This was *Sensory Overdrive*. There was something still missing even if the colors were changed from Manson's cover idea. It was Michael's own eye. No stock photo eyes. And Michael's crazy painted nails had to be in the picture too. Mikko von Hertzen took a picture of Michael's eye and sent it to Kii Arens, and that's how the album cover came together.

I kicked off a different kind of trip down memory lane in Finland that February. Joose Berglund, the owner of punk label Stupido Records in Helsinki, suggested getting the original lineup of Pelle Miljoona Oy back together just for a tour. The band talked it over and agreed because it sounded like an interesting idea.

We organized a rehearsal at Nosturi, a club in Helsinki: Pelle, Tumppi, me, Andy, and Taskinen. What do you wanna play? "Olen kaunis" (I'm beautiful)? We started playing, everybody cracked up! After thirty years, it sounded just as scabby as when we played together before. It was exactly the same. It was incredible. There's really something to be said about band chemistry—some people just sound a certain way together. Some are better than others, but it's the sum of all parts that matters. And thank God Pelle and Tumppi's drumming hadn't changed at all.

We didn't play the *Moottoritie on kuuma* album from start to finish on the reunion tour, we played the set we played over the summer of 1980. That setlist. "Mulla menee lujaa." We played Tumppi's songs from Problems. "Ei tää lama päähän käy." The songs from *Moottoritie* started to take shape in the spring of 1980, and most of the songs were in rotation during the summer tour. But songs like "Meille kävi näin" we never played live. We gave it a go, and it turned out great for the live set.

Singing duties were split fifty-fifty: Tumppi's set and Pelle's set. Whoever wasn't singing was on drums. The change didn't happen song by song, but maybe three to five songs at a time.

Andy didn't remember all the Pelle songs anymore. We rehearsed, but they just didn't stick in his head. I had to run across the stage and yell "F!" I got to know just from the look on Andy's face if he didn't remember the next part coming up. And then I'd go running again. "G!"

Andy had been more focused on painting than band stuff recently. Maybe getting a band together and touring wasn't something he wanted to do anymore after the second Hanoi. Who knows?

We did more reunion shows over the summer. Pelle played the punk stage at the Ruisrock Festival in Turku, Finland. It was a small stage in the corner of the meadow. Twenty thousand people showed up. And every one of them sang along with all the songs. It was an amazing vibe. Joose wouldn't have guessed that Pelle Miljoona Oy would have been a big band that summer. The next time we played Turku, it was booked at a three-hundred-capacity venue. The presales were so good that the show moved to a bigger venue, the Caribia. The organizers thought that maybe five hundred people would show up. That sold out too. Over three thousand people. All the shows that summer were like that. Every single last one.

The eight months I'd spent in Pelle Miljoona Oy thirty-six years before had been most excellent, and we remained lifetime friends. Pelle asked me sometime in the late nineties if I knew of a place for rent in New York where he might be able to come write a book. I lived in Brooklyn, Williamsburg, back then and knew a Finnish girl named Lubna who lived a couple of blocks away. She had a vacant room, and that's where Pelle spent a month and a half writing. I sang backup on one of Tumppi's last solo records, *Sivupersoona*, in exchange for use of his daughter's Jopo bicycle while I was in Helsinki.

I don't know what Taskinen has been doing all these years other than experimental music, but is he even releasing any of it? I'm also not too clear on when Taskinen left Pelle, because we left Finland and our contact with Finland was pretty much cut off. We played gigs in Finland, but it was just work. I'd have time to check in on my family, but I didn't hang out anywhere. We'd go back to Stockholm as quickly as possible. I really lost touch with Finland for quite a while. But it's come back since the beginning of the 2010s with Monroe's band. I've spent more time in Finland now than I have in the last thirty years.

I've seen new Finnish artists, met lots of people, and gotten the news that a lot of old friends like Musta Paraati and others are touring again. Finland isn't in black and white anymore, and the scale of the music scene has changed.

HIM and Rasmus were both bands Seppo Vesterinen managed. Seppo had trained for world domination with Hanoi. It was good practice for him. The best school possible. Years ago, I saw HIM play a big concert in New York when they—or Seppo—had made a deal with Sire Records. There was a big turnout, *Spin* and *Rolling Stone* magazine and everyone of any importance in the NYC music biz was there, and of course Seymour Stein and Michael Goldstone from Sire, who signed both Jetboy to MCA and now HIM to Sire.

I met up with Seppo during soundcheck at the bar downstairs and again in the VIP section when the show was starting. When I ran into him prior to the show, he had two cigarettes in his hands and was losing it. "FUCK! Sami, I already went through this shit with you guys. Do I REALLY have to go through it AGAIN? That fucking singer has been up all night, he's lost his voice and is fucking wasted."

The Irving Plaza was sold out. Ville Valo basically fell onstage. He was pretty much only able to wheeze. The show didn't get any better. It was pretty embarrassing. I got up, clapped Seppo on the back, and said, "Fucking good band. See you later!"

×××

Sensory Overdrive came out in Finland in March and went to number one. The record came out at just the right moment, after the new Hanoi broke up. And now Michael Monroe was back and *strong!* "Michael Monroe" now was a band and not Michael and his backup band.

During the record release tour, it started to rub Ginger the wrong way that he was just the rhythm guitarist. The attention is always on the middle of the stage, and he's used to being there; he's been the lead singer and center of attention for a looong time. The crowd was mostly focused on Michael, which apparently bothered Ginger, even though he'd specifically joined the band to escape the attention of being the lead singer and he said he just wanted to play the guitar.

Ginger played on my side of the stage, in Nasty Suicide's spot, but he wanted to play on Steve's side, which Steve was not down with. Then Ginger wanted to take over my spot to be closer to Michael's spotlight. But I've been used to playing next to the drums since 1978. I have to be able to hear the bass drum and see the drummer out of the corner of my eye.

But it's not like I have an X marked on the stage that I won't leave. Ari Taskinen tried that one time in Pelle; one time, he drew a box with chalk because I ran around the stage too much and got in his way. "Don't step outside of your box!"

We were playing a club show in Turku, and I said okay fine, let's check it out. Ginger took my spot next to the singer and the drummer and I moved all the way to stage right. The whole show sucked; the sound on stage was imbalanced. We moved our spots back, but Ginger never got over it. There seemed to always be something wrong. On top of it, Ginger and Virpi had some bad beef between them. Ginger was just looking for a way out.

After a show in Madrid, Ginger and I were the last men standing. Both of us had had a lot of beer before switching to whisky, and we were both getting twenty sheets to the wind. I asked why he was always complaining and said that he should do something about it. Ginger snapped and threw a drink in my face and stood up. I threw a drink back in his face and stood up. We glared at each other for a second and busted out laughing. Then we sat back down and hugged it out, another shot of whisky perhaps? Shit happens on tour.

I love and respect Ginger, but I got pissed off because I saw that he was pulling away little by little.

We did a joint tour with Motörhead. Ginger's last show with us was in Brighton.

Ginger knows he's mostly to blame for the whole thing. He's not the easiest to be in a band with, but on the other hand, he's a genuine and warm guy. I was sad that such a gifted and great guy was leaving, but on the other hand, I was also surprised that he made it a whole year and a half. I think he joined the band to recharge his batteries and to find the spark again to do his own thing. After taking a break and some distance from the Wildhearts with us, he was ready to go solo.

After his time with the Monroe's, Ginger did a VERY successful pledge campaign. His English fan base is very solid and fully behind him. Ginger wanted to put out a triple record, and the fans who donated to support got to decide the order of the songs. Crowdfunding, like PledgeMusic, is a reasonable way to get past the fuckin' labels, the music industry, and the stiff old structures of the business, but you've gotta be prepared to do a lot of work yourself. Pledge and other fan-funded campaigns are as in now as using social media for marketing and info sharing. It brings the artists closer to his or her audience. Hats off to Ginger.

Richard Fortus had a year-and-a-half-long tour with Guns N' Roses coming up. We couldn't count on him as a replacement for Ginger. Our second option for a guitarist was Dregen, who Michael had asked to join back before Todd Youth. Backyard Babies had just fallen apart, and Dregen wanted to put out a solo record. This solo record hadn't materialized a year and a half later. So we called him again.

Dregen agreed. From June on, there'd be another bolt of energy in the band aside from Michael. Dregen didn't care if he was stage left or stage right because he just ran around the stage like a headless hyena anyway. We also got a new sonic gift from Dregen; his playing style is so much his own that you can recognize him from just one riff. Just like Neil Young, Johnny Thunders, and Malcolm Young had their own thing going on, Dregen is a riff and rhythm guy who built his own world from scratch.

I met Dregen in 1995 when Backyard Babies opened for Demolition 23. It was in Gothenburg, the show when Nasty quit. Dregen and I clicked, and I'd meet up with Dregen when I was in Stockholm if he was around. Backyard Babies came to New York in 1999 to record, and me, Karmen, Michael, and Joey Ramone and a bunch of others sang backup on their song "Friends."

I thought Dregen joining the band was cause for celebration. Now there was another Swede besides Karl, and Dregen didn't exactly spit in the bottle. The four of us became the Buffoons, much to the chagrin of the managers, bookers, roadies, and Michael Monroe. But it wasn't an all-day headache, just a half-day one. And hopefully it was mostly a good vibe.

Poor Michael. He's had a lot of bands with a bunch of crazy people. Michael does not imbibe, does not suit him at all. In Birmingham, at the end of the *Sensory Overdrive* tour, the whole band went to the pub in the afternoon. Except for Michael, of course. We got the great idea to play the Damned's "Smash It Up," with the whole long intro and everything. And of course, as a surprise for Michael.

At the show we realized that playing wasn't really working, our fingers were not moving as nimbly as they should have, thanks to drink. We really had to concentrate and pull ourselves together so the rest of the show wouldn't be a complete disaster. And of course, Michael let us have it later on about how selfish we were. A couple of beers is gig juice, but playing drunk never works. Might seem like a good idea before the gig, but no, it never works.

The Classic Rock Awards has as categories album of the year, the band of the year, the best new band of the year, and so on. *Sensory Overdrive* won the album of the year, so we traveled to London for the honors. Ginger was invited too, also for his pledge campaign, if I remember correctly, much to the surprise of the whole English music business.

The tables at the Camden Roundhouse were full of nominees and winners. Deep Purple was sitting over there, and Brian May, Roger Taylor, Jimmy Page, Rat Scabies, Chrissie Hynde, Jeff Beck over there on those tables… This cream of the crop and my childhood heroes all smiled and clapped when we got up to collect our award. It was kind of an out-of-body experience. I saw Bob Ezrin for the first time in almost thirty years at that party. He was there because he was getting an award for Outstanding Contribution. His first question was, "You still doing Mad Juana?" I was totally surprised that he was still following up on what I was doing. He raved about the band and urged me to keep going.

I asked Bob Ezrin to produce Mad Juana. He asked if I had a Bob Ezrin budget.

2012

No Reservations

On the corner of Avenue B and Fourteenth Street is a rock 'n' roll tiki bar called Otto's Shrunken Head where Mad Juana played a lot. One of the owners of the bar, Nell, called me up in the fall of 2011. Anthony Bourdain's *No Reservations* production team had asked if she knew anyone from Finland because Bourdain was planning to do one of his culinary trips to Finland. I met up with Anthony Bourdain's producer to hear what they had in mind, even though I thought I was the wrong guy. I'd left Finland back in 1980, what did I know about Finnish food culture?

I told them that I didn't remember Finland being any kind of culinary paradise so they better be prepared. We didn't go to restaurants at all back in the seventies. When the first Chinese restaurant came to Tapiola, we went there a grand total of once with the family. I think I ate a hot dog because nothing else on the menu looked good to a nine-year-old.

I knew that Finland had become more multicultural since then, but it's not really interesting to see things that you can find anywhere, like pizza or Nepalese cuisine. I suggested some nice, old classic restaurants in Helsinki like Salve and Elite, but I also told them that they definitely had to stop at a late-night junk food kiosk. You rarely get punched out at a restaurant, but it happens all the time at the junk kiosks, maybe they'd get to record some action. They were down: sounds like good TV.

Another call came after the first: We want you to be on camera in the Finland episode. Okay, but when were they going to Finland? Right after the new year. Well, that worked for me. I'd already be in Finland after the Monroe New Year's show, and January is totally dead as far as touring.

Bourdain's show—like we were with *Sound Tracker*—was totally dependent on local fixers who'd show the ropes and get things done. When a food show goes to Italy, you take it for granted that it's going to be a great experience and episode. However, the Italy episode was one of Bourdain's most boring episodes. Bad fixer can ruin everything.

Anthony and the production team came to Helsinki in the beginning of January, and the shoot turned into a good ol' time. Wherever we went, there was vodka. Anthony liked to imbibe, so I figured, let's imbibe. The host of Radio Rock in Helsinki pulled out a bottle of Salmiakki Koskenkorva (a Finnish liquor that tastes like salty black licorice) at nine in the morning. What are we supposed to do, say no thanks, it's too early? Absolutely not. We say now we're talking, thank you for your hospitality.

Anthony compiled a ten-song playlist for the Radio Rock broadcast, and it easily could have been my own: songs from *Raw Power*, *Exile on Main Street*, *Dead Boys: Young, Loud and Snotty*—my man!

I had no idea there'd be a little scandal over the episode in Finland. Some people—mostly nouveau riche golfing types—took it really fucking seriously. "How dare you present Finland in this way?" Hey, open your eyes: we didn't make anything up for the episode. "You could have come in the summertime and showed a proper sauna on a lakeshore." I've always been more interested in the underbelly of every society. I want to find the one-legged, one-eyed bartender in Mexico. I want an electric shock from the homemade shock box in an Ensenada cantina. The Beats from the fifties feel more real than the rest. The dark side feels like the real side to me.

After joining the Monroe band, I flew a lot between New York and Helsinki, and the flights were, of course, full of Finns. After the Bourdain episode, someone always came up to me to give me his or her opinion. Never before the flight, but always somewhere in the middle of it, after a couple of rum and cokes. When I saw someone walking up the aisle to me, I'd try to guess if it was going to be a "so ridiculously good" or a "how the fuck dare you." I haven't met anyone who thought the *No Reservations: Finland* episode was just okay.

The episode showcased my friend Santeri Ahlgren's Päämaja pub, which got some people complaining about why there were Romanis in the episode and how Romanis weren't Finns. Totally unbelievable. Finland is a racist country and still has a long way to go. Other people asked me how I found that "horrible family." Horrible? We got a gracious invitation into a home with a daughter, mother, and grandmother who busted out incredible food. On top of the meal, we got some shots of Pöytäviina, "table booze." I think this is hospitality at its finest and a pretty normal thing for a Finnish dinner party.

It's important to remember, this kind of TV is meant for entertainment. Bourdain's team isn't interested in fine dining or places like Salve, Elite, or Kosmos in Helsinki. "We don't do white tablecloths" was their first rule.

A month after the episode aired, I was writing new songs with the Monroe band in Los Angeles. We were walking along Santa Monica Boulevard when a sixty-something couple walked past. They stopped me. "Oh my God, it's that guy from Anthony Bourdain's show," the woman raved. "Honestly, I have never even thought about going to Finland, but after seeing that episode, it looked like a fun and strange place. Me and my husband, we want to go there now!"

Surprises do happen. Finnish Tourist Board, I'm talking to you.

While filming the Bourdain episode, it occurred to me: Why has no one ever done this with music? Multiple TV channels have tens of chefs at any given moment flying all over the world showing the globe's culinary wonders, but nothing like that existed for music. If food is physical nourishment, music is spiritual nourishment, which is just as diverse and necessary for the world.

My question was answered immediately. Two days later, when I'd gotten back to New York from Finland, I got an email from Otso Tiainen. I'd met him once, when Mad Juana had done an episode of his show *Off the Record*, and I'd liked his out-of-the-box thinking right away.

Otso wrote: *Hey, what if we did this kind of TV show about the music of the world...*

Exactly!

Both of us were thinking about something bigger than some dry, academic, ethnographic show about music. The show had to live and breathe the local vibe. The musicians could talk about the society they lived in, where the cracks are, and we'd immerse ourselves in the culture as best we could. We wanted to capture both men and women, the young and old, street musicians and legends.

We decided to make a demo for the Finnish network Yle. It must have been March when Michael Monroe was on tour in Finland, and I was sitting in a Mexican bar with Otso after soundcheck. I gave a two-minute monologue for the camera about the kind of show we wanted to make and what the idea was.

Otso thought we should go contact the creators of the Finnish TV show *Madventures*. He sent the video to Jari Lähteinen, who was a producer at Gimmeyawallet, Riku Rantala and Tunna Milonoff's production company. We got them interested, next we had to make a better demo for Yle Radio. I thought we could shoot ten artists in New York and make it look like we'd gone to Bulgaria, Cuba, and India. Gimmeyawallet took care of the expenses, and Otso flew out to stay with me for a week.

We filmed a couple of Sikh musicians at an Indian restaurant on Sixth Street, a group that has played—and gone gray—in the same spot for the past thirty years. Yuri Yunakov, a Bulgarian Romani saxophone virtuoso, happened to play at a wedding at a bar called Mehanata on Ludlow Street. A Cuban band played every Sunday at the Thompson Hotel. We got a five-minute demo together, sent the video forward, and waited.

×××

Michael was busy with filming *The Voice of Finland* TV show in the early spring. He was free again after April, and in May, we played some shows on the East Coast and in South America. We toured the European and Scandinavian festivals over the summer.

Just when *Sensory Overdrive* was at the end of its touring cycle and it was time to start making the next record, Michael agreed to another season of

The Voice of Finland. When Michael makes a commitment to something, it is a full dedication, but no one is able to give one hundred percent to two separate things at the same time. So we wrote and rehearsed a lot without Michael. Steve Conte took over Ginger's main writing spot and became a driving force, especially as far as lyrics. Steve kept asking Michael about the song subjects and ideas, can you sing about that or from this perspective. These kinds of conversations helped move the record forward.

Dregen is from the world of riffs; riffs are more important to him than solos. Old blues, funk, soul, Keith Richards, Malcolm Young. There's one song where Dregen played a one-note solo. That's musicianship, a good sign in a guitarist. One note can have more to say than a thousand and one notes.

We left to record in Stockholm in November. Not just any studio, but Park Studio, where Hanoi's first record was recorded almost thirty-two years before. When Michael and I walked in together we were like *fuck*, because the place hadn't changed at all, only the control room had gotten a facelift.

It was cheaper for us to live in rental apartments than a hotel during the recording. Karl lives in Upplands Väsby, north of Stockholm, so he'd come in on his own. My routine was to take the tunnelbana from Skanstull to Gullmarsplan after breakfast, and then continue on from there by bus to Älvsjö. Same thing all over again; I'd make the same commute to Park Studio in 1981 on public transportation. But back then I had to go to Odenplan from Solna, twice the trip I had to do now.

Stockholm has changed less in the last thirty years than Helsinki, because Stockholm was already a more international city in the early eighties, but maybe a little less clean than it is now. Stockholm has gotten a little more homogenous in the way that all global cities are becoming the same Starbucks kind of cities. I'm no nationalist, but I miss the peseta, lira, marks; but at the same time, I understand that Europe has some tough competition with US and other markets, so from an economic perspective it makes sense. Or is the EU just a corporate vassal, doing the bidding of giant multinationals?

An American producer with a big name was picked to produce the second Monroe album. After the recording sessions, the guy went back to California at the end of November and prayed that Monroe wouldn't follow him to the mixing sessions, which he wanted to do. The producer had noticed how intense Michael is; he needs to be hands on with all aspects of the postproduction.

So we sat around waiting for the good sire's first mix. There was a clause written in the contract that was pretty nuts: He'd send us one mix, after which we were allowed to follow up with one email. He'd make the fixes listed in the email. If the mix wasn't satisfactory after those fixes were made, every additional one would cost a grand.

That's an impossible arrangement. Especially in the beginning, when you're getting the first few songs in the place and looking for the overall sound of the album, you have to go back and forth a little bit until you reach that aha moment where you see where the album is heading, sonically speaking. After the first mix of one song, you can't really say exactly where you're going.

Working that way, the entire tour and video budget would have been eaten up by mixing. We decided that we wouldn't have the producer mix the record, and we asked him to send us the files, to who else but Petri Majuri at Seawolf, who ended up fixing yet another American name producer's work.

2013

Horns and Halos

The Finnish National Television Yle's arts and culture channel Yle Teema had liked the idea for *Sound Tracker*. They gave us a budget that was doable for the project. It could have been bigger, but its success wasn't going to depend on expensive guest stars. You can make an interesting show with a small amount of money as long as you have the inspiration, a good team, and a solid production company.

There was some talk about filming the show the next year, 2014. To me that was a horrid idea. I really had to push *Sound Tracker* forward. If I sit on an idea too long, I run out of steam and interest, the shit has to be done now. There was a lot of work to be done, the trips had to be planned, the preproduction work done, and finding the right fixer! We couldn't just show up in Spain and ask around where we could find some real flamenco.

We had to work around the Monroe schedule, so the first trip wasn't until January 2013. We went to Spain first, since I had longstanding ties to the country. The New York Dolls had played in Seville in 2006, and it was then I got to know the flamenco legend Raimundo Amador's rhythm guitarist Marco Aguilar. We asked Marco to be the fixer for the Spain episode, and with his help, we got into places that would have been closed to us otherwise.

Flamenco was born in the triangle between Lebrija, Morón, and Seville. It started off as a vocal tradition; the guitar came in much later on. Flamenco was like the blues to the Romani and southern Spain's impoverished field laborers, a way of letting go over drinks at night, singing and screaming out the pain and frustration.

El Cabrero, a goat farmer and political singer, doesn't usually grant interviews, but he did one with us anyway because of Marco Aguilar's involvement—Marco's father and El Cabrero went to the same school. When we went to film him, El Cabrero shoveled goat shit and told us parables. He's a tough but gentle and learned guy who isn't interested in self-promotion or pleasing the powers that be. He'll play to a full house at the Olympia in Paris, and then go back home to his goat farm.

Oren Kaplan opened the doors for us in Granada; he had been in Gogol Bordello and was doing sound for Mad Juana at Baby Jupiter the night when the snake show scared off the audience. Oren was an old friend.

We filmed Antonio Heredia, Oren's flamenco guitar teacher, first in Granada. It's a family band; the wife sings and is the manager/agent, the husband plays guitar and takes home the money, and the kids and cousins dance, clap, and sing. This is an age-old tradition within the flamencos. Flamenco guitar is very technical, precise, and demanding; the chords are extensive, the scales and rhythm complex, it's not something that is easily mastered. And a lot of these old masters don't necessarily know how to read or write.

Aside from the local fixer(s), our crew was only four people: I was the host and interviewer, Otso was the director and cinematographer, Juge Heikkilä was the main cameraman, and Jukka Uitto was the sound guy. We traveled with as little gear as possible; a quick setup was often necessary, and we found ourselves many times in cramped places.

We flew to Argentina and Uruguay for ten days in March. We wanted to find out where tango really came from, but we didn't exactly get the answer. The 1930s tango star Carlos Gardel always comes up, as does the question of if he's really from Argentina or Uruguay, or maybe France? Tango started off as guitar music, but in the beginning of the 1900s, the German bandoneon came into use; it's an accordion with a big sound that was a replacement for organs in poor churches in Germany. Tango absorbed influences from the different immigrant workers from all over Europe.

It's a forever-changing art form and continues to mutate to this day; it hasn't gotten totally stuck as some dancehall institution. For example, Orquesta Tipica Fernández Fierro is a band started by a bunch of street musicians in Buenos Aires; they now perform in their own big club, a former warehouse that was transformed into a performance space by the band, friends, and family. Tango has morphed into spoken word and even punk in their hands, which isn't always to the liking of the old guard. The older generation has forgotten that pure tango has never existed, because it's the sum of many layers and keeps changing generation to generation. We came across candombe in Montevideo, the drum music of African slaves brought to Uruguay; tango is also heavily influenced by its polyrhythms.

×××

The record release for Michael Monroe was behind schedule due to the American producer's unreasonable conditions. The mix of the first song was all kinds of fucked up even after the fixes we asked for were implemented. Since every fix after that would cost a grand, each song could easily rack up four thousand extra. We put the brakes on the whole process, which meant pushing back the release of *Horns and Halos* from May to August. There's no point in releasing anything in the middle of the summer, unless you're U2.

The delay messed up the summer tour. The tour had to be canceled and needed to be rebooked all over again. Our international agent also changed. The timing was messed up, and it took all kinds of adjustment that went on even a couple years after. The next agent had to try to come to the rescue after everything the previous one had abandoned.

We were most interested in going to Central Europe, especially Germany, which is a big and important market, the most important after the US and UK. But Germany has always been a tough nut to crack.

Hanoi never broke through in Central Europe because we never toured much there. We had the UK, Scandinavia, Japan, and the US to some extent. And those have always also been Michael's territories.

×××

Sound Tracker went to Brazil in June. There was a changeup in the crew because the sound guy Jukko Uitto stepped out. Svante "Svane" Colerus replaced him. He did all the *Sound Tracker* trips after Brazil.

We decided to focus on Pernambuco in Southeast Brazil since I'd gotten into that music when I'd been in Recife for the festival the New York Dolls played with Bad Brains. The festival organizer and label head, Paulo André M. Pires, was a clear choice for Brazil/Pernambuco fixer.

There was an explosion in the Pernambuco music scene in the mid-nineties, a fusion, where bands like Nação Zumbi and Mundo Livre S/A were mixing together maracatu, forró, ciranda, coco, hip-hop, and punk.

Recife is one of the most dangerous cities in the world with an unbelievable degree of poverty and an unbelievable degree of wealth. One of the hallmarks of the city is high garden walls topped with barbed wire and glass shards. The penniless street punks build their own instruments from scrap metal.

Forró is kind of like Brazil's or maybe just Pernambuco's answer to country. Everyone listens to it, and forró festivals draw hundreds of thousands of attendees and hundreds of performers. Maracatu is fast-tempo Carnival music with lots of horns and drums and long, hypnotic songs. A crowd will form following the band and dance away while the sugarcane booze cachaça is flowing.

Thanks to the filming, we got closer to the music and the musicians than the average observer. Our trip to Brazil was above and beyond what any typical holiday trip would likely have been.

×××

The pressure on Dregen to work on his solo album grew during the spring. He had thought he'd be able to write during Michael Monroe touring, but that rarely works. In the summer, Dregen announced that he was leaving the band, at least for a break; his head wasn't in it, and he was under a lot of pressure with a kid on the way as well. He had a meltdown at a festival that...didn't end well.

We had to find someone for the tour. We knew that Dregen had to get his own record out of his system, but we also knew that a temp wasn't good enough; we needed someone who could commit to the band.

Rich Jones joined us at the end of the summer. Rich was Ginger's former sidekick and had played in the Black Halos and Amen and had been on board with Monroe from the beginning. He'd designed the logos and the live album and the cover for *Horns and Halos*.

After two gifted and lovable madmen, we were now joined by an even-keeled and always, more or less, positive dude. The majority of musicians are emotional creatures who only react to everything. Not Rich. He's an even-keeled mad man with reason. How is that possible?

So the third album and third rhythm guitarist—the Monroe band was a rotating door with guitarists coming in from stage right. The cool thing about the change in lineup is that every record feels fresh.

Horns and Halos went gold in a few days, even faster than *Sensory Overdrive*. Rich ended up promoting a record on tour that he didn't play on. Dregen's record came out at the same time, and he was on the road too. We ended up doing some shows together, all in the family.

×××

My birthday—September 4—was coming up. There was a reason to do something a little bigger than usual, or a lot bigger, because I was turning fifty.

A couple years before, my old landlord John Stavros had invited me, Mina, and Mina's son over to his loft for dinner. Greek-style fish was on the menu, and Stavros told us, "There's twelve different spices. Whoever guesses what all of them are gets to use this space for free." It was a five-thousand-square-foot loft space on the fourteenth floor of a building in Midtown Manhattan. I tasted carefully—concentrate, concentrate—because this would be the perfect party spot for my fiftieth. Stavros rented it out for parties, weddings, bat and bar mitzvahs, or whatever for a lot of dough.

I listed off the spices one after another, and every single one was spot on.

So two years later, I called up Stavros: Remember the twelves spices? Stavros hemmed and hawed at first, but kept his word and handed over his loft for the party. Paul, the head chef of the Jamaican restaurant Negril, promised to do the food. The night's entertainment, an awesome Brazilian Pernambuco band, came by way of a bar in Brooklyn called Miss Favela.

The guest list was over two hundred names long, the same New York guys who are still my friends: David Johansen, Bob Gruen, Jesse Malin, the Mad Juana gang, and all the Finns, Nuutti Kataja, Maukka Palmio, Lada Ferrari. My son flew in from Stockholm. The party lasted for the better part of a week, but on my actual birthday, we were all together at Stavros's loft. And how do Finns conduct themselves at a party? They end up in the kitchen around a bottle of Finnish vodka. "This isn't enough for everybody."

The afterparty in the early hours of the morning went on at the Bowery Electric, which Jesse Malin owned; the entire downstairs was reserved for us, with an open bar.

But every party has to have a troublemaker. My son tried to intervene in a drunken fight, and he got an ashtray banged on his head. Nicke will rarely have a beer, much less two beers, and doesn't like to get wasted. This time, he had drunk the Finnish vodka and woke up on my sofa with a horrible hangover and a bump on his head. "Fuck! What a fucking birthday!"

×××

We did the fourth trip for *Sound Tracker* in September. We were thinking about the countries in the Balkans, until we finally decided on Serbia, mostly because we had a contact ready to go there: Dragan Ristić from KAL. There's no denying Mad Juana's Balkan influences, and in Serbia, I got a chance to immerse myself in this incredible musical culture and ask a lot of questions about the position of Romanis in Serbian society.

The same thing happened in Serbia as in Andalusia: The concept of time is a bit different than ours in Scandinavia, and we couldn't really schedule interviews with musicians in advance, because there was no scheduling anything anyway. That was how we lived each day; in the morning, we didn't know how the day would go. And that wasn't the last time our *Sound Tracker* adventures went that way.

We filmed the Eddie Van Halen of the accordion in a Romani village called Stublina; the guy's name was Pilosh, he wanted to get paid with a pig, beer, and some *slivovitsa*. The pig was roasted, and the filming turned into a party; all the villagers showed up, and Pilosh started playing the old songs everybody knew. Sorrow and joy go hand in hand in Balkan songs, they're not just sad moan-and-groaners.

The Balkan wars in the early nineties tore families and friends apart. The Bosnian Serbs were driven out of Sarajevo, and some of them landed in Belgrade, which was our hub during the trip.

We interviewed brass bands that were straight out of an Emir Kusturica movie, and also Ljupka Stevic, a singer who performs a highly questionable kind of music: turbofolk. It's folk music mixed with techno, and is loved and apparently funded by gangsters. We went to a turbofolk club that was full of Botoxed women and their bald gorilla boyfriends; the vibe was pretty hardcore. Dragan felt that turbofolk was hick music but made sure we weren't making fun of it on the show; *Sound Tracker* would be sold to Serbian TV, and he could get into trouble with the gangsters, he had to live there.

But we just showed it and didn't pass any judgment. People can make their own decision about turbofolk.

Belgrade is a depressing city. The daytrips to the southern Serbian countryside were full of generosity and warmth, even if the people were poor and didn't have much opportunity to dream. The only person who spoke English in the entire Romani ghetto of Zagužane was a nine-year-old "Trumpet Ninja" who was a huge fan of Real Madrid and was learning languages to get out of the ghetto and hopefully to a better life.

2014
Sound Tracker

Our film crew went to Ethiopia next. I had come across a collection of records called *Éthiopiques* that was a compilation of Ethio-Jazz and other interpretations of American music from the fifties to the eighties. It also had its share of original ethnic music from Ethiopia. The mixed-up combo was truly special: a heavy Motown influence on top of horns running up a pentatonic scale, which is the foundation of Ethiopian music.

My old contacts panned out here too: Tommy Gobena, the bassist from Gogol Bordello, was born in Addis Ababa. Tommy came along on the trip as a fixer, and we were able to film some old Ethio-Jazz veterans at his brother's jazz samba club. Alemayehu Eshete, the "Ethiopian James Brown," told us about the bad blood between the tribes, which had never turned into civil war. Ethiopia has eighty-two different tribes, which means a lot of different customs, languages, and religions, but in the end, there's room enough for everyone to live side by side and by their own convictions.

Going to a service in a church carved into rock was a memorable experience. The pilgrims came from far away to Lalibela for the Christmas mass, which took place in January and lasted for a week. Eight hundred pastors swayed and prayed in the upper part of the church, and the accompanying hum of drums in the whinstone cave created this intense, hypnotic experience.

The bègèna is a sacred instrument; it's also called King David's Harp, because David playing its low drone cured King Saul's insomnia and might have been the first fuzz bass in the world. We got to meet the bègèna master Alemu Agan at his business, a kitchen wholesale shop. We went to the shop's backroom, and Alemu played us a long, chill song there that basically hypnotized Svane—you could only make out the whites of his eyes. Just behind a couple of walls, Addis Ababa's farmer's market and traffic were bustling.

Svane snapped out of the spell of David's harp, but our camera guy, Juge, got infected with skin bacteria. His lungs filled up with fluid, and he ended up in a coma for three weeks. We were in a rush to get him back to Finland. He was shaking like a leaf from the fever, and he got an abscess the size of a tennis ball on his neck. We didn't know what was wrong for quite some time, and we were worried sick. We canceled our February trip to Trinidad for the Carnival because we wanted to keep the show going with Juge, if he was still able to keep going at all.

And then one day Juge called up. "When are we leaving?"

Otso wanted an episode in the States. And I answered absolutely not. It was too obvious an idea. But then I thought we could rent a tour bus and film a road trip. In the end, the America episode turned into two episodes.

Latin culture is a big part of the US. Nico Camargo, who had played trumpet in Mad Juana, was originally from El Paso, right on the border with Mexico. We traveled to El Paso and filmed mariachi tradition as well as some local punk pioneers and an artist who mixes it all, Kiko Rodriguez. We drove the bus to Austin where we met up with my friend, the great Alejandro Escovedo, and the alt-country star Dale Watson. We continued on to New Orleans, where we got to the heart of the song-making process by following Ivan Neville to the studio, where he alternately wrote lyrics and recorded the vocals. In Como, Mississippi, we filmed a gospel sermon at a country church and the afterparty, where young and old guitarists played the blues while sitting on amps, and the crowd drank out of paper bags. We went on to Nashville from there. As a musician, it's easier to open up to other musicians, and I heard a lot of stories about how impossible it feels to break out in that old capital of American music, where the competition is tough; talent and experience are no guarantee for success or even just to get by.

Most important of all, my old Choctaw buddy Cochise rode around on the bus with us. We went to his reservation and to some sacred Choctaw sites. There would have been no grounds for an America episode without including Native Americans and their music.

Our final destination was New York. And of course, the toughest place to fix, to make it all happen, was my hometown. Friends bailed the day before because they were supposedly busy. At least David Johansen was reliable, and he graciously took part in our session. We also talked to the jazz trumpeter, Roy Hargrove, who isn't much of a talker, but he even managed to get a laugh in our company.

New York rappers and their managers expected so much money just to sit down and talk that we decided to ditch 'em. We got down to the street level and talked to a rapper and teacher from Brooklyn, Chris Faust, who performed for us at a basketball court. The beat was booming from a boombox, and a crowd of little kids showed up to dance. It was beautiful, and it was the last shot of the US part of *Sound Tracker*.

Me, Otso, Juge, and Svane learned something. The first trips the year before—Spain, Argentina, Uruguay—had been a logistical nightmare, total trial and error. The next trips we lowered the number of destinations and left one day open for filming just the city shots.

At the beginning of the Argentina episode, I'm walking, then I get into a car, then I get out of the car, and in that short clip I managed to have three different sets of clothes. We only noticed it in editing.

Honestly, the whole first season was one big educational process for all of us. I struggled with the writing and narrating, and Otso and the master editor looked for the right visual language. We threw twenty hours of Spain footage at Jussi, out of which he was supposed to whip up a fifty-minute episode. Jussi gave us the middle finger. "Thanks, assholes!"

The first edit was still too slow, far from what flamenco really is. Otso and company had succeeded in the impossible: They got flamenco to look melancholy, depressing, and gray. The complete opposite of Spain—I've watched enough Kaurismäki movies for one lifetime. The episode came to life when we closed in on the feet and hands on the intro. It set a strong vibe right off the bat. We found the look, style, and the vibe for the whole series.

×××

It had been a good five years with Mina. However, the last two years were also really rough. From 2013 to 2014, I was on the road about two hundred days out of the year and at home for only short spurts at a time. We didn't know how to give the other what they needed, and both of us probably had unrealistic expectations. There were worries and grief to deal with in the day-to-day, and those matters took precedence.

I spent the whole summer living in my father's painting studio upstairs from him in Helsinki. He was eighty-four. I hadn't spent that much time in Finland since leaving, and there had always been some distance and tension between us, even if our relationship was cordial. And now I was seeing Dad every morning. I saw how frail and little he had gotten.

Sound Tracker was edited and was coming out in the fall, and so was the associated book. There was a lot of work to do after the fact. I had to spearhead it, give the show, a face and do all the press and marketing, plus do the Monroe summer tour. Everything was happening fast. The wall started to go up.

Things just got worse when I got back to New York in September. I had to head to the studio in October and on tour in November. I had been on tour nonstop for twelve years since the 2000s. Joan Jett, the Dolls, Monroe, *Sound Tracker*. I was not in a good place.

I was fifty-one. Through my dad, I'd started to come to terms with my own aging and the life that I had left. Where I wanted to spend it and how. I'd lived the last five years in New York because of Mina. New York wasn't what it used to be for me any longer—the place that nourished my curiosity and gifts, that gave more than it took. New York had been my home for more than twenty years. It will always have part of my heart.

×××

I had to somehow find the time to make the third Michael Monroe record. Steve Conte was again responsible for a lot of the songwriting, but Rich Jones also brought whole songs to the table. Michael got his own songwriting tap flowing, which was fucking beautiful. His creativity came back, along with his joy for doing things. "R.L.F.," rock like fuck, was my music from start to finish and so were half the genius words for the chorus. Michael built the song lyrics around his own adage, "Rock like fuck," adding my own very deep line, "Fuck shit up."

I was going through some difficult personal stuff, so my heart wasn't completely in these writing sessions. Not at first, at least. *Horns and Halos* had been really varied, full of different ideas and musical approaches; we'd thrown in reggae breakdowns and other stuff. All of a sudden, we now just had punk songs from start to finish. I stepped back and thought, all right, I'll play and support as best I can, and it's good that there's ideas flying about, but are they good ideas? Maybe I was going through a phase where I was questioning everything, from my love life to making a record. Making a record is weird and beautiful because you never know what the end result is going to be. There are always surprises both ways. Some filler track turns into a gem in the studio, and on the other hand, one of the initial favorites can get ruined by bad production.

When we left to record in Gothenburg in November, I still wasn't sure about the songs. We recorded eighteen backing tracks with Karl in four days. That's more than you normally need for an LP, but we used all of them, because some territories wanted bonus tracks. The English and the Japanese like their extras, and there's always gotta be bonus tracks on the vinyl version, and the Americans want their own special bonuses.

As soon as my bass parts were done, I was ready to take off. I didn't have time to stay and take part in the overdubs or to listen to how the record would turn out. I had to get my new living situation in order.

I had taken the step and gotten myself an apartment in Mallorca. I really needed a change of scenery, with lots of space and quiet. After the incessant running around the world, touring, TV, etc., I needed a place to settle down and think about how the fuck I was doing and what was really going on with me.

2014–2016

Mallorca

"I don't have the slightest idea
about how many shows I've done.
Thousands, five thousand, whatever."

2014

Head, heart, mountains, and the sea

In November, I moved to Mallorca with my few meager possessions. I wanted—and I got—to be in peace, and all by myself. My sister lived two hours away, on the other side of the mountains. It wasn't easy to get there, but there are phones and a bus too. The main thing was to spend some time by myself and figure out my head and my heart. After all the traveling and touring, I was back in a quiet village in the middle of nature.

It's always helped in moving that I don't really put too much value into material possessions. I'm not interested in furniture or dishes. My record collection was gone back when I bought my first bass. Later on, I've passed on my records and books to friends. All my old clothes are gone, except one pair of pants from Hanoi and the blue kimono I wore on the cover of *Two Steps from the Move*. But I think even those are in storage at a friend's in San Diego.

Stuff is a pain in the ass. That being said, I'm of two minds about the digital world: it's wonderful not to have to lug around and store physical records, but at the same time, I remember loving as a kid the smell of vinyl and the big covers. All your senses are rewarded. And vinyl just sounds better.

It had been a good year—and also hellish. Mina and I started talking through things civilly, because there was no lack of love between the two of us. Life had just gotten in the way, and we were both dealing with heavy stuff.

We both wanted to keep trying. Instead of one, we had two apartments at our disposal, and both were so cheap that we were able to keep them both. The rent for the apartment in Mallorca was some hundreds a month, with a terrace opening up to a view of the sea that was worth a lot more than that.

Moving to Finland has always come to mind from time to time, but when I come to visit, I lose interest. I was thinking about it seriously the summer of 2014, when I was living in my dad's atelier. I looked at the cost of rentals, but because I had to hang on to the New York apartment, I could only get a closet in Helsinki on my budget. I could get a big apartment in Mallorca for the same money. There are good flight connections to my son in Sweden and my family in Finland. I left Finland so young, I was just barely seventeen, that in my heart, I didn't have time to put down deep roots. You learn languages so fast when you're young, I was able to hold a conversation in Swedish after a couple of months in Stockholm. The lasting interest in other countries and cultures probably came from when I was eleven or twelve and my parents divorced. One of them took me to Italy and Greece and the other to Stockholm.

Sound Tracker was airing on Finnish TV in August, and a book about the travels with the same name came out in October. *Sound Tracker* went up for awards in Finland for Best Music Program of the Year. Mad Juana did a little tour of Finland at the same time. Probably thanks to *Sound Tracker*, people were suddenly curious to hear what kind of music I made, how the global influences from all those years were flowing, and the shows sold really well.

2015

Blackout States

Michael asked me to join the filming of *The Voice of Finland* in January. I said in advance that I wouldn't be a suck-up, that I would say what I thought.

Some of the singers were incredibly young. You could hear that some of them could go really far with a lot of work. But a breakthrough isn't going to happen right away. There are no shortcuts. You have to get frustrated and tear your hair out and give up every now and then but keep going anyway and spend hours just singing scales over and over or yodeling along with records. All this effort is to make your voice stronger.

Sweden has had the culture of singing for decades; that's why so many top-notch singers come from there. In Finland, children are scared silent in school with song tests. We don't really have a lot of technically good soloists. Marjo Leinonen from Balls has been the only one to rep the Aretha Franklin school. In America, you can go to some bar in Kentucky, and you'll quickly find a singer who will knock you on your ass with their gospel background.

The Voice of Finland is encouraging, doesn't judge. I can dig that. But there's gotta be alternative programming to all this competition stuff. The bottom line for TV networks is always of course money. There were years where I only watched reruns on TV: *Twilight Zone* reruns, *Star Trek* reruns, *Honeymooners* reruns. Yle TV in Finland has a lot of open-minded programming. I was amazed one time in a hotel room while touring Finland to get acquainted with Yle Teema: Finland has an arts TV channel now? There was absolutely no BS, every program was interesting.

×××

Sound Tracker won a big award in January, the Golden Venla (local Grammies) for Best Music Series, which is a big deal. Yle Teema had agreed to produce another season, so Otso and I had already started planning more trips during the first season. We decided to focus on the East. We were interested in filming Indian and Indonesian music, and we wanted to go to Turkey, right on the East/West border. The Bosphorus divides Istanbul into two sides; one is in Europe and the other in Asia.

But first we had to get to Jamaica. There's an Eastern influence there too. When slaves were shipped from West Africa to the Americas, the hard cases were dropped off in Jamaica, and the island culture got new blood.

As soon as we arrived to Inna de Yard, the backyard sessions of Earl "Chinna" Smith, who had played with Bob Marley and was the house guitarist for Lee Scratch Perry, I was sat down with my bass. I jammed for hours with the old bearded rastas while the chalice was passed around. It was pretty damn far-out and extremely beautiful.

Jah9 came to attention from Inna de Yard; she sings fiery conscious reggae and, through her recordings, has toured in the US, Europe, and all the way to Japan. The next to be interviewed was the politically aware rising star, Kabaka Pyramid, whose background is in hip-hop. The conditions of the poor in Kingston slums are a longtime grievance. The longtime tradition of singing about society's ills continues with artists like Kabaka.

You can also temporarily get away from misery with proper parties. Mento is a kind of music related to calypso, which is the basis of a lot of the music on the island. We talked to the old men from the Jolly Boys, who had founded the band in the fifties. The foundation of mento is a five-note bass made from scrap wood and discarded saw pieces. It's related to the African finger harp kalimba and mbira, but bigger, much bigger. The Jolly Boys rhumba box master Derrick "Jonny" Henry built me one and painted MENTO, SOUND TRACKER, and JOLLY BOYS on the front. I cherish that instrument.

Of course we had to get some dancehall in the program. At its best and weirdest it's a minimalistic and polyrhythmic infectious groove machine, at its worst the auto-tuned hyper-commercial made-by-numbers music that permeates the airwaves the world over. The dancehall street parties in Kingston late at night were an experience I will not soon forget. Motörhead-loud music was blaring out of a giant SUV that had been equipped as a huge sound system, and gyrating bottoms and sync dancing groups of young men partied until the sun came up. We left after hours long open-mike battles where everyone got to express themselves.

We drove up to the Blue Mountains range and walked the rest of the way up the winding path through coffee bushes. There was a religious service happening in a Rastafarian commune. Giant bass drums created a thunderous heart-shattering trance, while the sound of lightning-fast hand drums swirled in the air in the midst of the sacred marijuana smoke, simultaneously a joyful and deep event. This Rastafarian community lived free from the influence of the outside world, as self-sufficiently and healthily as possible, using herbal medicine, singing, drumming, grass, and meditation as their arsenal for their chosen way of life.

We filmed the first season of *Sound Tracker* in fifteen months. The pace was tightened for the second season, and we went through all five countries in seven months. This was possible because we were deliberately taking it easy with Michael Monroe. We played fewer shows and smaller festivals so we wouldn't wear ourselves out.

Sound Tracker sought the legends, the street level, and was looking for the roots of the countries' music. We took off for Senegal, to the origins of a lot of Black Americans and also the basis of hip-hop: tassou is an ancient form of spoken word poetry set in musical rhythm. We were going to go to the so-called birthplace of blues in Mali, we'd gotten our visas and other permits together, but the political situation in the country was very volatile, and the Finnish foreign ministry plainly told us that we should not travel to Mali.

Through Mina's sister's husband Serge, we got a man named Amadou Faye as our Senegal fixer, who had managed Youssou N'Dour briefly and had been married to one of Youssou's daughters. Amadou had tons of contacts, but Senegal is Senegal; sessions were constantly getting canceled. The whole thing went sideways within a couple of days, and Otso calmly tore up the script. We realized that we'd just have to improvise, go with the flow, and see if we could pull together an episode on Senegal. The country doesn't really have an organized music business. There's no way of promoting shows because they're not planned in advance. We had to use the backup plan for our backup plan on several days, and our nerves were getting a bit frazzled. Some thugs stopped us from filming a sabar, a colorful street party where the Muslim women get to let loose for a change. We got a lot of great footage despite the problems: a band of three brothers from Dakar who mixed traditional music with rap called Bideew Bou Bess; a group of women drummers from the Serer tribe in the Sahara Desert; and Assiko Band de Gorée's four-cornered drummers from the Gorée island, where slaves were gathered to be shipped off to America.

Spoken word takes a very different shape in Senegal. Tassou, an ages-old women's lyrical tradition, did not always include instruments. Griots are improv troubadours who also used to spread the flow of news and tell of historical events that go back hundreds of years. Contemporary Senegalese hip-hop mixes American and local influences. The free expression of words is the most narrow in countries where there are the most subjects to talk about. One of the rappers we were looking for was in prison.

Even though our show isn't based around talking with stars, getting Baaba Maal on board was a big deal. Because Baaba isn't some watered-down world music guy but a fucking intense, single-minded, Paris Conservatory–trained master musician. He recorded electronic music with Brian Eno, but not just to get a name in popular music, but because he couldn't get the sounds that were playing in his head to come out with traditional instruments.

By April, we were already on our third shoot. The birthplace of Romani music is in the Thar Desert in Rajasthan. According to legend, that's where the Romani walked through the Middle East, Turkey, and Balkans to Spain and elsewhere in Europe. In addition to Rajasthan, we wanted to raid Mumbai, where I'd last been with Hanoi in 1983. The biggest point of interest in Mumbai to us was Bollywood and the film music industry there, which was at its peak in the seventies: hundreds of musicians sitting on standby twenty-four-seven as the writers and arrangers wrote music for them to play. There were film composers and copyists, a big hierarchical system—a caste system within a caste system.

Mumbai had cleaned up in thirty years, which means the same thing as Rudy Giuliani's clean-up when he was mayor of New York: The undesirable elements don't disappear, they just get moved elsewhere, away from view. Snake charming is illegal these days, and almost no one is ready to admit to knowing a snake charmer. But we managed to find one anyway, in the Pushkar Romani ghetto.

Hijra—third gender—people have fallen from their station in the Maharajas' palace to the bottom ranks of society. The English arrived in the 1800s and were horrified by what they saw and deprived trans people of their station and human rights. We were able to interview members of the hijra community, who believe with high hopes in the return of equal rights and justice to the trans people. As for now, they mostly earn a living through begging and prostitution.

What's the reason for their fall? The Christian sexual taboos brought over by the English colonialists. In that tradition, heterosexuality is supposedly the only healthy and acceptable type of sexuality, and everyone who broke from it was sick, immoral, and worthy of judgment. Hinduism is exceptional as a religion in that it adopts elements from other religions, not believing itself to be the only true way. It doesn't judge. Hinduism keeps the door open, and that's why all faiths are represented in India.

Hundreds of years ago, women would sing about daily life while going to fetch water. That slowly developed into its own thing, panihari, where the act of filling jars has specific choreography. And when the animal protection agency outlawed the use of snakes in flute performances, the Sapera Nath Romani lost their living. They came up with the idea to dress up a woman in black and get her to move to the music like a cobra. This is how Kalbeliya dance was born. The Indian government has organized Kalbeliya performances all around the world, in large concert halls all the way to the United States. When these Romani people come back from the tour to their slum dwellings, they have only a pittance of the pay. The hard-earned concert tour income disappears into someone else's pockets.

I didn't drink at all during the filming trips at the beginning of the year. I found myself again in a place where I was sick of alcohol, and since my brain had fried from everything that had happened the last fall, I wanted to keep thinking over things with a clear head. I stayed sober until December, when I went from the Monroe Tavastia gig in Helsinki to the afterparty in the Gimmeyawallet office, where I cracked open a beer.

×××

Michael Monroe did only one or two festivals a weekend over the summer, and Ruisrock in Finland was the only big one.

Nasty covered for Steve Conte in Pori and Ruisrock, and Nasty always handles the job with honors. We've been playing together since we were seventeen. Those are the formative years for rock and roll: seventeen, eighteen, nineteen. That's when you play with raw teenage energy, and if you're lucky, you can do it with the same group. Five years at that age is like fifteen now. It's a long time where a lot of growth and everything else happens.

So as soon as Nasty plugged into his amp and started playing, it was like putting on an old pair of boots: *Now*, I feel good. This is where it's at… it's a warm, fuzzy feeling. You can't help but grin like an idiot. We created ZZ Top–like dance moves in the Hanoi days just to have a laugh, and those old steps fell out of the old memory bank with ease.

Nasty played in Steve Conte's spot this time, too far away and in the wrong spot. Help! Where you at? Nasty always played next to me, stage right. Nasty is so solid, there's no bullshit with that man, no pretenses, no agenda. Nasty is out of his mind, but he's still solid. Firmly rooted to the ground.

×××

We did the last two trips for the second season of *Sound Tracker* that summer.

Indonesia has a really big, strong metal scene that kicked off more or less around when Metallica played there in 1993. Metal is a much-needed lifeline in a totalitarian country. Bands release music on cassette tapes because cassette tapes are still a huge thing there. Even though there's a demand for it, Jakarta's clubs don't usually book metal or punk bands.

Metal bands sing in their own languages about Indonesian mythology, which teems with ghosts, horror, slaughter, and curses. There's one band that has a member whose only job is to shuffle around the front of the stage in a white cloak. Our Jakarta fixer, Indra, was a band manager, but this band was something else entirely. White Shoes and the Couples Company plays light, stylish samba-influenced pop, with a twist.

The traffic chaos of Jakarta wasn't so dangerous compared to Mumbai; it's just endless sitting around in traffic. Jakarta is an oppressive city just because of its sheer size. It was a relief to get on a train to Badung.

Karinding Attack mixes metal and Javanese Karinding bamboo vibraphone. The biggest bass vibraphones are so low that they're basically percussion. The rumble and drone come from the jaw harp and the didgeridoo, which is called a gon tiup in Javanese.

We filmed Karinding Attack in a pitch-dark bamboo forest in Badung. The only source of light was the haphazardly placed ritual oil candles. The low rumble created this shaman vibe, and whenever I talk about this night later on, my hairs stand on end all over again.

SambaSunda showcases the Javanese gamelan. The typical instrumentation is siter, flute, and conga drums. The drum skins are hit with the thumb, and the height of the hit changes the sound, same as the Indian tabla. The Javanese gamelan is light and relaxed, whereas the Balinese gamelan is an aggressive beat that is played with instruments like the metallophone and the jegogan that is made of ten different types of metal.

From Badung, we drove to Yogyakarta, which is Indonesia's biggest university town. Noise bombers are art students that bring amps and effects pedals to the street corner and start making noise. Sometimes they stop traffic and the cops show up to shoo them away. The students spread the word, gather their gear, and soon enough, the noise bombing will continue somewhere else. The kids have built their own effects and instruments, and one setup strongly reminded me of the table lamp spring drone experiment from my childhood. This instrument's springs were so much bigger that marbles could roll around inside. A spring and mike had been attached to a board, and the sound was distorted through fuzz and delay.

I got my chance to bomb too. I asked the bombers for the signal chain distortion—delay, distortion, delay—and I plugged my bass into it. I stepped on and off the pedals and was able to make some noisescapes people seemed to trip to. The noise bombing in Yogyakarta reminded me of New York's no wave movement back in the early nineties, back when New York's street and club culture was unpredictable and diverse.

We went to Bali from Java. We were able to film a kecak group at a holy site, in front of Kebo Iwa's giant home cave. Kecak has at least sixty people divided into three concentric circles, each one with their own consonant to shout.

We got to see a lot of things that tourists don't, but one thing remained a mystery: water singing. Our Bali fixer, Anom Baris, admitted that he knew of it, but wouldn't tell us anything more. Apparently water is played with cupped palms on the calm surface of a pond, but the Balinese kept mum about it. Bali is very spiritual, full of temples built for the spirits that are all around us. We had to content ourselves with the silence.

Sound Tracker had yet to dive into Middle Eastern culture. We directed ourselves to Turkey next, which isn't exactly the Mideast but in the neighborhood, and took off for Istanbul, because the age-old tradition of Islam is alive and well there. And at the same time, it's the edge of the West, so we were expecting to hear music with both Eastern and Western influences.

My old friend, Cerdar Ihan, is the owner of New York's Drom club, where all of Turkey's biggest names have come to perform. Cerdar agreed graciously to be the fixer for the Turkey episode. The preproduction started haltingly, we didn't seem to get on the same wavelength of what we were looking for. At first Cerdar offered us postcard kind of stuff, polished music, where we were more interested in the streets and rougher stuff.

Usually, Romani people all over the world are pushed to the outskirts of the city, out of sight. Sulukule is the Romani ghetto in Istanbul. As the city expands, Sulukule has become if not quite the city center, still not an area to be left to its poor inhabitants. The shanties are bulldozed and up pop residential areas for rich people. The Turkish news keeps quiet about Sulukule and the problems of its residents. Drug-trade-related shootings are a daily occurrence. We had to leave the place in a hurry when the rap group we were interviewing told us that the situation was getting a bit hot and we needed to get into the car.

Selda Bağcan is a singing legend famous for decades of protest songs and critical of the Turkish government, and she did three stints in prison in the eighties. We interviewed her in her office and had planned on filming her show later on. Then Selda lost her voice, and she went out to her place in the country to recover. We rearranged the schedule for the end of the trip, but nothing came out of it. It was disappointing. But we were able to compensate for the music of rebellion otherwise. In Turkey, all performers down to the belly dancer are very politically aware. They started to rail on the government as soon as there was a mike in front of them.

Kardeş Türküluer is a big lineup of Turks, Kurds, Romanis, and Armenians. The band's message is that we're all people and all equal. It seems obvious, but even in places like Finland, it's not.

Otso filmed the band BaBa ZuLa's show while in a trance himself: This is going to be the best shot ever! He almost hurled the camera against the wall when he noticed that the memory card had been full since the middle of the performance. BaBa ZuLa played a kind of Turkish dubfunk. I got so influenced by it that I went to buy myself an electric bağlama the next day. Or in fact, you don't go and buy something in Turkey. First you sit down for tea, chitchat, and haggle until the seller agrees to the price.

One of the most memorable experiences with *Sound Tracker* was to be let inside a mountaintop mosque where imam Ahmet Muhsin Tuzer gave us a demonstration. He sings the call to prayer during the day and in a rock band at night. This had initially triggered some resentment against him, but the higher-ups decided to let him do his thing; it's easier to let go rather than making a big deal about it. Sufis aren't really big moralizers.

We made a book about this season as well, in both my and Otso's voice: *Sound Tracker at the Roots of Rebel Music*. The book came out in the fall, just before the show started to air.

All in all, *Sound Tracker* has been one of the most enriching and beautiful experiences of my life. I'm grateful that Gimmeyawallet and Yle Teema gave the idea the green light.

×××

Billy from Jetboy called me in December to ask if I remembered Andy Moraga, one of Jetboy's roadies from the late eighties. Andy was coming to Helsinki with his new girlfriend, Margaret Cho. Margaret had been a Gen X figure at the beginning of the nineties with her sitcom, *All-American Girl*, and she's a known Chinese-American comedian. I had gotten the idea from somewhere that Margaret isn't into men, but now our old roadie was getting married to her and was coming to Helsinki for his concert. Billy sent over a new bass he'd built for me with Andy, and I picked it up from a restaurant. The bass was named Margaret.

Margaret has some Fender parts: the neck and body of a 1968 Jazz. Billy's partner in biz built the mikes, and they're a little hotter than usual. It plays about ten times louder than my real Fender '68 Jazz bass. I always have to crank it up…but the sound that comes out of that thing when it's turned all the way up! Heaven. Thank God this bass Billy built is so light; I can throw it around, and my back isn't all crooked after a show.

When you find a good bass, what's the point in changing? I learned from the bad changes I made as a kid. Guitarists are crazier than bassists in this way; they've always gotta have this ridiculous row of guitars. I bought a blue Washburn Delta a little before I moved to Mallorca. It's cheap, but it's good, does the job.

With big record deals usually come endorsements. Sponsorships require you to show off your axe in a photoshoot. The Gibson/Jetboy sponsorship came through MCA. When the New York Dolls did Conan O'Brien's show, a Fender rep came to say hi to Steve Conte, but Steve is a Gibson guy. I grunted, "Hey…ME…" and I got a good bass out of it. But to be honest, I sold that one later on. If I notice that I'm not really into playing the instrument, I don't want it to go to waste, taking up space at home—I'll sell it to someone who actually needs it.

Hanoi had a deal with Aria, orchestrated by either Vesterinen or Bishop. I got weird-colored, weirdly shaped basses from Aria, but they looked more like weapons, like I had a fucking crossbow around my neck. A lot of instrument brands came to talk to us during the Japan tour. One gave me a stick bass. Goddamn, how did they dare make something so awful…we played cricket with it in the hotel hallway, using beer cans for the ball.

I played the Gibson Thunderbird for a long time in the early eighties. The Thunderbird is pretty neck-heavy: If you let go of your hand, the neck will swing to the ground. I played all of *Back to Mystery City* with the Mott the Hoople bassist Overend Watts's '64 Thunderbird. Those old ones have a good sound. The factory changed the mikes later on, with a smaller bridge and headstock, so the newer Thunderbirds are a different thing altogether.

When all these LA bands in late eighties started to play T-birds, I switched to a '68 Fender Jazz bass, which is what I play to this day.

2016
The road bends

After the new *The Voice of Finland* tapings, I was able to go home to Mallorca in January to rest. Really rest. For the first time in three years, I got to spend an entire month waking up in my own bed every day.

Daily life on an island has its own problems. The winter is so dry that water has to be brought in from the peninsula at the beginning of the year, and there's the threat that the water won't last to summer. There was a similar kind of situation twenty years ago because of the drought. You'd only get water from the tap three hours out of the day, the pipes were turned off otherwise.

Unfortunately, my relationship with Mina had come to an end. We had tried to get it to work for the last year and a half—we really tried—but we threw in the towel around the new year and went our separate ways.

I'm not an easy person to live with, because I'm gone a lot. My partner's got to understand that I'm traveling all the time and that it takes me a couple days to adjust when I come back. I've always lived in the moment without worrying too much about tomorrow or having the need of putting roots down anywhere.

I've been really lucky that I've stayed friends with Nicke's mom and with Karmen. I hope that the same bond stays intact with Mina and her family. Time will tell.

×××

I started to compile all the songs I'd recorded with whoever, and I started to think about new collaborations. I wanted to tour Brazil at the end of the year, and I wanted to record with locals, get different singers together to sing in their own language. It didn't have to be just English or Spanish. Why not sing in Swedish, if Thåström joined in? The project wouldn't necessarily have anything to do with rock.

The idea was brewing. It wasn't a Mad Juana in question, but a solo in a way, something I'd wanted to do for a long time.

I wrote music for a movie too in January. I was asked to make music for a twelve-minute-long short. I used my intuition and instruments from around the world that I kind of knew how to play, like the mento box and bağlama, and I liked what I heard. Danny Garcia, the guy who made the *Looking for Johnny* documentary, is making a Spaghetti Western in Almería, where Sergio Leone made his classics. That's a possible project. Movie scores are something interesting to me, how the sound complements the visuals and sets up the events. One of the nicer things about *Sound Tracker* was making the background and theme music. The show's theme got its start in Mallorca, when I wasn't yet living there. I went there to see my sister and my nieces, Sara and Noemi, and I decided to check in on how my old friend Puter was doing. I had recorded a demo with Puter's band the Satellites, and later on produced their record too.

Puter had found his deceased father's whisky stash from the seventies. The stuff was as tolerable as Spanish bootleg whisky could be. I had just come back from filming in Brazil, and I still had Pernambuco beats playing in my head. We tasted the stash, and Puter played a marimba made from Mallorquin stone, and I beat on a drum all night until I found a riff. This was the embryo of the *Sound Tracker* theme, which I finally scraped together in New York.

It looked like we'd be making the third season of *Sound Tracker* in 2017. I dubbed all the episodes up to now into English in March, because the show was going to be sold abroad.

I organized a tour of Spain with Sylvain Sylvain in April, because I missed Syl so much and the only way to see him nowadays is to plan a joint project. I asked Stevie Klasson and Chris Musto to come along, who had played with Johnny Thunders in the final years, and they were happy to join us. We made stops in Bilbao, Madrid, Murcia, Barcelona, and Valencia. We played under the name Sylvain Sylvain and the Trash Cowboys, and we played songs from our joint history: the Dolls, Hanoi, Thunders, Syl's seventies solo stuff. An overabundance of the setlist was inevitable.

This lineup proved that old relationships can be brought back to life. It's normal that people will have disagreements, and I don't believe in cutting ties, except in the most extreme of circumstances. It's healthy to let go of relationships that are only destructive and bring bad energy.

Mad Juana is in the process of activation too. Karmen has lived in Mexico for the last six years and came out to Mallorca in April. It was time to sit down side by side with our guitars and go through our ideas and demos that we'd been sending each other over the last years. We've got to get a record together. A pledge campaign or some other kind of crowdfunding is one possibility, but I'm not closed off to the idea of a more traditional record deal.

We went to the States in February with Michael Monroe. West Coast, East Coast, and this five-day cruise called Monsters of Rock: Shredders from the Deep. It sounds ridiculous, but it was such good money and fun that we couldn't say no.

We ran into Bam from Dogs D'Amour on the boat, Sebastian Bach, Chip Z'Nuff, Danny Nordahl for the Throbs—it was like an eighties class reunion. The organizer of the whole Monsters of Rock cruise was Harlan Henrickson. Back in the day, I had produced a record for Harlan's band, the Dogtown Balladeers. So around and around we go.

Monroe gigs are like being on the playground—a lot of weird running around. Grown men acting like little brats and loving every second of it, playing rock and roll together. I always try to toss the pick and catch it with my mouth onstage, like some trained fucking seal, I haven't succeeded a single time in five years. Practice makes perfect, maybe.

The current lineup has a healthier balance than with Conte and Dregen or Conte and Ginger. Rich has played in some great bands. Even with

Tricky. You'd get an entire book just out of Rich's experiences on Tricky's Romanian tour.

I knew Rich was a songwriter, but I had no idea how fucking great he was.

I've been playing with Steve Conte continuously for longer than with any other musician. It's coming up on twelve years of touring and making records. He has become like a brother and is one bad mofo on guitar, vocals, and writing.

I've found a partner in riddim in Karl. He's pure energy and stamina, but he can also get sensitive and play the piano. The big guy also makes musical score for movies and video game music. He's an exceptionally talented guy whose other talents include singing country and western and nineties Seattle's vocal stylings. Wait for his grunge and western solo album. He's also out of his mind and the best company possible on a tour.

Michael is totally my brother from another mother. Our connection was born on the streets of Stockholm in 1980, and we've gotten over all our shit. I love the man as a human being and as a musician. As the frontman, he's one of the best in the world, and he deserves all the good things. But there's one thing that he doesn't listen to: when I tell him to take it easy.

The *Blackout States* tour kept going to the end of the year. When that cycle finished up, it was time to start writing the next record.

×××

There's a lot of travel time that goes into each year. Going from place to place can take up a lot of time and that's when you realize the importance of your travel company not complaining about small stuff and their ability to wait. The touring life is mostly just waiting around, and then it's HURRY UP!! You've got to do interviews at the gigs when you don't feel like it, you haven't slept for days, and you are starving and stink. So sometimes there's grumbling and fuses get blown. Musicians are musicians, and there isn't any more time or energy to set up your own gear like in the beginning. Roadies are the ones that keep the show going. When I start to get sick of sitting with the band, I go sit in the techs' car.

It used to be that roadies were a beast of their own, colorful half-insane characters, but that field is becoming more homogenized too. There's a big need for roadies, the straight, decent ones. The whole thing has become such a biz that they can't be called roadies anymore, but technicians or something like that. The lighting guy is the lighting designer and the guitar roadie is the guitar technician. We've had some snobs with us that look down on musicians, who thought they were superstars because they had been around and done some tours with "bigger" bands. Just a bunch of big whiners, nothing's ever good enough for them. Dedication and commitment to a band aren't the same as they used to be either, when the roadie would have taken a bullet for the band. Now they'll just move to a better-paying gig for a less-interesting band.

The musicians that are rude to the crew are complete assholes. Being respectful of the hard work they do should go without saying. This goes both ways: The crew makes the show technically possible, but the show wouldn't happen without the band. Roadies are looking at the same goal from a different perspective. Everyone wants a successful show.

Pelle's roadies, Puosu and Illi, were incredibly important. Big Hell's Angels–looking dudes that weren't afraid of anything, but at the same time, big-hearted guys, kind of like two dads to their sixteen-year-old child, me. I'm still in touch with both of them. It feels like it all happened yesterday, that's how intense those nine months with Pelle were.

Helge and Spede were our roadies in the early days of Hanoi, until Helge ended it all and Timppa Kaltio took his place. Nasty said that Timppa lived in Rinkeby or somewhere else close to Stockholm. We went there, and Nasty knew approximately which house it was. We saw Timppa through the first-floor window as he was sitting on the couch and watching TV. The balcony was on the ground floor and the door was cracked. I climbed in and went inside. Hi! He was surprised.

Timppa dressed the same way we did, and a lot of people thought he played in Hanoi too. This Helsinki brother is a very important person in my life. He lived in LA in the late eighties, and now he lives in London.

When we moved to London, Hanoi got a merch guy, or is it now merchandising retailer? Anyway, a guy named Cod from the East End, a smart, interesting guy, but one who didn't know how to read or write. This certainly says something about the British educational system. Cod was out with Bon Scott the night he died.

Mick Staplehurst was the front of house mixer, a really cheerful lovely guy, and Lurch, like from the Addams Family, was our big pig farmer stagehand. He always appeared from out of the dark. "Is everything olroight?"

Jetboy's roadies were Andy Moraga and Tim Allyn. Andy really was getting married to Margaret Cho, I don't know if that happened by the time of this book coming out. Tim's wife is the Hollywood producer, Cathy Schulman. I found this out watching the Oscars. The camera swiped across the front row: Denzel Washington, Brad Pitt, Angelina Jolie, Tim. Wait…go back…. Why was our good old roadie Tim sitting in the middle of that crowd? I shot him a text. Tim answered: "Yeah, I'm at the Oscars. My wife won an Oscar for *Crash*!"

Joan Jett and the Blackhearts was full of old hands. The mixer Billy was a good-tempered Sicilian American who would bring duct tape on flights to get sleep. He would tape the loudspeakers over above him and crash out. And do not wake him up, there's hell to pay.

Michael got to know the mixer Nite Bob some time in 1989, and Nite Bob toured with Demolition 23. David Johansen was surprised. "He's still around?" Nite Bob did the Stooges' shows at Max's Kansas City in 1969 and 1970, and at one point he was mixing the Stooges, MC5, and the Dolls. Then he toured with Aerosmith from 1974 to the early eighties, when the band started to go downhill. Nite Bob was enough of an authority that he slapped a confused Steven Tyler in the face. "Sorry, Bob. Thank you for that. I needed it!" That's a man with more than enough stories to tell, when's that book coming out?

If Nite Bob hears that Mad Juana is playing a show in New York, he comes to do the sound for free. Musicians and roadies are constantly helping each other out. Nite Bob is one of the few to not get sick of always being on the move.

Michael Monroe has a good crew nowadays. Pekka Kupiainen mixes, Bobby Nieminen takes care of the guitars, and Tomi Nivala the drums and Michael. Total pros and not a single whiner. They're not bothered by watching over the band or the periodic insanity that permeates the bus; they'll put their headphones on or keep watch or jump into the mess too.

×××

A band and roadies are an important family; you share your thoughts and experiences with them, and at its best, being with them is creative and organized. But blood relatives are the root note of everything. It's important that my sister and her family live on the same island. I always say hi to my mom when I'm in Finland. And Jone too, if he's around. Family stuff isn't always easy. I always had a bit of a weird relationship with my dad. He was a threatening figure when I was a kid; he was busy, distant, and short-tempered. Sure, he had to take care of a family of five. But even though my dad was always a critic, he also was a big support. He definitely saw how demanding a musician's life was.

Nicholas lives in Stockholm. He's a kickboxer and personal trainer and the best man I know. My sister didn't see Nicke for almost twenty years, and Nicke and I had a three, four-year break ourselves.

How can my boy be in his thirties? He's got the same face he did as a baby. He's a wonderful person who I love from the bottom of my heart. We've talked through everything together. We speak a mix of Swedish and English.

Now that I'm in my fifties and am looking back, I have the feeling that someone else has lived this life here and there. Was that really me? What the fuck was going on in my head when I decided to do this or that?

Decades-old memories get twisted and those changes become memories. When Michael and I are talking about the same situation, both of us remember it sometimes a totally different way, from a different angle: Don't you remember? Michael remembers from the India trip that we were splashing our feet in the water when the captain yelled out about the sharks, but I remember that he wasn't on the boat with us at all.

There's an old Romani saying: The road bends. What makes life interesting is not knowing what's around the corner.

1980–2015

Annotated Discography

"There's no need to be so fucking serious!
Experimentation and playfulness keep a band alive.
That's why it's a shame that singles are going away
because so too are the B-sides, where there's more room for
experimentation."

Pelle Miljoona Oy
Moottoritie on kuuma (1980)

We made the single *Olen kaunis / Älä äiti itkee* (I'm beautiful / Mother, don't cry) first. Pelle and Taskinen didn't share the songs until we were in the studio. There's no count-off at the beginning of "Olen kaunis." Pelle just starts it off, and then the rest of us charge in. That was the spirit; we spent four hours max at Finnvox Studios. It was a seminal single obviously, showing off the new band. *Viimeinen syksy* had been a big record. But Pelle didn't care about that. Punk.

We joked around that Taskinen wrote the B-side about me: "Don't cry, Mom. Your son will be a good boy when he finds his place in the world." That could be; you write about what's around you, after all.

We recorded the LP in between all the weekend gigs. It was ready in May, if not already in April. We didn't spend a lot of time massaging it out. The first or second take: that's it, it's not going to get any better. We didn't go looking for anything too crazy for the keyboards; Taskinen had already found the sounds he wanted back at our practice space at the school in Herttoniemi.

I listened to the record for the first time in decades in 2011 just before the reunion tour, and it was incredible; I really like it. I'm wearing checkerboard pants I bought at Clotz in Stockholm on the back cover. They're my two-tone ska pants.

Hanoi Rocks
Bangkok Shocks, Saigon Shakes, Hanoi Rocks (1981)

The single for *I Want You* was the first attempt, a demo we recorded and didn't know if this would turn into a band. "Tragedy," taken from the LP, was effectively our calling card, and it sold pretty well.

Did the band go to the studio too soon? It's never the right time. Sometimes you get a good result when you go halfway prepared to the studio and throw all your energy at it. But sometimes it's possible to be over-rehearsed, everyone knows the beat even in their sleep, and you're not necessarily going to get any good surprises then. We were seventeen, eighteen, and *Bangkok Shakes* was our foot in the door. And the back cover… oh man, what a crew. Our moms must have been proud of their sons.

Hanoi Rocks
Oriental Beat (1982)

We were chasing a big global sound, and we totally failed. This one has the worst sound of all the Hanoi records, and it probably has the band's best songs, which is just typical. We didn't do justice to the good songs until we played them live. Seeing the UK Subs had taken our energy up a notch. The live shows were explosive, and part of that is getting lost. You never knew when you were gonna fall.

The cover concept was shot at Lepakko, our palms against clear plastic. It was lifted from the Stones' *Through the Past, Darkly*, the compilation with an octagonal cover. The back cover is a picture of Anna's tits.

Hanoi Rocks
Self Destruction Blues (1982)

This one is better than the official LPs. The songs are all singles, and the B-sides have this who-gives-a-fuck kind of vibe. The pressure to put out a hit is off. We made "Malibu Nightmare" and "Do the Duck," and we straight-faced told Atte and Seppo that this was our new direction. Nasty played the bass on "Do the Duck" because I only made it in to sing backup. I woke up hungover in some lady's apartment, and it took me a while to remember that we had sessions scheduled.

I love "Beer and a Cigarette." There's something genius in its idiocy. It has probably Andy's best solo on record. "Taxi Driver" became a mainstay later on. It's the simplest song in the world, and it's been hanging on in Monroe's setlist through all these years.

Razzle had already joined the band and is on the cover, even though Gyp played on all the songs. Riipinen took the picture at the bar Vanha in Helsinki. The bar was right behind the door. When it was time for setup and a break, we ran to the bar, and by the end of the shoot, we were so hammered that we were lucky to be able to keep our eyes open.

Hanoi Rocks
Back to Mystery City (1983)

Razzle's first album. Good songs, but weird production, so it doesn't exactly swing. I like that the record is imaginative and has good energy. We were still really close as a band then, even though the drugs were already starting to tear us apart. Not junk yet—that was still waiting around the corner. Two songs were done with a drum machine because we needed a robotic rhythm, and that wasn't something Razzle could do; he had too much of a swing. One of those songs was "Mental Beat."

Hanoi Rocks
All Those Wasted Years (1984)

Live double album, recorded at the Marquee in London in 1983. I broke a string on my Thunderbird right on the first song, and I had to play the rest of the show on an Aria, which doesn't sound or look as good. The gig was captured on film as well and was released on VHS. The backstage was full of people after the show: members of the Cockney Rejects, the Anti-Nowhere League, UK Subs, and Gary Holton. The OG Punks Stiv Bators and Brian James showed up as well.

The next day we had to do some closeups for the edits. We were hungover posing for the cameras as if in the middle of the show, duck walk and the like. We had to wear the same clothes, of course, without the sweat.

We had to do some overdubbing for the record. The microphone on Andy's amp had been turned away, and Nasty wasn't recorded very well either. The guitars had to be played over again in part at Nick Lowe's studio. But what can you do? I had to play the first song over, the one where my string broke, but other than that, all the bass and drum parts are the originals and most of Michael's vocals, too.

Live albums can easily get too cleaned up, be too aware of the recording and everything. My favorite live albums are Motörhead's *No Sleep 'til Hammersmith*, MC5's *Kick Out the Jams*, and Iggy Pop's *TV Eye Live and Ramones: It's Alive.* They're tough, magical, chaotic records that make you wanna go nuts.

Hanoi's downward spiral was entirely mental. The shows were hard all the way to the very end. The *Nottingham Tapes* from sometime in the spring of 1984 are animalistic.

Fallen Angels
Fallen Angels (1984)

Knox, the front man of the Vibrators, had become a friend of Hanoi and wanted to do a solo record under a band name. He asked me, Razzle, and Nasty to play on the record. Which was a huge honor; Knox was really important to me. Back in the seventies, Saku Paasiniemi had had the Vibrators' single for "Baby Baby," which blew my mind, that song is legendary.

We only practiced the Fallen Angels songs for a day. Really, we sat in the pub, and Knox wrote the chords out on a piece of paper and told us about the songs. We spent three days in the studio for the backing tracks including the rhythm guitar. Michael came to play sax and the harmonica, and Andy had a solo, so the whole family was there. Right about this time, the end of 1983, was when Richard Bishop started to manage Knox.

Greenhouse Studio was right across from Waterloo Station and the pub where we sat after every take. One song done, another hour in the pub. That evening, after ten pints, it was hard to muster the energy to play again. I solved the problem by playing while lying down. You can't tell by listening to the record.

It was nice to play someone's songs other than Andy's for a change. The record has never gone out of print. Knox has a store in Camden Town nowadays and still plays gigs.

Hanoi Rocks
Two Steps from the Move (1984)

I like it and I don't. It's great that the songs are well produced for a change. "Boiler" was done in the spirit of "Do the Duck," but with ZZ Top's "Gimme All Your Lovin'" in mind; it was our homage to ZZ Top and on the other hand to Cockney bands, as well as the English gent in our band.

Bob Ezrin's contract had a clause that if there was any drug use during the sessions, he could walk away from the project with his advance in hand.

And his advance was $50,000. So we only drank beer, barely even smoked weed, so we didn't fuck up the whole thing when there was a lot of money riding on it.

It's this record that gave birth to Guns N' Roses and the whole LA scene. Axl and Izzy were big Hanoi fans, and they knew the earlier records too. We fell apart a couple of years too early. If we had gone to the US in 1986 and made something like this…who knows.

The name came from Bobby Bland's *Two Steps from the Blues*. Andy introduced the record to both me and Michael, and we fell for it so hard that we both bought it for ourselves. It's Bland's first record, and some of his later albums like *His California Album* is untouchable. Andy was into the fact that behind the title was an obscure early sixties blues record.

In the fall of 1985, Hanoi put out a live album that I don't play on even though my picture is on the back cover: *Rock & Roll Divorce*. It was recorded during Hanoi's last tour with René Berg and Terry Chimes. It's not worth listening to.

Sam Yaffa—Pelle Almgren
Sam Yaffa—Pelle Almgren (1986)

The album cover photo is pretty fucking bad. The songs were good though, but it was no success by any measure. Seppo Vesterinen funded it and took care of the publicity. He wanted to do just a four-song EP first. We probably would have made a full-length if the EP had sold better. We recorded half in Stockholm at Marcus Music, which had changed a lot since the Hurriganes made *Roadrunner* there. We finished the recording sessions at Finnvox in Helsinki with the Finnish musician and producer T.T. Oksala.

We did a short summer tour of Finland. Pelle and I got into some sort of a squabble, I don't even remember what about, and that was that, we stopped playing together after the tour.

After taking a break from playing, it had become clear that I had to support myself by doing what I love. At that point, I had held onto my '76 Thunderbird and Gibson EB3L, which is the long-neck bass Jack Bruce played. My Hanoi brothers had sold all my other instruments.

Jetboy
Feel the Shake (1988)

The title says it all. Well, the band is from the land of earthquakes, so it's fair to call it that. Jetboy formed in 1985, right after Hanoi, and the guys had had tickets to the San Francisco show. Which never happened.

I joined right in the middle of everything, just weeks before recording, and I pretty much only had enough time to help out in the writing process of "Locked in a Cage." The record was skillfully put together rock and roll for the time, but the lyrics are like a caricature of rock, with song titles straight out of a *Saturday Night Live* sketch: "You're like a bad disease."

The rhythm guitarist Billy Rowe plays like Malcolm Young and the drummer, Ron Tostenson, like John Bonham. Jetboy really came together live; even Monroe said as much when he saw us. But the record hasn't aged well.

Jetboy
Damned Nation (1990)

Musically, it's more varied and mature. But the lyrics are what they are. It didn't rise above rhymes; the lyrics didn't go any deeper, they just stayed on the level of simple rhymes.

The producers had good ears, and I learned to listen to music in a different way during these sessions. I learned some about mikes and compression, and how even the smallest tweaks could change everything. During Hanoi, I didn't give a shit about either business or production, as long as we went in there and killed it.

Damned Nation wasn't any worse than some Faster Pussycat record, which sold half a million, whereas this capped out at 150,000. When the record came out, I was already living in New York. Jetboy toured with their new bassist for a few months until they got dropped by the label. Grunge was coming, and it had changed everything. The labels decided to kill all their glam projects and move forward with the Seattle scene.

Jerusalem Slim
Jerusalem Slim (1992)

Really promising at the demo stage, but the end result is poop. I absolutely cannot listen to it. The goal was to make a raw, back-to-basics record, but all the plans we'd agreed on with Steve Stevens mysteriously disappeared as soon as the guitar hero stepped over the threshold of the studio. The control freak was so obsessive in his direction of the drummer that after the first week of recordings, we had just done the drums. For the price of this slicked-up cock rock turd, you could produce thirty great punk rock records.

Alison Gordy
Mad As Hell (1993)

The Oddballs were Johnny Thunders's last band, and its core group of members were Alison Gordy, Chris Musto, Stevie Klasson, and Jamey Heath. I played shows with Alison from 1991 to 1994. I played the standup bass on a few songs, which meant I had to haul it to every show. And back home after the show, which was really fun for me since I lived in the sixth-floor walkup of a tenement building with no elevator. I was hauling the contra upstairs once at five in the morning while a little bit drunk, and I kept banging it into the walls, waking up the whole building. "Stop playing that fuckin' big bass, Sammy!"

Alison had a big Mae West attitude on stage: a tall blonde, cigarette in hand, nightgown. It's a great record that should see the light of day. It's probably up to Alison since the record was self-released. Labels weren't interested in that kind of sixties R&B, but Alison wanted to get her own music out and took care of business herself.

Demolition 23.
Demolition 23. (1994)

This album could be a commentary on the previous one: we learned from the shit. It's that kind of record. I'm referring to *Jerusalem Slim*. Before this record, me, Michael, and Nasty recorded "Disappointed in You" for the Johnny Thunders tribute album. The song had the rough edges and attitude that we wanted, and it was the springboard for the sound of *Demolition 23*.

Yeah, *Jerusalem Slim* was supposed to be simple, simple, simple. Michael's *Not Fakin' It* wasn't simple, nor was Jetboy's *Damned Nation*. We were hungry to make this kind of record, no frills, simple down-to-earth production and great songs. That material still works great live with Monroe.

Jan Stenfors
Vinegar Blood (1996)

Nasty Suicide had gotten his life together after being lost for a while; he quit drinking, went back to school, and picked up budo. He started to feel imprisoned by "Nasty Suicide." So he made a solo record under his own name, and it was clearly freeing for him. It's a good album, I dig it. It was nice to get to play some rock for a change. I had been in another headspace than rock out in Mallorca.

Mad Juana
Skin of My Teeth (1997)

I dig this a lot, absolutely one of my favorites. I'd think about mixing it again if the opportunity arose. The low end isn't quite right, even though Jimi Sumén and I mixed them a couple times. The soundscape on this one isn't exactly the easiest thing to get a grip on. The elastic parts are the best, where the tempo sways like a drunken sailor: the wah-wah children's accordion, wah-wah bongos, two basses, and no guitar.

Affe Forsman's twenty-six-inch bass drum played with a big mallet was layered on top of the rattle recorded in Spain. "Let's fucking double it." Affe is a genius. The man is an amazing musician, I saw him in Pen Lee back when I was a kid. Affe should have gone out into the world playing with big artists; he would have killed it in anything at all. He's an intuitive player that can jump into any genre. Affe was in Krakatau with my brother.

Pep Banyo & the Blues Devils
Live (1997)

I had to get the whole set rehearsed in one day, twenty-something songs, my brother Maukka had an emergency, and I had to jump in and cover for the departed bass player. My goal for the gig was to get my bass to sound like a standup. I turned down the treble and used the front mike only and played with my fingers above the neck to get that sound. This album, which was recorded in one night at the Bluesville club in Palma de Mallorca, remains the best-selling record put out by a local band.

Mad Juana
In Your Blood (2001)

This was self-released, meaning people sent their money in the mail, and I sent them a CD-R. You'd have to send MP3s nowadays I guess. It was recorded at the end of 2000, first at home, then at Transporterraum studios. I made the beats on a drum machine and built it up from there. I wanted the drummer to play the same beats in the studio. But the studio was still under construction with a limited amount of outboard gear. We were struggling with drum sounds.

Jimmy Goodman played vibraphone for Mad Juana, which works really well with all the electronic sounds. The result was pretty sensual, nocturnal and velvety. A lot of couples told us the record is to blame for their pregnancies. We were in the middle of a gig in San Francisco when I happened to look up at the mezzanine, which was closed off from the audience that night, and there was a lady and a gent copulating. So maybe there's some truth to these claims.

We made the album covers at Kinko's. Black and white copies were cheaper, but black text on white would have been boring, so that's why *In Your Blood* became our Black Album—gray text on a black background. But that turned out also a bit boring. Why didn't I doodle something, like I did for all the Mad Juana flyers and posters?

Mad Juana
Acoustic Voodoo (2002)

Just like the name suggests, we'd moved away from electric. The only electric instrument was Lenny Kaye's guitar.

Most of the album was made in our Tenth Street apartment on my first laptop. Someone had given me Cubase, which I learned how to use by pulling my hairs and cursing violently. I had three mikes: a Shure 57, 58, and some other cheap ribbon mike. And that's what we used for the whole album. Tony Mann and I built the percussion tracks. Playing the bass drum by hand was starting to become a habit.

I'd found a new G-tuning for the guitar that I hadn't seen before in books: GGDDBG. Not B flat, but B—or "H" in Finnish—so Dorian mode. We built two songs around that tuning. We also did a cover of the Velvet Underground's "Venus in Furs," and later a French version, when a French label was interested in us. Karmen had studied French in school, but speaking French is a different thing altogether. When Karmen started singing, the French engineer asked, "I'm sorry, but what language are you singing?"

We got a record deal. Diesel Motor put out *Acoustic Voodoo* in the UK. I haven't seen a single royalty statement to this day.

New York Dolls
One Day It Will Please Us to Remember Even This (2006)

One day David Johansen announced to us, "Well, I have this idea for the title…" We had been waiting for the right name for the title. Here it comes, something amazing! or so I thought, everyone was quiet. And out came that sentence…it felt like it would never end. It was a little stupefying. David continued, "I think it's a great title for the album. And I think it's true."

And it's true: it pleases me to remember even this. Good rock and roll, something old and something new. Now it's the favorite title for any album I've ever been involved with. The rehearsals and recording were a great experience from start to finish. It was a little painful for Sylvain, he fought with a couple of the songs. Sylvain took the Dolls legacy seriously, and he wanted to do justice to that without straying away too far. But then again, if you stick to it too much, the band would become its own tribute band. You've got to give yourself enough room to move, so things don't get stagnant. We found a great balance on this one.

Jesse Malin
Glitter in the Gutter (2007)

Jesse had been listening to a lot of seventies soft rock, and you can tell from the songs. I went looking for influences for the bass and rhythms, there's quite a stew in the seventies recordings: Fleetwood Mac's *Rumours* has a lot of air and colors on the low end, seventies Elton John stuff is nuts, amazing bass lines, almost like soloing through entire tracks. So that's why it was a bit of a surprise that two metal dudes like Eddie Wohl and Rob Caggiano, the latter of whom had played in Anthrax, were picked for this kind of singer-songwriter seventies vibe type of music. I can't stand metal as a genre. It was a totally incomprehensible choice.

The metalheads' mix wasn't cutting it for Jesse, so he decided to use a different mixer. After all the teeth clenching, the record turned out really good.

Mad Juana
Bruja on the Corner (2008)

This record was made in San Diego, and the proximity to the Mexican border is palpable in the vibe of the music. I recorded and mixed it again at home and a record label guy's home with my own gadgets, but unlike *Acoustic Voodoo*, *Bruja* didn't suffer at all from the home mix. I'd bought a JBL home monitor system that was a lifesaver. It was the first time home recording sounded good even when listened to with other systems. I was able to trust my mix.

Karmen is incredibly gifted, but it would have been great if she'd put as much time into making music as going to yoga. She'd run off to yoga while I was taking care of the record and touring and funding. A lot of times I had to push Karmen to get the lyrics out of her.

Rick Ballard released *Bruja* on his own label, Acetate. This time we didn't have to run to copy places to print out the covers or mail the album out ourselves.

New York Dolls
Cause I Sez So (2009)

I like the record. A lot of people don't, for some fucking reason. But the people that just want another copy of the first Dolls album still wouldn't be happy if they got what they wanted, they would find something to bitch and moan about. "But we don't like this." People stuck in the past aren't ever happy with anything, so why bother wasting your time.

I wrote "Temptation to Exist" with Johansen. Conte came up with the intro melody, which turned into the vocal melody. The album didn't have a whole lot to do with the old Dolls, it was more like a sixties Motown album, but different. Only three songs are really rock 'n' roll, the rest are ballads or rhythm and blues. Playing that kind of bass in Hawaii sessions was a blast.

Michael Monroe
Another Night In the Sun (2010)

This album was recorded live at a show at Tavastia in Helsinki and released right away in the fall.

The band paid for the recording without knowing how we'd put it out or who would release it. That's how we were able to introduce the new band. It tells a lot about the strength of Demolition 23. songs, there's five of them on this one. And the band was supposed to be more like Demolition 23. than Hanoi.

Mad Juana
Kumpanía (2011)

A lost gem that was recorded in 2009, finally released in January of 2011, but only on iTunes. It's a daring record, lots of horns and violins and storyline that pretty much follows the unrealized Romani musical.

Kumpanía has been promoted by the likes of me and me alone, and it's rare that anyone even knows about it. It hasn't been enough to post on Facebook that hey, we put out a record. Social media is important, but it can't do all the work.

Kumpanía is the last Mad Juana release for the time being. We have enough demos for a record, and we've started work on another. Just gotta find a couple of months to work in peace and enough money so that I can bring the musicians out to Mallorca or go back to the States myself.

Michael Monroe
Sensory Overdrive (2011)

It was important for both me and Michael to get to work together again. We both had a lot of enthusiasm from the get-go. The record shows a good range of songwriting. It was a real joint effort: We sat around with our instruments at the rehearsal place and worked together on the riffs and arrangements. When Lemmy came and sang on "Debauchery as a Fine Art," I was surprised by how high he sang. You think he's singing low because of the tone of his voice but the actual note is pretty damn high.

I'm proud of these Michael Monroe records, especially the fact that we didn't get stuck in the eighties. The sound is timeless in a way. The only thing I don't dig is that *kursschht* snare. Petri Majuri ended up fixing the mistakes made at the recording. He had to use the snare trigger, which can get a bit monotone.

Michael Monroe
Horns and Halos (2013)

Sophomore album. For real. Our history aside, funnily *Horns and Halos* feels like it's Michael's and my second album. "Now we gotta show everybody that we're not just a one-album wonder."

Sadly the timing was wrong because the record got held up and didn't come out until the beginning of the fall, so the touring schedule got fucked up. Shit happens sometimes. Michael and I have looked at each other on occasion like, are we just cursed? Did we do something bad? As much as you might want to plan things out, you can't predict everything. The business is unpredictable, people are unpredictable.

Rob Carlyle & the Compulsions
Dirty Fun (2015)

I also found the time to be in this New York rock and roll lineup with current Guns N' Roses members Richard Fortus and Frank Ferrer in addition to me and Rob. Recorded over a long period of time from sometime in the spring of 2013 to the summer of 2014. The cover was the tackiest I've seen since the eighties: a chick's ass in lace underwear. "Well done, you put an ass on the cover. Doesn't that make you an ass, Rob?" But it's good stuff, worth checking out if you can get your hands on it and not feel filthy.

Michael Monroe

Blackout States (2015)

More even that the last one, more cohesive. I just have the problem that I like it when a record goes all over to surprising places. Like *Electric Ladyland*. I didn't totally believe in all the songs in the studio in the beginning, and there are some elements that I still don't feel at home with. But overall, it's good.

Everyone in the music business likes this one the most. Says it's Michael Monroe's best ever. And it always makes me nervous when record execs like something too much. The new generation doesn't seem to know shit about music, and they're only in the biz because it's cool or they're making bank. A&R guys don't even listen to demos or go see bands, they just look up how many Facebook likes, listens on Spotify, or views on YouTube something has. Bands get signed by the thumbs alone.

The mainstream is always begging for a backlash, and that's what keeps music alive. Middle-of-the-road shit doesn't know it's the spark and the reason for revolt. When you look at the Billboard lists from 1975, it's all Captain & Tennille, the Carpenters, the Osmonds. But this and the pathetic, proggy fart music had the merit of giving birth to punk.

The other reason was societal. New York in the mid-seventies was a bankrupt warzone, and it was a fucking dangerous place to be. There were strikes and a general uproar in London; there was a garbage strike and piles of shit on the streets and high unemployment. No future for me. Young people reacted by making music that they were passionate about and that meant something to them.

Acknowledgments

I'd like to thank the following people, in no order of preference, who made this book possible and who have been important to me along my journey: Aila, Ingrid, Jone and Lasse Takamäki, Nicholas Jederby, Ingeborg Kesäluoto, Tommi Liimatta, Krista Sarasti, Päivi Paappanen, Michael Monroe, Nasty Suicide, Andy McCoy, Razzle, Jeppe Sporre, Pelle Miljoona, Tumppi Varonen, Ari Taskinen, Steve Conte, Karl Rockfist, Rich Jones, David Johansen, Sylvain Sylvain, Brian Delaney, Karmen Guy, Joan Jett, Thommy Price, Dougie Needles, Jesse Malin, Danny Ray, all the men and women of Mad Juana, the Jetboy dudes, and the hundreds of musicians with whom I've had the pleasure of playing and those who have been a big influence on me as both a musician and a person, Otso Tiainen, Juge Heikkilä, Svante Colerus, Riku Rantala, Tunna Milonoff, the Yle Teema team, Rane Raitsikka, Timppa Kaltio, Mina and Quest Soliman, Puosu, Illi and the hundreds of other roadies/techs that have made everything possible, Seppo Vesterinen, Richard Bishop, Virpi Immonen, Atte Blom, Maukka Palmio, Ginger Wildheart, and Dregen, my brothers and sisters in London, Los Angeles, New York, Spain, Sweden, and Finland (you all know who you are), Justin Thomas, Alan Rand, Hilary Hulteen, and Meeri Koutaniemi. You're all important, and it's been a BIG honor to have you all in my life. With humble thanks. Sami